It is important to reconsider the problem of social context, given the intensity of contemporary concern about relational, situated, historical conceptions of social practice and activity, the self and subjectivity, and their located everyday character. Through vivid accounts of human endeavors as diverse as psychotherapy, artificial intelligence research, and blacksmithing, *Understanding Practice* offers creative approaches to the question of the role of context in human action and interaction. The excitement and fascination of these chapters lies in part in their pursuit of a closely interrelated set of theoretical quandaries *through* rich portraits of everyday practices. Further, the authors set out from the beginning to present the most formidable and different approaches to the contextual character of human activity.

Understanding practice

Learning in Doing: Social, Cognitive, and
Computational Perspectives

Founding Editor
JOHN SEELY BROWN, Xerox Palo Alto Research Center

General Editors
ROY PEA, *SRI International, Center for Technology
in Learning*
CHRISTIAN HEATH, *The Management Centre,
King's College, London*
LUCY A. SUCHMAN, *Centre for Science Studies and
Department of Sociology, Lancaster University, UK*

Continued on page following the Index

Understanding practice

Perspectives on activity and context

Edited by
SETH CHAIKLIN
Aarhus University

JEAN LAVE
University of California, Berkeley

CAMBRIDGE
UNIVERSITY PRESS

CAMBRIDGE UNIVERSITY PRESS
Cambridge, New York, Melbourne, Madrid, Cape Town, Singapore, São Paulo

Cambridge University Press
The Edinburgh Building, Cambridge CB2 2RU, UK

Published in the United States of America by Cambridge University Press, New York

www.cambridge.org
Information on this title: www.cambridge.org/9780521392631

© Cambridge University Press 1996

First published 1993
First paperback edition 1996
Reprinted 2000, 2002, 2003

A catalogue record for this publication is available from the British Library

ISBN-13 978-0-521-55851-8 paperback
ISBN-10 0-521-55851-4 paperback

Transferred to digital printing 2006

Contents

Part IV   Conclusion

Series foreword

The *situated* nature of learning, remembering, and understanding is a central fact. It may appear obvious that human minds develop in social situations, and that they use the tools and representational media that culture provides to support, extend, and reorganize mental functioning. But cognitive theories of knowledge representation and educational practice, in school and in the workplace, have not been sufficiently responsive to questions about these relationships. And the need for responsiveness has become salient as computational media radically reshape the frontiers of individual and social action, and as educational achievement fails to translate into effective use of knowledge.

This series is born of the conviction that new and exciting interdisciplinary syntheses are under way, as scholars and practitioners from diverse fields seek to analyze and influence the new transformations of social and mental life, and to understand successful learning wherever it occurs.

Computational media include not only computers but the vast array of expressive, receptive, and presentational devices available for use with computers, including interactive video, optical media such as CD-ROM and CD-I, networks, hypermedia systems, workgroup collaboration tools, speech recognition and synthesis, image processing and animation, and software more generally.

These technologies are dramatically transforming the basic patterns of communication and knowledge interchange in societies, and automating the component processes of thinking and problem solving. In changing situations of knowledge acquisition and use, the new interactive technologies redefine–in ways yet to be determined–what it means to know and understand, and what it means to become "literate" or an "educated citizen."

The series invites contributions that advance our understanding of these seminal issues.

Roy Pea
John Seely Brown

Contributors

Seth Chaiklin
Institute of Psychology
University of Aarhus
Risskov, Denmark

Ole Dreier
Psychological Laboratory
University of Copenhagen
Copenhagen, Denmark

Yrjö Engeström
Laboratory of Comparative
   Human Cognition
University of California, San
   Diego
La Jolla, California

Urs Fuhrer
Department of Psychology
University of Bern
Bern, Switzerland

Edwin Hutchins
Department of Cognitive
   Science
University of California,
   San Diego
La Jolla, California

Charles Keller
Department of Anthropology

University of Illinois
Urbana, Illinois

Janet Dixon Keller
Department of Anthropology
University of Illinois
Urbana, Illinois

Steinar Kvale
Institute of Psychology
University of Aarhus
Risskov, Denmark

Jean Lave
Graduate School of Education
University of California,
   Berkeley
Berkeley, California

Harold G. Levine
Graduate School of Education
University of California,
   Los Angeles
Los Angeles, California

R. P. McDermott
School of Education
Stanford University
Stanford, California

Hugh Mehan
Department of Sociology

University of California,
  San Diego
La Jolla, California

Norris Minick
Department of Communication
  Sciences and Disorders
Northwestern University
Evanston, Illinois

Roger Säljö
Department of Communication
  Studies
University of Linköping
Linköping, Sweden

Lucy A. Suchman
System Sciences Laboratory
Xerox Palo Alto Research
  Center
Palo Alto, California

Randall H. Trigg
Institute of Computer Science
University of Aarhus
Risskov, Denmark

Jan Wyndhamn
Department of Communication
  Studies
University of Linköping
Linköping, Sweden

Part I

Introduction

1 The practice of learning

Jean Lave

The problem with "context"

This book grew out of the work of a two-part conference in which the participants came together to consider what we initially

Seth Chaiklin and I initiated this project, but we discussed it with Steinar Kvale very early on and he has been our colleague and advisor on the project ever since. Roger Säljö was exceptionally kind and efficacious in organizing the second meeting of the conference and arranging to fund it through his department at Linköping University, Sweden. The Spencer Foundation generously provided travel support for conference participants. William Schonfeld, dean of the School of Social Sciences at the University of California, Irvine, funded the first meeting. This is just one example of his steady support over the years, for which I am grateful. At UCI, Norma Mendoza did a wonderful job of organizing the whole enterprise. Together, she and Kathy Girvin created the warm ambience that made it a matter of course that fellowship and intellectual openness would prevail.

In the spirit in which all of the authors have written their chapters with the help of "editorial boards" consisting of three other conference participants, Steinar Kvale has read many versions of this introduction, and provided the encouragement without which I might never have finished it. Ole Dreier, Paul Duguid, Martin Packer, Carol Stack, Lucy Suchman, Randall Trigg, and Etienne Wenger have generously given it critical readings. I am grateful also to participants in the 1991 summer course, sponsored by the Qualitative Research Center of Aarhus University under the direction of Steinar Kvale, at Mols Laboratoriet for their thoughtful reading and suggestions for revisions. Thanks are in order to each of them. A special acknowledgment to our editor, Julia Hough, is also in order; her kindness, patience, and insightful encouragement have contributed greatly to the fruition of the project.

Much of the value I have derived from the project has come from collaborating with Seth Chaiklin. In order to make sure that our introductory and concluding chapters give two separate commentaries on the book, we have not read or commented on drafts of each other's chapters. This explains why the introduction does not discuss Seth's closing chapter, and vice versa. The process of writing the introduction is the only part of the conference and the book that has not benefited directly from Seth's deep knowledge and his long, critical view of the historically situated practice of social science research.

3

called "the context problem." All of us were involved in research on socially situated activity. We were concerned about conventional limitations on various approaches to the study of activity. In particular, we wished to explore questions about the "socially constituted world" – the context of socially situated activity – that our work often seemed merely to take for granted.

I had tried in previous research to understand how math activity in grocery stores involved being "in" the "store," walking up and down "aisles," looking at "shelves" full of cans, bottles, packages and jars of food, and other commodities. My analyses were about shoppers' activities, sometimes together, and about the relations between these activities and the distractingly material, historically constituted, subjectively selective character of space–time relations and their meaning. Both Seth Chaiklin and I knew that other people conceived of the problem in quite different terms. We decided to hold a collective inquiry into these old, but still perplexing questions (e.g., Bartlett, 1958; Goffman, 1964; Barker, 1963, 1968; Birdwhistell, 1970; and more recently Dannefer, 1991; Haraway, 1988; Rommetveit, 1987, 1988; Hanks, 1990a, 1990b; Goodwin & Duranti, 1992). The time seemed appropriate for such a project, given that theoretical approaches to the study of situated activity, and hence to its situations, had fairly recently become surprisingly diverse and increasingly informed by rich empirical research. The traditions behind the work in this book include activity theory, critical psychology, Barker's ecological psychology, cognitive anthropology, and ethnomethodological perspectives. The contributors include psychologists, sociologists, and anthropologists from Sweden, Denmark, Finland, France, Switzerland, and the United States.

We met first without prepared papers in hand, in order to establish the grounds for a broad discussion of our quite different approaches to the study of situated activity. We assembled again several months later to discuss papers drafted in the interim. We then worked for two years more to develop the papers in ways that reflect the impact of these interchanges on our research.

Why would a diverse group of students of the human condition participate over months, and even years, to try to understand each other's perspective? Seth Chaiklin and I initially proposed the following rationale: Theories of situated everyday practice insist that persons acting and the social world of activity cannot be separated (cf. Minick, 1985). This creates a dilemma: Research on everyday practice typically focuses on the activities of persons acting, although there is agreement that such phenomena cannot be analyzed in isolation from the socially material world of that activity. But less attention has been given to the difficult task of conceptualizing *relations* between persons acting and the social world. Nor has there been sufficient attention to rethinking the "social world of activity" in relational terms. Together, these constitute the problem of context.

The participants in the conference agreed to this set of priorities, with the obvious proviso that relational concepts of the social world should not be explored in isolation from conceptions of persons acting and interacting and their activities. That proviso gradually took on a more central meaning and, as a result, our conception of the common task crystallized into a double focus – on context and, to our surprise, learning. A focus on one provided occasions on which to consider the other. If context is viewed as a social world constituted in relation with persons acting, both context and activity seem inescapably flexible and changing. And thus characterized, changing participation and understanding in practice – the problem of learning – cannot help but become central as well.

It is difficult, when looking closely at everyday activity as the authors in this volume have done, to avoid the conclusion that learning is ubiquitous in ongoing activity, though often unrecognized as such. Situated activity always involves changes in knowledge and action (as Keller & Keller, this volume, argue) and "changes in knowledge and action" are central to what we mean by "learning." It is not the case that the world consists of newcomers who drop unaccompanied into unpeopled problem spaces. People in activity are skillful at, and are more often than not engaged in, helping each other to participate in changing ways in a changing world. So in describing and analyzing people's involvement in practical action in the world, even those authors whose work generally would be least identified with educational foci (e.g., Suchman & Trigg or Keller & Keller, both this volume) are in effect analyzing peoples' engagement in *learning*. We have come to the conclusion, as McDermott suggests (see also Lave & Wenger, 1991) that there is no such thing as "learning" sui generis, but only changing participation in the culturally designed settings of everyday life. Or, to put it the other way around, participation in everyday life may be thought of as a process of changing understanding in practice, that is, as learning.

Learning became one focus of our work, even where unintended, partly because of our concern with everyday activity as social and historical process and with the improvisational, future-creating character of mundane practice; partly, also, because those of us whose research has touched on educational questions have come to insist on denaturalizing the social processes that unfold within educational institutions by turning them into analytic objects. So whether the researchers here have approached the problem of context through its temporal dimension, as activity (or practice), or whether they have looked at institutions of learning as contexts, learning has become a central issue.

In the next section a brief description of the chapters provides an opportunity to show how they developed around the issues of context and learning. Next I shall explore at greater length issues concerning the character of learning as situated activity, especially its heterogeneity – the various scopes of social processes (of learning) simultaneously enacted in everyday settings, and their open-ended character. The point is to show how the meaning of "learning" in the research discussed in these chapters differs in significant ways from conventional views of learning. But what, given unconventional conceptions of learning, becomes of the concept of context? The fourth section lays out the views of "context" that assume changing understanding and situated practices to be part and parcel of the lived social world. The discussion of context suggests a problem, however: Conventional theories of learning and schooling appeal to the decontextualized character of some knowledge and forms of knowledge transmission, whereas in a theory of situated activity "decontextualized learning activity" is a contradiction in terms. These two very different ways of conceiving of learning are hardly compatible. Nonetheless, a belief that the world is divided into contextualized and decontextualized phenomena is not merely an academic speculation that can be discarded when found theoretically inadequate or incomplete. This dualistic view of the world has a lively presence in our everyday lives. This dilemma motivates two developments in the book: On the one hand, these chapters reflect a growing sense of responsibility for historical explanation of central theoretical traditions; it is not accidental that conventional theory here is treated as part of the activity we are studying, rather than as a contrastive object to be discarded (cf. Chaiklin's concluding chapter). On the other hand, much of the analysis in the book is focused on the mechanisms by which decontextualization practices are generated in situated ways in everyday life.

Craftwork learning and social production

Traditionally, learning researchers have studied learning as if it were a process contained in the mind of the learner and have ignored the lived-in world. This disjuncture, which ratifies a dichotomy of mind and body, sidetracks or derails the question of how to construct a theory that *encompasses* mind and lived-in world. It is not enough to say that some designated cognitive theory of learning could be *amended* by adding a theory of "situation," for this raises crucial questions about the compatibility of particular theories (cf. Soviet psychologists' discussion of the "match" between psychologies and sociologies in the 1920s: Davydov & Radzhikovskii, 1985, p. 49). Nor is it sufficient to pursue a principled account of situated activity armed only with a theory of cognition and good intentions. Without a theoretical conception of the social world one cannot analyze activity in situ. A more promising alternative lies in treating relations among person, activity, and situation, as they are *given* in social practice, itself viewed as a single encompassing theoretical entity. It is possible to detect such a trend in most if not all of the research traditions represented in this collection – these chapters are working toward a more inclusive, intensive development of the socially situated character of activity in theoretically consistent terms.

Theories of situated activity do not separate action, thought, feeling, and value and their collective, cultural-historical forms of located, interested, conflictual, meaningful activity. Traditional cognitive theory is "distanced from experience" and divides the learning mind from the world. This "release" from the narrow confines of body and immediate experience is rejected on varied grounds in the chapters collected here in favor of more complex relations between person and world. The idea of learning as cognitive acquisition – whether of facts, knowledge, problem-solving strategies, or metacognitive skills – seems to dissolve when learning is conceived of as the construction of present versions of past experience for several persons acting together (Kvale, 1977; Cole, Hood, & McDermott, 1978; Hutchins, this volume). And when scientific practice is viewed as just another everyday practice (Latour & Woolgar, 1979; Latour, 1987; Suchman, 1987; Lave, 1988), it is clear that theories of "situated activity" provide different perspectives on "learning" and its "contexts."

Participants in the conference agreed, on the whole, on four premises concerning knowledge and learning in practice.

1. Knowledge always undergoes construction and transformation in use.
2. Learning is an integral aspect of activity in and with the world at all times. That learning occurs is not problematic.
3. What is learned is always complexly problematic.
4. Acquisition of knowledge is not a simple matter of taking in knowledge; rather, things assumed to be natural categories, such as "bodies of knowledge," "learners," and "cultural transmission," require reconceptualization as cultural, social products.

David Pear argues that to explore the meaning of "knowledge" you must begin with what is not knowledge (1972); the present book has taken up this strategy as well. The first chapters are about work, which is not usually conceptualized as learning. A number of other chapters are about failure to learn, which is usually assumed to be something other than learning. If learning is taken to be an aspect of everyday practice, however, such distinctions dissolve.

Several themes that emerge in Part II of the book, "Learning craftwork," help to reformulate the meaning of learning. These chapters are concerned with what we have dubbed *craftwork*. They are about adults engaged in culturally, socially, historically defined forms of ordinary, productive activity. "Learning craftwork" includes Hutchins's study of the careers and work practices of navigators on a U.S. Navy helicopter transport ship. Engeström presents his research on changing medical practice in public clinics in Finland, and Dreier discusses his research on therapist–client relations. The work of artificial intelligence practitioners, viewed as craft practice, is the focus of Suchman and Trigg's chapter, while the craft of blacksmithing is the topic of Keller and Keller's. Fuhrer examines the uncommon hazards of unfamiliar activity for newcomers to a career placement center who are trying to track down information about jobs in an unfamiliar setting. The settings for these studies lie outside conventional educational institutions, and away from the usual research populations of children and other academic novices; they focus on prosaic everyday practices.

It should be said that the conceptions of craftwork in most of the chapters bear little resemblance to the small-scale problem-solving tasks typical of cognitive learning research: Forging a cooking utensil, or taking part in the work of a national university examination committee are substantial, meaningful forms of activity. In all cases the work described takes on meaning from its broader interconnections with(in) other activity systems.

Authors in Part II of the book have (re)conceptualized what might be meant by learning-in-practice. They address the question, "if people learn in activity in the seamless way suggested by investigations of situated activity, how does this come about?" They begin by shifting from terms such as *learning* (given its traditionally narrow connotations) to concepts more akin to *understanding* and *participation in ongoing activity*. *Understanding* is assumed to be a partial and open-ended process while at the same time there is structure (variously conceived) to activity in the world. Thus, the indeterminacy and open-endedness of understanding are not viewed as infinite or random. Finally, authors argue that knowledge and learning will be found distributed throughout the complex structure of persons-acting-in-setting. They cannot be pinned down to the head of the individual or to assigned tasks or to external tools or to the environment, but lie instead in the relations among them.

Paradoxically, learning craftwork may appear easy in the chapters in Part II, whereas in Part III it often seems nearly impossible to learn in settings dedicated to education. But appearances are deceptive: Studies in the second half of the book suggest that it is as easy to learn to fail in school as it is to learn to navigate a ship. On the other hand, the studies in Part II show that what people are learning to do is difficult, complex work. The learning is not a separate process, nor an end in itself. If it seems effortless, it is because in some sense it is invisible.

If learning-in-practice is ubiquitous, what are we to make of educational institutions, formal methods of learning and teaching, and of failure to learn? Part III of the book, "Learning as social production," explores different approaches to the analysis of institutionalized education, to learning identities *as a process,* to learning identities *as products,* to teaching, and to participants' beliefs about knowledge and the everyday world. These chapters focus on how institutional arrangements (such as schools) generate "learners," "learning," and "things to be learned" – in practice. They analyze the processes by which these products of situated activity are socially produced.

Part III focuses on Western cultural institutionalized arrangements for learning and failing to learn. Success and failure at learning are viewed, not as attributes of individuals, but as specialized social and institutional arrangements. There is a strong emphasis on the problematic and differentiated character of what gets learned (e.g., Säljö & Wyndhamn; Kvale); it depends on the subjective and intersubjective interpretation of the how and why of ongoing activity. National examination systems, placement processes for children nominated for special education, and learning disabilities are analyzed respectively by Kvale, Mehan, and McDermott as what might be called rituals of legitimation or degradation and exclusion. (Latour's analysis of the centralization of control achieved through the mathematization of science offers a complementary analysis of institutional arrangements for knowledge and legitimacy [1986].) Likewise, Levine focuses on the social organization of mild mental retardation, arguing that it is the product of a cultural process of ritualized exclusion of some in the name of a normality that, once turned into a goal, becomes unobtainable (Levine & Langness, 1983). Levine, Säljö and Wyndhamn, and Minick trace the changing meanings of tasks for learners and teachers alike, and build a rich picture of the situated character of knowing, doing, and learning identities for all those involved.

These chapters provide evidence of the *sociocultural* production of failure to learn (Kvale; Levine; McDermott; Mehan; Minick; Säljö & Wyndhamn). They are about how people learn identities and identify the situated meaning of what is to be learned, and the specific shaping of people's identities as learners. Thus, Levine insists on the sociocultural construction of retardation within the family in terms compatible with Mehan's analysis of a school system's construction of educationally handicapped children. He shows how parents restrict the experience of developmentally delayed children and are silent to them about the general and extended meanings of everyday activities, a theme that resonates through other chapters as well. Kvale argues that university comprehensive examinations are, from one perspective, tests of students, measuring what they have learned or failed to learn. At the same time, the national system is the means by which representatives of academic disciplines, acting in examination committees, establish what will constitute legitimate academic knowledge, and what lies outside its boundaries. Students who fail (and perhaps the most successful as well) are the sacrificial lambs whose fates give material form to legitimate knowledge. Further evidence that school accomplishments (including failure) are situated and collective is to be found in demonstrations that a child's "handicap" may be reformulated when it turns out to be incompatible with class scheduling requirements (Mehan, Hertweck, & Meihls, 1986), and in McDermott's argument that learning disabilities acquire the child, rather than the other way around. McDermott argues that people are so knowledgeably experienced in detecting, diagnosing, highlighting, and otherwise contributing to the generation of such identities that the society produces its quota of nonactors, or flawed actors, as they participate in the everyday world. As for identifying the meaning of things-to-be-learned, understanders' "conceptions," Säljö and Wyndhamn (also Säljö, 1982) demonstrate the different meanings students assign to a single task when the task is embedded in different situational frameworks. Minick explores early attempts of primary-school teachers to induct children into a distinctive form of school discourse. These authors provide evidence that tasks are viewed differently, and responded to differently, with characteristic variations in success and failure, when things to be learned are situated differently.

Relations with theory past: Some paradoxes and silences of cognitive theory

Silences and paradoxes are generated in any theoretical problematic: questions that cannot be asked and issues for which no principled resolution is possible. At least four such issues trouble traditional cognitive theory. They concern those conventional divisions alluded to earlier, between learning and what is not (supposed to be) learning. Resolutions to these difficulties have been anticipated in the four premises concerning knowledge and learning in practice mentioned earlier. The problems include, first, an assumed division between learning and other kinds of activity. Second, both the invention and reinvention of knowledge are difficult problems for cognitive theory if learning is viewed as a matter of acquiring existing knowledge. Third, cognitive theory assumes universal processes of learning and the homogeneous character of knowledge and of learners (save in quantity or capacity). This makes it difficult to account for the richly varied participants and projects in any situation of learning. Finally, there is a problem of reconceptualizing the meaning of erroneous, mistaken understanding in a heterogeneous world.

First, how is "learning" to be distinguished from human activity as such? Within cognitive theories it has been assumed that learning and development are distinctive processes, not to be confused with the more general category of human activity. This involves two theoretical claims that are in question here: One is that actors' relations with knowledge-in-activity are static and do not change except when subject to special periods of "learning" or "development." The other is that institutional arrangements for inculcating knowledge *are* the necessary, special circumstances for learning, separate from everyday practices such as those described in Part II. The difference may be at heart a very deep epistemological one, between a view of knowledge as a collection of real entities, located in heads, and of learning as a process of internalizing them, versus a view of knowing and learning as engagement in changing processes of human activity. In the latter case "knowledge" becomes a complex and problematic concept, whereas in the former it is "learning" that is problematic.

A second, related issue concerns the narrow focus of learning theories on the transmission of existing knowledge, while remaining silent about the invention of new knowledge in practice. Engeström argues that this is a central lacuna in contemporary learning theory (1987). Certainly, any simple assumption that *transmission* or *transfer* or *internalization* are apt descriptors for the circulation of knowledge in society faces the difficulty that they imply *uniformity* of knowledge.

They do not acknowledge the fundamental imprint of interested parties, multiple activities, and different goals and circumstances, on what constitutes "knowing" on a given occasion or across a multitude of interrelated events. These terms imply that humans engage first and foremost in the reproduction of given knowledge rather than in the production of knowledgeability as a flexible process of engagement with the world. Engeström's conceptualization of how people learn to do things that have not been done before elaborates the idea that zones of proximal development are collective, rather than individual, phenomena and that "the new" is a collective invention in the face of felt dilemmas and contradictions that impede ongoing activity and impel movement and change.

Further, part of what it means to engage in learning activity is extending what one knows beyond the immediate situation, rather than involuting one's understanding "metacognitively" by thinking about one's own cognitive processes. Critical psychologists of the Berlin school (e.g., Dreier, 1980, 1991; Holzkamp, 1983, 1987, 1991) insist on the importance of a distinction between experiencing or knowing the immediate circumstances ("interpretive thinking," "restricted action") and processes of thinking beyond and about the immediate situation in more general terms ("comprehensive thinking," "extended, generalized action"). Together, in a dialectical process by which each helps to generate the other, they produce new understanding (see Wenger, 1991).

Doing and knowing are inventive in another sense: They are open-ended processes of improvisation with the social, material, and experiential resources at hand. Keller and Keller's research illustrates this: The blacksmith's practices as he creates a skimming spoon draw on rich resources of experience, his own and that of other people, present and past. But his understanding of the skimmer also emerges in the forging process. He does not know what it will be until it is finished. At one point he spreads one section of the spoon handle for the second time but goes too far and, in evaluating the work, finds it necessary to reduce the width of the handle again. "It is as though he has to cross a boundary in order to discover the appropriate limits of the design" (Keller & Keller, this volume).

The work of researchers in artificial intelligence appears to have the same character: Suchman and Trigg (this volume) describe it as "a skilled improvisation, organized in orderly ways that are designed to maintain a lively openness to the possibilities that the materials at hand present." And "analyses of situated action ... point to the contingencies of practical action on which logic in use, including the production and use of scenarios and formalisms, inevitably and in every instance relies."

Fuhrer (this volume) emphasizes the varying emotional effects of the improvisational character of activity. These effects are perhaps most intensely felt by newcomers, but he equates newcomers' predicaments with those of learners in general. He insists that in addition to cognitive and environmental dimensions, there is an emotional dimension to all learning. He argues that "to some degree, all individual actions within everyday settings, especially those of newcomers, are somewhat discrepant from what is expected; the settings change continuously. Most emotions within social situations, such as embarrassment, audience anxiety, shyness, or shame, follow such discrepancies, just because these discrepancies produce visceral arousal. And it is the combination of that arousal with an ongoing evaluative cognition that produces the subjective experience of an emotion."

Given these considerations, Fuhrer raises the question of how people manage and coordinate "the various actions that arise from cognitive, social and environmental demands or goals." Old-timers as well as newcomers try to carry out the usual activities in given settings, but they are also trying to address many other goals, among which are impression management and "developing interpersonal relations to other setting inhabitants. . . . Thus the newcomers simultaneously pursue several goals and therefore they may simultaneously perform different actions."

The third issue, the assumed homogeneity of actors, goals, motives, and activity itself is challenged in many chapters, replaced with quite different assumptions that emphasize their heterogeneity. I believe this view is new to discussions of learning. It derives from an intent focus on the multiplicity of actors engaged in activity together, and on the interdependencies, conflicts, and relations of power so produced. These views are elaborated in this volume by several authors: Keller and Keller argue that "the goal of production is not monolithic but multifaceted ... based on considerations aesthetic, stylistic, functional, procedural, financial, and academic as well as conceptions of self and other, and material conditions of work." Dreier proposes that "different participants' interpretations are based on different contextual social positions with inherent differences in possibilities, interests, and perspectives on conflicts arising from different locations." Suchman and Trigg describe artificial intelligence research as a socially organized process of craftsmanship consisting of "the crafting together of a complex machinery made of heterogeneous materials, mobilized in the service of developing a theory of mind." And McDermott proposes that, "by institutional arrangements, we must consider everything from the most local level of the classroom to the more inclusive level of inequities throughout the political economy (preferably from both ends of the continuum at the same time)." These statements refer to a wide variety of relations, but each challenges research on knowing and learning that depends implicitly on a homogeneity of community, culture, participants, their motives, and the meaning of events.

The heterogeneous, multifocal character of situated activity implies that conflict is a ubiquitous aspect of human existence. This follows if we assume that people in the same situation, people who are helping to constitute "a situation" together, know different things and speak with different interests and experience from different social locations. Suddenly assumptions concerning the uniformity of opinion, knowledge, and belief become, on the one hand, matters of common historical tradition and complexly shared relations with larger societal forces (whatever these might mean – now an important question) and, on the other hand, matters of imposed conformity and symbolic violence. Analysis focused on conflictual practices of changing understanding in activity is not so likely to concentrate on the truth or error of some knowledge claim. It is more likely to explore disagreements over what is relevant; whether, and how much, something is worth knowing and doing; what to make of ambiguous circumstances; what is convenient for whom, what to do next when one does not know what to expect, and who cares most about what. There are always conflicts of power, so mislearning cannot be understood independently of someone imposing her or his view. There is, of course, and at the same time, much uniformity and agreement in the world. The perspectives represented here differ about whether this is always, or only much of the time, a matter of one party imposing assent, subtly or otherwise, on others.

The fourth and final issue concerns "failure to learn." In mainstream theorizing about learning this is commonly assumed to result from the inability or refusal on the part of an individual to engage in something called "learning." The alternative view explored here earlier is that not-learning and "failure" identities are active normal social locations and processes. The latter generates further questions, however: If failure is a socially arranged identity, what is left to be said about the making of "errors"? Given that several of the authors provide novel construals of failure to learn, question the meaning of "consensus," and call attention to the deficiencies of claims that knowing unfolds without conflict and without engaging the interests of involved participants, does the term *error* still have meaning? The answer depends on whose socially positioned point of view is adopted, and on historically and socially situated conceptions of erroneous action and belief. Several of the chapters in this volume develop powerful ways of conceptualizing socially, historically situated nonlearning or mislearning. They discuss nonlearning activities that occur when embarrassment is too great or that result from anxiety, from the social delegitimation of learning or the learner, and from the retarding effects of denying learners access to connections between immediate appearances and broader, deeper social forces, or to concrete interrelations within and across situations (e.g., Fuhrer, Levine). Mehan explores the discoordination of voices in interactions between school psychologist, teacher, and parent, who speak in different "languages" – psychological, sociological, and historical – and between physicians and patients. Engeström locates unproductive encounters between patients and physicians in the mismatch among historically engendered discourses – thus, in practice, among the biomedical and psychosocial registers or voices the physician and patient use for communicating about medical issues.

Hutchins's analysis raises questions about the location of error-making in historical systems of activity and in relations among participants. He describes what it is possible for novice navigators to learn in practice in terms of task partitioning, instruments, lines of communication, and limitations and openness of access for observing others, their interactions, and tools. He argues that these define the portion of the task environment that is available as a learning context to each task performer – this constitutes the performer's "horizon of observability." The density of error correction (which helps to make learning possible) depends on the contours of this horizon.

In sum, the assumptions proposed here amount to a preliminary account of what is meant by *situated learning*. Knowledgeability is routinely in a state of change rather than stasis, in the medium of socially, culturally, and historically ongoing systems of activity, involving people who are related in multiple and heterogeneous ways, whose social locations, interests, reasons, and subjective possibilities are different, and who improvise struggles in situated ways with each other over the value of particular definitions of the situation, in both immediate and comprehensive terms, and for whom the production of failure is as much a part of routine collective activity as the production of average, ordinary knowledgeability. These interrelated assumptions run deeply through the work presented here.

Context as situated activity

Common concerns – theories of person–activity–world and their intrinsic heterogeneity, and a commitment to the investigation of everyday practice in detail – by no means determine a single theoretical position on the question of "context." Roughly speaking, there are two major viewpoints represented here, built upon these commonalities but differing in their conception of the relations that constitute the contexts, or perhaps more precisely the contextualization, of activity. One argues that the central theoretical relation is historically constituted between persons engaged in socioculturally constructed activity and the world with which they are engaged. Activity theory is a representative of such theoretical traditions. The other focuses on the construction of the world in social interaction; this leads to the view that activity is its own context. Here the central theoretical relation is the intersubjective relation among coparticipants in social interaction. This derives from a tradition of phenomenological social theory. These two viewpoints do not exhaust the positions taken by authors here, but cover the majority.

Analysis of "context" in the activity theory perspective begins with historically emerging contradictions that characterize all concrete social institutions and relations. Unlike some other traditions inspired by Marxist principles, activity theory emphasizes the nondeterminate character of the effects of objective social structures. Differences in the social location of actors are inherent in political-economic structures, and elaborated in specific sociocultural practices. Differences of power, interests, and possibilities for action are ubiquitous. Any particular action is socially constituted, given meaning by its location in societally, historically generated systems of activity. Meaning is not created through individual intentions; it is mutually constituted in relations between activity systems and persons acting, and has a relational character. Context may be seen as the historically constituted concrete relations within and between situations. As Engeström (this volume) puts it: "Contexts are activity systems. An activity system integrates the subject, the object, and the instruments (material tools as well as signs and symbols) into a unified whole ... [that includes relations of] production and communication, distribution, exchange, consumption." Dreier (this volume) argues that, "The situation stands in particular connections with the overall societal structure of possibilities, meanings, and actions that produce and reproduce the concrete social formation. ... So the immediate 'internal' connections of the situation are also societally mediated in a concrete and particular way."

Activity theorists also take issue with assumptions that minute actions are the proper object of psychological study. This should not be surprising, given their insistence on the complex interrelations of activity systems and persons engaged in lived practice. In activity theory the term *operation* is most closely equivalent to the conventional meanings of *an action*. But whereas action is typically viewed as a direct, unmediated connection between person and environment, in an activity theory perspective there is always a more complicated relation that mediates between them. In particular, operations, the way in which the goals of actions are implemented or carried out under particular situated circumstances, have no intrinsic meaning of their own. Meaningful actions, entailing complex relations with(in) societal activity systems, give meaning to operations. All of this together constitutes the smallest possible meaningful unit of study in activity theory.

Minute actions are by no means the constitutive elements of "interaction" in social constructionist approaches either. This book contains rich descriptions of the unfortunate *effects* of beliefs that "meaningful activity" is composed, building-block fashion, out of operations (see Suchman and Trigg's description of the artificial intelligence researchers' approach to action, Mehan's description of the assumptions and procedures of school psychologists, and Levine's chapter and his research more generally on approaches to mental retardation).

Säljö and Wyndhamn offer a good example of relations among actions, operations, meaning, and systems of activity (though they might not use these terms). They describe how children's engagement in action (finding the correct postage for a letter from a postal table) is realized through different operations (e.g., calculating amounts of postage to several decimal places, determining which is the right-priced stamp) in different settings (math classes, social studies classes, and in the post office) in which the situated "sense" of the task differs. The meaning of the postal task cannot be defined independently from the activity within which the problem is posed, and the children's assumptions about what are the relevant premises for action.

The conception of "context" in the phenomenological perspective, in contrast with that typical of activity theories, begins with the premise that situations are constructed as people organize themselves to attend to and give meaning to figural concerns against the ground of ongoing social interaction. Silence, erasure, the construction of boundaries, and collusion are constitutive here (e.g., Latour & Woolgar, 1979; and, in this volume, Suchman & Trigg; McDermott; and Mehan). The figure–ground metaphor highlights the key relation of context and meaning – both determined by the relation and determining of it. McDermott argues that "context is not so much something into which someone is put, but an order of behavior of which one is a part" (see also McDermott, 1980). He draws on Birdwhistell's view of context:

I like to think of it as a rope. The fibers that make up the rope are discontinuous; when you twist them together, you don't make them continuous, you make the thread continuous. . . . The thread has no fibers in it, but, if you break up the thread, you can find the fibers again. So that, even though it may look in a thread as though each of those particles are going all through it, that isn't the case.

Mehan points out that a social constructionist research tradition is concerned with

how the stable features of social institutions such as schooling, science, medicine, and the family are both generated in and revealed by the language of the institution's participants. . . . People's everyday practices are examined for the way in which they exhibit – indeed, generate – the social structures of the relevant domain. . . . Inferences about social structure are permissible only when the workings of the structure can be located in people's interaction.

The major difficulties of phenomenological and activity theory in the eyes of the other will be plain: Those who start with the view that social activity is its own context dispute claims that objective social structures exist other than in their social-interactional construction in situ. Activity theorists argue, on the other hand, that the concrete connectedness and meaning of activity cannot be accounted for by analysis of the immediate situation. Thus, Dreier points out a widely held assumption that the context of activity is the immediate surround of specific persons' actions – that the context of action is "the characteristics of immediate interaction and/or participating personalities." Much of his chapter is devoted to argument concerning how this view distorts not only therapeutic relationships but also the analyses typically carried out by social scientists who study therapeutic and other kinds of face-to-face relations, as it erases historical processes, both large and small (cf. Latour & Woolgar, 1979).

The chapters by Suchman and Trigg and by Mehan represent innovative responses from phenomenological researchers to criticisms of the self-contained, ahistorical character of much of that tradition. In fashioning a transitive analysis of social projects, they raise questions about the ground against which meaning in particular contexts is configured, a ground that goes beyond the immediate situation. This involves following projects across interrelated interactional events. (For Mehan the project is the school's decision-making process about where to assign particular students. Objects are the children who become objectified in the bureaucratic work of designating them "learning disabled." For Suchman and Trigg, the artificial intelligence researchers' project is to find a solution to a theoretical problem in their field; the result is an emerging artificial intelligence program.) Suchman and Trigg address the issue of how particular craftwork is both constrained by, and takes resources from, the intersection of several existing practices. They analyze connections among what they call the ancestral traditions of artificial intelligence as it organizes its projects around "scenarios" (short, programmatic, storylike proxies for the everyday-world problem the program is supposed to address), and the work of generating formalisms that can be turned into computer programs that will resolve the artificial intelligence problems that motivate the scenarios. "The scenario serves as a coordinating device for project activities distributed in time and space." The segment of work that they analyze "is located in a stream of activities whose concerns are both historically given and projected forward in time." At each step in their analysis they consider how the work in which the researchers are engaged both mediates and is mediated by past and future steps in realizing the project. Suchman has recently suggested that concern with historical mediation has become a point of convergence between activity theorists and phenomenological analysts: The latter are beginning to recognize that immediate situations include historical artifacts, practices, and routines, and that historical practices and artifacts provide resources, interactionally, to be garnered and employed on next occasions (personal communication).

I have sketched two views of the context of activity and tried to indicate some of their implications for conceptualizing action and the mediated interconnections that partially produce its meaning. Both theoretical viewpoints expand the horizons of conventional analysis of situated activity, especially in temporal, historical terms. Rather than contrast them in terms of the original unit of analysis proposed earlier – persons in activity in the social world – it now seems more appropriate to sum them up, respectively, as exploring how it is that people live in *history*, and how it is that people *live* in history. Activity theory reflects the former, and with it the importance of the partially given character of an objectively structured world. Phenomenological views emphasize the latter and with it the partially cogenerated character of a meaningful world.

This seems an odd, felicitous, but still preliminary outcome of our attempts to come to grips with the "context" of activity. The emphasis on the historical mediation of activity in context may provide a clue as to how to proceed. The chapters stress the importance of interrelations among local practices; they give hints that local practices must inevitably take part in constituting each other, through their structural interconnections, their intertwined activities, their common participants, and more. The next step may be to reformulate the problem of context: Instead of asking, What is the constitutive relationship between persons acting and the contexts with which they act? the question becomes, What are the relationships between local practices that contextualize the ways people act together, both in and across contexts? The work represented here has succeeded in producing this new sense of the problem and, with it, an insistent and appealing recommendation to investigate those interconnections in a concentrated fashion.

Decontextualization as local practice

Usually, contextualized learning is not discussed alone, but as part of a duality of which decontextualized learning forms the other half. But the theories of context discussed in the previous section are intended to apply broadly to *all* social practice: They claim that there is no decontextualized social practice. Such a claim commits us to explaining what has often been taken to be "decontextualized knowledge" or "decontextualized learning" *as* contextualized social practices. This may not be a simple task: To discuss decontextualization it is first necessary to establish just what is meant, conventionally, by the term *context.* For there has as yet been no discussion of its most common dualistic conception, as a static, residual, surrounding "container" for social interaction. Given the formalist character of this view it should not be surprising that the head is often also conceived to be a container, in this case, for knowledge, while more general knowledge is the container of more particular knowledge, and language is an inert container for the transmission of meaning. Reminded by a flurry of defining gestures during the conference, Latour pointed out that when most people talk about context, they sketch in the air a shell about the size and shape of a pumpkin. Nor should this come as a surprise:

In all commonsense uses of the term, context refers to an empty slot, a container, into which other things are placed. It is the "con" that contains the "text," the bowl that contains the soup. As such, it shapes the contours of its contents; it has its effects only at the borders of the phenomenon under analysis. . . . The soup does not shape the bowl, and the bowl most certainly does not alter the substance of the soup. Text and context, soup and bowl . . . can be analytically separated and studied on their own without doing violence to the complexity of the situation. A static sense of context delivers a stable world. (McDermott, this volume)

That this sense of context (and with it common senses of decontextualization) is deeply held and embodied should remind us that a formalist view of context is a key conception in conventional theories of action, thinking, knowing, and learning, with, significantly, deep roots much more generally in a Euro-American worldview.

The prevailing view of context furnishes the ground against which conventional views of decontextualization take on meaning. In fact, a detached view of context seems prerequisite for an analytic conception of decontextualization. In spite of its derivative character, however, we must not lose sight of the fact that decontextualization is the more salient and highly valued of this asymmetric, dualistic pair. Until quite recently it has been more significant in the prevailing lexicon than context, especially where knowledge and learning are at issue.

To decontextualize knowledge is to form-alize it (to contain it, pour it into forms) at a more inclusive level. To formalize is to contain more forms. It follows that abstraction from and generalization across "contexts" are mechanisms that are supposed to produce decontextualized (valuable, general) knowledge. Along with this way of talking about decontextualization go several other claims. First, that movement toward powerful (abstract, general) knowledge is movement away from engagement in the world, so that distance "frees" knowers from the particularities of time, place, and ongoing activity. Second, that language contains and can express literal meaning (Minick, this volume, discussing Rommetveit). Rommetveit (1988) reminds us of "the intuitive appeal of pervading pretheoretical notions such as, for instance (Goffman, 1976, p. 303), 'the common sense notion . . . that the word *in isolation* will have a general basic, or most down-to-earth meaning.' Such presuppositions seem to form part of the myth of literal meaning in our highly literate societies." A third assumption accompanying claims for the possibility (and power) of decontextualization is that we live in an objective, monistic world. Minick elaborates this point:

Just as the myth of literal meaning posits a language that has meaning independent of local concerns, interests, and perspectives – independent of the formation of "temporary mutual commitments to shared perspectives" – the myth of the "monistic real world" posits a world that can be described and comprehended in isolation from such local concerns, perspectives, and commitments.

Once the separate, inert, objective character of the world is assumed, along with the neutral, disinterested character of knowledge (because it brackets out local concerns), it is entirely consistent to think of institutions in the same terms. From this, assumptions are derived about the privileged character of schools and of therapeutic encounters as sites where knowledge is produced, where learning takes place, but where what is learned is independent of, and not affected by, the circumstances in which it is produced. Further, it is assumed that what is learned is of a general nature and powerful because it is *not* embedded in the particularities of specific practices. These assumptions are brought into question simultaneously once learning is conceived as situated practice.

McDermott, Minick, and other authors would surely agree that the pair of terms, context and decontextualization, has been borrowed unreflectively from the culture more generally, rather than derived analytically or theoretically. Also, according to the authors in this book, the dualistic division and categorization of experience that privileges "decontextualization" does not offer an adequate explanation of thought or action. Nonetheless, this pervasive perspective leads a robust existence *in practice*, in the contemporary world. Euro-American culture instantiates it, and in many ways is predicated upon it. Beliefs, institutions, and a great deal of action operate in its name. A theoretical account of (de)contextualization as situated practice should account for how such formalist views of the world are sustained in practice. Accordingly, authors here have raised the question, How are conventional conceptions of context and decontextualization, and the myth of an objective, disinterested, asocial world, *made* part of our social practices, in situated ways? And how do conventions (beliefs and practices) that enact contextual dualism shape other social practices? I have come to see these questions and ethnographic explorations of this issue as among the most novel and interesting contributions of the book.

Minick provides an example of a situated practice that inculcates belief in a monistic world and in literal meaning. Teachers' use of what he calls "representational speech" reflects the belief that complete, explicit, unambiguous representation in language should be sufficient to convey meaning. This is, of course, one way to subscribe to the myth of literal meaning. It has a crucial corollary: that if complete representation of meaning in language is possible, then the student, the receiver of explicit communication, need attend to nothing except its "literal" meaning. Minick argues that "the introduction of representational forms of speech to primary-school children is . . . a study of their introduction to social and mental activities that take place in this 'mythical' monistic real world."

Minick uncovers situated, cultural political mechanisms that produce "decontextualized" representational interactions. One of these is the switching from commonsense interpretations to representational directives: He describes a grade-school teacher leading children through a lesson, saying "Did I say raise your hand when you finished or did I say put your pencil down?" when the original sense of her instructions had been "Let me know when you're done." There is conflict between situational sense and representational directives; this creates uncertainty for children and anxiety about what is the right thing to do; it creates grounds for blame from the teacher, and dependency of children on the teacher because only the teacher can resolve the ambiguity-through-decontextualization she has created along with conflict between situational and "desituated" meaning.

There are numerous ways, then, in which the specific social practices involved in interactions around literal meaning are means by which teachers maintain control of classrooms and move pupils through activities in an efficient and mechanical fashion. (These practices themselves are, of course, situated in other relations that make control of children and their activities a customary, even required, aspect of teachers' everyday lives.) One of the ironies of this is that the very act of attempting to turn language into the only site of meaning creates at one and the same time ambiguities of meaning and a basis for controlling learners. It reduces what is being communicated to operations (in activity theory terms), with predictable results. There is a second irony as well: It was emphasized earlier that improvisation, ambiguity, and openendedness are essential aspects of activity.

Teachers' attempts to disambiguate directives to children are no exception. Attempts to decontextualize – to achieve self-contained precision and thereby both generality and literalness of meaning – create ambiguity in the process of stripping away meaning. Thus, teachers' decontextualizing practices have (unintended) effects, which change practices and shrivel the meaning of learning for all concerned.

Representational speech is not, of course, limited to the classroom. Mehan focuses on this and other mechanisms for turning myth into reality in practice. "When technical language is used and embedded in the institutional trappings of the formal proceedings of a meeting, the grounds for negotiating meaning are removed from under the conversation." Under such circumstances, institutionally grounded representations predominate (e.g., psychiatrists' representations prevail over patients' and, as Kvale demonstrates, examination committees' prevail over students'). The effect of technical language (its technologism is not accidental) is to bracket and delegitimize the situated understanding of other participants, including parents and teachers. Further, this particular "universalizing language, as invoked in settings such as meetings to decide on the classroom placements of children with learning difficulties," decontextualizes the (absent) child by reducing her or him (beforehand and elsewhere) to a collection of discrete variables. Mehan argues that this technical, psychologistic, scientistic language is a common source of power and authority in many contemporary settings. Patterns of removal and alignment across socially constructed boundaries (classroom, testing the child, discussing the child's placement) are material aspects of decontextualization processes.

Although there are many other ways of demonstrating the absurdity of claims that educative institutions such as school and therapeutic relations are privileged "noncontexts" for context-free learning, the examples here of the specific, situated practices of decontextualization are surely among the most dramatic. Further, they offer clues as to lines of historical work within which to locate future analyses of the situated practices of craftwork and the nature of learning identity formation described throughout the book.

There are yet other mechanisms for giving material existence to the myth of monistic realism: Dreier describes two such processes, one of them "desubjectification":

Reasons for action are constitutive of human agency, but clients' subjective rationality only appears from an external perspective – the therapist's interpretation. . . . The therapist couches the subjective rationality of his own actions from the external perspective of his client's needs (purporting to have no needs or interests of his own). The consequence is the desubjectification of therapist–client relations.

He goes on to describe processes of "deinstitutionalization," which also help to privilege therapy as "the building of an anywhere and nowhere." As Suchman and Trigg describe them, the careers of artificial intelligence researchers follow a path of decontextualization (and recontextualization) through increasingly specialized communities – positioned mediations that distance the everyday practice of artificial intelligence research from some of its claimed constituencies, and insinuate it into closer connections with others. "In the course of their work, researchers selectively reproduce, make relevant, extend, and transform problems and solutions *given by their membership in progressively more specialized technical communities*, each with its own assumptions, commitments, and identifying technologies" (emphasis mine). This work, Dreier's, and that of other authors here as well offer clues as to the relations between specialization and professionalization and specific social practices of decontextualization.

The authors here take situated activity to be far more complex and contentful than formal notions of context could contain. They locate learning throughout the relations of persons in activity in the world. From this point of view decontextualization and appeals to it are active, interested denials of contextual interconnections (i.e., they are processes of erasure, collusion, and domination). Most broadly, decontextualization is a key process in the production of the culture of monistic realism, the historically located societal formation in which, as Mehan observes, there is consensus around psychological, technological, and institutional means for objectifying persons and legitimizing "generalization."

Conclusion

As the conference drew to a close, we tried to sum up our common endeavor. Three guidelines emerged for organizing the introduction to this book. The conference participants preferred not to emphasize learning because the traditionally narrow genre of research conjured up by the term might get in the way of readers' interest in our work. They hoped I would convey the spirit of the commitment we forged in the time we spent together to the value of the *differences* among our theoretical positions. These differences offer multiple possibilities for interrogating social experience and this is a central intention of the book. And we all hoped to produce chapters reflecting movement forward, motivated as little as possible by opposition to other views, which surely has driven us too much in the past. We intended to produce positive accounts of our changing understanding of how to investigate social practice.

I have not complied very well with any of these guidelines, and each one deserves comment. First, I have indeed given singular attention to questions of learning. The chapters clearly warrant it: They provide the most positive possible answer to fears that learning is a dessicated topic. The authors have produced fascinating analyses of learning as situated practice. In doing so they have opened out the scope of studies of learning, erasing old barriers between learning and participation in ongoing social practice, and locating failure to learn squarely in the latter.

Second, there is a remarkable variety of theoretical positions represented in the book. I initially intended to recount these differences more thoroughly, but found myself drawn to other issues instead, and have tried to demonstrate that a coherent account of understanding in social practice is to be found among the diverse analyses of these chapters. Together they demonstrate that learning and not learning, contextualization and decontextualation, are socially situated and socially produced. To the extent that my argument for coherence is convincing, however, it obscures our intention to focus on the significance of the disjunctions among our positions. The book would repay reading in two ways: for its strong common argument and for the resources of diversity it offers as well.

Finally, we have been trying to explore new approaches without miring ourselves in the burdens of defending the value of doing so, and we have tried to go beyond mere critique of dominant theories. There are reasons to question the feasibility of this goal. If our relations with currently dominant theoretical positions are difficult to escape, the problem may be one of rethinking *how* to struggle with such hegemonic theoretical practices. It seems useful to stop treating mainstream theoretical positions simply as unmediated alternatives to our own practice and start looking at them as historical manifestations of the sociocultural formation in which we are participants, and to which we have concrete connections of various kinds (cf. Chaiklin, 1992; Kvale, 1992).

There are not many precedents for doing this. Prevailing theory concerning learning, thinking, and knowing is for the most part ahistorical and acontextual in its understanding of itself. Further, so little has been done to denaturalize and historicize its analytic categories and questions that the assumptions and concepts of mainstream theories (though not the jargon) are difficult to distinguish from folk beliefs and practices. This should serve notice that the everyday, situated practices that the authors here set out to describe may be significantly intertwined with the theory we are trying to transcend. We are left with the task of historical analysis and explanation of how rationalist, individualist, empiricist conceptions of learning, knowing, and the social world are kept alive and well in the culture at large.

This book does not offer such an analysis of Euro-American culture. Some of the studies analyze detailed aspects of specific changing social practices. Others assume that what they have to say about Euro-American culture is incidental, a means through which to explore conceptions of socially situated activity. In neither case do I detect a keen sense that the crucial "move" in these projects is to lay bets on what constitutes the most important cultural underpinnings of the world in which we live, so as to study those in particular.

In the previous section, however, I argued that these studies examine sociocultural processes of participation, production, myth and sense making, inculcation, and (de)legitimation, in situated processes that *are* central to Euro-American practices and worldview. Furthermore, I argued that the central cultural significance of the understanding practices that have been analyzed in these chapters is not accidental. The question is, How did authors in the book come to investigate processual mechanisms by which mainstream, hegemonic, theoretical practices help to constitute the societywide underpinnings of belief and action about thought, knowing, learning, and the world?

It may be that the answer lies in our inability to escape from

"saying no" to older theoretical practices: Existing theoretical perspectives contribute in a serious way to the sustenance of the existing
social formation; to take them on, to turn mainstream theories into
objects of analysis and critique, while accounting for their crucial
role in organizing and justifying numerous Euro-American social
practices, is to take on the culture more broadly. In short, there may
be advantages as well as drawbacks to our unsuccessful struggles to
stop grappling with old paradigms.

This suggests a program for the developing practice of studying
situated activity and learning. It might begin with a conception of
learning as an aspect of culturally, historically situated activity. It
would focus on the content of and the ways people participate in
changing social practices singled out for study *because* they appear to
lie at the heart of the production and reproduction – and transformation and change – of the sociocultural order. The present work
furnishes strong beginnings for such a project.

References

Barker, R. (1963). On the nature of the environment: Kurt Lewin memorial award
  address 1963. *Journal of Social Issues, 19,* 17–38.
Barker, R. (1968). *Ecological psychology: Concepts and methods for studying the environ-
  ment of human behavior.* Stanford, CA: Stanford University Press.
Bartlett, F. (1958). *Thinking: An experimental and social study.* New York: Basic Books.
Birdwhistell, R. (1970). *Kinesics and context.* Philadelphia: University of Pennsylvania
  Press.
Chaiklin, S. (1992). From theory to practice and back again: What does postmodern
  philosophy contribute to psychological science? In S. Kvale (Ed.), *Psychol-
  ogy and postmodernism.* London: Sage.
Cole, M., Hood, L., & McDermott, R. (1982). Ecological niche picking: Ecological
  invalidity as an axiom of experimental cognitive psychology. In U. Neisser
  (Ed.), *Memory observed: Remembering in social contexts* (pp. 366–373). San
  Francisco: W. H. Freeman.
Dannefer, D. (1991). On the conceptualization of context in developmental dis-
  course: Four meanings of context and their implications. In D. L. Featherman,
  R. M. Lerner, & M. Perlmutter (Eds.), *Life-span development and behavior*
  (Vol. 11). Hillsdale, NJ: Lawrence Erlbaum.
Davydov, V. V., & Radzhikovskii, L. A. (1985). Vygotsky's theory and the activity-
  oriented approach in psychology. In J. V. Wertsch (Ed.), *Culture, commu-
  nication and cognition* (pp. 35–65). Cambridge: Cambridge University Press.
Dreier, O. (1980). *Familiäres Bewusstsein und familiäres Sein: Therapeutische Analyse*

einer Arbeiterfamilie [Family being and family consciousness: Therapeutic analysis of a working-class family] (Texte zur Kritischen Psychologie Bd. 11). Frankfurt am Main: Campus.

Dreier, O. (1991). Client interests and possibilities in psychotherapy. In C. W. Tolman & W. Maiers (Eds.), *Critical psychology: Contributions to an historical science of the subject* (pp. 196–211). Cambridge: Cambridge University Press.

Engeström, Y. (1987). *Learning by expanding.* Helsinki: Orienta-Konsultit.

Goffman, E. (1964). The neglected situation. *American Anthropologist, 66*(6)2, 133–136.

Goodwin, C., & Duranti, A. (1992). Rethinking context: An introduction. In A. Duranti & C. Goodwin (Eds.), *Rethinking context: Language as an interactive phenomenon.* Cambridge: Cambridge University Press.

Hanks, W. F. (1990a). *Referential practice: Language and lived space among the Maya.* Chicago: University of Chicago Press.

Hanks, W. F. (1990b). *Meaning and matters of context.* Dean's Inaugural Lecture, Division of the Social Sciences, University of Chicago, May 16.

Haraway, D. (1988). Situated knowledges: The science question in feminism and the privilege of partial perspective. *Feminist Studies, 14,* 575–599.

Holzkamp, K. (1983). *Grundlegung der Psychologie* [Foundations of psychology]. Frankfurt: Campus.

Holzkamp, K. (1987). Critical psychology and overcoming of scientific indeterminacy in psychological theorizing (L. Zusne, Trans.). In R. Hogan & W. H. Jones (Eds.), *Perspectives in personality* (Vol. 2, pp. 93–123). Greenwich, CT: JAI Press.

Holzkamp, K. (1991). Societal and individual life processes; Experience of self and scientific objectivity; Psychoanalysis and Marxist psychology. In C. W. Tolman & W. Maiers (Eds.), *Critical psychology: Contributions to an historical science of the subject* (pp. 50–101). Cambridge: Cambridge University Press.

Kvale, S. (1977). Dialectics and research on remembering. In N. Datan & H. W. Reese (Eds.), *Life-span developmental psychology: Dialectical perspectives on experimental research* (pp. 165–189). New York: Academic Press.

Kvale, S. (1992). Postmodern psychology: A contradiction in terms. In S. Kvale (Ed.), *Psychology and postmodernism.* London: Sage.

Latour, B. (1987). A relativistic account of Einstein's relativity. *Social Studies of Science, 18,* 3–44.

Latour, B., & Woolgar, S. (1979). *Laboratory life: The social construction of scientific facts.* Beverly Hills, CA: Sage.

Lave, J. (1988). *Cognition in practice: Mind, mathematics and culture in everyday life.* Cambridge: Cambridge University Press.

Lave, J., & Wenger, E. (1991). *Situated learning: Legitimate peripheral participation.* Cambridge: Cambridge University Press.

Levine, H., & Langness, L. (1983). Context, ability and performance: Comparison of competitive athletics among mildly mentally retarded and nonretarded adults. *American Journal of Mental Deficiency, 87,* 528–538.

McDermott, R. P. (1980). Profile: Ray L. Birdwhistell. *Kinesis Report, 2*(3), 1–4; 14–16.

Mehan, H., Hertweck, A., & Meihls, J. L. (1986). *Handicapping the handicapped: Decision making in students' educational careers.* Stanford, CA: Stanford University Press.

Minick, N. (1985). *L. S. Vygotsky and Soviet activity theory.* Unpublished doctoral dissertation, Northwestern University.

Pear, D. (1972). *What is knowledge?* Oxford: Basil Blackwell.

Rommetveit, R. (1987). Meaning, context, and control: Convergent trends and controversial issues in current social science research on human cognition and communication. *Inquiry, 30,* 77–99.

Rommetveit, R. (1988). On literacy and the myth of literal meaning. In Roger Säljö (Ed.), *The written world: Studies in literate thought and action.* Berlin: Springer-Verlag.

Säljö, R. (1982). *Learning and understanding.* Göteburg: University of Göteburg Press.

Suchman, L. (1987). *Plans and situated actions.* Cambridge: Cambridge University Press.

Wenger, E. (1991). *Toward a theory of cultural transparency: Elements of a social discourse of the visible and the invisible.* Unpublished doctoral dissertation, University of California, Irvine.

Part II

Learning craftwork

2 Learning to navigate

Edwin Hutchins

The navigation activity

At all times while a naval vessel is underway, a plot of its past and projected movements is maintained. Day and night, whenever a ship is neither tied to a pier nor at anchor, navigation computations are performed. In a long passage, the navigation activities may be continuously performed for weeks or even months on end. Most of the time the work of navigation is performed by one person working alone, but when a ship leaves or enters port, or operates in any other environment where maneuverability is restricted, the computational requirements of the task may exceed the capabilities of any individual. In such circumstances, the navigation duties are carried out by a team of individuals working together.

The work described here is a continuation of my long-standing interest at looking at cognition in the real world. In earlier work on litigation in the Trobriand Islands (Hutchins, 1978, 1980), and on navigation without instruments in Micronesia (Hutchins, 1983; Hutchins & Hinton, 1984), I was mainly concerned with the influence of culture on the cognition of individual actors where their activities, while socially situated, were considered primarily as individual cognitive accomplishments. Looking at navigation as it is actually conducted aboard ships, however, brought home to me the extent to which cognitive accomplishments can be joint accomplishments, not attributable to any individual. Another absolutely apparent feature of this setting is the extent to which the computational accomplishments of navigation are mediated by a variety of tools and representational technologies.

Developmental arenas in navigation

The activity of ship navigation is continuously developing in several senses.

First, navigation as it is practiced today is part of a tradition that can be traced back more than two thousand years. Many of the star names used in modern navigation, for example, were used by Egyptian astronomers. When a modern navigator does celestial navigation, he is seeing a sky (at least the northern sky) composed of constellations that were grouped and identified by navigators in the Mediterranean thousands of years ago. Between the early attempts at measurement and map making and the present day, there lies a rich history of technological innovations. In a typical hour of navigation activity, a modern navigator may utilize technologies that range in age from a few years to many hundreds of years. The time scale of the development of navigation practice may be measured in centuries.

A second developmental line in the world of navigation unfolds in the careers of navigation practitioners. In the U.S. Navy, navigation is performed by sailors of the quartermaster rating. Quartermasters begin their careers with rather limited duties and advance to more complicated procedures as they gain expertise. The time scale of this aspect of development may be measured in years.

A third developmental aspect concerns the microgenesis of individual cognition in social interaction. Because people jointly perform the task of navigation, and do so with differing levels of expertise, much of the learning of navigation skills takes place in interaction. The time scale of this aspect of development may be measured in minutes.

The final sense in which the activity of navigation is to be understood as a developmental process involves a return to the first point: the microgenesis of the embedding culture in the conduct of the activity itself. While every navigator and every navigation team depend upon the long tradition that precedes them to structure their task environment, they also are part of the tradition for those who follow. The innovations that change the shape of the navigation activity come into being in the practice of navigation and their development can be studied in the microstructure of the interactions among people, tools, and task. We can see patterns of technological change over the long run, but we can also see the details of the process of innovation in the minutia of actual practice.

The principal focus of this chapter is the nature of the navigation activity as a context for thinking and learning. In particular I will try to show how certain aspects of the conduct of navigation work contribute to the development of the quartermasters' navigation expertise.

The navigation task setting

An important fact about this setting is that the primary function of a peacetime military is what is called "the maintenance of readiness." The military establishment is a big institution full of terrifying weapons systems and other artifacts. The glue that holds the artifacts together, which makes the separate ships and planes and missiles and bombs into something more than a collection of hardware, is human activity. But there are high rates of personnel turnover in the military. The human parts keep passing through the system, so that even though the system is ready to make war one day, it will not be ready the next unless the expertise of the people departing is continually replaced by newly acquired skills of those who have more recently entered. This high turnover of personnel and the resulting need for the continual manufacture of replacement expertise make the military a fertile ground for research into the nature of learning in cultural context. So, in some sense, my discussion concerns the microstructure of maintaining the readiness of the human component of the war machine.

The events described in this chapter took place aboard a ship called an amphibious helicopter transport. Its warfare mission is to transport marine troops across the seas and then deliver them to the battlefields in the 25 helicopters that are carried on board. The helicopters also bring troops back to the ship, which has a small hospital and a complete operating theater on board.

Ships of this class are often mistaken for true aircraft carriers of the sort that carry jet planes. As is the case with true aircraft carriers, the hull is capped by a large flat flight deck, which creates an overhang on all sides of the ship. But this flight deck is only 592 feet

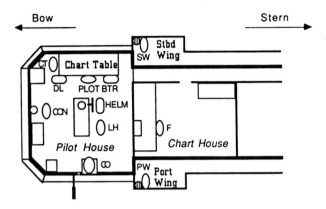

Figure 2.1. Watchstander positions for sea and anchor detail.

long – just over half the length of a carrier deck and much too small to handle fixed-wing aircraft. About halfway between bow and stern, jutting up out of the smooth expanse of the flight deck on the starboard rail, stands a five-story structure called the island. The island occupies the rightmost 20 feet of the flight deck which is about 100 feet wide. Three levels above the flight deck in the island is the navigation bridge or "pilothouse" where most of the navigation work takes place. Also in the island are the air operations office from which the helicopters are controlled, and a flag bridge where an admiral and his staff can work. The top of the island bristles with radar antennae.

The ship extends 28 feet below the surface of the water and weighs 17,000 tons empty. It is pushed through the water by a single propeller driven by a 22,000-horsepower steam turbine engine. These properties of the ship are important to the navigation task because they describe a vehicle of very limited maneuverability. The normal crew compliment of the ship is 44 officers and 608 enlisted men. Because the ship is primarily a troop transport vessel, it also has accommodations for more than 2,000 troops.

The physical layout of the spaces in which navigation is practiced is shown in Figure 2.1. This is a plan view of the navigation bridge, which is in the island three levels above the flight deck. The bow of the ship is to the left. The heavy line indicates the skin of the ship, whereas medium-weight exterior lines indicate railings on exterior walkways and medium-weight interior lines indicate interior walls. The elliptical shapes are duty stations for the members of the navigation team.

The navigation computations

The central computations in navigation answer the questions, Where are we? and If we proceed in a certain way for a specified time, where will we be? Answering the first question is called "fixing the position" or "getting a fix." Answering the second is called "dead reckoning." It is necessary to answer the first in order to answer the second, and it is necessary to answer the second to keep the ship out of danger. This is especially true for large ships that lack maneuverability. In order to make a turn in restricted waters in a big ship, it is not good enough to know when one has reached the point where the ship is to make the turn. Because of the lag in maneuvering response of such a massive object, when a ship reaches the turn point, if it has not already taken action to make the turn, it is too late to do so.

Position fixing by visual bearings

The simplest form of position fixing, and the one that concerns us here, is position fixing by visual bearings. For this we need a chart of the region around the ship, and a way to measure the direction, say with respect to north, of the line of sight connecting the ship and some landmark on the shore. The direction of a landmark from the ship is called the landmark's bearing. Imagine the line of sight between the ship and a known landmark. Although we know that one end of the line is at the landmark and we know the direction of the line, we can't just draw the line on the chart that corresponds to the line of sight between ship and landmark because we don't know where the other end of the line is. The other end of the line is where the ship is and that is what we are trying to discover.

Suppose we draw a line on a chart starting at the location of the landmark on the chart and extend it past where we think the ship is, perhaps off the edge of the chart if we are really unsure. We still don't know just where the ship is, but we do know it must be somewhere on that line. Such a line is called a "line of position." If we have another line of position, constructed on the basis of the direction of the line of sight to another known landmark, then we know that the ship is also on that line. And if the ship is on both these lines at the same time, the only place it can be is where they intersect.

Each line of position thus provides a one-dimensional constraint on the position from which the landmark was observed. The intersection of two lines of position uniquely constrains the location from which the observations were made.

The nautical chart

This computation could be realized in terms of many types of representations. For example, the lines of position could be expressed as equations of lines in a coordinate space, and the location of the intersection of the lines could be computed analytically by solving the simultaneous equations of the two lines of position. That is in fact how the problem is represented in some navigation computers, but it is not the way it is most often done. In our tradition of navigation, the central representational and computational artifact is the navigation chart. The chart is a spatial analogy to the large-scale space surrounding the ship. Locations on the chart correspond to locations in large-scale space. On a chart, lines of position are represented as pencil lines, and the location of the intersection of lines of position is computed graphically by drawing the lines on the chart. Although any two intersecting lines of position will uniquely specify the position of the ship, in practice, three lines of position are normally obtained for a fix. The intersection of the three lines forms a small triangle. (See Figure 2.2 for an example of a position fix with an acceptably small triangle.) If all of the observations are accurate and the lines are carefully plotted, the triangle formed will be very small. A navigator's anxiety is roughly proportional to the area of the fix triangle. Big triangles are bad. They mean that there is a problem somewhere in the processing of the information.

The computation of where we will be if we move in a particular direction at a particular speed for a specified time is also answered by geometric construction on a chart. A track line begins at a known

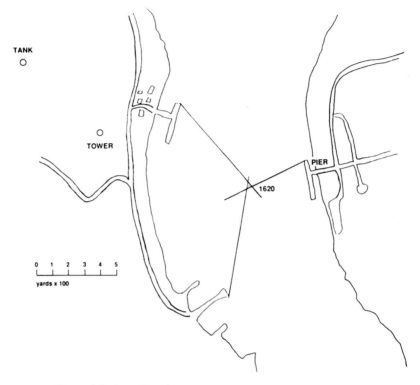

Figure 2.2. A position fix.

position and is extended in the direction of travel. To compute a projected position at a particular time in the future, for example, one multiplies the ship's speed by the time interval in question to get a prediction of the distance that will be traveled. This distance from the known starting point is then spanned on the track line to determine the predicted position. Figure 2.3 shows a dead reckoning track line extended from the fix.

From these two simple examples, it can be seen that a chart is much more like a coordinate space in analytic geometry than it is like the casual maps we draw to direct friends to our homes or offices.

Mercator projection charts are specially constructed computational artifacts that support this computation. In particular they are made so that angular relations among positions are preserved. The preservation of angular relationships is required if position is to be estab-

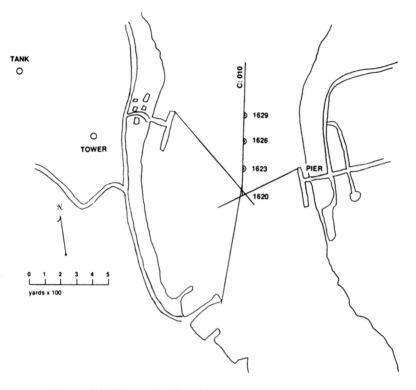

Figure 2.3. The projected track.

lished by visual lines of position. Other desirable chart properties are sacrificed on the Mercator projection in order to preserve the one property that makes this kind of navigation possible. Many people know that the relative size of areas on Mercator projection charts does not correspond to area in the world. Greenland appears as large as South America on some charts, despite the fact that the area of South America is many times that of Greenland. Mercator projection charts also lack a constant distance scale. Away from the equator, a displacement on the chart that represents 10 miles in the east–west orientation will represent a much shorter distance in the north–south orientation. This is not to say Mercator projection charts are accurate or not accurate, only that they are tuned for some kinds of navigation, and not for others.

It is difficult to overestimate the importance of the development and use of external representational media in this task. The contrast with navigation in nonliterate societies where it is carried out without the aid of external representations is striking. The task and its computational properties are determined in large part by the structure of the tools with which the navigators work.

The fix cycle

The necessity for continuously plotting the ship's position, projecting the track, and preparing to plot the next position is satisfied by a cycle of activity called the "fix cycle." As long as a ship is underway, it is continually executing this cycle. If it is away from land and other dangers, the cycle may be completed at a leisurely pace of, say, once every half hour. When the ship is in restricted waters, however, it may be necessary to complete the cycle on 1-minute intervals. Under these conditions, no single person could make all of the observations and do all of the computations required to complete the cycle in the amount of time available.

When the ship is operating in restricted waters, the work of the fix cycle is distributed across a team of six people.[1] The duty stations of the members of the team in the configuration called Sea and Anchor Detail are shown in Figure 2.1 as ellipses. We can follow the fix cycle by following information through the system.

New information about the location of the ship comes from the bearing takers on the wings of the ship (positions 1 and 2 in Figure 2.1). They find landmarks on the shore in the vicinity of the ship and measure the bearings of the landmarks (direction with respect to north) with a special telescopic sighting device called an alidade. An illustration depicting the view through such a sight is shown in Figure 2.4. The bearing takers then report the measured bearings over a telephone circuit to the bearing timer-recorder.

The bearing timer-recorder (position 3 in Figure 2.1) stands at the chart table inside the pilothouse and records the reported bearings in a book called the bearing log.

The plotter (position 4 in Figure 2.1) plots the bearings that are reported by the bearing takers. He normally has no direct communication with the bearing takers, but is either told the bearings by the bearing timer-recorder, or reads them out of the bearing book as

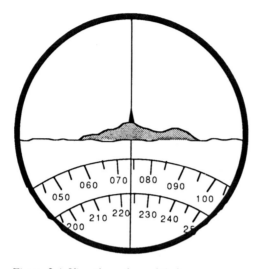

Figure 2.4. View through an alidade.

they are written down. Once he has plotted the ship's position, the plotter also projects where the ship will be at the time of the next few fix observations. To do this he needs to know the heading and speed of the ship. The plotter normally reads these from the deck log, which is lying on the chart table beside him.

The keeper of the deck log (position 5 in Figure 2.1) maintains the deck log in which all events of consequence for the ship are recorded. He records all commands given by the conning officer to the helmsman concerning the course to steer, and all orders to the lee helmsman concerning the speed to order from the engine room.

When the projected position of the ship has been plotted, the bearing timer-recorder consults with the plotter to decide which landmarks will be in appropriate position for the next fix, and assigns the chosen landmarks to the bearing takers by talking to them on the phone circuit. In choosing landmarks, the plotter and the bearing timer-recorder are looking for a set of three landmarks such that the lines from the three landmarks to the projected position of the ship intersect at reasonably steep angles. If the lines from any pair intersect at a shallow angle, then a small angular error in either one will move their point of intersection (one corner of the fix triangle) considerably and add uncertainty to the fix. If the angles of the intersections of the lines of position are steep, then small errors in the observations themselves will have small effects on the locations of the intersections.

The bearing timer-recorder uses a wristwatch to time the fix intervals, and about 10 seconds before the next fix time, he says "Standby to mark." This alerts the bearing takers that they should find their landmarks and aim their telescopic sights at them.

The fathometer operator (position 6 in Figure 2.1) sits in the chart house and is connected on the phone circuit with the bearing takers and the bearing timer-recorder. When the timer-recorder gives the "standby to mark" signal, the fathometer operator reports the depth of water under the ship. This is recorded in the bearing log and is later compared with the depth of water indicated on the chart at the plotted position. This comparison provides an additional check on the quality of the position fix.

At the time chosen for the fix observations, the bearing timer-recorder says "Mark," and the bearing takers observe and report the bearings of the landmarks they have been assigned. Thus the cycle begins again.

Learning to navigate

The developmental trajectory of the quartermaster

It takes about a year to learn the basics of the quartermaster's job. For a young person learning to be a quartermaster, there are many sources of information about the work to be done. Some go to specialized schools before they join a ship. There they are exposed to basic terminology and concepts but little more. In some sense, they are "trained" but they have no experience.[2] Most quartermasters learn what to do and how to do it while on the job. Some of the experience aboard ship is a bit like school with workbooks and exercises. In order to advance to higher ranks, the novice must work through a set of formal assignments that cover the full spectrum of navigation practice and are used for evaluation of the student's progress. They must be reviewed and approved by a supervisor before the student can progress to the next rank in the rating.

Novice quartermasters participate in joint activity with more experienced colleagues in two contexts: standard steaming watch, and sea and anchor detail.

Standard steaming watch

When the ship is far from land, where the requirements of navigation are relatively light and the time pressures are relaxed, navigation is conducted in a configuration called "standard steaming watch." In this condition, a novice may stand watch "under instruction" with someone who is qualified to stand watch alone. Depending upon the level of experience of the novice, he may be asked to perform all of the duties of the quartermaster of the watch. While under instruction, his activities are closely monitored by the more experienced watch stander who is always on hand and can help out or take over if the novice is unable to satisfy the ship's navigation requirements. However, even with the help of a more experienced colleague, standing watch under instruction requires a significant amount of knowledge, so novices do not do this until they have several months of experience.

The task for the novice is to learn to organize his own behavior such that it produces a competent performance. Novices who are not capable of such organization by themselves can contribute to a competent performance if the missing organization of action is provided by the more experienced supervising watch stander. In the following example, a novice quartermaster, Seaman D, was standing watch under instruction of C. The tasks were to fill out routine position and compass report sheets. The position report requires the current latitude and longitude of the ship. D was unsure how to proceed, so C asked him to measure the latitude and longitude of the ship's current position on the chart and dictate the values to C, who recorded them on the position report sheet. Here, the labeled blank spaces on the form provide some of the structure of the task, but that structure is presented explicitly to D by C who assigns the subtasks.

Later, while working on the compass report, D was again unsure what to do. The task is to make sure the gyrocompass and the magnetic compass are in agreement. This is done by taking simultaneous readings from the two compasses and then applying corrections to the magnetic compass reading and seeing whether the corrected magnetic heading is the same as the observed gyrocompass heading. The magnetic compass reading is called the checking head, and the corrections to the magnetic compass include a quantity called deviation. While C filled in the form, they had the following conversation:[3]

C: What's our checking head?
D: 090 and 074 [reading the gyrocompass and magnetic compasses at the helm station].
C: What's the table deviation for 074?
D: One East [reading from the deviation card on the binnacle].

In asking D these questions, C is not only getting him to practice the subtasks of reading headings from the compasses and finding deviation in a table, but is also guiding D through the higher-level task structure. D did not know what to do – how to organize his actions to get the task done. Some aspect of the organization of action required is present in the labeled blank spaces on the compass report form, but D was, by himself, unable to make use of that structure. C interprets that structure for D by asking the questions that are implied by the spaces. With C providing the organization, D becomes part of a competent performance. As D becomes more competent he will do both the part of this task that he did in this instance, and also the organizing part that was done in this instance by C. Next time D may use the structure of the form itself to organize his actions. When D becomes a fully competent quartermaster, he will not need the form at all for its organizing properties, will be able to say what the form requires without consulting it, and will use the form only as a convenient place to do the computation of corrections. I have discussed elsewhere (Hutchins, 1986) a model of psychological processes by which such organizing structure in the environment can be acquired by the individual. It is an important issue to which I will return in the discussion of the social origins of navigation competence.

Sea and anchor detail

Long before they are ready to stand watch under instruction in standard steaming watch, novice quartermasters begin to work as fathometer operators and bearing takers in sea and anchor detail. The procedural decomposition of the task in this work configuration permits unskilled people to participate in complex activities. The jobs in sea and anchor detail, in order of complexity, are:

- monitoring the fathometer
- taking bearings
- keeping the deck log
- timing and recording bearings
- plotting fixes and projecting the dead reckoned track

During their individual careers, novice quartermasters move through this sequence of positions, mastering each before moving on to the next. This ordering also describes the flow of information from the sensors (fathometer and sighting telescopes) to the chart where the information is integrated into a single representation (the position fix). The fact that the quartermasters themselves follow this same trajectory through the system as does sensed information, albeit on a different time scale, has an important consequence for the larger system's ability to detect, diagnose, and correct error. To see why this is so, however, we need to consider the distribution of knowledge that results from this pattern of development of quartermasters.

System properties

The distribution of knowledge

Knowledge in cooperative tasks is frequently assumed by analysts to be partitioned among individuals in an exhaustive and mutually exclusive manner such that the sum of the individual's knowledge is equal to the total required, and there is little or no overlap. Consider the knowledge required to perform just the input portion of the basic fix cycle. This requires the knowledge of the bearing takers, the bearing timer-recorder, and the plotter. We could imagine designing an experiment along these lines by training individuals to perform each of these roles and then putting the people in interaction with each other. This assumes no history for the participants except that each is trained to do his job. This would result in a distribution of knowledge as shown in Figure 2.5. Here the knowl-

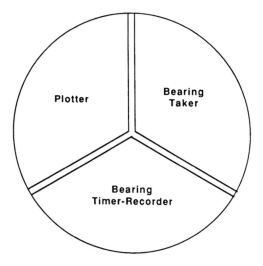

Figure 2.5. Nonoverlapping distribution of knowledge.

edge required to do each of the jobs is represented by a nonoverlapping region in the pie shown in Figure 2.5.

It is certainly possible to organize a functional system along these lines, but, outside of experimental settings, this pattern of knowledge distribution is very rare. More commonly, there is substantial sharing of knowledge between individuals with the task knowledge of more expert performers completely subsuming the knowledge of those who are less experienced. At the other end of the knowledge distribution spectrum, one can imagine a system in which everyone knows everything about the task. This too is a rare pattern because it is expensive. Splitting the task into coordinated fragments permits relatively less skilled people to contribute to task performance.

In many human systems, as people become more skilled they move on to other roles in the task performance group, making way for less skilled people behind them and replacing the more expert people before them who advance or leave the system. This is what we observe in the case of the development of navigation skills among quartermasters. A competent bearing taker knows how to do his job, but because of his interaction with the bearing timer-recorder, he also knows something about what the timer-recorder needs to do (see Figure 2.6a). The bearing timer-recorder knows how to do his

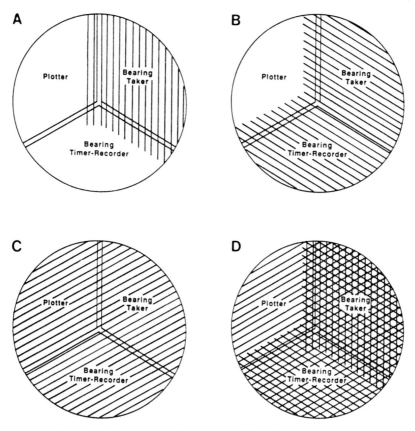

Figure 2.6. Overlapping distributions of knowledge.

job, but he also knows all about being a bearing taker, because he used to be one. Furthermore, he knows a good deal about the activities of the plotter because he shares the chart table with the plotter and may have done plotting under instruction in standard steaming watch. What the bearing timer-recorder knows is shown in Figure 2.6b. Finally, a competent plotter knows how to plot, but he also knows everything the bearing timer-recorder and bearing takers know because he has done both of those jobs before advancing to plotting. What the plotter knows is shown in Figure 2.6c, and the distribution of knowledge that is the sum of these individual expertises is shown in Figure 2.6d. Thus, this movement through the system with increasing expertise results in a pattern of overlapping expertise, with knowledge of the entry-level tasks most redundantly represented and knowledge of expert-level tasks least redundantly represented.

Task decompositions

The structure of the distributed task provides many constraints on the learning environment. The way a task is partitioned across a set of task performers has consequences for both the efficiency of task performance and for the efficiency of knowledge acquisition. For example, if the decomposition into subtasks cuts lines of high-bandwidth communication (i.e., if two processes that need to share information often in order to reach completion are distributed across different task performers), the task performance may suffer from the effects of a bottleneck in interpersonal communication. The question of what parts of the process need to communicate with which other parts and how much information per unit time must be communicated is an important determinant of optimal task partitioning. This problem is evident when inexperienced bearing takers attempt to find landmarks in the world. If the bearing taker already knows how to find the landmark in question, then little information needs to be passed. The name of the landmark may be all that is required. If the bearing taker is unsure of the location or appearance of the landmark, more information may be required. For example, in the following exchange, the starboard bearing taker needs additional information to resolve an ambiguity. Here, SW is the starboard-wing bearing taker and S is a qualified watch stander working as bearing timer-recorder.

SW: (Is it) The one on the left or the one on the right?
S: The one on the left, OK?
SW: Yah, I got it.

When the confusion or lack of knowledge is more profound, it is simply impossible to communicate enough information over the phone circuit, and someone has to go in person to the wing to show the bearing taker where to find the landmark. A little later in the same exit from port, the starboard bearing taker was unable to find the north end of the Tenth Avenue terminal. The plotter C, who is also the most qualified and highest-ranking member of the team, went onto the wing to point it out to him. On the wing, C put his arm over SW's shoulders and aimed his body in the right direction.

C: The north one, all the way up.
SW: OK.
C: If you can't see the light, just shoot the tangent right on the tit of the, the last end of the pier there.
SW: OK, that pier, where those two . . .
C: Yah, all the way at the end.
SW: Alright.
C: There should be a light out there but if you can't see the light out there at the end of the pier (when we get in position), just shoot the end of the pier.

The horizon of observation

Lines of communication and limits on observation of the activities of others have consequences for the knowledge acquisition process. This is so because they define the portion of the task environment available as a learning context to each task performer. Let us refer to the outer boundary of the portion of the task that can be seen or heard by each team member as that person's horizon of observation.

Open interactions. On a previous at-sea period, L, the deck log keeper had served as bearing timer-recorder, but his performance there was less than satisfactory. That is the job that was next in line for him, though, and he was anxious to acquire the skills required to perform the job. One of the most important aspects of the bearing timer-recorder's job is knowing when particular landmarks will be visible to the bearing takers on the wings. One complication of this judgment is the fact that a large convex mirror is mounted outside the pilothouse windows just in front of the bearing taker on the port wing. The mirror is there so that the commanding officer, who sits inside the pilothouse, can see all of the flight deck. Unfortunately, the mirror obstructs the port bearing taker's view forward and the bearing timer-recorder must be able to judge from his position at the chart table whether or not the port-wing bearing taker's view of a chosen landmark will be blocked by the mirror.

The plotter, C, the bearing timer-recorder, S, and L, were all standing at the chart table. The ship had just entered the mouth of the harbor and the team was running the fix cycle on 2-minute intervals. The previous fix taken at 36 minutes after the hour, called "time thirty-six," was complete and C had just finished plotting the dead reckoned track out through times 38 and 40. S indirectly solicited C's assistance in deciding which landmarks should be shot for the next round of bearings. L stood by watching what S and C were doing. All of the pointing they did in this interchange was to the chart itself.

1. S: Last set still good? OK. Ballast Point, light Zulu.
2. C: Here's (time) 38 [pointing to the DR position on the chart].
3. S: So it would be that [pointing to light Zulu], that [pointing to Bravo Pier] . . .
4. C: One, two, three. Same three. Ballast Point, Bravo. And the next one . . .
5. S: (Time) 40 should be, Ballast Point . . .
6. C: Front Range, Bravo.
7. S: And Balla . . .
8. L: He may not be able to see Front Range.
9. S: Yah.
10. C: Yah, he can. Once we get up here [pointing to the ship's projected position for the next fix].
11. S: Yah. Up there OK.
12. C: Down here [pointing to ship's current position] he can't. It's back of the mirror, but as you come in it gets enough so that you can see it.

Because what S and C are doing is within L's horizon of observation, L has a chance to see how the landmarks are chosen. Furthermore, the fact that the decision about which landmarks to shoot is made in an interaction opens the process to him in a way that would not be the case if a single person was making the decision alone. In utterance 8, L raises the possibility that the port-wing bearing taker may not be able to see the landmark. Three days earlier, on another sea and anchor detail, L had made the same suggestion about the mirror blocking the port-wing bearing taker's view and C had agreed with him. In the present circumstances, however, L's caveat is inappropriate. S and C have already anticipated the problem raised by L, and they jointly counter L's objection, each building on what the other has said. Clearly, if L did not share the work space with S and C or if there was a strict division of labor such that people did not monitor and participate in the actions of their fellows, this opportunity for L to have even peripheral involvement in that task that will someday be his would be lost. Furthermore, L's horizon of observation is extended because the decision making about landmarks is conducted as an interaction between S and C.

Open tools. But being in the presence of others who are working is not always enough by itself. In the preceding example, we saw that the fact that the work was done in an interaction between members opened it to other members of the team. In a similar way, the design of tools can affect their suitability for joint use or for demonstration and may thereby constrain possibilities for knowledge acquisition. The interaction of a task performer with a tool may or may not be open to others depending upon the nature of the tool itself. The design of a tool may change the horizon of observation for those in the vicinity of the tool. Because the navigation chart is an explicit graphical depiction of position and motion it is easy to "see" certain aspects of solutions. The chart representation presents the relevant information in a form such that much of the work can be done by perceptual inferences. Because the work a chart does is performed on its surface – all at the device interface as it were – watching someone work with a chart is much more revealing of what is done to perform the task than watching someone work with a calculator or a computer.

The openness of a tool can also affect its use as an instrument in instruction. When the bearing timer-recorder chooses a set of landmarks that results in lines of position with shallow intersections, it is easy to show him, on the chart, the consequences of his actions and the nature of the remedy required. Figure 2.7 shows a fix that resulted from landmark assignments made by the bearing timer-recorder. Bearings off to the side of the ship rather than ahead or astern are called "beam" bearings. When the plotter plotted

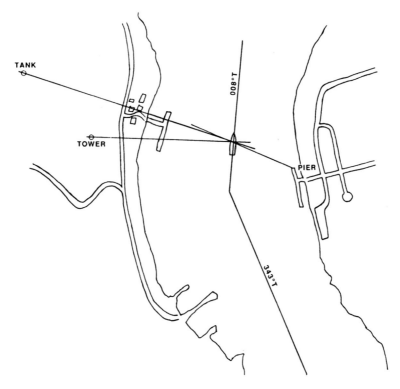

Figure 2.7. Three beam bearings.

this fix and saw how it came out, he scolded the bearing timer-recorder.

C: What did you take a bunch of beam bearings for? Why ain't you
        shooting up there [points out the front window of the bridge] some
        place? Look what you did [points to the chart]! You shot three
        beam bearings. You shot three beam bearings. You better tell 'em
        to shoot from up ahead some place.

Once the fix was plotted, of course, it was easy for the bearing timer-recorder to see the nature of his error. Imagine how much more difficult it would be to explain the inadequacy of the landmark assignment if the lines of position were represented as equations to be punched into a calculator rather than as lines drawn on the chart.

Errors and performance feedback

The structure of the task and the extent to which the behavior of the participants is available to each other also have consequences for error detection. In the following example, the team had shot Front Range, Silvergate, and Light 2 on the previous round. S begins to make a shift that will drop Front Range on the port side and pick up North Island tower on the starboard side. He instructs PW to drop Front Range, but then discovers that SW can't yet see North Island tower. Only a request for clarification from another sailor making a redundant plot in combat information center (CIC) makes it clear that S has decided not to shift landmarks at all and that PW has misunderstood the situation.

S: [to PW] OK, shift to Silvergate John.
PW: Drop Front Range.
S: Drop Front Range. [to SW] Steve, pick up . . . ah, just stick with number 2.
PW: Alright.
CIC: [to S] Okay, John, you're gonna shoot Light 2, Silvergate, and the Front Range, right?
S: Yah, Light 2, Silvergate, and Front Range.
CIC: OK.
PW: I thought we dropped Front Range.
S: No, picked that up because he couldn't see the tower on this side here [starboard].
PW: The Front Range and Silvergate, right?
S: Yah.

The point of this example is that the density of error correction possible depends on the horizons of observation of the team members. Here PW is on the phone circuit with CIC and S. In this case, this problem would surely not have been detected had the communication between S and CIC not been available to PW.

Supervisors are not the only ones to correct one's behavior; a competition among peers doing similar tasks may develop. Feedback can be provided in attempts to show competence as in the following example in which PW faults SW's reporting sequence.

S: Standby to mark time 14.
F: Fifteen fathoms.

SW: Dive Tower 034.
PW: He didn't say mark.
S: Mark it . . . I've got the Dive Tower Steve, go ahead.
PW: Point Loma 339.

Here, SW was supposed to wait for the "mark" signal, but blurted out the bearing of Dive Tower when he heard the "standby to mark" signal. PW jumped on him. S then gave the "mark" signal and waited for reports, but the earlier confusion seemed to have disrupted the coordination of the reports and no one said anything for 2 seconds. When getting bearings, "the show must go on." Stopping to fix the situation would ruin the fix because the near simultaneity of the observations would be violated. S minimizes the damage by acknowledging the early report on Dive Tower and asking PW to report.

If errors in the upward propagation of sensed data are not caught in the lower levels, they are likely to be noticed at the chart table by the plotter. The value of the third line in the fix is that if an error is present, it is likely to show up as an enlarged fix triangle, which will be detected by the plotter. It is, of course, possible for independent errors to conspire to produce a nice tight fix triangle that is actually in the wrong place, but such an event is quite unlikely. Now, the importance of the distribution of knowledge produced by the over-lapping careers of a set of quartermasters following a career trajectory that coincides with the flow of sensed information can be stated. When an error is detected, it is detected by someone who has, at some time in his career, performed all of the transformations to which the information at hand has been subjected. This gives each task performer a much better basis for diagnosing the possible causes of any observed errors than would be the case in a system with discrete knowledge representation. When a bad bearing is reported, the plotter can examine it and may develop hypotheses about, for example, whether the bearing taker misread the gyrocompass scale, or the bearing timer-recorder mistranscribed it into the bearing book. These hypotheses are based on his experience in each of these roles.

Finally, the trainee is not the only person to benefit from error correction. Depending on the structure of the task, when feedback is given, it can be observed by others involved in the task, and their knowledge of the task system as a whole can be improved. In the previous example, for example, the fathometer operator, who has not yet worked as a bearing taker, can learn a good deal about the task by sharing the phone circuit with the bearing takers and witnessing their mistakes and the corrections to them. In a system populated by novices and experts, many errors are likely to occur, but because there are many sources of error correction, most errors are likely to be detected. This observation leads to the somewhat paradoxical conclusion that some nonzero amount of error may actually be functional on the whole. A low level of error that is almost certain to be detected will not in ordinary circumstances harm performance; however, every error correction event is a learning context not just for the person who commits the error but for all who witness it.

Flexibility and robustness

These examples also illustrate the robustness of the system of distributed knowledge. If one human component fails for lack of knowledge, the whole system does not grind to a halt. If the task becomes difficult or communications break down, the navigation team does not have the option of stopping work. The task is event-driven and must be performed as long as the ship is underway. In response to breakdowns, the system adapts by changing the nominal division of labor. It is the bearing taker's job to find the landmarks, for example, but if he is unable to do so, some other member of the team will contribute whatever is required to ensure that the landmarks are found and their bearings observed. This robust property is made possible by the redundant distribution of knowledge among the members of the team, the access of members to each other's activities, and the fact that the individual workloads are light enough to permit mutual monitoring and occasional assistance. Both the knowledge required to do the task and the responsibility to keep the system working are distributed across the members of the navigation team. We can think of the team as a sort of flexible organic tissue that keeps the information moving across the tools of the task. When one part of this tissue is unable to move the required information, another part is recruited to do it.

The social formation of navigation competence

In considering a novice under instruction in standard steaming watch, we observed that the structure required for the novice to organize his behavior in a competent performance was sometimes provided by the supervising watch stander. Similarly, when the quartermasters work as a team in sea and anchor detail, they each provide the others, and the others provide each, with constraints on the organization of their activities. A good deal of the structure that a novice will have to acquire in order to stand watch alone in standard steaming watch is present in the organization of the relations among the members of the team in sea and anchor detail. The computational dependencies among the steps of the procedure for the individual watch stander are present as interpersonal dependencies among the members of the team. So to the extent that the novice participant comes to understand the work of the team and the ways various members of the team depend on each other, perhaps especially the ways he depends on others and others depend on him, he is learning about the computation itself and the ways its different parts depend on each other. Long before he knows how to choose appropriate landmarks to shoot, the bearing taker learns that landmarks must be carefully chosen and assigned prior to making observations.

This point is closely related to Vygotsky's notion of the social origins of higher mental functions. Vygotsky (1960/1981) says:

Any higher mental function necessarily goes through an external stage in its development because it is initially a social function. This is the center of the whole problem of internal and external behavior. . . . When we speak of a process, "external" means "social." Any higher mental function was external because it was social at some point before becoming an internal, truly mental function. It was first a social relation between two people. (p. 162)

Vygotsky was of course aware that internalized processes were not simple copies of external processes: "It goes without saying that internalization transforms the process itself and changes its structure and functions" (p. 163). For the sake of clear explication no doubt, and perhaps because the primary concern has been with the development of young children, many of the examples provided in the activity theory literature present cases in which the structure of the external activity is evident and where the required transformations are fairly simple. What happens if we consider adults learning more complicated thinking strategies in more complex social settings where the primary goal is successful task performance rather than education?

If social processes are to be internalized, then the kinds of transformations that internalization must make will be in part determined by the differences between the information-processing properties of individual minds and those of systems of socially distributed cognition.

Let us consider just two such differences that were raised in the discussion of the navigation activity in its individual and socially distributed forms. First, socially distributed cognition can have a degree of parallelism of activity that is not possible in individuals. Although current research tells us that much of individual cognition is carried out by the parallel activity of many parts of the brain, still, at the scale of more molar activities, individuals have difficulty simultaneously performing more than one complex task or maintaining more than one rich hypothesis. These are things that are easily done in socially distributed cognitive systems. Ultimately, no matter how much parallelism there may be within a mind, there is the potential for more in a system composed of many minds.

Second, lacking mental telepathy, communication among people in a socially distributed system is always conducted in terms of a set of mediating artifacts (linguistic or other) and this places severe limits on the bandwidth of communication among parts of the socially distributed system. Systems composed of interacting people have a pattern of connectivity that is characterized by dense interconnection within minds and sparser interconnection between them. Cognitive processes that are distributed across a network of people have to deal with the limitations on the communication between people.

Because society has a different architecture and different communication properties than the individual mind, it is possible that there are interpsychological functions that cannot ever be internalized by any individual. The distribution of knowledge described here is a property of the navigation team, and there are processes enabled by that distribution that can never be internalized by a single individual. The interpsychological level has properties of its own, some of which may not be the properties of any of the individuals who make it up. This, of course, is no challenge to Vygotsky's position. He did not say that every interpsychological process would be internalized, only that all the higher mental functions that did appear would get there by being internalizations of social processes.

That leads one to wonder whether there might be intrapsychological processes that could not be transformations of processes that occurred in social interaction. Finding such a process would be a challenge to Vygotsky's position, but unless there are constraints on the possible transformations, then there is no way to identify such a process.

Clearly there are higher mental processes that could never have been realized in their current form as interpsychological processes simply because they exploit the rich communication possible within a mind in a way that is not possible between minds. Here is an example we have already encountered. The task of reconciling a map to a surrounding territory has as subparts the parsing of two rich visual scenes (the chart and the world) and then establishing a set of correspondences between them on the basis of a complicated set of conventions for the depiction of geographic and cultural features on maps. As performed by an individual, it requires very high bandwidth communication among the representations of the two visual scenes. This task appears very occasionally as a socially distributed task when a bearing taker has no idea how to find a particular landmark. In that case, the restricted bandwidth communication between the bearing taker, who can see the world, and the bearing timer-recorder, who can see the chart, makes the task virtually impossible. The spatial relations implied by the locations of symbols on the chart are simply too rich to be communicated verbally in such a way that the bearing taker can discover the correspondences between those relations and the relations among the objects he can see in the world.

Of course, it may be that the real difficulty here is simply with the volume of information to be processed and that the actual technique for reconciling map and territory was an internalization of a social activity in an environment that was informationally sparser. Without a much more detailed account of the acquisition of this process, it will be impossible to decide this case. For now, all that is possible is to raise the question of whether internal processes might exist that are not internalizations of external processes. And doing that seems to throw the spotlight squarely on the nature of the transformation that occurs in the internalization process.

A problem of attribution

I used to subscribe to the view that all of cognitive science is basically an attribution problem. Our topic of study is, after all, a set of phenomena that are not directly observable, but only inferred from other behavior. I have now changed my mind about that. Systems of socially distributed cognition such as the navigation team seem to me to be excellent units of cognitive analysis in their own right, and understanding their operation is largely a matter of observation rather than inference.

Still, the nature of my change in mind does not change the fact that in America, at least, cognitive science in general and the current coalition between cognitive psychology and artificial intelligence in particular have adopted a theoretical stance that leads to serious overattribution of knowledge to individual actors. The basic tenet of this line of thought is that an adequate theory of cognition is one that is sufficient to account for the computational behavior observed. That in itself is not bad, but when the context of cognition is ignored, it is impossible to see the contribution of structure in the environment, in artifacts, and in other people to the organization of mental processes.

If the individual mind itself is the only locus considered for the structures that organize thinking, then everything that is required to create a sufficient account of cognitive activity has to be crammed into the individual mind. This leads the followers of this view to try to put more in the individual mind than belongs there. The properties of groups of minds in interaction with each other, or the properties of the interaction between individual minds and artifacts in the world, are frequently at the heart of intelligent human performance. But attributing them to individual minds hides them from analytic view and distorts our understanding of the processes that do belong to individual minds. As long as the nature of the shaping of thought by context is not seen, the organization of mental function that must be attributed to individual minds to account for observed performances will not be of the right sort.

Notes

1. On other ships, and on this ship in different circumstances, the team may be somewhat larger or smaller depending on the availability of qualified personnel.
2. In fact, the two quartermaster chiefs with whom I worked most closely said they preferred to get their trainees as able-bodied seamen without any prior training in the rate. They said this saved them the trouble of having to break the trainees of bad habits acquired in school.
3. This example and all of those that follow come from a corpus of video and audio recordings collected by the author during fieldwork aboard U.S. Navy ships. All of the events described are the activities of a real navigation in real operations.

References

Hutchins, E. (1978). Reasoning in Trobriand discourse. In R. Casson (Ed.), *Language, culture and thought* (pp. 481–489). New York: Macmillan.

Hutchins, E. (1980). *Culture and inference.* Cambridge, MA: Harvard University Press.

Hutchins, E. (1983). Understanding Micronesian navigation. In D. Gentner & A. Stevens (Eds.), *Mental models* (pp. 191–225). Hillsdale, NJ: Lawrence Erlbaum.

Hutchins, E. (1986). Mediation and automatization. *Quarterly Newsletter of the Laboratory of Comparative Human Cognition, 8*(2), 47–58.

Hutchins, E., & Hinton, G. (1984). Why the islands move. *Perception, 13,* 629–632.

Vygotsky, L. S. (1981). The genesis of higher mental functions. In J. V. Wertsch (Ed. and Trans.), *The concept of activity in Soviet psychology* (pp. 144–188). Armonk, NY: M. E. Sharpe. (Reprinted from *Razvitie vysshikh psikhicheskikh funktsii,* 1960, 182–223).

Developmental studies of work as a
testbench of activity theory: The case of
primary care medical practice

Yrjö Engeström

Introduction

When I write about *the* theory of activity, I am using a
double-edged notion. On the one hand, it is necessary to emphasize
the unique and self-consciously independent nature of the Soviet
cultural-historical research tradition, which today is commonly called
activity theory (see Leont'ev, 1978; Leontyev, 1981; Wertsch, 1981).
On the other hand, this tradition is not a fixed and finished body of
strictly defined statements – it is itself an internationally evolving,
multivoiced activity system.[1]

Rumors about activity theory have been around in Western behavioral and social sciences for some time. But in many ways, this
theoretical approach is still one of the best-kept secrets of academia.
This is partly due to language barriers, partly to the epistemological
foundations of activity theory, which are not immediately transparent
to scholars unfamiliar with classical German philosophy and dialectics (see Ilyenkov, 1982; Lektorsky, 1980/1984; Mikhailov, 1980 –
and Bakhurst, 1991, for a careful Anglo-Saxon interpretation). And
when a Western researcher begins to realize the impressive dimensions of theorizing behind the activity approach, she or he may well
ask: Is it worth the trouble? Can it be used to produce something

The research reported in this chapter has been funded by the Board of Health of
the City of Espoo and by the Academy of Finland. The collaboration of Ritva
Engeström, Jouni Helenius, and Kirsi Koistinen has been invaluable in the course
of the research. When I use the pronoun we in the text, I refer primarily to our
research group.

The editorial comments of Seth Chaiklin and Jean Lave as well as critical
discussions with other authors of this volume are acknowledged with gratitude.

interesting? How does one do concrete research on the basis of activity theory?

This chapter aims at answering those questions, if only partially and sketchily. Others have begun such bridge building in the fields of education (Moll, 1990), language socialization (Ochs, 1988), design of computer interfaces (Bødker, 1990), and explanation of skilled action (Keller & Keller, this volume). I shall focus on expert work as collective, institutionally organized activity.

The chapter has a fourfold structure. First, I discuss three general principles of activity theory. Second, I present a concrete activity setting – a health center providing primary medical care – and an item of discourse data obtained from that setting. Third, I work out and apply specific analytical instruments that will bridge the gap between the general principles and the data. Fourth, I discuss the implications of this type of work research for the applicability and further evolution of activity theory.

Three principles[2]

How can one analyze and interpret data that record and describe human behavior and discourse? From an activity-theoretical viewpoint, three basic principles should be observed. First, a collective activity system can be taken as the unit of analysis, giving context and meaning to seemingly random individual events. Second, the activity system and its components can be understood historically. Third, inner contradictions of the activity system can be analyzed as the source of disruption, innovation, change, and development of that system, including its individual participants.

The entire activity system as the unit of analysis

In *Cognition in Practice*, Jean Lave (1988) discusses the concept of context in a refreshing manner. She points out that a determinist environmental view, such as Roger Barker's notion of behavior settings, excludes the *relation* between persons' acting and settings. Though powerful for purposes of classifying forms of human behavior, this approach leaves little room for the human construction of novel contexts. Contexts are easily conceived of as containers of behavior, untouched in themselves by human actions.

The standard cognitivist view identifies the given problems and knowledge domains – or the given individual's mental models and cognitive structures – as the context of problem solving, thinking, and learning. This view excludes the societal and cultural aspects from its notion of context.

Finally, various phenomenological and ethnomethodological analyses focus on dyadic interaction, attempting to define contexts as social situations, as spaces of interactive experience, or as fields of discourse. Although contexts are here seen as interpersonal constructions, they are commonly treated as purely linguistic, symbolic, and experiential entities. This makes contexts look like something that can be created at will by two or more persons in interaction, as if independently of the deep-seated material practices and socioeconomic structures of the given culture. In sum, "one has system without individual experience, the other experience without system" (Lave, 1988, p. 150).[3]

There is a deep-seated common feature in all the notions of context just discussed. In all of them, the individual experience is described and analyzed as if consisting of relatively discrete and situational *actions*, be they motor movements, attempts to solve a problem, or conversational turns. On the other hand, the system, or the given objective context, is described as something beyond individual influence – if described at all.

Activity theory contends that such a notion of context beyond our influence is fiction, a fetish. It is true that the arenas of our everyday life are usually not *directly and visibly* molded by our actions. But they are constructed by humans, not by superhuman agents. If we take a closer and prolonged look at any institution, we get a picture of a continuously constructed collective *activity system* that is not reducible to series or sums of individual discrete actions, although the human agency is necessarily realized in the form of actions (Leont'ev, 1978). "The whole approach to individual cognition can only benefit from recognizing the individual person's involvement with institution building from the very start of the cognitive enterprise" (Douglas, 1986, p. 67).

The pressing theoretical and practical problem of our time is the very indirectness of institution building, that is, the indirect or even hidden influence of individual actions on the creation and reproduction of activity systems.

> The ends of the actions are intended, but the results which actually follow from these actions are not intended; or when they do seem to correspond to the end intended, they ultimately have consequences quite other than those intended. Historical events thus appear on the whole to be (. . .) governed by chance. But where on the surface accident holds sway, there actually it is always governed by inner, hidden laws and it is only a matter of discovering these laws. (Engels, 1976, p. 366)

For activity theory, contexts are neither containers nor situationally created experiential spaces. Contexts are activity systems. An activity system integrates the subject, the object, and the instruments (material tools as well as signs and symbols) into a unified whole.

An activity system incorporates both the object-oriented productive aspect and the person-oriented communicative aspect of the human conduct. Production and communication are inseparable (see Rossi-Landi, 1983). Actually a human activity system always contains the subsystems of production, distribution, exchange, and consumption.

A model of the basic structure of a human activity system is presented in Figure 3.1 (see Engeström, 1987, for further grounding and elaboration of the model). In the model, the *subject* refers to the individual or subgroup whose agency is chosen as the point of view in the analysis. The *object* refers to the "raw material" or "problem space" at which the activity is directed and which is molded or transformed into *outcomes* with the help of physical and symbolic, external and internal *tools* (mediating instruments and signs). The *community* comprises multiple individuals and/or subgroups who share the same general object. The *division of labor* refers to both the horizontal division of tasks between the members of the community and to the vertical division of power and status. Finally the *rules* refer to the explicit and implicit regulations, norms and conventions that constrain actions and interactions within the activity system. Between the components of an activity system, continuous construction is going on. The human beings not only use instruments, they also continuously renew and develop them, whether consciously or not. They not only obey rules, they also mold and reformulate them – and so on.

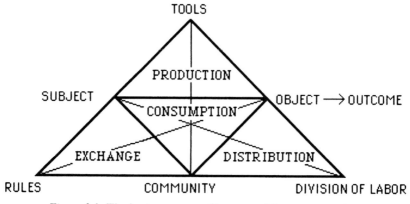

Figure 3.1. The basic structure of human activity.

But the life of activity systems is also discontinuous. Besides accumulation and incremental change, there are crises, upheavals, and qualitative transformations. An activity system is not only a persistent formation; it is also a creative, novelty-producing formation.[4]

An activity system is not a homogeneous entity. To the contrary, it is composed of a multitude of often disparate elements, voices, and viewpoints. This multiplicity can be understood in terms of historical layers. An activity system always contains sediments of earlier historical modes, as well as buds or shoots of its possible future. These sediments and buds – historically meaningful differences – are found in the different components of the activity system, including the physical tools and mental models of the subjects. They are also found in the actions and object units of the activity.

Historicity as the basis of classifications

A social or behavioral scientist cannot avoid using yardsticks of development. When we classify and evaluate responses or cognitive structures, forms of action or organizational patterns, how do we know which ones are more advanced than the others? Our judgments are inevitably based on an implicit or explicit theory of development.

Closed, linear theories of development claim that there is only one correct course or sequence of development, leading to a fixed end point of mature fulfillment. For these views, history and intellectual development appear as advancement from the primitive society (and primitive thought) to the developed Western civilization (and formal-logical thinking). Also the Marxist conception of socioeconomic formations is often misinterpreted as a doctrine of a mechanically predetermined course of history. Marx and Engels saw it otherwise: "History does nothing, it 'possesses no immense will,' it 'wages no battles.' It is man, real living man who does all that, who possesses and fights; 'history' is not, as it were, a person apart, using man as a means to achieve its own aims; history is nothing but the activity of man pursuing his aims" (Marx & Engels, 1975, p. 93).

It is the merit of researchers like Michael Cole, Jack Goody, Ed Hutchins, and Sylvia Scribner to have shown that intellectual development does not follow a linear course (for a synthesis, see Cole, 1988). Highly complex and abstract forms of thought and communication are found in vital activities of the so-called primitive societies. But this does not necessarily imply that there can be no direction or "progress" in history.

Marx found the criteria of progress in the development of the productive forces, in humanity's ability to overcome scarcity and toil. As industry and automation replace direct handwork, the human subject becomes a "watchman and regulator" of production and human intercourse. Humanity's collective mastery of these complex processes, the development of the subject as "a social individual," becomes the true measure of progress (Marx, 1973, pp. 704–706). But this is not a question of linear quantitative growth of wealth and rationality. To the contrary, the increasing "systemness" of society (Beniger, 1986) is both an overall developmental direction and, at the same time, an unresolved challenge of qualitative reorganization. It should be interpreted in terms of emerging "zones of possibility" (Holzkamp, 1983) rather than as a predetermined course of events.

One may distinguish between *modes* and *historical types* of the given activity. The mode refers to the way the activity is actually organized and carried out by its participants at any given time. The mode resembles a continuously evolving mosaic, consisting of various parallel interests, voices, and layers. But the activity system as a whole also represents some historically identifiable ideal-typical qualitative pattern or constellation of its components and inner relations. As a highly generalized conceptual framework for identifying and analyz-

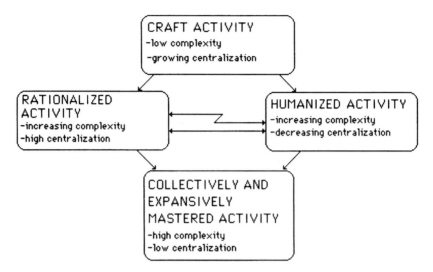

Figure 3.2. General historical types of activity.

ing such historical types, we may use the categorization depicted in Figure 3.2. The vertical dimension signifies generalized historical time downward from the past to the future.

The activity types in Figure 3.2 are characterized with the help of two variables: degree of complexity and degree of centralization. These are related to the notions of complexity and coupling as they are used by Perrow (1984) in his analysis of organizations and technological systems.

The classic unit of craft activity is a workshop with minimal specialization of labor. The apprentices work under the close supervision and tight control of the omnipotent master. In this sense, the unit, although small in scale, is already highly centralized. This ideal type is commonly posed as the lost form of work that truly corresponded to the human nature – a stance most effectively criticized by Touraine (1965).

The classic unit of rationalized activity is the industrial factory, and subsequently the bureaucratic office. The machinery and size of the organization entail complex interactions. In the name of efficiency, division of labor and centralization of control are brought to the utmost.

Humanized activity is a contemporary and counterpart of rationalized activity. The double arrows between rationalized and humanized activity in Figure 3.2 signify their mutual hostility and mutual dependency (for a discussion of this dual relationship reflected in psychological theories, see Kvale, 1976). Classic attempts at humanization are found in the semiautonomous industrial work groups, propagated by the "quality of working life" movement and by theories of sociotechnical systems. Complexity of interactions is so high that centralized control and extreme division of labor create serious motivational and quality problems. However, the ensuing decentralization is limited to partial control over procedures, timing, and division of labor in groups, whereas the strategic contents of tasks and products remain essentially untouched (for an overview, see Rose, 1988).

Collectively and expansively mastered activity is a hypothetical construct, based on tendencies and emerging possibilities found in a number of recent studies (e.g., Hirschhorn, 1984; Kern & Schumann, 1984; Noyelle, 1987; Projektgruppe Automation und Qualifikation, 1987; Stanback, 1987; Zuboff, 1988). As complexity increases, it seems that the inherent cognitive, communicative, and motivational contradictions of both rationalized and humanized activity systems press toward novel solutions. Essential in these solutions is that decentralized work teams begin to reconceptualize and plan the *objects* and *products* – and thereby also the organizational forms – of their work on a long-term basis. Instead of asking only, How? as in humanized activity, teams and work communities start asking also Why? For whom? Where to? As a consequence, work teams and communities are engaged in modeling and reconstructing their own entire activity systems. This implies that high-level theoretical and conceptual instruments are collectively developed and employed as part of the everyday activity. Hirschhorn (1984) uses the notions of "second-order work" and "developmental work" to characterize the growing importance of design and planning "from below."

Inner contradictions as the source of change and development

An activity is not a stable and harmonious system. Ideal types, such as those depicted in Figure 3.2, are "pure" types. If imposed upon concrete data from "top down," they tend to eliminate multivoicedness and contradiction, thus rendering transitions and development incomprehensible. Development can be understood by tracing disruptions, troubles, and innovations at the level of concrete modes of the activity, both historical and current. The analysis of such data leads to hypothetical identification of the internal contradictions of the activity system. Such a hypothetical model is actually a depiction of the activity system at the level of ideal types – only this time the inner contradictions are built into the ideal-typical model from "bottom up."

Thus, the ideal types depicted in Figure 3.2 provide no excuses or shortcuts in concrete research. As an instrument, such a classification of ideal types has to be challenged and reconstructed anew through data-driven historical and empirical analyses of the specific activity system under scrutiny. Such analyses are guided by the notion of contradictions.

Activity systems are characterized by inner contradictions. The primary inner contradictions reflect the basic contradiction characteristic to the socioeconomic formation as a whole. In capitalism, the basic contradiction is the dual nature of commodities, the tension between the use value and the exchange value. In different activity systems, this fundamental tension appears in different forms, as the primary contradiction of that particular activity. This primary contradiction resides in each component of the activity system. For example, in bureaucratic and rationalized medical work activity, physicians typically experience a constant latent tension between their role as gatekeepers and cost-efficient producers on the one hand, and as healers or consultants on the other hand.

The activity system is connected to other activity systems through all of its components. When a strong novel factor is "injected" into one of the components and it thus acquires a new quality, pressing secondary contradictions appear between that component and some other components of the system. For example, when new types of patients begin to enter a medical activity system, the doctors' material and conceptual tools for diagnosis and treatment may become inadequate. A secondary contradiction thus arises between the novel object and the traditional instruments of the doctors' work activity.

These secondary contradictions of the activity are the moving force behind disturbances and innovations, and eventually behind the change and development of the system. They cannot be eliminated or fixed with separate remedies. They get aggravated over time and eventually tend to lead to an overall crisis of the activity system. In this process, practitioners may experience them as overwhelming "double binds," dilemmas where all available alternatives are equally unacceptable.

General practitioners in a health center

The activity setting in our case consists of two health stations that together form a service district of the health center of the city of Espoo in Finland. In 1986, the city of Espoo had 153,000 inhabitants. It is located near the capital, Helsinki. The health center and the health station are the present organizational units of primary medical care in Finland. The legislation behind the system was passed in 1972. It requires that every municipality offer the primary medical services to its inhabitants free of charge.

In 1986, the health center of Espoo had 10 health stations. The service district chosen for our project had 36,500 inhabitants. The health stations in our study had 10 and 6 full-time general practitioners, respectively. The bigger one is the main station of the district. It serves both acute cases coming without appointments and also patients with appointments. The smaller station is a subsidiary one, serving mainly patients with appointments. Both stations are equipped with their own laboratories and physiotherapeutic services, the bigger one also with modern x-ray technology. During the first 6 months of 1986, the two stations had 33,433 patient visits, averaging 5,572 per month.

There are certain widely discussed visible surface problems in the functioning of health centers. Especially in larger cities, the waiting times and lines are often frustratingly long. Private medical centers offer competing services with little waiting, and patients often experience these centers as giving better service. General practitioners are mostly young – large numbers of them have been trained in universities after the reform of 1972. Within the medical profession, general practitioners are often considered an inferior category – the highly specialized hospital physician is still the ideal.

The general practitioner is under direct daily pressure from four sides: (1) the national and municipal administrative bureaucracies, which demand more output and effective adherence to a growing number of rules and regulations (as well as paperwork considered excessive and unnecessary by practitioners) – and simultaneously more satisfied patients; (2) the patients and the general public demanding more time and better care per patient and – paradoxically – shorter lines and waiting periods; (3) the nurses demanding independent professional status and refusing to be subordinated by physicians, while also criticizing physicians for inability to cooperate and to take a holistic view of the patient care; (4) the hospital specialists demanding that really serious cases (e.g., cancer) be screened and found earlier and more reliably, while on the other hand the flow of patients sent by general practitioners to specialists should be restricted. Under these pressures, the physician may question his or her professional identity and ability to give any real medical help (besides routine prescriptions and sick leaves) to the patients.

In Espoo, the patient records have recently been computerized. All health stations use a central program called FINSTAR. In the organizational framework of 1986, patients were eligible to visit any of the 10 stations regardless of their location because their records are immediately available at any of the stations. The computerization has caused certain turmoil among the staff, and the new technology has been frequently criticized by the physicians. It has been argued, among other things, that the computerization increases the impersonal and bureaucratic nature of general practitioners' work. On the other hand, it is acknowledged that a single patient's dealings with the health care system are often so varied and complex that new and more effective means for collecting and handling information have become necessary.

The Ministry of Health and Social Services recently initiated a new reform in primary medical care, aiming at the realization of the so-called personal doctor system and based on the principle of population responsibility. According to this principle, each general practitioner gets a fixed list of his or her own patients. The list is compiled by dividing the population into segments according to their addresses or to their already existing care relations. Between 1985 and 1987, four cities tested variations of this system in the framework of a centrally organized demonstration, with the aim of finding out the administrative and financial implications of alternative arrangements. Experienced volunteer doctors in each city were chosen to test the new arrangements. The demonstration was limited to consultation work with sick patients. The Finnish Cabinet has subsequently decided that the personal doctor system shall be implemented in all municipalities within a few years.

Espoo did not participate in the centrally administered demonstration of the personal doctor program. Our project had the task of creating a working model of the principle of population responsibility from below, based on the efforts and needs of the general practitioners and other staff of the two health stations. Our project aimed at producing theoretical tools for the practitioners themselves. In contrast to the centrally administered demonstration, all doctors and staff were involved, and the analyses and interventions covered the full range of tasks, including preventive work.

The project was completed at the end of 1989. From the beginning in May 1986, our project emphasized the contents of the actual daily practice in health stations. The project proceeded in three, partially overlapping phases. In the first phase, the historical development and the present mode of the work activity were analyzed. In the second phase, a new model for the work of the center was designed by the general practitioners and other staff. In the third phase (1988–1990), the new model was put into practice in the two stations. In all stages, our research group had the dual task of documenting and analyzing on the one hand, providing feedback and interventions on the other hand.

Thus, our research did not aim at producing analytical academic reports only. It aimed at grasping developmental potentials and dynamics by initiating, supporting, and recording qualitative changes in the practical work activity itself. That is why this approach is called developmental work research.

An item of data from general practitioners' work

The following item is a part of the data collected in the first phase for the analysis of the initial (1986) mode of activity. In that phase, all the 16 doctors and 23 representatives of the other staff were interviewed thoroughly. Moreover, 5 or 6 patient consultations of each doctor, totaling 85 consultations, were videotaped. After the consultation, the patient and the doctor separately viewed the videotape and gave a stimulated recall interview on the consultation. In addition, each of the 85 patients was interviewed at length about his or her health and related topics.

The item is a verbatim transcript of one videotaped consultation. I have chosen it primarily to illustrate gaps and discoordinations in the interaction between the doctor and the patient. It also illuminates certain aspects of the "invisible work" going on in all work settings, as has been pointed out by Strauss, Fagerhaugh, Suczek, and Wiener (1985) and Star (in press).

In the transcript of the videotaped consultation there are bracketed indications about "topic" and "voices." The reader is asked to ignore them at the moment; I shall return to them later. In the transcript, interruption is indicated with an asterisk (*), and unclear or incomprehensible talk is indicated with the sign (. . .). Explanations added by the author are in bracketed italics.

CONSULTATION # VI/22 (TRANSCRIPT OF THE VIDEOTAPE)
June 4, 1986
[A 31-year-old male patient comes in and shakes hands with a male doctor, giving him an envelope that contains an epicrisis of a surgery performed on him 6 years earlier in a hospital.]

(TOPIC 1: VOICES 4A ← 4A)
001 P: (. . .) about the operation on the neck, the neck was operated on,
002   but I can't retain any food in the morning, (. . .)*
003 D: I just looked at the old information [*in the computerized record*],
004   you've been feeling sick in the morning* . . .
005 P: Yes, (. . .) I can't keep anything down, it's been getting worse and
006   worse during this spring, I've been feeling sick every now and then
007   for many years, but . . . now I've been losing weight about eight
008   kilos during the last couple of months.
009 D: Do you have the feeling that it gets stuck there or does it go first in
010   the stomach and come out only after that?
011 P: It goes first in the stomach.
012 D: Then you feel sick and . . .
013 P: Yes . . . it comes suddenly . . . it comes in fits so that I don't have it
014   all the time, but when I eat something in the morning, it will always
015   come up by lunch (. . .)*
016 D: Is it . . .
017 P: It is much better in the evening, in the afternoon it already calms
018   down (. . .)

019 D: Does it matter what you eat or is there some food which comes up
020   more easily?
021 P: It doesn't matter ... I've tried if it's some particular dish but it's
022   almost anything.
023 D: Do liquids come up as well, if you drink coffee or something in the
024   morning, do you vomit it, too?
025 P: I don't drink coffee any more in the morning ... but I've also
026   drunk cocoa because I can't always eat as soon as I wake up in the
027   morning, it seems to come up, too, but I've managed to retain it
028   with difficulty.
029 D: Do you have pain in your stomach?
030 P: I don't have continuous pain, but sometimes after lunch I have
031   stabbing pains and sometimes I have a twinge of pain here, like a
032   stab of a knife, I've had a couple of times these twinges.
033 D: Is it heartburn?
034 P: I don't think it's heartburn, but ...
035 D: Do you have stomachache at night?
036 P: No, I don't.
037 D: It seems you've been here a month ago and ... doctor S has given
038   you A [*brandname of medicine*], liquid (. . .), have you tried it?

(TOPIC 2: VOICES 1→4A)
039 P: Yes, I've tried it, but it didn't help,* then I have something ...
040 D: Nothing.
041 P: ... due to cervical nerves and others, I've had an operation on my
042   neck, I brought these papers* [*gives a large envelope to the doctor,*
043   *containing a hospital report of a surgery performed in 1980*].
044 D: I looked, it seems to have been quite a big operation* [*refers to*
045   *information he obtained from the computerized record before the consul-*
046   *tation*].
047 P: It's quite (surprising) that I can't make out what was done in the
048   last operation.*
049 D: Do you mean that (. . .) [*reads the hospital report*]?
050 P: Yes, there, the back of the neck was operated on, there was an
051   unexpected finding* ... there was something ...
052 D: Let's have a look, there isn't anything particular in that operation
053   report. . . .
054 P: I had an operation on these cervical muscles* ... (. . .) operated
055   when I had compulsive movements ...
056 D: (. . .)
057 P: ... there were, the nerves were removed.

058 D: Yes, it was quite a big operation (. . .) a piece was taken away.
059 P: This is tense, the other part of the neck (. . .)* [*points to his neck*].
060 D: But the situation is still much better than before*. . .
061 P: Yes.
062 D: . . . these operations? This was the last one, wasn't it?
063 P: Yes, it was there earlier, somewhere there [*points his finger at the*
064   *hospital report*].
065 D: Well show it to me [*hands the hospital report over to the patient; starts*
066   *typing at his computer terminal while the patient seeks the crucial point*
067   *in the report*].
068 P: Here it is (. . .) [*points his finger at the hospital report*].
069 D: Oh, you mean that unexpected bleeding (. . .)
070 P: No, it's not that either.
071 D: That is only a technical problem concerning the operation, it has
072   bled from there . . .
073 P: There was something else, an unexpected finding (. . .)
074 D: Yes, yes, these certainly induce those compulsive movements.*
075 P: Yes.
076 D: Yes, there has been a structural defect in the head (. . .)
077 P: It's not congenital, however . . .
078 D: Yes . . . there's something . . . it has grown for some reason . . .
079 P: Yes . . .

(*TOPIC 3: VOICES* 2 → 3)
080 P: . . . could this stomachache be due to nerves?
081 D: It's possible that it's due to, say, psychic reasons.*
082 P: Yes.

(*TOPIC 4: VOICES* 4A ← 4A)
083 D: Still, if you've lost weight at the same time* . . .
084 P: Yes.
085 D: . . . then it's worth examining a little. You've been in laboratory
086   tests a bit earlier and there was nothing particular there.*
087 P: There was nothing.
088 D: But how about x-rays? Have they been taken?
089 P: Nothing has been taken.
090 D: They are worth taking, too, the gullet, this space, and then the
091   stomach. You can see there, for instance, if your lower orifice of
092   the stomach, I mean the juncture of the gullet and the stomach is
093   so wide that a flow is possible, or if there's a hernia (. . .)
094 P: Yes, it's worth taking (. . .)

(*TOPIC 5: VOICES* 4B ← 4B)

095 D: So we can get the x-ray photographs here. Where do you live?

096 P: I live in L.

097 D: Yes, they take x-rays on the second floor, all you must do is go

098   there and make an appointment.

099 P: Yes.

100 D: When we get the x-ray photographs, we'll talk about it.

101 P: Yes. Should I also make an appointment with the doctor?

102 D: You can call me up first.

103 P: Yes.

104 D: Yes, go and make the appointment right away, it may take a couple

105   of weeks before you can go there.

106 P: There isn't any referral . . .

107 D: No (. . .) straight there.

108 P: I see.

109 D: That's all.

110 P: Yes.

(*TOPIC 6: VOICES* 4A ← 4A)

111 D: You still use that Z [*brandname of medicine*] for the night, do you

112   have any other medicines?

113 P: No . . .

(*TOPIC 7: VOICES* 2 → 4A)

114 P: Nervous tensions (. . .) I get such surprising nervous tensions (. . .)

115   . . . such . . . every now and then I get them . . . my heart thumps

116   and I tremble (. . .)

117 D: Does it occur in some particular situation?

118 P: Yes, it comes in surprising situations.

119 D: Well, it's quite a normal reaction.

120 P: Yes . . . it's pretty common, of course, but . . .

121 D: It's annoying, that's the only nuisance.

122 P: Well, I guess so, it's not so serious* . . .

123 D: No.

(*TOPIC 8: VOICES* 4B ← 4B)

124 P: . . . yes . . . well, I go to make the appointment then and . . .

125 D: Yes, go to the second floor, too, I'll put that (. . .)

126 P: OK.

127 D: Then we'll return to this later.

128 P: Yes . . . goodbye.

129 D: Goodbye.

Analyzing the data from the viewpoint of the entire activity system and its inner contradictions

In the 1986 mode of the general practitioners' work activity, the consultation (the patient visit) was the central *object unit,* the typical chunk of tasks to be mastered and brought to conclusion time and again in the course of a day. In such central object units, the essential inner contradictions of the whole activity system are presumably repeatedly manifested in the form of troublesome discoordinations, and occasionally also as future-oriented initiatives or experiments.

In the following, I present a technique for identifying discoordinations in the doctor–patient discourse of the first data item presented already. The discoordinations found in that particular consultation are then discussed as possible manifestations of the inner contradictions hypothetically identified in the activity system of the health center.

To get a systematic picture of the discoordinations in our videotaped consultations, we developed a technique of identifying the *voices* in each topical phase[5] of the doctor–patient discourse. Elliot Mishler (1984) suggests that there are two basic voices in medical discourse: the voice of the *patient's lifeworld* and the voice of the *authority of medicine.*

As a preliminary gloss, the voice of the life world refers to the patient's contextually-grounded experiences of events and problems in her life. These are reports and descriptions of the world of everyday life expressed from the perspective of a "natural attitude." The timing of events and their significance are dependent on the patient's biographical situation and position in the social world. In contrast, the voice of medicine reflects a "technical" interest and expresses a "scientific attitude." The meaning of events is provided through abstract rules that serve to decontextualize events, to remove them from particular personal and social contexts. (Mishler, 1984, p. 104)

Both the doctor and the patient may use either one of the voices – a realization that makes this kind of an analysis less mechanical. Even so, as we went through our data, we found the schema of the two voices insufficient. Such a schema seems to reduce the tensions in consultations to the familiar asymmetric power relation between a professional expert and a lay client, ignoring possible tensions in the actual medical contents of the discourse. As Tuckett, Boulton, Olson, and Williams (1985) point out, this is the prevalent approach in the sociology of medical encounters. Emphasis has been on style and form, while contents have been largely evaded.

The classic dimension of difference and dispute in the substantive interpretations of health and illness is that of *somatic-biomedical* versus *psychic-social* explanation. This dimension, like the one between patient's lifeworld and medical authority, is easily interpreted in simplified moral terms, with the intention to demonstrate "the fallaciousness of the disease-oriented, organic approach" (Shorter, 1985, p. 256). Susan Sontag's *Illness as Metaphor* is a useful reminder of the pitfalls of such simplifications, demonstrating how "psychological theories of illness are powerful means of placing the blame on the ill" (Sontag, 1983, p. 61).

When these two dimensions are combined, the following framework for analyzing voices of medical discourse emerges (Figure 3.3). When a speaker in the consultation talks about somatic-biomedical contents with the criteria and terminology of the medical authority, that portion of the discourse is classified as representing voice 4A – and so on. Notice that we found it necessary to differentiate between the professional medical authority proper and the administrative or bureaucratic aspect of that authority (symbols A and B in voices 3 and 4).

We can now return to the transcript given previously as my first data item. Each topical phase of the discourse is characterized with the help of number symbols taken from the framework. The first number symbol always refers to the voice of the patient, the second to the voice of the doctor. The direction of the arrow between these two symbols indicates who has the initiative in that topical phase. If the arrow goes from the first symbol to the second, the patient has the initiative – and vice versa.

For example, in topic 1, the symbols 4A←4A indicate that both the patient and the doctor speak in or comply to the voice of somatically and biomedically oriented medical authority, and the doctor has the initiative. When both symbols are identical, we may say that the discourse between the doctor and the patient is coordinated. When the symbols are unidentical, there is a *discoordination* in the discourse. These discoordinations are of special interest for my analysis.

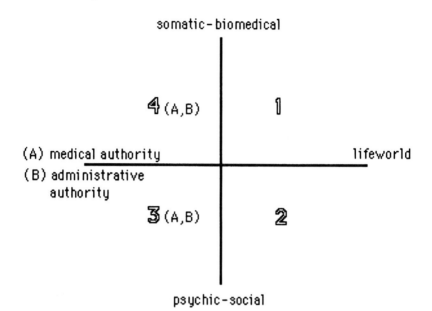

Figure 3.3. Framework for analyzing discoordinations in consultations.

The three discoordinations in my example are as follows. First (topic 2), the patient tries to get an understandable explanation (voice 1) of a report of a surgery he has undergone in a hospital – the doctor tries to give the explanation in medical terms (voice 4A) but fails. Second (topic 3), the patient suddenly asks whether his somatic symptom could have a psychic origin (voice 2) – the doctor answers affirmatively but formally (voice 3), not entering the realm of the psychic lifeworld of the patient, and quickly returns to the biomedical line of discourse (topic 5). Third (topic 7), almost at the end of the consultation, the patient suddenly takes up another psychic concern of his, namely "nervous tensions" as he calls them (voice 2) – the doctor again evades the psychic realm, coining the patient's symptom a "normal reaction" (voice 4A).

In the stimulated recall interview, the doctor admitted that he was not able to decipher the special neurosurgical terminology of the hospital report to the patient in topic 2. The patient's request momentarily revealed the inadequacy of the conceptual and communicative *instruments* at the doctor's disposal. However, there is a deeper problem with the doctor's instruments than just lacking mastery of neurosurgical jargon. Instead of asking the patient *why* he worries about the old surgery report, the doctor sticks to his role as an expert interpreting biomedical findings. In the stimulated recall interview, the doctor actually confirmed that he felt the psychic problems of the patient were not within his competence. In other words, the fundamental instrumental inadequacy here has to do with the lack of means for tackling psychic problems.

When questioned about the other two discoordinations (topics 3 and 7), the doctor said that he had consciously postponed the handling of the patient's psychic problems. He wanted first to rule out any biomedical causes of the symptoms and thus sent the patient to get x-ray pictures of his stomach. He further stated that if the x-ray pictures revealed no somatic problems, a quite different course of care should be chosen – he would send the patient to the psychologist of the station.

In this case, the patient had already gone through all relevant laboratory tests, and the doctor had read their negative results in his computer terminal. The doctor did no physical examination on the patient, presuming that it had been performed in previous visits. The duration of the consultation was only 572 seconds, whereas the average duration of our 85 consultations was 786 seconds. The doctor's time-conscious approach comes to surface twice in the stimulated recall interview. First, the interviewer asks what the doctor writes into his terminal while the patient is searching the problematic part in his surgery report (lines 054–055 in the transcript).

> Doctor: I write into it . . . information while the the patient is searching . . .
> Interviewer: You use the time effectively?
> Doctor: I do that usually always, for example, if the patient takes off his clothes, I write in the meanwhile.

The interviewer then asks whether the doctor is satisfied with his way of communicating with the patient. The doctor replies that maybe he should have handled the patient a little more softly.

> Interviewer: Could you have got some additional meaningful information from him?
> Doctor: It's quite possible. But I don't know, as he comes for the first time again to a new doctor, of course, if I had reserved one

> hour of time for him, maybe I would have got something from him. But that's of course not possible as it is, he coming for the first time.

It is difficult to avoid the interpretation that a central factor behind the discoordinations in topics 3 and 7 was actually the *rule* of rapid consultation, that is, the *time pressure* internalized by the doctor (see Horobin & McIntosh, 1983, and Shorter, 1985, pp. 207–210, for related points). Both topical phases in the discourse are almost abruptly cut short by the doctor. Entering the rather obviously offered domain of psychic problems would have taken much more time. "Ruling out" the biomedical causes (already quite well checked in this case) by sending the patient to x-rays is a convenient way to postpone more lengthy and perhaps troublesome discussions.

In his stimulated recall interview, the patient expressed concern over the quick pace of the consultation. Interestingly enough, he formulated his critique in terms of failing to "examine" the patient properly, as if trying to make his point in a medically valid form.

> Patient: When you come here the first time, they don't really examine you at all. And they prescribe some medicine and so on, and then it's quickly over. It just seems that they do it as quickly as possible, so that they don't much examine anything.

Actually, from a biomedical viewpoint, the patient had been examined quite thoroughly, and the x-rays were a further step in this direction. What was missing was discussion of the patient's worries and anxieties – something that was obviously difficult to formulate for the patient.

In this case, the rule of the rapid consultation was dictated by the fact that the patient came without appointment, as an urgent case. Such urgent cases could simply walk in and wait in the lobby to see the doctor who happened to be on duty. In the activity system of the health center, there was a strict division between such urgent consultations and consultations with appointment. Urgent consultations were meant for acute sicknesses, and only the chief complaint was supposed to be treated in such a consultation. Because of the excessive demand, the waiting time for a consultation with appointment was often several weeks. This created a situation where many patients used the urgent consultations as a way to avoid waiting. This in turn led to excessive use of urgent consultations, including many cases that the doctors did not regard as medically urgent. This further increased the time pressure on the urgent consultations, creating a veritable vicious circle. The average duration of an urgent consultation in our videotaped sample from 1986 was 517.2 seconds, whereas the average duration of a consultation with appointment was 939.7 seconds.

In other words, the time pressure in this activity was largely created by a rule separating two artificial categories: the urgent consultation and the consultation with appointment.

Now how should we interpret these discoordinations in the framework of the entire activity system, modeled in general form in Figure 3.1? First, discoordinations arising from the doctor's inability or unwillingness to handle psychic problems may be tentatively interpreted as manifestations of a deeper contradiction in health center work. This is the contradiction between the *novel object* represented by patients' changing problems and traditional biomedically oriented conceptual and communicative *instruments* at the doctors' disposal. In Figure 3.4, this contradiction is indicated with the letter *A*.

The novel object consists of altered patient problems that are not easily classified and treated in standard biomedical terms. This is a fuzzy and ambiguous kind of novelty. It is reflected in the fact that in 26% of the consultations we videotaped in 1986, psychic and social problems were manifestly taken up. In 48% of the consultations, the patient took up more than one complaint or problem. Only 16.5% of the consultations reached a nonambiguous diagnosis or operated on the basis of a previous diagnosis of such clear-cut nature. Shorter's characterization of the "postmodern patient" is in line with these findings. "Many patients, as they walk into the doctor's office, don't yet have a chief complaint. They have a collection of ill-defined symptoms and anxieties and desires for reassurance, all simmering together in an inchoate pot" (Shorter, 1985, p. 252).

Second, discoordinations arising from the time pressure may be tentatively interpreted as manifestations of a contradiction between patients' complex and ambiguous problems – *novel object* – and the administrative *rule* separating rapidly conducted urgent consultations and regular consultations with appointment, each with different criteria of access. In Figure 3.4, this contradiction is indicated with the letter *B*.

However, the consultation example suggests an additional third contradiction. The doctor saw in his terminal that the patient had been visiting several different doctors in the same station during the past 6 months.

> Interviewer: Now this guy will go to get the x-ray pictures and return to consultation. Have you any idea whether he will return to you or to some other doctor?
>
> Doctor: This is a little difficult, I mean he has visited nearly every . . . I guess those visits were all to doctors. He has lived in Espoo a fairly short time, it is sort of searching he's doing, what kind of health services are offered here. That is, he just goes and takes a look.

Later in the interview the doctor is asked what he typed into the computerized record about this particular consultation.

> Doctor: (. . .) In other words, I wrote fairly little. I do it of course wrong in that I don't put in so awfully much text. But so far, I trust my memory.
>
> Interviewer: Your own memory?
>
> Doctor: My own memory. That is, I only make a report for myself, not that much for another person.
>
> Interviewer: So if he comes again and seeks out another new doctor, in a way that new doctor has it. . . .
>
> Doctor: . . . It's of course more difficult for him to get into that.

And finally toward the end of the interview, the doctor is asked why he did not make it explicit to the patient that he should return to this same doctor.

> Doctor: Well. I did not say that he should reserve an appointment with me. But it's natural that you come to the same doctor. I usually never say it. I think it's self-evident that you return to the one who has given you the referral to the further examinations.

The doctor seems here to avoid a very crucial issue: cooperation and communication between doctors (and other staff). This patient has visited several different doctors within a relatively short period of time. This was actually not just an individual behavior pattern. Rather it was a structural feature in the division of labor of the health center. In principle, any patient could choose to use the services of any of the doctors. In practice, the patients were arbitrarily distributed to doctors according to whomever happened to have free time slots in the appointment calendar or be on urgent duty. This meant that the continuity of care was very low.

Instead of seeing this as a challenge to cooperation and communication, the doctor explains it as common search behavior. Considering the patient's complaints and history, this seems quite an understatement. The only effective means of patient-related communication between the doctors is the computer record. But the doctor admits he uses that means as a support of his personal memory, not as a means of communication. Finally, the doctor expects this patient to act "naturally" and return to him – regardless of the patient's recent history of changing doctors constantly.

These discoordinations in cooperation and communication between practitioners are not directly visible in the consultation transcript. They emerge as potential breakdowns when one contextualizes the consultation with the help of data from the stimulated recall interviews (for a further analysis of such breakdowns, see Engeström, Engeström, & Saarelma, 1988). These discoordinations may be tentatively interpreted as manifestations of a third contradiction in the health center work. This is the contradiction between the patients' complex problems demanding cooperative attention – *novel object* – and the *division of labor* that distributed patients arbitrarily to doctors in the health station. Moreover, the doctors were effectively compartmentalized and isolated from each other. In Figure 3.4, this contradiction is indicated with the letter *C*.

In Figure 3.4, the primary contradiction of the health center work as we found it in 1986 is characterized in the form of dilemmas within each component of the triangle (e.g., subject: effective bureaucrat vs. counselor and helper). The three secondary contradictions – *A*, *B*, and *C* – all originate in the object component, indicating that the patients' novel problems and demands are the factor that initially brought about those contradictions.

In their preliminary form, the three secondary contradictions were initially identified and formulated as an outcome of historical analysis

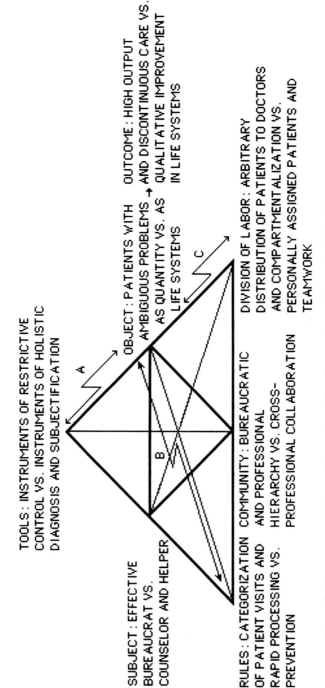

TOOLS: INSTRUMENTS OF RESTRICTIVE
CONTROL VS. INSTRUMENTS OF HOLISTIC
DIAGNOSIS AND SUBJECTIFICATION

OBJECT: PATIENTS WITH   OUTCOME: HIGH OUTPUT
AMBIGUOUS PROBLEMS → AND DISCONTINUOUS CARE VS.
AS QUANTITY VS. AS   QUALITATIVE IMPROVEMENT
LIFE SYSTEMS   IN LIFE SYSTEMS

SUBJECT: EFFECTIVE
BUREAUCRAT VS.
COUNSELOR AND HELPER

DIVISION OF LABOR: ARBITRARY
DISTRIBUTION OF PATIENTS TO DOCTORS
AND COMPARTMENTALIZATION VS.
PERSONALLY ASSIGNED PATIENTS AND
TEAMWORK

RULES: CATEGORIZATION   COMMUNITY: BUREAUCRATIC
OF PATIENT VISITS AND   AND PROFESSIONAL
RAPID PROCESSING VS.   HIERARCHY VS. CROSS-
PREVENTION   PROFESSIONAL COLLABORATION

Figure 3.4. Inner contradictions of the work activity of general practitioners in the health center.

of the evolution of primary care practice in Finland (Engeström, Engeström, Helenius, & Koistinen, 1987; Engeström & Engeström, 1988). Our analyses of discoordinations in the videotaped doctor-patient consultations have several times forced us to elaborate, change, and refine our initial hypothetical picture of the contradictions. However, discoordinations manifesting these three contradictions are repeatedly and consistently found in our consultation data from 1986. No other potential contradiction has emerged with a power anywhere near to that of the three identified earlier.

Obviously this does not "prove" that the three contradictions depicted in Figure 3.4 are the only feasible ones. It might even be argued that we have found only what we wanted to find, simply because qualitative discourse data can always be interpreted in a way that pleases the researcher. This argument misses the point of this type of research endeavor. Rather than proving or disproving a preset hypothesis, the idea is to bring the data and the hypothesis into such an interaction that the latter can be improved and gains in explanatory power. To succeed in this without acquiring a blind faith in the hypothesis elaborated, intermediate theoretical instruments are needed. The function of such instruments is to break the direct imposition of the hypothesis upon the data, to provide for detachment and possibilities for alternative explanations. Here I have presented a framework for analyzing voices and discoordinations in consultations as one such intermediate theoretical instrument.

Analyzing the data from the viewpoint of historicity

In this section, I look at doctor–patient consultations as historically layered object units of medical practice. The consultation already presented will be scrutinized again.

There is a large body of empirical research on the doctor–patient relationship (see Fisher & Todd, 1983; Pendleton & Hasler, 1983; Stewart & Roter, 1989; Stoeckle, 1987). The constantly repeated finding is that the relationship is characterized by asymmetry, professional dominance, and subtle repression of the patient's concerns. Recommendations for improvement seem to stem mainly from general egalitarian and humane concerns. But there is very little evidence that such recommendations have had any notable effect on the daily practice.

Hardly ever is this relationship analyzed in historical terms. Picturing the doctor's work as a self-evident historical constant in need of egalitarian and humane improvement effectively prevents one from seeing the actual inner dynamics of change in the work activity. The first step toward grasping this dynamics is to identify historically evolved successive types of doctor–patient relationship.

An exception among the generally ahistorical studies of doctor–patient relationships is Jewson's (1976) important paper on the "disappearance of the sick-man from medical cosmology." Jewson traces the emergence of three successive historical types of medical cosmology: bedside medicine, hospital medicine, and laboratory medicine. In bedside medicine, the object was the person with his or her total psychosomatic disturbance. In hospital medicine the object is the case, with its organic lesion as the focal point. In laboratory medicine, the object is a cell complex and the biochemical processes within it.

Jewson's analysis indicates that the prototype of modern medical practice used to be specialized hospital care and is currently laboratory research. While this is certainly one dominant line of development, there are obviously other, parallel lines. One such line is the transformation from private fee-for-service practice to corporatized and rationalized doctoring, aptly analyzed by McKinlay and Stoeckle (1987). They summarize key differences between physicians at the beginning of the century and today as depicted in Table 3.1 (I have selected only the characteristics most relevant for the present analysis).

Corporatized medicine emphasizes "rationalization, productivity, and cost efficiency" (McKinlay & Stoeckle, 1987, p. 74). In Jewson's hospital medicine the object is an anonymous case with a lesion, a physically located disease. In corporatized or rationalized medicine, the object is even more anonymous: It is treated as an input–output unit that fulfills the requirements of accounting (a visit, a procedure, a hospital day). However, within the *genus* of corporatized/rationalized medicine, it is important to differentiate between two species, the privately owned corporatized medicine operating for profit, and the publicly owned bureaucratic and rationalized medicine striving for cost efficiency.

Table 3.1. *Differences between physicians' work around 1900 and today*

	Physicians in small-scale fee-for-service practice (1900)	Physicians in bureaucratic practice today
Autonomy over the terms and content of work	Work typically more generalized and controlled by the individual practitioner himself	Work typically segmentalized and directed by administrators in accordance with organizational constraints (profit) and government regulations
Object of labor	Patients usually regarded as the physician's "own patients"	Patients are technically clients, or members of the organization, whom physicians share with other specialists
Tools of labor	Equipment typically owned or leased by the practitioner and employees are hired by the practitioner	Technology typically owned by the employing organization and operated by other bureaucratic employees

Source: McKinlay & Stoeckle, 1987, p. 81.

Alongside with corporatization and rationalization, another competing line of medical thought and practice has emerged. It is variously characterized as *holistic medicine, psychosomatic medicine,* or *humanistic medicine.* In the literature on the doctor–patient relationship, Szasz and Hollender's (1956) model of "mutual participation" represents an early formulation of this direction. Arney and Bergen (1984) provide a rather comprehensive critical treatise of this line. Again, within the same *genus,* two species are found: that of psychoanalytically oriented humanization emphasizing deep emotional conflicts, and that of sociopsychologically and communicatively oriented humanization, emphasizing skills of interpersonal understanding and empathy.

When these partly successive, partly parallel lines of the historical development of medical practice are combined, we get the picture depicted in Figure 3.5. Very little is known of the empirical manifes-

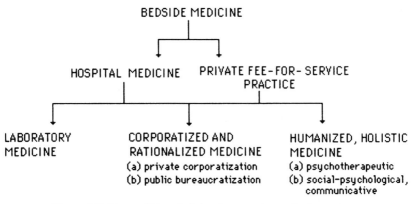

Figure 3.5. Lines of historical development in medical practice.

tations of these lines of development in actual doctor–patient encounters. Stoeckle and Billings (1987) recently attempted to interpret historically the existing literature on medical interviews. While their analysis is a useful beginning, it is severely limited by the ahistorical nature of available empirical studies. The cultural-historical theory of activity claims that history is present in current practices. In other words, manifestations of basic historical types of thinking and practice, such as those depicted in Figure 3.5, coexist as layers within one and the same current activity system.

The historical lines depicted in Figure 3.5 may be read as a concretization of the more general schema depicted in Figure 3.2. Bedside medicine, hospital medicine, and private fee-for-service practice may be regarded as different forms of craft activity. The hospital system certainly brought the medical craft to the peak of its professional authority – but skilled craftsmanship still remained the operational core of medical work (Waddington, 1973).[6] Corporatized medicine and laboratory medicine may be regarded as forms of rationalized activity – machines and division of labor finally took over the organization of work, if not the minds of the practitioners. And humanistic, holistic medicine may obviously be seen as a form of humanized activity.

What is missing in Figure 3.5 is lines equivalent to the "collectively and expansively mastered activity" of Figure 3.2. Such lines would have to represent a combination of high complexity and low centralization – something seldom witnessed in today's medical practice dominated by huge conglomerates and bureaucracies (Jones, 1988). Consumerism (Haug & Lavin, 1983), self-care movements, and new forms of community-based medicine may be forerunners of such emerging lines of development in medical practice.

To create a workable intermediate theoretical instrument for historically oriented analysis of doctor–patient encounters, the tentative historical types identified here are not enough. Crucial substantive dimensions or aspects of the encounter must be identified. Expanding upon the suggestions put forward by Hennen (1975), we formulated a set of five qualitative dimensions of the doctor–patient relationship. These are (1) knowledge about the patient's social life conditions, (2) psychosomatic comprehensiveness and integrity of diagnosis and care, (3) subjectification and activation of the patient, (4) provision for coordination and cooperation with other providers involved in the care, and (5) time perspective of the care. Combined with the historical types of medical practice tentatively identified, these five dimensions provide us with a matrix for interpreting and classifying data from consultations (Figure 3.6).

We thus have a table of 45 empty cells that represent qualities potentially found in the videotapes and associated stimulated recall interviews. Before these empty cells can become substantive categories, a reasonably large sample of consultations must be analyzed and their outstanding properties must be placed in the most fitting cells. In the end, a number of cells will contain a substantive basis for the formation of categories. Some cells will probably remain empty or ambiguous, and some findings may require changes in the matrix itself.

Let us now take another look at the consultation example given as data item 1 earlier in this chapter. This time, I will follow the five dimensions presented in Figure 3.6, drawing from both the transcript and the associated stimulated recall interviews.

Knowledge about the patient

In the stimulated recall interview, the doctor says he looked through all information on the patient in the computer before the patient arrived. As relevant background information thus acquired, he first mentions the recent visits of the patient, characterizing them

	KNOWLEDGE ABOUT THE PATIENT	INTEGRITY AND COMPREHENSIVENESS OF CARE	SUBJECTIFICATION OF THE PATIENT	PROVISION FOR COOPERATION WITH OTHER PROVIDERS	TIME PERSPECTIVE
BEDSIDE MEDICINE					
HOSPITAL MEDICINE					
PRIVATE FEE-FOR-SERVICE PRACTICE					
LABORATORY MEDICINE					
CORPORATIZED MEDICINE					
BUREAUCRATIZED MEDICINE					
PSYCHOTHERAPEUTIC MEDICINE					
SOCIAL-PSYCHOLOGICAL MEDICINE					
ELEMENTS OF EXPANSION					

Figure 3.6. Matrix for identifying characteristics of consultations.

as caused by vomiting. He also mentions the data on the earlier surgery. He then also mentions the patient's psychic problems and the recorded history of such problems. During the consultation, the doctor *never enters the patient's social background*. In the stimulated recall interview, his only comment to that direction is the following.

> Doctor: I think this guy is one of those timid newcomers from the countryside, so to speak. So he was content with the suggestions he got. In other words, I guess he has come from the K region [a rural part of eastern Finland] and he has somehow pondered these difficulties. But in these earlier documents there was nothing on that vomiting. . . .
> Interviewer: You mean in the documents he holds in his hand?
> Doctor: Yes. So they are probably symptoms that have appeared here.

Toward the end of the interview, the doctor is asked whether he would have changed anything in his way of leading the consultation.

> Doctor: No, certainly not. Perhaps only that I should have said something more about the psychic aspect, after all.
> Interviewer: What could that have been?
> Doctor: Perhaps inquiring about what I saw [in the terminal] about that earlier psychosis, something about him having these psychic catastrophes earlier. Or why have you moved here from that region, when have you moved – along those lines.

Integrity and comprehensiveness of care

The doctor's intention to avoid and postpone the handling of psychic and social issues has already been documented and commented upon. The doctor takes a strictly biomedical approach to diagnosis during the consultation. The somatic problem is disconnected from psychic issues. The doctor's essential model is that of *ruling out*.

As a matter of fact, the patient did call the health station to ask for the results of the x-ray pictures. The doctor of our example was not present, so another doctor gave the patient the negative results. The patient has not returned to the health center after that. The procedure not only ruled out organic causes, it effectively "ruled out" the entire patient.

Subjectification of the patient

The doctor does not take measures toward activating the patient as subject of his own care. In the stimulated recall interview, he characterizes the patient as follows.

> Interviewer: Was this a difficult or an easy patient in your opinion?
> Doctor: On the other hand, I found this difficult in that he took so, or submitted really to what he was told. He was easy in that he has been examined already so much, so one doesn't have to start from the very beginning of time. Technically an easy patient.

One wonders to what extent the doctor's own actions contributed to reproducing the docility or acquiescence he criticizes.

Provision for cooperation with other providers of care

The doctor's rather compartmentalized approach has already been documented and discussed. In this case, his interaction with other staff is reduced to referring or "sending off" the patient to x-rays. Similarly, in the interview he points out that he would refer the patient to the psychologist if the x-ray pictures were negative.

Time perspective

The doctor's intention to save time has been documented and discussed above. This seems to be connected with an abstract belief in patients' rational behavior. Recall that the doctor considered it "natural" that the patient return to him, in spite of contrary evidence from the patient's recent history, just cited by the doctor himself. Perhaps we are here not dealing so much with a belief in how patients really act but rather with a normative idea of *how patients should act*. This belief or normative idea relieves the doctor from the burden of guiding the patient or planning the future steps of care together with the patient.

The qualitative features of the doctor–patient relationship found

KNOWLEDGE ABOUT THE PATIENT	INTEGRITY AND COMPREHENSIVENESS OF CARE	SUBJECTIFICATION OF THE PATIENT	PROVISION FOR COOPERATION WITH OTHER PROVIDERS	TIME PERSPECTIVE
no entry in patient's social background	"ruling out" the somatic causes	docility found and reproduced	referring, "sending off" the patient	saving time; normative belief in patient rationality

Figure 3.7. Qualities of doctor–patient relationship in consultation VI/22.

in this consultation can be summarized in Figure 3.7. This characterization would be a candidate to fill the sixth row – bureaucratized medicine – in Figure 3.6. A central underlying theme seems to be the pursuit of restrictive screening and effective management of the patient flow. Recently Terry Mizrahi (1985) has analyzed some aspects of this orientation in a hospital context, calling it provocatively the *Getting Rid of Patients (GROP)* model. Being just one case, the data presented here are naturally an insufficient basis for categorization. But they seem to illustrate quite well some central qualities and inherent mental models of a particular historical type of rationalized doctor–patient relationships.

Conclusions and implications

The data analyzed so far do not seem to justify great optimism concerning development of the general practitioners' work activity toward what I have called the collectively and expansively mastered type. The choice of the data has been intentional: simplicity for the sake of clarity. The case discussed so far has been quite straightforward and homogeneous. The picture becomes much more varied and contradictory as soon as one enters other patients' consultations with the same doctor, not to mention the other doctors' consultations and broader observations of discoordinations and innovations going on in the setting (see Engeström, 1990).

Activity theory is not a specific theory of a particular domain, offering ready-made techniques and procedures. It is a general, cross-disciplinary approach, offering conceptual tools and methodological principles, which have to be concretized according to the specific nature of the object under scrutiny.

I have described three principles of activity theory: (1) using a collective activity system as the unit of analysis; (2) searching for internal contradictions as the driving force behind disturbances, innovations, and change in the activity system; and (3) analyzing the activity and its constituent components and actions historically.

To turn these principles into workable research procedures, intermediate theoretical instruments are needed. In this chapter, I have demonstrated two such instruments, a framework for analyzing discoordinations in doctor–patient discourse, and a matrix for identifying qualitative features of medical consultations. The former intermediate instrument serves to bridge the gap between principles (1) and (3) and the data. The latter intermediate instrument serves to bridge the gap between principle (2) and the data.

The substantive analyses and findings reported in this chapter are limited to small fragments of data collected over three and a half years in a health center setting. As such, they are mainly demonstrations of an approach. The key objective of this type of research is to produce conceptual tools for practitioners. The application of those tools in the self-organization of the activity system puts them in rigorous tests of validity. The adoption and elaboration of those conceptual tools in a growing number of related activity systems is a measure of their generalizability.

Developmental work research may thus be regarded as a testbench of activity theory. However, this testbench is not just the "applied end," receiving theoretical propositions and hypotheses from the heights of the basic research. The epistemology of activity theory transcends the dichotomy between the basic and the applied. I see developmental work research, and other serious attempts at empirical activity-theoretical research, as a laboratory in which new theoretical concepts and methodological principles are created, not only tested. In this sense, the testbench is in the center of the theoretical endeavor.[7]

Notes

1. A comprehensive set of surveys of the reception and development of activity theory in various parts of the world was prepared for the 1st International Congress on Activity Theory held in Berlin (West), 1986; see Hildebrand-Nilshon and Rückriem (1988). A new volume edited by Lektorsky (1990) contains a comprehensive collection of Soviet debates around the concept of activity. In West Germany, already the fifth volume in a series of anthologies on activity

theory was recently published (Holodynski & Jantzen, 1989). A similar collection of Danish research has also appeared (Hedegaard, Hansen, & Thyssen, 1989).

2. These principles should be examined against the dialectical philosophical tradition behind activity theory. Especially Hegel (1966) stressed the idea that substantive theory and the methods of study are genetically intertwined, not separate. Methods should be developed or "derived" from the substance, as one enters and penetrates deeper into the object of study. In this sense, the principles put forward in this chapter are essentially "methodological" principles.

3. Lave herself puts forward the notions of setting and arena as suggested units of analysis. "The supermarket, for instance, is in some respects a public and durable entity. It is physically, economically, politically, and socially organized space-in-time. In this aspect it may be called an 'arena' within which activity takes place. The supermarket as arena is the product of patterns of capital formation and political economy. It is not negotiable directly by the individual. It is outside of, yet encompasses the individual, providing a higher-order institutional framework within which setting is constituted. At the same time, for individual shoppers, the supermarket is a repeatedly experienced, personally ordered and edited version of the arena. In this aspect it may be termed a 'setting' for activity. Some aisles in the supermarket do not exist for a given shopper as part of her setting, while other aisles are rich in detailed possibilities" (Lave, 1988, pp. 150–151). For Lave, a setting is generated out of the person's activity and at the same time generates that activity. But this dialectical and constructive relation seems to stop short as we enter the arena. "There is a distinction to be made between the constraints imposed by the supermarket as arena and the constructable, malleable nature of the setting" (Lave, 1988, p. 151). Symptomatically, in her detailed analysis of the practice of grocery shopping, Lave concentrates on the level of individual actions of problem setting and problem solving. The formation of the arena (the supermarket) is left practically unanalyzed, as something given from above. In other words, Lave has both the individual experience and the system – but they remain only externally, mechanically related to each other.

4. In their discussion of the creative mind, Findlay and Lumsden (1988, pp. 14–15) present a model structurally identical with Figure 3.1. With this model they demonstrate the general difference between hierarchical and heterarchical organization – the latter being characteristic to human societies and complex innovative processes. "From the above considerations, it follows that the isolation of a particular component for analysis totally *ex situ* is justified only if the functional complexity of the system is at most hierarchical. For creative activity, this amounts to asserting that the step from cognitive state to discovery is causally independent of the step from discovery to innovation, and *vice versa*. Intriguingly, such simplicity does not prevail" (Findlay & Lumsden, 1988, p. 15).

5. The notion of topic is problematic in itself (see Brown & Yule, 1983, chap. 3). Here, I use it pragmatically, to signify the changes in the contents of the discussion between the doctor and the patient.

6. Craft professionalism in physicians' work has been eloquently characterized by Freidson (1970, chap. 8) in his analysis of the "clinical mentality." He quite

convincingly crushes the Parsonian myth of professions, showing that there is no principled difference between the "professions" of a plumber and a physician if one uses the criteria put forward by Parsons himself. But he never explicitly uses the notion of craft in his analysis of doctors' work. Would that be a consequence of an implicit hold of the professional myth even on Freidson?

7. It is perhaps this combination of high theoretical ambition and rigorous striving for practical relevance that has made developmental work research itself somewhat a snowball phenomenon in Finland and Scandinavia. Time will tell whether this approach has generalizability beyond the cultural borders of those countries.

References

Arney, W. R., & Bergen, B. J. (1984). *Medicine and the management of living: Taming the last great beast.* Chicago: University of Chicago Press.

Bakhurst, D. (1991). *Consciousness and revolution in Soviet philosophy.* Cambridge: Cambridge University Press.

Beniger, J. R. (1986). *The control revolution: Technological and economic origins of the information society.* Cambridge, MA: Harvard University Press.

Bødker, S. (1990). *Through the interface: A human activity approach to user interface design.* Hillsdale, NJ: Lawrence Erlbaum.

Brown, G., & Yule, G. (1983). *Discourse analysis.* Cambridge: Cambridge University Press.

Cole, M. (1988). Cross-cultural research in the socio-historical tradition. *Human Development, 31,* 137–157.

Douglas, M. (1986). *How institutions think.* Syracuse, NY: Syracuse University Press.

Engels, F. (1976). *Anti-Dühring.* Moscow: Progress.

Engeström, Y. (1987). *Learning by expanding: An activity-theoretical approach to developmental research.* Helsinki: Orienta-Konsultit.

Engeström, Y. (1990). *Learning, working and imagining: Twelve studies in activity theory.* Helsinki: Orienta-Konsultit.

Engeström, Y., & Engeström, R. (1988). Seeking the zone of proximal development in physicians' work activity. In M. Hildebrand-Nilshon & G. Rückriem (Eds.), *Proceedings of the 1st International Congress on Activity Theory* (Vol. 2, pp. 471–496). Berlin: Hochschule der Künste.

Engeström, Y., Engeström, R., Helenius, J., & Koistinen, K. (1987). *Terveyskeskuslääkäreiden työn kehittämistutkimus. LEVIKE-projektin I väliraportti* [Developmental study of the work of health center physicians. First interim report of Project LEVIKE]. Espoo: Board of Health.

Engeström, Y., Engeström, R., & Saarelma, O. (1988). Computerized medical records, production pressure, and compartmentalization in the work activity of health center physicians. *Proceedings of the Conference on Computer Supported Collaborative Work.*

Findlay, C. S., & Lumsden, C. J. (1988). *The creative mind.* London: Academic Press.

Fisher, S., & Todd, A. D. (Eds.). (1983). *The social organization of doctor–patient communication.* Washington, DC: Center for Applied Linguistics.

Freidson, E. (1970). *Profession of medicine.* New York: Dodd, Mead.

Haug, M., & Lavin, B. (1983). *Consumerism in medicine: Challenging physician authority.* Beverly Hills, CA: Sage.

Hedegaard, M., Hansen, V. R., & Thyssen, S. (Eds.). (1989). *Et virksomt liv: Udforskning af virksomhedsteoriens praksis* [An active life: Research on the practice of activity theory]. Aarhus: Aarhus Universitetsforlag.

Hegel, G. W. F. (1966). *The phenomenology of mind.* London: George Allen & Unwin – Humanities Press.

Hennen, B. K. (1975). Continuity of care in family practice. Part 1: Dimensions of continuity. *Journal of Family Practice, 2,* 371–372.

Hildebrand-Nilshon, M., & Rückreim, G. (Eds.). (1988). *Proceedings of the 1st International Congress on Activity Theory* (Vols. 1–4). Berlin: System Druck.

Hirschhorn, L. (1984). *Beyond mechanization: Work and technology in a postindustrial age.* Cambridge, MA: MIT Press.

Holodynski, M., & Jantzen, W. (Eds.). (1989). *Persönlicher Sinn als gesellschaftliches Problem* (Studien zur Tätigkeitstheorie 5) [Personal sense as a societal problem (Studies in activity theory 5)]. Bielefeld: Universtität Bielefeld.

Holzkamp, K. (1983). *Grundlegung der Psychologie* [Foundation of psychology]. Frankfurt am Main: Campus.

Horobin, G., & McIntosh, J. (1983). Time, risk and routine in general practice. *Sociology of Health and Illness, 5,* 312–331.

Ilyenkov, E. V. (1982). *The dialectics of the abstract and the concrete in Marx's* Capital. Moscow: Progress.

Jewson, N. D. (1976). The disappearance of the sick-man from medical cosmology, 1770–1870. *Sociology, 10,* 225–244.

Jones, R. (1988). *The supermeds: How the big business of medicine is endangering our health care.* New York: Scribner.

Kern, H., & Schumann, M. (1984). *Das Ende der Arbeitsteilung* [The end of the division of labor]? Munich: Beck.

Kvale, S. (1976). The psychology of learning as ideology and technology. *Behaviorism, 4,* 97–116.

Lave, J. (1988). *Cognition in practice: Mind, mathematics and culture in everyday life.* Cambridge: Cambridge University Press.

Lektorsky, V. A. (1984). *Subject, object, cognition* (S. Syrovatkin, Trans.) Moscow: Progress. (Original work published 1980)

Lektorsky, V. A. (Ed.). (1990). *Activity: Theories, methodology and problems.* Orlando, FL: Paul M. Deutsch.

Leont'ev, A. N. (1978). *Activity, consciousness, and personality* (M. J. Hall, Trans.) Englewood Cliffs, NJ: Prentice-Hall.

Leontyev, A. N. (1981). *Problems of the development of the mind* (M. Kopylova, Trans.) Moscow: Progress. (Original work published 1981)

McKinlay, J. B., & Stoeckle, J. D. (1987). Corporatization and the social transformation of doctoring. *Sosiaalilääketieteellinen Aikakauslehti, 24,* 73–84.

Marx, K. (1973). *Grundrisse: Foundations of the critique of political economy (rough draft).* Harmondsworth: Penguin Books.

Marx, K., & Engels, F. (1975). *Collected works.* Vol. 4. Moscow: Progress.

Mikhailov, F. T. (1980). *The riddle of the self.* Moscow: Progress.

Mishler, E. (1984). *The discourse of medicine: Dialectics of medical interviews.* Norwood, NJ: Ablex.

Mizrahi, T. (1985). Getting rid of patients: Contradictions in the socialization of internists to the doctor–patient relationship. *Sociology of Health and Illness, 7,* 214–235.

Moll, L. (Ed.). (1990). *Vygotsky and education: Instructional implications and applications of sociohistorical psychology.* Cambridge: Cambridge University Press.

Noyelle, T. (1987). *Beyond industrial dualism: Market and job segmentation in the new economy.* Boulder, CO: Westview Press.

Ochs, E. (1988). *Culture and language development: Language acquisition and language socialization in a Samoan village.* Cambridge: Cambridge University Press.

Pendleton, D., & Hasler, J. (Eds.). (1983). *Doctor–patient communication.* London: Academic Press.

Perrow, C. (1984). *Normal accidents: Living with high-risk technologies.* New York: Basic Books.

Projektgruppe Automation und Qualifikation (1987). *Widersprüche der Automationsarbeit: Ein Handbuch* [Contradictions of labor under automation: A handbook]. West Berlin: Argument-Verlag.

Rose, M. (1988). *Industrial behavior: Research and control* (2nd ed.). London: Penguin Books.

Rossi-Landi, F. (1983). *Language as work and trade: A semiotic homology for linguistics and economics.* South Hadley, MA: Bergin & Garvey.

Shorter, E. (1985). *Bedside manners: The troubled history of doctors and patients.* New York: Simon & Schuster.

Sontag, S. (1983). *Illness as metaphor.* Harmondsworth: Penguin Books.

Stanback, T. M., Jr. (1987). *Computerization and the transformation of employment: Government, hospitals, and universities.* Boulder, CO: Westview Press.

Star, S. L. (in press). The sociology of the invisible: The primacy of work in the writings of Anselm Strauss. In D. Maines (Ed.), *Social organization and social processes: Essays in honor of Anselm L. Strauss.* Hawthorne, NY: Aldine de Gruyter.

Stewart, M., & Roter, D. (Eds.). (1989). *Communicating with medical patients.* Newbury Park, CA: Sage.

Stoeckle, J. D. (Ed.). (1987). *Encounters between patients and doctors: An anthology.* Cambridge, MA: MIT Press.

Stoeckle, J. D., & Billings, J. A. (1987). A history of history-taking: The medical interview. *Journal of General Internal Medicine, 2,* 119–127.

Strauss, A., Fagerhaugh, S., Suczek, B., & Wiener, C. (1985). *The social organization of medical work*. Chicago: University of Chicago Press.

Szasz, T. S., & Hollender, M. (1956). A contribution to the philosophy of medicine: The basic models of the doctor–patient relationship. *AMA Archives of Internal Medicine, 97*, 585–592.

Touraine, A. (1965). *Sociologie de l'action*. Paris: Éditions du Seuil.

Tuckett, D., Boulton, M., Olson, C., & Williams, A. (1985). *Meetings between experts: An approach to sharing ideas in medical consultations*. London: Tavistock Publications.

Waddington, I. (1973). The role of the hospital in the development of modern medicine: A sociological analysis. *Sociology, 7*, 211–224.

Wertsch, J. V. (Ed.). (1981). *The concept of activity in Soviet psychology*. Armonk, NY: M. E. Sharpe.

Zuboff, S. (1988). *In the age of the smart machine: The future of work and power*. New York: Basic Books.

4   Re-searching psychotherapeutic practice

Ole Dreier

In this chapter I shall outline an approach to the analysis of psycho-therapeutic practice. The resulting analytic framework is geared to be a countermeasure against the current impasse of research and practice and to redirect its development. The analytic categories for this "re-search" are provided by the historical paradigm of "critical psychology" (systematically exposed by Holzkamp, 1983). They are employed upon three interconnected avenues of empirical inquiry:

1. Studies of audiotaped casework, including regular interviews with clients and other parties, directly or indirectly involved, concerning relations between their everyday life contexts and the ongoing therapy.[1]
2. Studies of audiotapes and notes from my practice as a therapist and supervisor (Dreier, 1980, 1986a, 1987a).
3. Studies of transcripts from a series of regular conferences between researchers and practitioners, analyzing issues of professional psychological practice on the basis of critical psychology (Dreier, 1983, 1986b, 1988a, 1989; Dreier, Kleinmanns, Konitzer-Feddersen, Michels, & Raitola, 1988; Holzkamp, 1988; Markard, 1988; Moll, Böhm, Vathke, & Dreier, 1985).

I shall not particularize my analysis of these data here. Instead, I shall build a multilevel argument resting upon them. In the course of laying out this argument, I shall introduce a number of central analytic categories from critical psychology deployed to construct it. It is the objective of these analyses to capture both what is the matter with current therapeutic practice and what the parties involved need to think about and do to improve it. My argument will highlight issues at four levels of analysis in turn: the participating subjects,

104

their situated interaction, the societal mediation of what takes place, and the restriction versus the extension of the subjects' practice.

The subjects

According to widespread ideologies, psychotherapy is an eminently subjective enterprise. In striking contrast hereto, representations of therapeutic practice, typically, are desubjectified. To put it more precisely, the subjectivity of the parties involved is captured in a restricted and distorted manner. Their subjective reasons for doing what they do, facing one another and the therapeutic process in which they take part, are not exposed directly and comprehensively. Neither party appears coherently in "first-person singular," in his own right and perspective. Yet subjective reasons for action are constitutive of individual human agency (Holzkamp, 1983, pp. 342–356). On the one hand, the premises of reasons for action are founded upon each participant's experience of the meaning of the situation at hand, that is, upon its action possibilities as they appear to him. On the other hand, the premises of these action possibilities rest upon his experienced needs, interests, and ability to pursue them in that situation. Notions about therapeutic practice that are restricted in that manner do not enable us to arrive at an encompassing and systematic comprehension of the participants' subjective rationality (Dreier, 1987b/1991, 1988a, 1988b, 1990). Moreover, the "desubjectification" is cast in differing forms for client and therapist respectively because of their different social positions, perspectives, and interests in the therapeutic process.

Within therapy the subjective reasons for the client's actions and problems are not exposed systematically from his own point of view (Dreier, 1987b). This is so despite the fact that the essential subject matter of the whole psychotherapeutic endeavor is to disentangle the problematics and conflicts of his subjective reasons for action – including their cognitive, emotional, and motivational aspects. A proper understanding, as well as a challenge to, and change of, those conflicting phenomena presupposes that they are analyzed upon the very level of their subjective rationality. Instead, client actions and problems appear from the external perspective of the therapist's – or an eventual researcher's – interpretations thereof, which, in turn, play a crucial part in the way in which therapists account for their actions vis-à-vis the client. Clients do, of course, supply more or less limited, induced, and directed descriptions. But they are interpreted by the therapist, and these interpretations are, possibly, used to direct the process, including future descriptions. Perspectives for description and interpretation are separated and distributed between the two parties. In that way clients are construed, even downright contrived, from a "proficentric" perspective.

The therapist, for his part, couches the subjective rationality of his own actions from the external perspective of his client's needs and other similar factors – as if the reasons for the therapist's actions were, in fact, totally objectively determined by and derived from his client's characteristics, needs, and problems and the demands they pose upon him as therapist. He purports to be a person who has no needs or interests of his own, except those of serving his client's, and whose own actions, therefore, rest solely upon somebody else's premises. To put it more precisely and in a way that emphasizes the obscure relationship of those views to the reality of the matter: The therapist's actions are accounted for, neither on the premises and perspectives of his own situation, nor on the premises and perspectives of the client's situation, but on the premises of the therapist's interpretation of his client's needs. It goes without saying that the subjective rationality of professional action cannot be accounted for on such a confounded and narrow basis. We are in need of a more comprehensive theory about professional therapeutic subjectivity and agency (Dreier, 1988a, 1988b). The current crisis of professionalism is partly caused and aggravated by this deficiency.

Doing and thinking therapy in that way, the two parties' perspectives and interests become thoroughly entangled, confused, and blurred. It becomes impossible to identify the actual differences between and combination of their respective possibilities, difficulties, tasks, problems, conflicts, needs, and interests within and during the therapeutic process. Representations of the process uncontrollably switch to and fro and confound perspectives. For instance, it may go unnoticed that the therapist's (or researcher's) perspective, interests, motives, and reasons for action influence interpretations of client problems. Ultimately, both parties may, in a sense, end up being dissolved as subjects in their own right: The client is transformed into a mere "interpretation" of his therapist, and the therapist into a subordinate part of the "story" about his client. The desubjectification of the client merges as he becomes an object of interpretation and treatment while the desubjectification of the therapist eventuates in the process in which he "deposits" his subjectivity in the service of his client. Whatever the therapist may hold back as subjectivity "of his own," is relegated to the external arenas of supervision and treatment planning (Dreier, 1987a, 1988b). Incidentally, this relegation in the interests of service to a client is not tantamount to giving up influence upon and power over the process, but only of obscuring it to the client and the public.

We can conclude that a more viable analysis of psychotherapeutic practice must include both parties as subjects and consider them as two of a kind, evenhandedly, and without privileged perspectives. The main reasons why this is rarely done have to do with problems at other levels of analysis, which we shall address in this paper. Like any concrete problem, this particular problem is characterized by and constituted in the overall connections of which it is a part.

Situated interaction

Merely striving to include both parties as subjects is not sufficient in itself. Human subjectivity and action are always displayed in relationship to an objective, social world. Subjective rationality can only be comprehended when seen in such connections. Subjective reasons for action are mediated by the meaning of existing, objective action possibilities. If not so construed, they will be envisioned as bereft of objective direction and momentum – in that sense, construed as irrational and deobjectified. Moreover, individual subjectivity and action are always located. They can only be properly studied in relation to a peculiar social context. Nevertheless, psychotherapeutic activity is often displayed as if it occurs in a vacuum or in a peculiar, even privileged, idealized space without any firm connections with an objective, social world. It is conceived as taking place anywhere and nowhere in particular. Predominant notions about therapy are decontextualized. Behind all this lies the general, implicit premise that the concrete context is without significance. It has no meaning for what goes on within it.

Within the immediate, therapeutic context, each other participant is part of everyone's conditions, possibilities, tasks, problems, conflicts. The others are part of my subjective reasons for participation, and for saying, thinking, and doing what I do. Furthermore, the meaning and impact of particular actions, events, and results are not constituted on a purely individual basis, but intersubjectively – that is, supraindividually. Accordingly, everybody makes observations and interpretations and directs actions on the basis of processes of which they are themselves a particular part and upon which they exert a definite influence. They must reflect on their relations to and influence upon this supraindividual process in order to determine their particular possibilities and tasks, as well as the perspectives from which they interpret what is going on. In that way they ground their individual intentions in ongoing interaction. They link them up with the meaning of their actions for the overall interactional process, for other particular participants, and for themselves. Most tasks are, indeed, common ones. They are not even distributed to a single individual, but carried out by a particular combination of individuals – through interaction. Particular, individual parts of such tasks are interlinked, intersubjectively defined and coordinated.

All this makes it impossible to predict the results of individual actions and the overall process on the basis of notions about intention and action that are entirely and purely individual. Such widespread notions about a purely individual, professional, therapeutic agency are untenable. They do, nevertheless, keep on playing a crucial part in the way in which professional, therapeutic accountability and responsibility is displayed and represented (Dreier, 1988a, 1988b). But the overall outcome is irreducible to the actions of a single, participating individual. It is not produced by an individual "maker" but by a composition effect of everyone's doings.

I have emphasized that the meaning of objective action possibilities in a particular, concrete context and the subjective reasons for action formed in trying to cope with life in relation to them are essential, defining features of human action and subjectivity. Issues of – intended or unintended – meaning are basic to a theory about human action and interaction. They must be basic to a conception about therapeutic practice as well. It is the special subject matter of psychotherapy to deal with particular inter- and intraindividual conflicts about subjective reasons and about the meaning of existing possibilities (Dreier, 1985, 1987b/1991, 1990). They must be of vital concern for therapeutic analysis and practice. Yet many therapeutic conceptions do not assign to them the central status they require in the analysis and exposition of therapeutic interaction in context. This paradox deserves further elaboration.

One form of such neglect consists in regarding therapeutic interaction and conversation as an execution of a general set of elementary mechanisms and procedures (Dreier, 1988c). Interaction is construed as a summation of those building blocks. But that takes our analysis one level below the level of human action and interaction – to the level of elementary, human operations (Holzkamp, 1983, pp. 269–304). They certainly are the means by which we carry out actions and which enable us to realize particular goals. But neither the objective meaning, nor the subjective reasons for the actions carried out by means of particular operations, can be identified at the very level of operations. It does not include this essential peculiarity of human subjectivity and of the objective, human world. Reasons for selecting particular operations are incomprehensible on the basis of an analysis of operations alone. On the contrary, the choice among particular operations is made on the basis of the meaning and reasons of human action and interaction. So variations among therapeutic situations, or among such situations and other types of situations, can be observed but not comprehended at an operational level. This applies equally to the comprehension of the significance of definite events and outcomes, as well as which interests are at stake, supported or impeded, and which goals are realized. Indeed, a definite goal and interest can be pursued by means of different operations, and a particular operation can be used to realize different goals. In other words, the significance and efficacy of therapeutic action cannot be univocally determined through an analysis at the level of operations, nor can the significance of some detail within the process – say, the "hidden secret" of therapeutic effects – be discovered at that level. Whatever the significance of an operation may be, an analysis at the level of action is required to establish its actual meaning.

When therapeutic practice, nevertheless, is presented and analyzed at an operational level, its interpretation must, strictly speaking, remain open. In practice it is, thereby, turned over to the therapist, subsequently some researcher or reader. Interpreting actions on the basis of observations about operations, therapists or researchers implicitly build hypothetical assumptions containing their own opinion about the meaning of the participants' possibilities and the subjective reasons for action (Dreier, 1988c; Holzkamp, 1987b).

A typical form of therapist interpretation consists in anchoring meanings and reasons exclusively in characteristics of the immediate interaction and/or of the participating personalities. Myriads of notions and studies about therapeutic practice do precisely that. This is what they mean by social context. Possibly, they add to the present context the idea that reality consists of a series of such immediate situations and expressions of personality characteristics, each understandable from within or from their immediate interconnections (Holzkamp, 1987a). However, in this way they bracket off more comprehensive social structures of possibilities and meaning, together with the corresponding, more comprehensive, social mediations of subjective reasons for action. In other words, such interpretations presuppose that mediated social conditions – and often even immediate material conditions – have no meaning for the events of interaction. What counts is only the persons and their immediate interchange. That is why this kind of interpretation is full of short circuits about significant, more comprehensive connections. They lead to a personalization of subjective affairs. In the case of therapy, they mostly eventuate in some kind of blaming of victims for their sufferings, characteristic of therapeutic subjectivism. In critical psychology such short-circuited thinking within the boundaries of immediate situations is termed an interpretative mode of thinking (Holzkamp, 1983, pp. 383–402). Because of its restricted scope, it must remain ambiguous as, indeed, abundantly evidenced in therapeutic practice and literature.

Interpretative ambiguity is conspicuously expressed in the inextricable conceptional and interpretational disagreements among therapists. This is, however, but a special part of the even more impressive disagreements in the preceding steps of interpretation concerning each case. Here various forms of differences of interpretation between therapist and client, among clients, and among other persons somehow involved in the same case are ubiquitous. Rather, it appears that the plurality of involved subjects is paralled by a plurality of interpretations. In fact, we must approach this crucial plurality from another angle: Differences of interpretation among involved parties are of systematic significance for comprehending the subject matter of therapy. They depend upon pertinent differences in contextual social position with inherent differences in possibilities and interests, and in the subjective meaning of and perspective upon existing conflicts among them. On that background the whole therapeutic endeavor and particular events within it have different meanings to them. Their reasons for action in relation to it differ, and so does the direction of their interests, intentions, and goals.

The concept of inter- and intrasubjective conflicts, and their foundation in contradictions of possibilities, interests, and reasons among subjects, must, therefore, be a key concept for therapeutic analysis (Dreier, 1985, 1986a, 1987b/1991, 1988b, 1990; Holzkamp-Osterkamp, 1976). Particular forms of such conflicts in, for, and among individual subjects are the special subject matter of therapy. Living in contradictory relations implies developing self-contradictory individual reasons, emotional evaluations, and motives. Individual intentions of action, their subjective reasons and their meaning to others, become an object of inter- and intrasubjective strife and conflict. Disputes of interpretation arise over them. Attempts are made to impose and monopolize interpretations about "what's really the case." They involve personalizations of responsibility and blame about "what's really the matter." Conflicts, thus obscured and repressed, lead to blurred and confused reasons and meanings, to disorientation of action.

Client and therapist interpretations are, in other words, themselves products of interaction. At the same time, they are a particular part thereof, played by their interpreter. In a more or less obscure and confounded way, they express and pursue his particular perspective upon, interests in, and evaluation of the conflicts in question. They are a more or less predominant part of that conflict. On those grounds they can and must be challenged as problematic. To be able to do so, the diversity of interpretations must be made publicly available to everybody concerned, in that way, for example, putting an end to the representation of some parties solely through the predominant interpretations of others. Voicing one's own reasons must take the place of others' interpretations thereof. It must be acknowledged, and made a subject of discourse and clarification, that events are differently interpreted – and for good reasons. Each subject must consider his own reasons and interpretations as arising out of the conflictual relationships and in relation to those of others. Then the connections between them, including the conflicts between them – and the changeability of these connections and conflicts – can be made an object of discourse and reflection. Therapeutic practice is meant to supply one kind of arena, safeguarding and promoting the discourse over, reflection on, and working through of such contradictions.

This approach to conflictual reasons and interpretations provides us with a basis for comprehending subjective rationality in connection with those social relations of which it is a part. We can reconstruct the immediate problem appearance as an expression of conflicts that are particular, located aspects of social contexts. In accordance with this, the generalization of reasons and interpretations has a social dimension. It rests upon the generalization of the parties' possibilities and interests. Until that is achieved, interpretations remain diverse and opposed for good reasons. Therefore, our analysis is directed toward clarifying individual interests as well as the possible transformation and overcoming of conflicts of interest, in order to open up, redirect, and extend action possibilities. They elucidate how individuals stand in their own and each others' ways while pursuing their interests in contrary ways. It is a crucial feature of conflictual relations based upon opposed interests that each person, while pursuing his own interests, simultaneously impedes those of others who, therefore, react and retaliate against him. In that way, he hampers his own interests in the long run, together with the general interest of all. Possibilities for generalizing interests must be identified and realized in order to overcome those conflicts and their inherent restrictions. Then each person's actions can simultaneously promote everyone's interests – including his own. The pursuit of such joint interest and common good implies the generalization and joint extension of action possibilities, instead of an alternating, dividing, or compromising pursuit of special interests. Until then conflicts, strictly speaking, remain unresolved. They are not overcome. Only their relative relations of strength and forms are changed.

Our analysis opens up a wider perspective on the conflicts that people suffer from, and for which they may seek the service of a therapist. It is more firmly and comprehensively anchored in the social world of subjects than are operational, personalized, or narrowly interactional notions. We can now recognize that those notions reflect *restricted* modes of action (Holzkamp, 1983, p. 374). By that term is meant a mode of action where people in conflict take the boundaries of the existing, immediate situation as the premises of their action and think about it in a concomitant interpretative way. It is a restrictive way of dealing with existing conflicts precisely because it disregards and precludes the alternative of changing the present boundaries by (jointly) extending the scope of possibilities and, thus, overcoming those conflicts. In other words, restrictive modes of action, thinking, and emotion express the subjective rationality of a particular way of reacting to existing conflicts. Of course, this applies not only to clients but to therapists as well (Dreier, 1986b, 1988a, 1988b). In their practice therapists may resort to restrictive modes of action and thinking, faced with the precarious task of unraveling conflicts in and among people while being (made) responsible for improving the problematic client's well-being. Against that background they may interpret their clients and themselves in personalizing ways.

The remaining two sections of this chapter highlight the societal mediation of client and therapist action possibilities and reasons for action, together with the alternative of a restricted versus an extended or generalized mode of action and the corresponding interpretative versus comprehensive modes of thinking (Holzkamp, 1983, pp. 356–415).

Societal mediation

We have emphasized that our understanding of the connections between the actions of human subjects and the objective world cannot be restricted to envision "an individual-in-his-immediate-situation." On the contrary, such conceptions and methodologies perpetuate interpretative ambiguity and arbitrariness. It is, actually, not even possible to analyze empirical phenomena that are immediately present in a particular situation without, implicitly or explicitly, employing fundamental categories about the sociohistorical "man–environment–context" as criteria with which to think about and identify what is to be taken as essential features among the infinite variety of relevant phenomena (Holzkamp, 1987a).

The existing connections in an immediate situation are not merely constituted in and out of that situation. They rest on a societally mediated scope of present possibilities. The immediate situation has particular connections with the overall societal structure of possibilities and actions that produce and reproduce the concrete social formation. It is a part of that structure of possibilities. In other words, the situation is embedded in extensive, societal connections. To an individual subject, the particular, concrete structure and appearance of these connections varies with the relation between his particular location and the overall social structure. So even the immediate "internal" connections of any situation are societally mediated in a concrete and particular way. We must, therefore, break with "the premise of immediacy" (Holzkamp, 1983, p. 193) and recognize the concrete, societal mediation of particular situations in particular locations. The scope of action possibilities, the meaning of those possibilities, and the subjective reasons for action formed in relating to them are of a mediated nature.

What is more, the subjects utilize and influence those mediated societal connections in their own immediate actions. That is precisely why they are able to direct their action possibilities and reasons beyond the boundaries of the immediate situation. They can direct them toward an intended or unintended mediated meaning at some other, somehow intermediately connected, level and location in the social world. Indeed, individuals also form reasons and realize actions that are directed at changing the present boundaries of their immediate situation itself and extending its scope of subjectively relevant action possibilities. The immediate situation contains mediated possibilities for doing so.

Needless to say, all this applies to the practice of therapy and its individual participants as well. Immediate therapeutic connections, formed in interaction at a particular location, in some way or other display and make use of particular, mediated action possibilities and structures of meaning. Let us elaborate this argument further, again starting with one of its parties at a time.

For clients (Dreier, 1980, 1986a, 1987b/1991, 1990) the very conflicts for which they seek therapy are of a mediated nature in relation to the therapeutic situation. They originate and primarily have meaning to them in other contexts. In order to come to understand those conflicts, the therapist must think beyond the boundaries of the immediate therapeutic situation. He must locate them within more encompassing structures of clients' lifeworld and reconstruct particular therapeutic appearances on that basis. Those client actions, reasons, and emotions that appear within the therapeutic situation can, of course, be observed there. However, they must be understood the other way around. Client motives for entering therapy and the reasons for client actions inside and outside, but in relation to it, are mediated. The way clients present and interpret their problems to the therapist cannot be understood only on the basis of the immediate relationship between them, but must be analyzed in the same way. All the features just mentioned depend upon the particular connections between the clients' therapy and their lifeworld as they see them and use them. It depends upon the localization of therapeutic practice in relation to subjectively relevant social structures, upon how, for what, by whom, and in whose interest such particular connections are used and imagined to be usable.

For the therapist (Dreier, 1988a, 1988b) we already noted that his actions within the immediate situation become part of the conflicts in and among participants and have different, indeed, contrary meanings to those involved. Furthermore, his actions mostly are made an object of interpretative conflicts and exploited by particular parties against others. In that way their emerging meaning is influenced beyond his control and even suspicion. This is also done in other contexts, at different times, and by other involved parties who might not even take part in the immediate therapeutic interaction. Actually, all this is not organized and done with the therapeutic interaction as, so to say, the center of events and control. Rather, it is organized from those contexts that are the most decisive and influential parts of client conflicts. So the therapist must reconstruct his own actions, his possibilities, emotional reactions, conflicts, and reasons in that perspective. He must analyze it all as part of those mediated, conflictual structures. He must come to understand the mediated meaning of therapeutic events for the clients in their relations in their lifeworld.

He must comprehend how the meaning of his actions spreads and is influenced via the particular net of connections that already exist and are used and changed by him, his clients, and other interested parties.

Of course, meaningful therapeutic action is produced in the immediate situation. Participants can influence its meaning therein according to its particular scope of mediated, situational possibilities. However, its meaning is not only determined therein, nor realized therein, but – hopefully – outside, elsewhere, in the clients' life contexts. After all, the overall objective of the therapeutic endeavor is to obtain meaning for client situations outside of its own immediate boundaries. If it was not able to achieve this, it would be futile, indeed, a meaningless endeavor. Actually, this is not a feature peculiar to therapeutic practice, but one it shares with many other social practices whose primary objective is to influence phenomena and events in other, outside contexts. So also therapeutic conceptions and methodologies must enable us to capture the mediated meaning of particular, immediate therapeutic inter-actions and of its overall outcomes. Just like the problems to be treated by means of it, therapy remains a particular aspect of extensive, societal connections.

Even the peculiarities of its immediate therapeutic possibilities, ways of functioning, and proceedings must be comprehended in that same perspective. The reasons to give therapeutic encounters particular contents and structure are constituted in that way. This is also true of the particular distribution and combination of possibilities, responsibilities, and tasks among participants in the therapeutic encounters, as well as of their particularities of discourse and routines. They all are particular, optional, and functional ways of coping with existing, conflictual scopes of therapeutic practice. What is more, these elements are changeable – and, indeed, must change – with its changing scopes. Immediate proceedings are often implicitly interpreted in the perspective we outlined, but this rarely is recognized explicitly at a conceptional and methodological level.

On the background of our arguments in this section, it is evident that neither therapist nor clients can restrict their thinking about therapeutic practice to its immediately "observable" interactions. The course of therapy cannot be conceived as a mere succession of immediate events and situations. Objective, immediate, and mediated, connections exist between situations and influence the course of events. We must include them when identifying the meaning of the actions and outcomes of a particular situation. Situations and contexts interact and interpenetrate in particular ways. Not all immediate manifestations of mediated structures are beyond the participants' influence. We are, therefore, faced with the task of identifying ways in which participants in the immediate interaction process may clarify, select, and utilize those connections with the aim of extending possibilities for serving client needs and interests. This amounts to discovering and realizing possible subjective influences upon relevant conditions, by the clients themselves as well as by the therapist. The therapist's influence upon this is predominantly indirect, mediated and carried through that which clients do about their problems out there. It functions by means of establishing and utilizing such possible connections with client options. In practice, its efficacy depends upon clarifying reasons for actions based on such connections and upon carrying them out.

Obviously therapist interpretations of client problems and their "realistic" solutions depend heavily upon the therapist's own experience of his possibilities and of the risks and conflicts that might be connected with their realization. His interpretations are accounts for the way he stands to his action possibilities in his context and for his corresponding reasons for action in relation to the case at hand. We shall pursue this issue further in the final section.

Restriction versus extension of practice

An interpretative mode of thinking directs a consonant restricted mode of action within the boundaries of the existing scope of action possibilities. Alternatively, a comprehensive mode of thinking is necessary in order to direct an extending and generalizing mode of action (Holzkamp, 1983, pp. 356–415). Naturally, this holds for everyone, for clients as well as for therapists. In this section we shall pursue it only as far as the therapist is concerned. Therapists become able to overcome widespread tendencies to personalize immediate contradictions and conflicts by analyzing the concrete societal mediation of the problems they deal with in their practice (Dreier, 1987a). They can then identify mediated possibilities for overcoming contradictions and resolving conflicts. In fact, only a therapeutic practice that addresses the concrete mediation of the conflicts for which clients seek therapy can (knowingly) meet client interests in anything but an immediate and restricted way. In accordance with the possibilities at hand, therapists must look for ways to cope with immediate, problematic situations directed at their extension. They must orient their practice toward their clients' discovery and extension of their action possibilities and toward the extension of their own possibilities for doing so. The therapists can influence such subjective possibilities in ways and degrees that depend upon the particularities of their present scope and pertinent action potence.

A comprehensive mode of thinking and extended or generalized mode of action stand contrary to widespread notions about objective determinism. Aimed at discovering and extending concrete scopes of possibilities, they run counter to a constraint model of human action and subjectivity. Of course, objective determinants do have an impact upon subjects, whether they realize it or not. And that impact is restricting as well as enabling. But it depends on whether the subjects realize their meaning and how they react to them. Their reactions may lead to a reproduction of existing, problematic conditions, or to a more or less optimal extension of their disposal over them and, thus, of their present scope. A constraint model, on the other hand, denies the existence of subjectively relevant, objective possibilities for exerting influence upon and extending one's disposal over existing conditions. It construes the social world one-sidedly as a mere constraint of human agency whereas what is objectively (made) possible to do is ascribed solely to the subjects or to the "internal" situation at hand as their "resources." That is, indeed, a constrained mode of thinking and acting, preoccupied with avoiding confrontation with societal contradictions. It produces local, individualized "need for control" (Holzkamp-Osterkamp, 1985), pursued in vain while "external events" keep upsetting things, or it leads to a total denial of the significance of external conditions. In that way, it may, eventually, take us back into a mere intersubjective constructivism that personalizes responsibilities for what happens, including the intersubjective meaning of events beyond the participants' current control. Then therapy may be regarded as a practice in which therapists are responsible for finding some solution within existing conditions to whatever sufferings are presented to them. It may be construed as a "private" practice, in the hope of escaping the merely negative influence of external constraints and obtaining "full autonomy" outside of the reach of the "external world." Indeed, therapy is often regarded in that way. Surprisingly, this is so whether it takes place as an immediate part of a particular institution in the domain or primarily has mediated connections with such institutions and "spiritual" links with the clients' social world. Yet even its private display remains a peculiar form of societal practice, characterized by peculiar social connections.

Notions about therapy typically are deinstitutionalized. They lose sight of existing interrelationships between immediate therapeutic interaction procedures and the institution within which or in relation to which they take place. It seems especially tabooed to reflect on the impact of interests, connected with institutionalized practice, upon immediate casework. Yet the therapist's own occupational context typically is some institution. That institution is the location of his particular practice, the particular scope of his occupational action possibilities. He has to cope with his practice within that scope, that is, among other things, to realize corresponding forms of casework.

Institutional demarcation, distribution, and coordination of tasks and of the concrete work with clients, makes the scope and meaning of an individual therapist's practice part of a supraindividual, institutional practice. Institutional practice and the interests behind it can be influenced and are not unitary. Within the institution, diverse and contrary staff positions and interests are played out in interchange with representations of external agencies of various, indeed contrary, kinds at various levels and with various strengths.

Moreover, the impact of various, optional kinds of particular connections between an institution and the social world of its clients must be identified. The scope and meaning of concrete therapeutic practice are framed through those connections. The adequacy of client service is influenced by them.

Finally, concrete practice with clients is part of interinstitutional chains and divisions of client care and treatment careers. It must be comprehended therein, and these structures analyzed so as to realize their impact upon client service. At issue is what kinds of service of client needs and interests they express, repress, or enable.

All this, then, is the necessary background for comprehending the adequacy of service and, thus, for redirecting and extending it toward improved service of client interests. Therapeutic action and subjectivity must be comprehended on the basis of such an overall frame of analysis about relations between client lifeworlds, structures of health care, institutional forms, professional agency, and casework interaction.

Inquiries into professional practice and subjectivity based on a generalizing mode of action and a comprehensive mode of thinking are regretably rare. Yet, if therapists do not determine and influence the meaning of their practice on the basis of such comprehensive connections, they merely leave it up to others to do so (Dreier, Kleinmanns, Konitzer-Feddersen, Michels, & Raitola, 1988). Often they even exaggerate the extent to which such external, planned determination is imposed upon them, or the extent to which they are inextricably caught up in institutional contradictions with negative implications for their service of client interests. They tend to interpret themselves one-sidedly as victims who have no alternative action possibilities. Still, we should not overlook a widespread peculiarity of therapeutic practice, that the demands and tasks directed at it mostly are astonishingly vague and therapeutic expertise insufficiently clarified.

On the one hand, this easily leads to a relatively disconnected and isolated therapeutic practice. In that way, every therapist is left with relatively restricted and individualized coping strategies. That makes it more likely that he will act in accordance with the prevailing ideology about his work as being motivated not by his own needs, interests, and conditions, but by service to his clients. The interests of the two parties are thus regarded as contrary, not generalizable.

On the other hand, however, the very vagueness of demands and expertise to an unusual extent leaves it to therapists themselves to shape and change the institutional levels, domains, and modes of their practice. In so doing, they will inevitably discover that the extension of their action potence and scope is part of the development of the organized institutional scope. After all, the kinds of tasks handed over to them are institutionally mediated. They do, for instance, depend upon what other staff members can cope with, or want assistance with.

The kind of empirical generalizations about therapeutic practice that we need are about typical scopes of action possibilities (Holzkamp, 1983, pp. 545–572). They include typical scopes behind client problems and their resolutions, combined with typical scopes of therapeutic practice dealing with them. Such knowledge can direct concrete practice with particular problems in particular contexts. Then scopes at hand need not be employed blindly but may be utilized and extended by comparison with typical, exemplary cases of realized scopes. It follows that the essential task of therapeutic practice is not only to comprehend client problems within their social world and to promote their extension of their action potences and possibilities therein. It is just as well a crucial feature of therapeutic expertise to comprehend the problems within their own practice as expressions of contradictory social structures of action possibilities. Then they can identify typical, current problems as expressions of typical, current, problematic scopes of possibilities. Theories about such typical scopes can be elaborated, generalizing strategies of action used while working within and while extending them. Research aimed at promoting the development of therapeutic practice must elaborate such analytic tools. It must produce concepts and methods for therapists to use when analyzing the scopes of their practice. It must elucidate the rationality and expertise employed to overcome contradictions and extend therapist and client scopes. In this sense, we are in need of a re-search of the particular rationality of therapeutic practice. At present we are in a crisis of theorizing and research in which the rationality of practice escapes comprehension. On the part of clients as well as of therapists, that rationality involves thinking about mediated connections – that is, transcending the boundaries of what is immediately observable. Actually, only then may the peculiar potentialities of human thinking be displayed. Research reflecting on that rationality, equally must conduct inquiries that transcend the boundaries of immediate situations. Research conceptions and methodologies must allow a systematic thinking about what people actually already do in their practice.

Because this kind of research is rarely done, theoretical notions about therapy either remain personalized or envision practice as a mere execution of a set of operations. Therapeutic theory and method become instrumentalistic, technicalized. They rest on the premise that correct, effective, and optimal therapeutic operations can be identified irrespective of the connections and scopes in which they are to be employed. They do not recognize that particular scopes allow for and make particular operations functional for coping with practice therein, nor that the concrete meaning ensuing their application arises out of and varies with the particular situation at hand. Such abstract generalizations do not promote our comprehension of concrete connections. Rather they misguide it and, therefore, cannot contribute to their development. They must remain abstract. At the same time, their kind of abstraction makes them suitable as normative prescriptions for correct procedures to be followed by practitioners in whatever peculiar, concrete scopes and tasks they may find themselves. They take on the status of normative prescriptions for professional agency from a point of view external to the particular situation in which they are to be employed. Adhering to them is purported to make practice accountable; deviating from them, to make it erroneous. A gap between prescription and description is installed in notions about practice and in the heads of therapists. Their thinking about their own practice turns into a self-contradictory double bookkeeping: Individual experiences about particular, concrete connections, contradictions, and possibilities exist in more or less generalized form beside, in conflict, or somehow entangled with "official" prescribed forms of explanation and account. What it means to be an expert remains self-contradictory and unclarified as well. Once again contradictions confront us with the alternative between a restrictive and an extending mode of thinking and action. On the one hand, these subjective contradictions may become an impetus for a concrete and systematic analysis of the possibilities in the therapist's own practice. They may lead in the direction of clarifying and extending that practice. On the other hand, they may lead therapists back into personalized modes of interpretation about their competence, typically offered them in current forms of their own training, supervision, or therapy (Dreier, 1987a, 1989).

Note

1. Supported by a grant from the Danish Research Council for the Humanities.

References

Dehler, J., & Wetzel, K. (Eds.). (1988). *Zum Verhältnis von Theorie und Praxis in der Psychologie* [On the relationship between theory and practice in psychology]. Marburg: VA&G.

Dreier, O. (1980). *Familiäres Sein und familiäres Bewusstsein: Therapeutische Analyse einer Arbeiterfamilie* [Family being and family consciousness: Therapeutic analysis of a working-class family] (Texte zur Kritischen Psychologie Bd. 11). Frankfurt am Main: Campus.

Dreier, O. (1983). Tagungsbericht [Conference Report]. *Forum Kritische Psychologie, 12,* 184–188.

Dreier, O. (1985). Grundfragen der Psychotherapie in der Psychoanalyse und in der Kritischen Psychologie [Fundamental issues of psychotherapy in psychoanalysis and in critical psychology]. In K.-H. Braun et al. (Eds.), *Geschichte und Kritik der Psychoanalyse* (pp. 127–152). Marburg: VA&G.

Dreier, O. (1986a). Persönlichkeit und Individualität in psychologischer Theorie und klinischer Praxis [Personality and individuality in psychological theory and clinical practice]. In H. Flessner (Ed.), *Marxistische Persönlichkeitstheorie* (pp. 256–277). Frankfurt am Main: IMSF.

Dreier, O. (1986b). Der Alltag der Therapeuten: Widersprüche und Entwicklungsmöglichkeiten [Therapists' everyday activity: Contradictions and possibilities of development]. *Verhaltenstherapie und psychosoziale Praxis,* 491–497.

Dreier, O. (1987a). Zur Funktionsbestimmung von Supervision in der therapeutischen Arbeit [Determining the function of supervision in therapeutic work]. In W. Maiers & M. Markard (Eds.), *Kritische Psychologie als Subjektwissenschaft: Klaus Holzkamp zum 60. Geburtstag* (pp. 44–56). Frankfurt am Main: Campus.

Dreier, O. (1988a). Der Psychologe als Subjekt therapeutischer Praxis [The psychologist as subject of therapeutic practice]. In J. Dehler & K. Wetzel (Eds.), pp. 113–138.

Dreier, O. (1988b). Denkweisen über Therapie [Modes of thinking about therapy]. *Forum Kritische Psychologie, 22,* 42–57.

Dreier, O. (1988c). Zur Sozialpsychologie der Therapie von Übergewichtigen. Bemerkungen zum Aufsatz von Haisch und Haisch [On the social psychology of the therapy of obesity. Some remarks to the article by Haisch and Haisch]. *Zeitschrift für Sozialpsychologie, 19,* 287–295.

Dreier, O. (1989). Fortbildung im Bereich psychosozialer Berufe als Einheit von Forschung und Praxis [Professional training within psychosocial practice as a unity between research and practice]. *Forum Kritische Psychologie, 24,* 48–84.

Dreier, O. (1990). Psychische Erkrankungen aus der Sicht der Kritischen Psychologie [Mental illnesses from the point of view of critical psychology]. In A. Thom & E. Wulff (Eds.), *Psychiatrie im Wandel. Wege zur Humanisierung der Psychiatrie im internationalen Vergleich.* (pp. 55–75). Frankfurt am Main: Psychiatrie Verlag & A. Barth.

Dreier, O. (1991). Client interests in psychotherapy. In C. Tolman & W. Maiers (Eds. and Trans.), *Critical psychology: Contributions to an historical science of the subject* (pp. 196–211). Cambridge: Cambridge University Press. (Reprinted from *Forum Kritische Psychologie*, 1987b, *20*, 66–83)

Dreier, O., Kleinmanns, M., Konitzer-Feddersen, M., Michels, H.-P., & Raitola, A. (1988). Die Bedeutung institutioneller Bedingungen psychologischer Praxis am Beispiel der Therapie [The meaning of institutional conditions for psychological practice exemplified by therapy]. In J. Dehler & K. Wetzel (Eds.), pp. 81–112.

Holzkamp, K. (1983). *Grundlegung der Psychologie* [Foundation of psychology]. Frankfurt am Main: Campus.

Holzkamp, K. (1987a). Critical psychology and overcoming of scientific indeterminacy in psychological theorizing (L. Zusne, Trans.). In R. Hogan & W. H. Jones (Eds.), *Perspectives in personality* (Vol. 2, pp. 93–123). Greenwich, CT: JAI Press.

Holzkamp, K. (1987b). Die Verkennung von Handlungsbegrñdungen als empirische Zusammenhangsannahmen in sozialpsychologischen Theorien: Methodologische Fehlorientierung infolge von Begriffsverwirrung [Mistaking reasons for actions as empirical assumptions about connections in social-psychological theories: Erroneous methodological orientation as a consequence of conceptual confusion]. *Forum Kritische Psychologie*, *19*, 23–58.

Holzkamp, K. (1988). Praxis: Funktionskritik eines Begriffs [Practice: Critique of the function of a concept]. In J. Dehler & K. Wetzel (Eds.), pp. 15–48.

Holzkamp-Osterkamp, U. (1976). *Motivationsforschung: Bd. 2. Die Besonderheit menschlicher Bedürfnisse – Problematik und Erkenntnisgehalt der Psychoanalyse* [Motivation research: Vol. 2. The peculiarity of human needs – problematics and validity of psychoanalysis]. Frankfurt am Main: Campus.

Holzkamp-Osterkamp, U. (1985). Kontrollbedürfnis [Need for control]. *Forum Kritische Psychologie*, *16*, 145–149.

Markard, M. (1988). Kategorien, Theorien und Empirie in subjektwissenschaftlicher Forschung [Categories, theories, and empirical materials in subject-scientific research]. In J. Dehler & K. Wetzel (Eds.), pp. 49–80.

Moll, M., Böhm, H., Vathke, H., & Dreier, O. (1985). Projekt "Theorie–Praxis–Konferenz" [Project "Theory–Practice–Conference"]. *Forum Kritische Psychologie*, *16*, 88–114.

5   Thinking and acting with iron

Charles Keller and Janet Dixon Keller

In theory

In 1957 Ward Goodenough created a new mandate for anthropologists. He directed our attention to knowledge and action by setting the anthropologists' task as that of accounting for "whatever it is one has to know or believe in order to operate in a manner acceptable to . . . [society's] members" (Goodenough, 1957, p. 167). This passage has been repeatedly cited but it is worth doing so again for, in spite of repeated citations, scholars in anthropology and related fields have typically focused on the first element of this phrase "whatever it is one has to know or believe" to the exclusion of an account of the second and equally important element, "in order to operate in a manner acceptable." What Goodenough's mandate requires is an account of knowledge and action in tandem: a dynamic approach to their complex interrelations. We argue that knowledge and action are each open to alteration by the other as behavior proceeds and that Goodenough's term *whatever* is not static and factual but is productive and conceptual.

In what follows we shall outline such an approach and apply it to a detailed example from blacksmithing in order to answer the question, What is it the smith needs to know in order to produce a specific artifact? Our goal in this research is to illuminate the complex interdependence of knowledge and action.

We start with the position that not only do ideas about the world affect action in the world, but ongoing perceptions of that action in the world affect the organization and content of ideas. This is one of the dynamic bases of an activity system. An activity system integrates phenomena of three kinds: social parameters, actions, and operations

125

(Wertsch, 1981). Activity is governed by social and collective parameters: rules, principles, guidelines. The social phenomena of an activity system include the distribution of knowledge and labor within a community and the social incentives for production. Actions refer to individual phenomena, to individual action oriented to a particular goal. Actions are strategic tasks. Operations are the routine aspects of production.

Our research focuses primarily on the interrelations of knowledge and action as individual phenomena, although the inclusion of individual action within a larger activity system requires that we draw on both social and routine elements. From this perspective neither the human organism nor the external world is solely responsible for developing knowledge about the world (Wertsch, 1981, p. 38). The key to a holistic view of knowledge is activity systems in which social, individual, and material aspects are interdependent (Leont'ev, 1972/1981, p. 48). The actions in which the human agent engages are functionally integrated in larger activity systems in which knowledge is simultaneously a prerequisite and a consequence of action and action is likewise a prerequisite and a consequence of knowledge. Knowledge and action in an activity system are themselves constituted by social, individual, and material phenomena.

By individuals' actions an object is transformed into its subjective form or image (e.g., a piece of metal into a replica of a 19th-century tool, or an individual into a husband). At the same time actions produce objective results and products (e.g., the actual artifact that is seen as a replica or the particular husband just produced). Viewed from this perspective, action emerges as a process of reciprocal transformations between one's image of a product associated with a plan for production and the properties of the material and social conditions of that production (Leont'ev, 1972/1981, p. 46). Internal activity that arises largely out of external, practical activity retains a fundamental two-way connection with that external world. Action continually brings the human into practical contact with objects that deflect, change, and enrich prior organizations of knowledge.

Crucial to this perspective is a treatment of subjective and objective that goes beyond a dichotomy of internal and external. On the objective side are physical and social objects not simply as material objects but the images particular actors have of them, that is, internal representations of objects and instruments from someone's perspective. On the subjective side are both the external acting and the knowledge relevant to this acting. One way to think about these dimensions and their interrelations is that the internal mental order, both the image of the object and other relevant knowledge, is continually transformed by external actions and their material constituents and results (Leont'ev, 1972/1981, p. 52).

We are focusing on knowledge and action within an activity system (Wertsch, 1981; Vygotsky, 1978), in which an individual's knowledge is simultaneously to be regarded as representational and emergent, prepatterned and aimed at coming to terms with actions and products that go beyond the already known (Dougherty & Fernandez, 1982, p. 823). Action has an emergent quality, which results from the continual feedback from external events to internal representations and from the internal representations back to enactment.

There is a tension to this process between the knowledge and the unfolding experience. Knowledge as organized for a particular task can never be sufficiently detailed, sufficiently precise, to anticipate exactly the conditions or results of actions. Action is never totally controlled by the actor but influenced by the vagaries of the physical and social world. Thus, in any given instance, knowledge is continually being refined, enriched, or completely revised by experience whereas external action accommodates unanticipated physical contingencies or previously unrecalled specifics of the activity.

In practice

To return to our initial question, What is it one needs to know or believe in order to operate . . . ? We need to identify a realm of things to be done, an activity in a general sense. Blacksmithing constitutes this realm for us: an activity system.

In the United States in 1987 blacksmiths can be divided into industrial and private smiths. Industrial smiths are employed in shipyards, lumber mills, and other heavy industrial contexts where they forge and repair machine parts and other items with the aid of an assistant and large air- or steam-actuated power tools. The primary criteria for production of work by house blacksmiths are physical and mechanical efficacy. Interestingly, some retired house smiths are finding a ready audience for their ironworking understanding and insights among private smiths.

Private blacksmiths work independently, although occasionally in multiperson shops. They may or may not earn their living by blacksmithing. They use lighter equipment than industrial smiths. Some are teachers in art departments or schools, some produce lines of products for wholesale or retail outlets (mail-order businesses, galleries), some specialize in architectural ironwork (gates, railings, window grates), some produce smaller ornamental or household goods, some replicate period tools or hardware, whereas others combine any or all of these activities. Still others blacksmith as a hobby during their spare hours.

Communication among private smiths takes place most commonly at moderate to long distance by telephone conversations between friends or in written form by magazine or newsletter articles. Books are a less common form of communication because of their expense. Face-to-face as well as printed communication is fostered by a number of organizations. One national organization, the Artist Blacksmith Association of North America (ABANA) has approximately 2,000 members, publishes a quarterly journal, and holds biannual meetings at which recent work is exhibited and various kinds of demonstrations, lectures, and slide shows are presented. Smaller regional organizations have newsletters and hold periodic workshops at which members or invited guests demonstrate particular techniques or styles of work.

The individual, private blacksmith operates in isolation but maintains a connection to the collective unit by a number of mechanisms. The social dimensions of the activity system in which the individual operates are available to the smith by seeing the work of others and by observing directly, at demonstrations or in work groups, or indirectly, from finished pieces, the techniques being utilized. Motivation for the private smith may be primarily economic or aesthetic but an underlying interest seems always to be a fascination with the transformations of iron while it is hot.

In developing our answer to Goodenough's question we focus on a task as dually structured with both an internal, mental and an external, active side. We use this dualism because it reflects a traditional dichotomy in the anthropological literature, which we hope to transcend. As we have indicated, activity theory allows us to focus on the integration of knowledge and practice.

The internal side of a task is problem definition and solution (Säljö, this volume): a conceptual structure selectively derived from prior knowledge with both its social and material aspects. The internal side of task is knowledge. In the case of blacksmithing, knowledge is brought to bear on problem solving in the production of an artifact. Relevant knowledge includes the internal image of the object or goal of production and the smith's conceptualization of the productive sequence. The external counterpart to knowledge is the actual actions in the world that produce a material end. We shall take you briefly through the forging of one item to illustrate the nature of the interrelations among knowledge and action for the practicing smith. Our emphasis in this effort is on the individual level of the activity system: on the nature of the dynamic relations among knowledge, imaged goals, conceptions of objective conditions both social and material, and explicit productive acts.

Our method combines participant observation and introspection. Charles Keller is simultaneously the practicing smith, whose knowledge and actions are the immediate subject of this study, and analyst bringing the insights of phenomenology and Soviet activity theory to bear on the practice of smithing. Janet Keller is participant observer and analyst, recording events during the production of an artifact in iron for subsequent analysis in which she draws on cognitive anthropology and Soviet activity theory. As practicing smith and analyst Charles Keller wears two hats in this research. We distinguish his remarks as practicing smith by putting them in quotations. When he speaks retrospectively as analyst, his comments appear as standard text.

The system we will examine is the production of a skimmer handle by Charles Keller, a relatively simple but not routine task for this smith. A skimmer is a long handled kitchen utensil with a shallowly dished, perforated bowl for removing residue from the top of bubbling, cooking liquids. On a previous occasion Keller had produced a skimmer but of a different and simpler style. Other utensils with some mechanical and functional similarities (ladles and spoons) had been produced routinely but, again, never with the stylistic parameters required for this skimmer. When a production has become routine much of the detail of the task becomes "taken-for-granted" and is difficult or impossible to articulate (Schutz, 1962; Polanyi, 1962). A novel production, however, involves a task with many problematic aspects that must be resolved. This process focuses the attention of the actor and makes the task more accessible for analysis.

In the case upon which we will focus Charles Keller is asked by a museum specializing in the American colonial period to provide a whitesmithed skimmer in the spirit of 18th- and 19th-century American skimmers. At occasional demonstrations of early American life styles where they do not wish to use an original museum specimen, the museum personnel have been using a chrome plated spoon attached to a stick to serve as a skimmer and find it functionally inadequate and aesthetically inappropriate. In presenting their request the museum staff shows the smith examples of period skimmers from the museum's collection and he notes characteristics of them such as a whitesmithed finish. The museum examples are, however, extremely simple. The smith hopes to produce an artifact with a more complex design yet still within the appropriate stylistic range. In the process of thinking out how to design the skimmer, the smith enriches this stock of exemplars from the museum collection by drawing on his previous knowledge of similar implements and reviewing literature depicting kitchen utensils of the appropriate period – that is, he takes advantage of socially distributed knowledge relevant to his task. He also recalls making a skimmer and similar utensils before. He considers roughly how much time and effort he will spend in production, given considerations of museum and personal reputation and financial constraints. Thus the goal of production is not monolithic but multifaceted. The smith draws on conceptions of his skills and the available material conditions for work. Ultimately he decides on a particular design for the handle alone, leaving development of the dished surface for later. It is in the production of this handle that we will examine the relations of knowledge and action. He represents this design constituting a part of the task conceptualization to himself both verbally and visually as illustrated in Figure 5.1.

Conceptions of task for American smiths are typically represented visually and may or may not have a verbal component. The visual image typically implies not only form but procedure. Our notion of

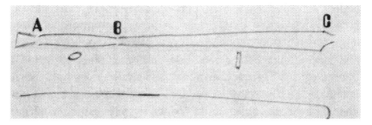

Figure 5.1. Skimmer handle. Design sketch of 19th-century skimmer handle by Charles Keller.

task in this chapter aims to capture this integration of the what and the how of production, which are so consistently coimplicational for the smith. The following excerpt from Francis Whitaker (1986, p. xiii), renowned American smith, emphasizes the importance of visualization (and tools) for the smith.

> If the eye cannot see it
> The hand cannot make it
> If the tongs will not hold it
> The hammer cannot hit it
> If you cannot remember it
> Forget it –

Let us return now to the development of the task conceptualization as given by Figure 5.1. What has led to this particular image is a combinatorial arrangement of selected bits of prior socially given knowledge stored in Charles Keller's head, in the heads of other smiths and museum staff, in the literature, and in exemplars. For purposes of analysis this knowledge may be analytically separated into sets of standards or domains relevant to the task at hand by virtue of the activity system in which the task occurs.

The products of private smiths involve multiple criteria for production. These are socially established dimensions of the activity system. One of these criteria is mechanical adequacy. Blacksmiths do not commonly consider their products purely as sculpture and therefore what they make must work to some degree. That is it must perform its job with reasonable adequacy. A second criterion is aesthetic, that is, the work must look good according to some system of aesthetic standards. These standards can vary from those of 18th-century housewares to late 20th-century art. In the case of period replicas, the modern replica is not usually supposed to be an exact copy of a particular specimen, but rather to look as if it could have been made during the period in question. A third criterion has to do with technique. The techniques blacksmiths commonly use take advantage of the fact that iron is plastic within a certain temperature range. The techniques used to accomplish transformations of the metal while in its plastic state are essentially those developed during the iron age in Europe (post 2000 B.C.) and they have been modified only slightly since then. Thus blacksmiths are supposed to achieve their mechanical and aesthetic ends using traditional techniques with minimal, if any, recourse to more recent technology such as gas or electric welding, or machine tools such as lathes or milling machines. When discussing potential solutions to a particular problem, one of Charles Keller's fellow smiths referred to "thinking hot" as a guide for decision making. For instance, if the problem is to make a hole in a bar, the preferred method would be to heat the bar and punch the hole rather than to leave the bar cold and drill the hole.

We recognize general aesthetics of design, the aesthetics of 18th- and 19th-century styles of housewares, mechanical adequacy or function, techniques or procedures, conceptions of self and other, material conditions, and financial constraints as crucial to task development in the instance under study. These dimensions operate as positive forces for action not determinants of outcome. We make no claims here that this particular arrangement of social dimensions as knowledge necessarily represents long-term organization of this information for the smith. That may or may not be the case but a determination of that issue is beyond the scope of this chapter.

We shall briefly exemplify the sorts of knowledge already referred to and exemplify the objective circumstances that indicate the pertinence of that knowledge to the task at hand. The museum's request that the product be in the spirit of 18th- and early 19th-century American skimmers calls upon the smith's representation of the concept skimmer and the particular functional standards implied – that is, the skimmer must serve to accomplish skimming. The handle must be long enough to prevent injury to the cook. It must be balanced with the bowl to facilitate use and be comfortable to grip. In addition, "in the spirit of" calls upon stylistic standards of the

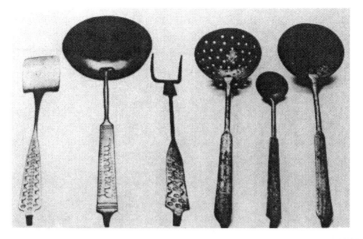

Figure 5.2. Illustrations of kitchen utensils from Jeannette Lasansky (1980), *To draw, upset, and weld: The work of the Pennsylvania rural blacksmith 1742–1935* (p. 71). Lewisburg, PA: Oral Traditions Project of the Union County Historical Society.

period: appropriate segmentations in the handle, cross-sectional contrasts, and transitions between them. It is in consideration of the dimensions of style that the smith gives form to the functionally defined concept labeled "skimmer" and translates this concept into iron and brass.

In turning to the literature the smith brings more general aesthetic criteria of line, proportion, contrast, elegance, and simplicity to bear in evaluating particular instances depicted with a view toward further refining the design of the skimmer at issue. He articulates "a desire to produce something more elaborate than the examples in the museum yet still in keeping with the period." Figures 5.2 and 5.3 illustrate the kind of reference material to which the smith turned.

One characteristic of examples from the literature is that they are represented in only two dimensions. This leaves the smith to construct his design in three dimensions without a template. Recall that the three-dimensional exemplars from the museum that the smith did have prior to production did not illustrate many of the design features at issue.

Stylistic and aesthetic criteria in turn call up questions of procedure and skill. How does one accomplish the various appropriate

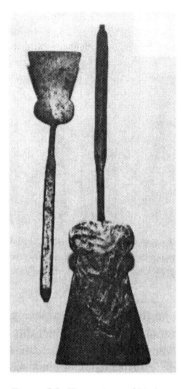

Figure 5.3. Illustrations of kitchen utensils from Jeannette Lasansky (1980), *To draw, upset and weld: The work of the rural Pennsylvania blacksmith 1742–1935* (p. 51). Lewisburg, PA: Oral Traditions Project of the Union County Historical Society.

designs? The items in the museum collection for example remind the smith that such utensils were whitesmithed. The feature of white-smithing requires filing the handle at the conclusion of forging to give the iron a silvery, smooth surface. In addition the relevant notions of line and contrast under consideration both carry with them questions of procedure.

The smith also recalls previous productions relevant to his task at hand. The task conceptualizations, actions, and operations that the prior productions involved now bear on the development of the task at issue here. These recollections suggest particular details, for example, of procedure, which were either successful or problematic. In addition the smith considers roughly how much time and effort to spend in production. This involves his conception of the client and his image of self as academic and smith. It also involves considerations of income and costs of production. Finally the smith draws on his conceptions of his own skill and the material conditions for work including the shop, available tools (with the possibility of producing new ones), and raw materials. In the end he articulates a decision "to make a skimmer handle like the left most example [in Figure 5.3], but with more obvious changes in cross section and in transition between the major thirds of the handle" labeled A, B, and C on Figure 5.1.

At this point an umbrella plan, an internal representation of goal and procedure, is established. The smith has crystallized a rough idea of the goal for production and developed a preliminary orientation toward goal attainment. The problem has been defined. The development of this umbrella plan has involved selective reliance on aesthetic, stylistic, functional, procedural, financial, and academic standards in conjunction with conceptions of self and other, and material conditions for work. This information was made available from prior knowledge held by the smith, recourse to relevant literature, and the examination of actual objective examples. The umbrella plan is so to speak momentarily complete as the smith is now on the verge of engaging directly in productive activity.

As we shall see, the umbrella plan will be detailed and enriched and altered as the smith's internal representations meet the objective conditions of the work. For each step of the way, constellations, microorganizations of task conception and material conditions, are developed in the act of production (Dougherty & Keller, 1985). It is in these specific productive steps that reorganizations of knowledge and action take place.

The level of the work upon which we shall focus in the remainder of this chapter is primarily that of actions (Leont'ev, 1972/1981, pp. 59ff.), the salient feature of which is goal orientation. These actions are neither so routinized as to be properly operations nor is the analysis so general as to be properly at the level of collective activity. We distinguish separate actions by transformations of the object, evaluation of the result, and transitions to the next action (Zinchenko & Gordon, 1972/1981, p. 93).

In what follows we shall detail particular actions in the task of producing a skimmer handle. We do this with two objectives in mind. First, we hope to show the relation of the internally represented umbrella plan to the structure of action. Second, we hope to make clear the effect of actual, ongoing actions and their material results on the internal organization and substance of knowledge. As blacksmiths communicate among themselves and are exposed to each other's products, this individual level of knowledge and action as a dynamic system comes into contact with and may influence or be further influenced by the social dimensions of the activity system.

Let us briefly elaborate on the handle as sketched by the smith prior to production and represented in Figure 5.1. We shall use this representation for reference to the handle segments throughout what follows. Segment A will be the bearing surface for the skimmer bowl, segment B a rounded midsection tapered at each end, and segment C a longer, flared flat section that culminates in a hook for hanging the tool. The sketch is only a vague image and leaves most of the detail particularly of proportions and transitions between segments as problems to be solved in the dynamic integration of knowledge and action which will occur in carrying out the task.

The umbrella plan conceptualization given in Figure 5.1 and already elaborated does seem to direct the initial stages of action. The smith selects the stock evaluating the possibilities against the requirements of the objective goal. "Since it is easier to make round stock flat than it is to make flat stock round, a piece of round stock is chosen. The diameter of the stock is approximately the same as the maximum diameter of the midsection of the handle, to keep forging to a minimum, but it must have enough mass to be spread in both end sections without getting too thin" as judged either functionally or aesthetically. The smith gets the fire ready. He gathers around the anvil tools he anticipates using in the early procedural steps. He lubricates the trip-hammer, which he has decided will facilitate the work and allow him to meet the constraints of time he has estimated as appropriate for this job. These preparations reflect a mental anticipation of the actions to follow based on the considerations that were relevant to developing the umbrella plan.

To this point the relationship is largely one of internal direction of action. But the process does not continue in a one-way fashion. As we examine goal-oriented actions in production, the significance of material conditions for directing the process becomes obvious. The object of the activity in general is the skimmer handle, but production of the object will require actions oriented to more particular goals, such as flattening and shaping sections A and C, forging the hook at the end of section C, tapering the round middle section toward each end, and forging the transitions between the segments. Each of these productive sequences will influence the conceptual plan and subsequent actions.

The smith begins with section A using both the trip-hammer and hand hammers to flatten the bearing surface. This action, seemingly straightforward at the outset, allows the smith to anticipate upcoming problems as he works the metal. We say this action is seemingly straightforward here because, to get ahead of ourselves just a bit, even bearing surface A is reforged several times at later points in the productive sequence as a result of evaluations of the results of subsequent actions. In any case, even in these early stages a lack of specificity in the image associated with the umbrella plan is apparent. While the smith is working to flatten the bearing surface of the skimmer handle, he is thinking not only about the shape that segment A should take but also about the transitions between segments. The selective blanks and rough outlines shown in Figure 5.1 suggest he is unsure exactly what form any of the segments or the transitions should take. These are the problematics to be resolved in practice.

As our discussion of production of the skimmer handle proceeds, we shall pay particular attention to the development of the transitions. The emergence of the transitions illustrates well the relations between knowledge and action in the task. However, the process by which the transitions take shape is repeated in principle for each step in producing the skimmer handle. The smith initially decides to "take care of the transitions when filing." Filing is the final stage of production and this decision leaves the most problematic details until later. As the smith continues to work to flatten segment A and then to taper section B, he reviews the decision to file the transitions. As he reflects, the smith considers that he "wants to file as little as possible, so . . . [he] must forge cleanly." This consideration has implications, for example, for the relevant procedures and tool inventory and leads him to select a wire brush for cleaning the iron after each heat; the brush is added to the tool inventory he previously accumulated for the task. He also comments that "forging is more interesting than filing so . . . [he] will forge as much as possible." (Forging more and filing less also are consistent with the value of "thinking hot.") Following on this consideration and in contrast with his earlier decision, the smith now decides he will forge the transitions. At this point he attempts a transition between segments A and B, which fails aesthetically. He corrects the offending bulge at the transition point and then leaves this point unfinished and goes on to continue work on the rounded section B, while he further contemplates the transitions.

While forging the segments, the smith examines the work often to get a sense of proportion, possible transitions, and straightness. He is trying to determine, for example, "how long [aesthetically, functionally] the tapered midsection should be. The two flat parts have to be about the same width and have enough contrast between them and the middle to show something's happening [in the change in cross section]." The smith articulates an aspect of the problem of proportion. "I can't make the round part too long because then its diameter would be too small at the transition to the flat parts. That would make it weak and make the contrast with the flat section too striking." These two features (length of segment B and diameter at the transition) must be balanced to produce a subtle but noticeable design contrast. Notice that although the smith is aware that balance is essential, the particular material balance comes not exclusively from the planned design but emerges as the smith responds to and evaluates the objective results of his actions.

Having tapered the round midsection, the smith articulates, "I'm close enough to where I want to be to start spreading the upper part [C]. There are still a few bad spots I'll have to get rid of [in section B] and I'm still not sure of the transition. I'll start spreading just above the round section [B] being careful not to spread too much at this point because otherwise there won't be enough mass at the top end [to continue the line appropriately]. I want to spread minimally at first to avoid having to reduce, because I can always spread more but its a hassle to reduce." During the next several heats, he spreads section C again using a combination of the trip-hammer and hand hammers. In this action sequence, he does ultimately take the spread too far and in evaluating the work finds it necessary to reduce the width of section C. It is as though he has to cross a boundary in order to discover the appropriate limits of the design. Again the form emerges as the smith evaluates the objective results of his actions.

Having spread and flared section C, the smith pulls out a tool not among those previously collected for the production of the skimmer handle. The tool is a spring fuller, which he will use in narrowing the flared end of section C at that point where the hook will begin. It is in the objective result (that being the material state and the smith's conception of it) of this action that he finally conceives of the appropriate transitions between segments A/B and B/C. Upon narrowing the flared end of segment C where the intended hook will begin, the smith creates a transition to the hook that results from narrowing the handle to the proper width for the hook and producing a 180-degree bend in the iron. He examines the artifact at this point and, in response to the current shape of the iron, he decides to work the other transitions to balance this transition to the hook. This decision is based on the form of the object itself at this stage and the image the object suggests for the final product. The forging of the transitions then proceeds rather quickly. This finally accomplished, he is finished forging the piece – hypothetically. For even after announcing that he has completed the forging of the skimmer handle and after he has gone on to the final whitesmithing stage, the smith is evaluating the object against the more detailed conceptual representation of it that has emerged in the process of production and against his general standards of aesthetics, style, and function. He returns at least twice to reforge segments of the handle, ultimately changing the shape and thickness of the bearing surface to provide a larger area for attachment of the skimmer bowl, and thinning section C as it approaches B to accentuate the contrasts between them. Figures 5.4 and 5.5 illustrate the completed handle and the subsequently completed skimmer.

In conclusion

We have argued that "what it is one needs to know or believe in order to behave appropriately" requires analysis of the activity system within which an individual's actions/behaviors take place.

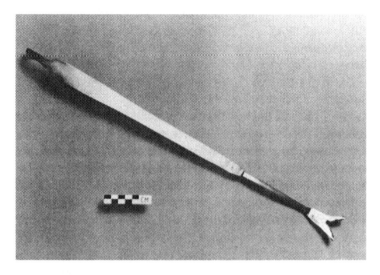

Figure 5.4. Skimmer handle by Charles Keller.

Figure 5.5. Completed skimmer by Charles Keller, 1987.

Rather than an exclusive emphasis on either the mental or the material, we have focused on the inherent integration of internal representations and external actions and objects in the accomplishment of a task. Rather than emphasizing the study of knowledge as a static and abstract entity, we have looked at conceptual organization in practice. "All you need to know" in order to make a skimmer handle includes but is not restricted to all the bits and pieces of knowledge that are subsumed under an umbrella plan. That knowledge is largely social and may have been already acquired by the subject in previous productive acts and stored as abstract standards or as vignettes of previous experiences or in any number of other ways. That knowledge may also be acquired in the process of plan formulation itself through various external sources such as literature and exemplars. Although we make no claims as to the organization of long-term memory, this organization of knowledge in performance may well be reflected there.

One needs, therefore, to know enough directly or indirectly to conceptualize an orientation toward a goal: to provide a combinatorial arrangement of previous knowledge in the service of a new, and therefore partially unknown, production. Beyond this point the goal and the actions and operations directed toward its attainment are intimately intertwined and what one needs to know to behave appropriately becomes a product of behaving. The umbrella plan, like the scenario discussed by Suchman and Trigg (this volume), provides an orientation for action. As the actions are carried out, any one or more of the dimensions of the umbrella may become problematic. At such a point, the internal representation is found wanting and may be enriched or altered as it is reconstructed on the basis of the results of action. "All one needs to know" is really only specifiable on the attainment of a goal. Any new production sequence will constitute a new event unique to a greater or lesser degree in terms of the knowledge required, the actions involved, and the outcome. Each such event is situated within an activity system in which the social dimensions and routine operations are more constant than individual action and knowledge, yet even these are not unchanging.

We argue here that one's initial concept of a skimmer handle, enriched by previously organized knowledge that the subject selects as relevant to the project at hand, becomes crystallized in an image of the object or goal of production and procedures for its realization. In the process of goal formulation, an umbrella plan encompassing the interaction of standards of form and procedure, and conceptions of self and other and material resources, is developed. This umbrella plan, which serves as the basis for initiating production, may then be elaborated, reorganized, altered, or simply hammered out. The on-going development of the conceptual task is fed by the smith's evaluation of the objective results of his actions. Blacksmithing as an instance of productive activity constitutes a system in which individual action and knowledge are integrally intertwined and interdependent, and in which these individual phenomena are influenced by and influence both the inventory of routine operations and the social dimensions of production.

References

Dougherty, J. W. D., & Fernandez, J. W. (1982). Afterword. Special issue on symbolism and cognition II. *American Ethnologist, 9*, 820–832.

Dougherty, J. W. D., & Keller, C. (1985). Taskonomy: A practical approach to knowledge structures. In J. W. D. Dougherty (Ed.), *Directions in cognitive anthropology* (pp. 161–174). Urbana: University of Illinois Press.

Goodenough, W. H. (1957). Cultural anthropology and linguistics. In P. L. Garvin (Ed.), *Report of the seventh annual round table meeting on linguistics and language study* (Monograph series on languages and linguistics, no. 9, pp. 167–173). Washington, DC: Georgetown University Press.

Lasansky, J. (1980). *To draw, upset and weld: The work of the Pennsylvania rural blacksmith 1742–1935*. Lewisburg, PA: Oral Traditions Project of the Union County Historical Society.

Leont'ev, A. N. (1981). The problem of activity in psychology. In J. V. Wertsch (Ed. and Trans.), *The concept of activity in Soviet psychology* (pp. 37–71). Armonk, NY: M. E. Sharpe. (Reprinted from *Voprosy Filosofi*, 1972, 9, 95–108)

Polanyi, M. (1962). *Personal knowledge: Towards a post-critical philosophy*. Chicago: University of Chicago Press.

Schutz, A. (1962). *Collected papers I: The problem of social reality*. The Hague: Nijhoff.

Vygotsky, L. S. (1978). *Mind in society: The development of higher psychological processes* (M. Cole, V. John-Steiner, S. Scribner, & E. Souberman, Eds.). Cambridge, MA: Harvard University Press.

Wertsch, J. V. (Ed. and Trans.). (1981). *The concept of activity in Soviet psychology*. Armonk, NY: M. E. Sharpe.

Whitaker, F. (1986). *The blacksmith's cookbook: Recipes in iron*. Vail, CO: Jim Fleming Publications.

Zinchenko, V. P., & Gordon, V. M. (1981). Methodological problems in the psychological analysis of activity. In J. V. Wertsch (Ed. and Trans.), *The concept of activity in Soviet psychology* (pp. 72–134). Armonk, NY: M. E. Sharpe. (Reprinted from *Sistemnie issledovaniya,* 1972, 82–127)

6   Artificial intelligence as craftwork

Lucy A. Suchman and Randall H. Trigg

> There are two ways in which the visualization processes we are all interested in may be ignored; one is to grant to the scientific mind what should be granted to the hands, to the eyes and to the signs; the other is to focus exclusively on the signs qua signs, without considering the mobilization of which they are but the fine edge.
>
> (Latour, 1986, p. 26)

The goal of research in artificial intelligence (AI) is to design runnable computer programs that replicate some aspect of human behavior. A common first step in the design process is to represent in some form the behavior to be replicated. In this chapter we consider representational practice in AI as the practical activity of two researchers working together at a whiteboard (i.e., a white "blackboard" used with colored markers).[1] In locating the science there, we aim to bring into focus its character as socially organized craftsmanship – the crafting together of a complex machinery made of heterogeneous materials, mobilized in the service of developing a theory of mind. In this effort we align ourselves with recent developments in the investigation and respecification of science as practice, beginning with Garfinkel's recommendations (1967) that we take sociology's subject matter to be the identifying details of particular forms of practical action, and Lave's analyses (1988) of the social and material structuring of specifically situated activity systems. Prior ethnomethodological studies of science orient us as well to the cen-

We are grateful to Phil Agre, Urs Fuhrer, Charles Goodwin, Brigitte Jordan, Bruno Latour, Jean Lave, and Susan Newman for their comments on earlier drafts. Seth Chaiklin and Jean Lave provided extremely valuable substantive as well as editorial suggestions. Most crucially we are indebted to researchers on the SIE project for allowing us to look in on their work.

trality of representational devices in the structuring of science practice (see, e.g., Garfinkel, Lynch, & Livingston, 1981; Lynch, 1985; Lynch, Livingston, & Garfinkel, 1983; Livingston, 1986; Lynch & Woolgar, 1990), as does Latour's notion of inscription devices (1986). Finally, we take inspiration from Latour's discussion (1986) of science as craftwork and Law's view (1987) of technological development as heterogeneous engineering.

Our objective here is to view the work of designing intelligent machines as a specific form of social practice – a form made the more interesting by AI's own concern with the delegation of social practice to machines (see also Dreyfus, 1979; Woolgar, 1987; and Collins 1987). We begin with an ethnomethodological interest in the "worldly observability of reasoning" as socially organized, embodied activity (Lynch et al., 1983, p. 206). With respect to science, this leads to a concern with the practical accomplishment of specific instances of scientific inquiry, "motivated by the attempt to rediscover the problem of social order in and as the real-world detail of scientific praxis" (ibid., p. 205). The interest in science, in other words, is not only an interest in a particular arena of human activity but in that arena as a window onto the general problem of the situated structuring of ordinary practice.

Of particular interest in science studies is the relation of scientific practice to various devices for seeing. Devices for seeing include re-representations of the world as texts, diagrams, formulas, models, and a host of other artifacts taken to stand for the structure of an investigated phenomenon. As proxies for the phenomena of interest, such artifacts underwrite the accountability both of the phenomena and of the claims to be made about them. Ethnomethodological studies of work, Lynch (1985) points out, "are distinguished by the way in which they topicalize embodied practices with 'paper,' 'pages,' 'blackboards,' and 'typewriter symbols' as of fundamental importance in studies of 'intellectual' activities" (p. 294). A major insight of such studies is that the practice of science and other "nonmanual" forms of labor crucially involves a material basis. Moreover, the use of representational devices organizes the conduct of such activities in a way that is methodical but also contingent and therefore necessarily ad hoc. The meaning of signs and the actions of scientists are mutually constituted, the intelligibility of each presupposing the other.

And insofar as the work of scientific inquiry comprises an emergent interaction between scientists and their materials, the structuring of scientific practice is a skilled improvisation, organized in orderly ways that are designed to maintain a lively openness to the possibilities that the materials at hand present.

Latour (1986) offers another insight into the role of representation in science and elsewhere. He calls for a view of science practice that "deflates grandiose schemes and conceptual dichotomies [e.g., of prescientific versus scientific culture] and replaces them by simple modifications in the way in which groups of people argue with one another using paper, signs, prints and diagrams" (p. 3). In particular, he points to the centrality of such inscription devices in the mobilization of credibility and other associated resources. What makes such devices efficacious, he argues, are their properties of "immutable mobility"; that is, their capacity to embody processes occurring at one time and place in a form that can be reproduced at another. At the same time, ethnomethodology's observations regarding the reflexive relation of activities to artifacts underscore the extent to which the persuasive power of such devices relies not on the devices themselves, but on the specific achievements of their design and use.

According to Law (1987) "the stability and form of artifacts should be seen as a function of the interaction of heterogeneous elements as these are shaped and assimilated into a network. . . . I call such activity *heterogeneous engineering* and suggest that the product can be seen as a *network* of juxtaposed components" (p. 113, original emphasis). Technology, on this view, is "a family of methods for associating and channeling other entities and forces, both human and nonhuman. It is a method, one method, for the conduct of heterogeneous engineering, for the construction of a relatively stable system of related bits and pieces with emergent properties" (p. 115). In this respect things engineered are not constituted as such once and for all, but rely upon the continuing cooperation of the world in which they are embedded.

In the case of artificial intelligence, the technology relies upon this cooperation at the same time that it is intended to participate successfully in the social order. The work of AI comprises a process by which researchers, drawing upon lived experience and their culturally constituted common sense of the social world, inscribe scenarios of activity as text, graphical formalisms, and computer programs intended to delegate human competence to machines. The process is not a simple encoding of behavior, but rather a series of transformations involving the simplification of action for purposes of its inscription, followed by implementation of the resulting inscriptions in the machine. The inscriptions produced must be interpretable with reference to common conceptions of rational action on the one hand, while meeting requirements of computability on the other.

We view the enterprise of designing intelligent machines as both "a cultural practice and an operationalization of beliefs about rationality" (Lave, 1988, p. 172). Lave warns that "constructing research in terms of mythological views of scientific thought insures blindness to questions of the structuring of everyday activities themselves" (p. 174). This study is a first attempt to replace mythological views of reasoning with the details of AI researchers' practice, as a contribution to the larger project of replacing mentalist myths about reasoning with an understanding of the structuring of embodied action. More specifically, our interest here is in understanding how AI researchers produce and reproduce the sense and sociality of scenarios, formalisms, and intelligent machines on the specific occasions of their creation and use.

The work's setting

The focus of this analysis is a particular episode of technical work in AI. The episode is located in a stream of activities whose concerns are both historically given and projected forward in time. The work makes use of certain resources, is accountable to persistent technical problems and concerns, and is judged in relation to common, albeit controvertible, conceptions of adequacy. In the course of their work, researchers selectively reproduce, make relevant, extend, and transform problems and solutions given by their membership in progressively more specialized technical communities, each with their own assumptions, commitments, and identifying technologies.

The field of artificial intelligence

Artificial intelligence is, most generally, a project to delegate human competence to computing machines. The possibility for such delegation depends on a starting premise of AI; namely, that the phenomenon of intelligent agency can be understood independent of its particular embodiment in human beings. For the case at hand, our practitioners follow what Searle (1980) calls the "weak AI programme," that is, they explicitly do not make claims for the psychological reality of their computer-based artifacts. The goal for them is rather to achieve effective delegation of competence; that is, to use the structure and functionality of computation to craft machines that are capable of participating successfully in interactions with the human world.

At this stage in the project, however, the goal is less to build a usable artifact than to develop a new formalism within a subfield of AI known as *knowledge representation,* and to demonstrate the formalism's efficacy to other practitioners. The enterprise of knowledge representation lies at the heart of AI:

> The notion of the *representation of knowledge* . . . has to do with writing down, in some language or communicative medium, descriptions or pictures that correspond in some salient way to the world or a state of the world. In Artificial Intelligence (AI), we are concerned with writing down descriptions of the world in such a way that an intelligent machine can come to new conclusions about its environment by formally manipulating these descriptions . . . just about every current AI program has what is called a 'knowledge base' containing symbolic descriptions represented in some 'representation scheme.' " (Brachman & Levesque, 1985, p. xiii)

But knowledge representations are more than inert data: "In AI, a *representation of knowledge* is a combination of data structures and interpretive procedures that, if used in the right way in a program, will lead to 'knowledgeable' behavior" (Barr & Feigenbaum, 1981, p. 143). It is the problem of combining structures and procedures to produce behavior that constitutes the work at hand. In this particular session, researchers focus on the means of interpreting and manipulating symbolic representations already given, rather than on designing the representations themselves. In the process, however, the representations are transformed.

The laboratory

The technological implications of artificial intelligence have led to industrial as well as academic interest in the progress of its work. The institution in which this work takes place is a corporate laboratory comprising activities that, though not directly related to a product line, can be argued to have potential relevance to the design of more powerful or more useful machines. This rationale supports the financing by the corporation of projects identified as "basic research": that is, research whose relevance to corporate profits is justified in the long-term and admittedly speculative future.

Work in the laboratory includes a range of projects involving the design of computer systems and the development of "system sciences" broadly defined. Although the prevalent field is computer science, there is value placed on multidisciplinary research; the laboratory includes cognitive psychologists, linguists, typographers and graphic designers, physicists, mathematicians, logicians, philosophers, and anthropologists. Self-organizing collaborations emerge through mutual interests discovered in everyday interaction as well as in more explicitly organized projects.

In addition, multiple ties to universities nationally and internationally are maintained through a steady stream of graduate students and members of the laboratory who hold joint industry–university appointments. Perhaps most salient to members of the laboratory is their identification with the academic community, as both resource and audience for their work.

The project

The AI project on which our analysis is based took place under the combined auspices of the laboratory and an affiliated institute at a nearby university. As described in the center's fourth-year report, "The Center for the Study of Language and Information is a research institute that aims to develop theories about the nature of information and how it is conveyed, processed, stored, and transformed through language and in computation" (CSLI, 1987, p. 1). Many of the center's projects are conducted jointly with the laboratory. One of these is the Embedded Computation (EC) project, described in the same report as having two goals: "(1) to develop a theory of computation that views computers as situated information processors, and (2) to design and implement specific computational architectures consonant with that theory" (p. 45). Researchers on the project see their efforts as leading to a significantly different view of computation than is standard in computer science. This view in-cludes the notion that computers are physically "embodied" and contextually "embedded," such that their abilities and limitations depend upon a physical substrate and a surrounding situation.

The project involves two related enterprises: (1) constructing sce-narios of activity that raise certain thorny representational issues in AI, and (2) designing and implementing a computer program that runs the scenarios, providing evidence that the behaviors (and prob-lems) identified there are realizable (and solvable) in a machine that could participate in the original activity. As with most work in AI, the project is expected to produce a running computer program that realizes and serves as a sufficiency test for the theories that stand behind it. The artifact created, accordingly, is designed to serve researchers' purposes of theorizing more than the purposes at-tributed to the projected user. At the same time, the program must ultimately succeed in the interactions it is designed for if it is to gain credibility for the theories on which it is based.

The EC project is distinguished by its stated commitment to modeling "situated inference" about time, place, persons, and the like. The model is to be tested through the design of a computer artifact called the Situated Inference Engine (SIE), intended to em-body ideas about "nonformal inference, situated language, parallel architecture, and representation" (p. 46). The report motivates the SIE subproject as follows:

Most models of computational inference – particularly those for which rigorous semantical analyses have been given – depend in large measure on theoretical notions from mathematical logic. These theories, however, typically sidestep consid-erations of various kinds of context. For example, mathematical proofs do not deal with such expressions as TO-THE-RIGHT-OF(TIGER,HIM,NOW), whose se-mantical interpretation depends on surrounding circumstantial facts. Human con-versation, however, systematically exploits exactly this kind of physical, temporal, and discourse relativity. (p. 50)

Researchers working on the SIE see as their goal the design of an "inference engine" capable of taking advantage of the implicit con-text and embedding circumstances of its interactions with a human user. The test case is to design a meeting scheduler capable of interacting with a hypothetical user to maintain a weekly calendar.

The first version of the SIE is intended to carry out simple "dialogues" with a human user about times, places, persons, and the like.

The scenario

The SIE's interactions with its user are modeled by a scenario which, standing as a proxy on behalf of the social world, conceives the activity of scheduling in terms of puzzles of logic and representation interesting from the point of view of AI. Scenarios are a particularly powerful form of what Latour (1986) calls "immutable mobiles"; that is, representations produced in one place and time, able to be transported more or less intact in order to be deployed again somewhere else:

> One example will illustrate what I mean. La Perouse travels through the Pacific for Louis XVI with the explicit mission of bringing *back* a better map. One day, landing on what he calls Sakhalin he meets with Chinese and tries to learn from them whether Sakhalin is an island or a peninsula. To his great surprise the Chinese understand geography quite well. An older man stands up and draws a map of his island on the sand with the scale and the details needed by La Perouse. Another, who is younger, sees that the rising tide will soon erase the map and picks up one of La Perouse's notebooks to draw the map again with a pencil. (p. 5)

Following Latour, we take a primary advantage of the inscription of an imagined activity into a scenario to be the latter's *simplicity, mobility,* and *immutability*. The scenario is crafted to pose just and only those problems that the scientist is, a priori, committed to solve. And rather than being contingent on the times and places in which others choose to act, the scientist using the scenario can have access to the problem whenever and wherever he or she chooses. Finally, an inscription has immutability insofar as it, or at least the basis for reproducing it, remains unchanged as it is displaced from one situation of use to a next. It is through these properties that the scenario serves as a coordinating device for project activities distributed over time and space.

At the same time, the mobility and immutability of the scenario are ongoing achievements of project participants, as they selectively reproduce the scenario's significance on successive occasions of its use. Through the scenario, received problems in the field are exem-

("us" = user, "ss" = system)

us > On Wednesday mornings I only meet with graduate students.
ss > OK

    ... later ...

us > Schedule a meeting with Tore for Wednesday morning!
ss > > Is Tore a graduate student?
us > > Yes.
ss > > How is 9:30?
us > > Fine
ss > Done.

Figure 6.1. Part of a scheduling scenario.

plified as simple invented interactions, which in turn establish requirements for the work at hand. In the meeting analyzed here, participants are concerned with the sequence from the scheduling scenario depicted in Figure 6.1. Their task is to extend the machinery of AI to handle the puzzles that the sequence poses.

The researchers in this meeting make extensive use of the scenario. Yet they do so constructively, transforming the scenario's opening statement, for example, to "Wednesday mornings are for graduate students" from the original "On Wednesday mornings I only meet with graduate students." The shorter form is equivalent for their purposes at hand, while it maintains the theoretical concerns that motivated the original scenario's design.[2] More specifically, for the researchers the first line of this sequence indexes the canonical AI problem of representing constraints on behavior, and it is that problem with which they are currently engaged.

Figure 6.1 shows a sequence of the scenario wherein the user informs the system of a scheduling rule, which it successfully makes use of at a later time. This piece of the scenario is made of a rule and directive and embedded question–answer sequence. The problem at hand is to encode the rule in such a way that the machine asks the embedded question regarding Tore's status if and only if the question has not previously been answered. The machine should not, in other words, act stupidly.

Work at the board

Where the physical sciences traditionally rely upon experimentation to produce the objectively accountable evidence of their phenomena and to test their theories, artificial intelligence relies upon the design of computational artifacts. Along with the computer, however, the representational technology of choice among AI researchers is the whiteboard. Whether the concern of the moment is theorizing or system design, much of laboratory activity on a day-to-day basis consists in talk that takes place in front of a whiteboard. Visitors to the laboratory often remark on the ubiquity of the whiteboard as a feature of the general decor. Whiteboards, some covering an entire wall from floor to ceiling, are to be found in "common" areas as well as in offices, conference rooms, and laboratories. Alongside the computer, the whiteboard constitutes the "bench" for the laboratory's work practices.

In the case at hand our focus is on a specific occasion of whiteboard work; namely, the production and use of the inscriptions depicted in Figure 6.2a and their development into Figure 6.2b. Ethnomethodological studies of lecturing and of mathematicians' work (Garfinkel & Burns, 1979; Livingston, 1986) have identified the essential, mutually constitutive relationship between marks and the activity of their production and use. Rather than analyze whiteboard inscriptions as such, therefore, we are interested in viewing them in relation to activity, through the use of video records. Viewed as free-standing signs left behind by the work, we assume that the sense of these marks is largely undecipherable. Viewed in relation to the activity of their production and use, in contrast, they come alive as the material production of "thinking with eyes and hands" that constitutes science as craftwork. Our task here is to provide for the reader, through text, a sense for the sense of these marks as the embodied practice of work at the board.

The analysis is based on video records of a 1.5-hour working session of two researchers, C and M, on the SIE project. Our focus in this analysis is on the design activity occurring after the construction of scenarios and before the creation of computer software. Given the world inscribed as a textual scenario, C and M employ a further device to re-represent the text in a form closer to the program they

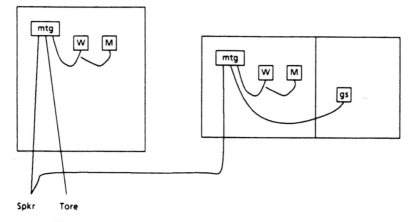

Figure 6.2a. Whiteboard at 1:01:06.

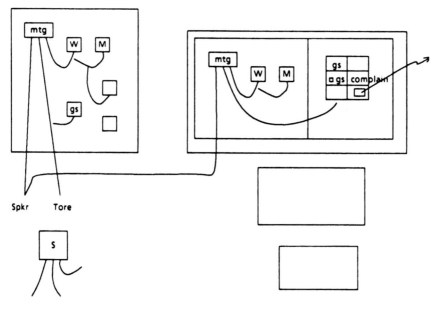

Figure 6.2b. Whiteboard at 1:21:48.

are eventually after. Previous work on the project, both their own and others', provides them with a graphical formalism and a set of representational conventions. With these, they construct the local setting for their work.

In the analysis we focus on a sequence near the end of the meeting, during which C and M deal specifically with the issues raised by the scenario of Figure 6.1. Though they continually hold their designs accountable to the scenario, and though they often look ahead to the requirements for implementation in a physical computer, the inscriptions with which they work are neither scenario texts nor computer programs, but hand-drawn diagrammatic representations written on the shared drawing space of the whiteboard.

The creation of the marks in Figure 6.2a occurs about an hour into the meeting.[3] In the course of their subsequent use, running for roughly 20 minutes until shortly before C and M conclude their work for the day, and resulting in the inscription depicted in Figure 6.2b, a design dilemma is posed, debated, and resolved. The problem is to design the mechanisms of SIE responsible for combining input from the user with prior knowledge and constraints inscribed in the system, in order to yield requirements on the system's response. In particular, C and M's immediate task is to design the behavior of the SIE system when a schedule command is received for which one or more scheduling rules or "constraints" are applicable.

The scenario posits that the part of the SIE that takes input from the user has just received the command, "Schedule a meeting with Tore on Wednesday morning." Among other "knowledge" captured in the SIE is a representation of the earlier directive, "Wednesday mornings are for graduate students." Combining this directive with the user's schedule command should yield a requirement that Tore be a graduate student:

58:14
001 C: So. Right so we, run the constraint about Wednesday mornings
002   being for graduate students, to get the requirement that Tore is a
        graduate student.

In this case, the slot in the user's weekly calendar corresponding to Wednesday mornings is constrained to be filled (if at all) with meetings with graduate students. As it turns out, the problem for C and

M is not how to represent this constraint. Rather, their struggle is over how and when it is to be applied.

At the outset of the sequence, in the space of 1 minute, C constructs all of the objects depicted in Figure 6.2a:[4]

59:54
031 C: (turns back to board) But so, we've got this, this isolated im-
032   impression structure (looks to M, who looks up at sketch)
033 M: //Right.
034 C: //That's come from the parser essentially. Now the lisp code that
035   runs scheduling could certainly make up (turns to upper left of the
036   wb) a piece (draws large box on left) of what it's going to melt into
037   the larger memory later (turns to M, waving hands in circular
038   motion around box.) (.) (back to box) which says you know meeting,
039   (draws smaller "mtg" box in upper left corner of large box)
040 M: Right.
041 C: Uh (line down from "mtg" box to "spkr" written outside large box)
042   Speaker. (another down from "mtg" box to "Tore") Tore. (draws
043   "w" and "m" boxes and connecting lines to the right of "mtg" box)
044   Wednesday morning.
045 M: //(inaudible)
046 C: (puts cap on marker, takes step back)//And then (.) (moves again
047   to board and draws second large box to right of the first) So, what's
048   going to be in the biplane, someplace else, outside, is you know
049   (filling in smaller boxes "mtg," "w," "m") meeting, Wednesday
050   morning (adds connecting line from "mtg" in large right-hand box
051   to "spkr" below large left-hand box, writes "gs" in box in right half
052   of large right-hand box, cap back onto marker, steps back).
053 M: Are for graduate students, ah right.

As with any occasion of work, C and M's work here is constructed in relation to, and makes use of the products of, previous activities. Most immediately, they have on hand a collection of graphical objects that they themselves have produced on the board earlier in this meeting – for example, the "impression structure" mentioned by C in lines 031–032 (not pictured). But those objects, in turn, are selectively reproduced from previous work of theirs, of others in their project, and of still others in the larger field of which they are members. Some of these objects are recreated by them here but treated, at least for present purposes, as closed. Others are the subject matter of their work now, open for invention or transformation. In either case, the objects produced and reproduced constitute the setting for C and M's subsequent activity.

The inscription of objects and the alignment of fields

Lynch and Woolgar (1990) propose that occasions of scientific practice distributed in time and space can be aligned, through the juxtaposition of inscriptions from one occasion with those produced on another. Relations between activities are thereby constituted through the relationship of their inscriptions:

Representations can represent other representations in complex socio-technical networks: the sense conveyed by a picture may derive as much from a spatio-temporal order of other representations as from its resemblance or symbolization of some external object. Relationships between representational objects and expressions are of particular interest for any effort to reveal the "social" organization of technical work in science. (pp. 5–6)

Similarly, Latour (1986) proposes that the progress of science relies upon scientists' successful deployment of a set of "well aligned and faithful allies," including techniques, technologies, arguments, and inscriptions. The alignment of these allies does not come without effort however, insofar as they comprise a heterogeneous mix of objects and processes drawn from a diverse collection of fields. For AI in general and for the SIE project in particular, the fields from which such allies are drawn include philosophy, psychology, linguistics, mathematics, electronics, computer science, and engineering. Figure 6.3 shows the fields brought to bear on constructing the SIE formalism and on the work at hand.

The scientists' problem is to transform this diverse collection of allies, through their superimposition and alignment, into a consistent theory or working artifact. That such alignment succeeds at all is largely due to the metaphorical quality of scientific language. That is, through their ways of talking and inscribing, researchers establish a metaphorical relationship between the various fields without having to say what exactly that relationship is (see Agre, 1990).

A requirement for C and M is to bring a particular set of heterogeneous devices – the scenario, the graphical formalism, the program

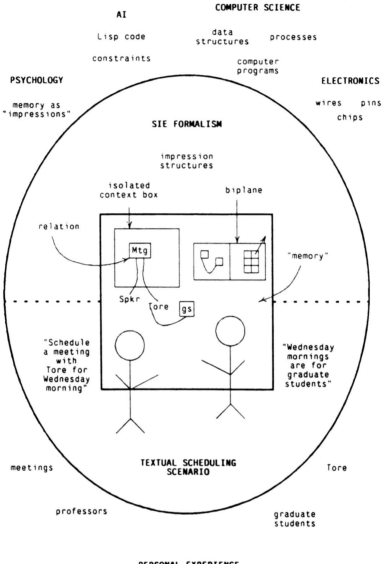

Figure 6.3. Objects and fields of origin.

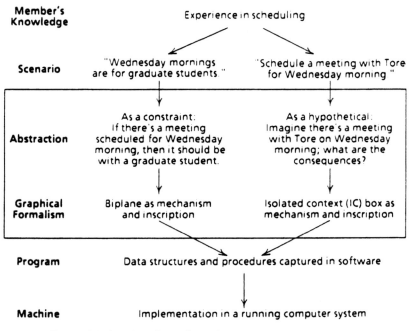

Figure 6.4. A series of transformations.

– into meaningful relationship. Each device is accountable to its adjacent fields. Figure 6.4 depicts their alignment as a series of transformations from activity to machine.

Experience is recast as scenarios, which are transformed into abstractions and graphical formalisms, transformed in turn into programs. To succeed, the scenario must be plausible as a representation of scheduling practices, at the same time that it sets up the conditions for their transformation to graphical formalisms. Graphical formalisms, in their turn, must inscribe the scenario, at the same time that they set up the conditions for its inscription as a program runnable on a machine.

The graphical formalism under development in this session at the board lies in some sense midway in the transformation from scheduling activity to program. Notions of scheduling are inscribed as passages in a scenario, reconceptualized in turn as abstractions (e.g., "constraints" and "hypotheticals"). These abstractions are recast as a formal notation inscribed as two-dimensional graphical objects (e.g., "biplanes" and "IC boxes") on the whiteboard, designed to be encoded as a computer program, to be implemented finally on a machine. The two-dimensionality of the whiteboard facilitates this appropriation of the social world to the world of machines. The crossing of boundaries between heterogeneous phenomena is made easier by the flatness and consequent homogeneity of their inscriptions, such that "realms of reality that seem far apart . . . are inches apart, once flattened out onto the same surface" (Latour, 1986, p. 27). Through this process of flattening and layering, the order of heterogeneous fields and their attendant phenomena are aligned.

Impression structures

The whiteboard is a medium for the construction of what we might call *concrete conceptual objects.* Constructs depicted on the board are conceptual in that they inscribe ideas, but they are also concrete objects – visible, tangible marks that can be produced, used, and transformed. The computer also is an inscribable medium at several levels. At the lowest level, computer software can be characterized as zeros and ones inscribed in the registers of the machine. For most programmers, however, the activity of creating software involves inscribing information in the computer by writing and storing instructions. The computer then "contains" the information so inscribed, in the same sense that the whiteboard contains the marks inscribed on it.

Impression structure is a generic term used in the SIE project to refer to any data inscribed in the computer's memory. Taking off from an early notion in psychology of memories as analogous to "impressions" made in soft wax, impression structure in the SIE formalism projects computational and psychological fields onto a single graphical object. Whereas the notion of computer "memory" itself superimposes computation over psychology, the terms used to denote the contents of memory in computer science traditionally do not draw on psychology. Rather than "memories," inscriptions in the computer are called "data structures," "records," "bytes." The notion that a computer's memory could be "impressed" upon, in contrast, not only allies computation with psychology and computers with minds, but implies a relation of the computer to the social world as the source of its inscriptions.

Isolated contexts

Assuming the inscription of the user's command to the SIE as an impression or data structure inside the machine, C creates the large box to the left in Figure 6.2a (lines 034–039). The box inscribes the text "Schedule a meeting on Wednesday morning with Tore" as a graphical formalism that represents the meeting itself, but in a way meant to assign it a provisional status. C describes the box he draws as, "a piece of what [the system's] going to melt into the larger memory later," that is once the meeting has been verified (lines 035–038). For now, the box and its contents must be "isolated" from the rest of the system's memory in case this meeting needs to be retracted from the schedule because it is found to violate some constraint.

To get at their provisional nature, such objects are referred to by project members as *isolated contexts* (ICs). An IC box contains a data or impression structure that is "isolated" from the rest of memory. One can think of the "walls" of such a box as a kind of one-way glass. From inside the box, the rest of memory is accessible for purposes of verifying the box's contents against the given constraints. From elsewhere in memory outside the box, however, the contents of the box are unavailable.

Boxes and wires

In lines 041–044, C draws several small labeled rectangles and connecting lines. Each small rectangle represents an association between objects. For example a (two-person) meeting ("mtg") is taken to be a relation between two people ("Spkr" meaning speaker, or the user of SIE and "Tore," the name of a graduate student), a time ("W" for Wednesday, "M" for morning), and a place.[5] *Relation instance boxes* capture this grouping through connecting *wires*. Thus the rectangle labeled "mtg" appearing inside the IC box (on the left in Figure 6.2a) has three wires connected to its bottom edge, one each for the two people meeting and one for the time of the meeting. The inscription "Tore" appearing below the IC box is not itself an entity in memory (thus the absence of a box) but rather indexes for purposes of talk at the board the totality of relations in which Tore participates – that is, a possibly complex but here left unspecified set of wires and connected boxes in the system's memory.

The device of boxes and wires aligns social, psychological, and computational relations through electrical engineering. Digital circuit design is a familiar activity to many computer scientists. Manipulating and constructing digital circuits are largely matters of linking (or wiring) together a number of chips (essentially "black boxes" with well-documented behavior) containing simple logical or processing elements. The goal is a network whose behavior can be "read off" of the resulting diagram.

Memory

In lines 046–052, C moves to the right of the IC box and draws a divided rectangle called a *biplane* (i.e., a flat plane divided in two) to represent the constraint "Wednesday mornings are for graduate students." As C begins to draw the biplane he says, "So, what's going to be in the biplane, someplace else, outside . . ." (lines 047–048). Both "someplace else" and "outside" convey his intention that the biplane exists outside of the hypothetical context represented by the IC box. In this case, the biplane is presumed to exist as an impression structure in the computer's "memory" before this particular schedule command is received. (The placement of "Tore" and "Spkr" outside the IC box suggests that they too have been inscribed in memory prior to receiving this command.) As boxes are drawn on the whiteboard, the memory – that which the IC box isolates the context from – becomes the space on the board surrounding the box. As a consequence, a decision about whether something is part of the hypothetical meeting or part of the memory is trivially reversible; one erases the object's inscription from outside the box and redraws it inside (or vice versa).

Constraints

The standard definition of *constraint* that comes closest to C and M's technical usage is "something that restricts, limits, or regulates" (*American Heritage*, 1976, p. 286). In this representation scheme the constraint takes the form of a logical if–then rule: If there is a meeting scheduled for Wednesday morning, then it must be with a graduate student. M's reading of C's inscription as "Are for graduate students, ah right" (line 053), however, reflects a preference among researchers in AI to represent constraints in a "declarative" rather than a "procedural" fashion; that is, independently of the mechanism by which they are enforced. The goal of representing constraints in a declarative fashion, in turn, reflects a more basic assumption in AI; namely, that there is a distinction between the knowledge one has and how one uses it. Knowledge of the kind "Wednesday mornings are for graduate students" should be represented in a form that is independent of the procedures comprising its use or application, so as to make the knowledge representation formalism independent of its implementation in a particular system. One should be able to read off from the representation the meaning of the constraint – that is, which objects are restricted to be in what relationships one to another – *without* having to know how the system will maintain such relationships, or what action will be taken if it finds them to be violated.

Designing the behavior of objects

We have noted that all of the objects of Figure 6.2a are reconstituted by C and M from prior work on the project. Rather than invent new objects, C and M's task on this occasion is to design the behavior of those already in hand. More specifically, they take as their task to specify the response of the system when a schedule command is received to which some previously specified rules of scheduling apply.

The scenario with which C and M are concerned prescribes an order of scheduling based on an allocation of times to social categories, for example, "Wednesday mornings are for graduate students." Social identity is at once a major organizing device for interaction and a practical problem for everyday interactants (Schegloff, 1972).

Institutional interactions, or interactions between strangers, frequently involve demonstrating one's own membership in a particular social category and inferring the membership of others. Various means are available for such demonstrations and inferences, including evidence provided by time, place, appearances, and talk. Troubles of uncertainty or misidentification are detected and resolved (more and less successfully) as they arise.

A basic requirement for successful interaction, remarkable only when trouble arises, is to know what constitutes adequate grounds for inference. For example, if I infer something about you based on appearance and turn out to be wrong, or if I question your status when the answer should be obvious, my own competence as a member of the local group is called into question. For C and M, the immediate question is how the system should combine the command "Schedule a meeting with Tore for Wednesday morning" with the requirement that anyone scheduled for such a meeting must be a graduate student. In this sense, their problem is first and foremost a members' one. That is, given the command to schedule a meeting with Tore, what inference regarding Tore's social status is warranted?

1:00:58
053 M: . . . And the problem here is that (.) we don't want to infer (3.0)
054   It's not supposed to be an inference.
055 (2.0)
056 C: What.
057 M: We're not supposed to infer that Tore is a graduate student, (C
058   sits down on table still holding marker) we're supposed to ask it.
059   That's one-
060 (7.0)
061 M: So::
062 (2.5)

In designing the SIE formalism C and M have a dual accountability, to the social world on the one hand, and to the world of computing on the other. Their problem becomes a technical one insofar as their commitment is to the capabilities of the computer – in particular, how to inscribe knowledge of the social world into the computer in such a way that it will appropriately combine the directive with the constraint. A standard approach to solving the problem is actually to inscribe in the machine some rules of conduct in the form of procedures that, when run, will reproduce the prescribed behavior. In what follows M proposes such procedures as a way of dealing with the constraints on meeting scheduling. More specifically, in lines 068–104 he describes what the computer would do under his plan:

1:01:31

062	C:	Right. (.5) Well, first of all, y'just more basically,
063	M:	Yeah.
064	C:	(stands up, moves to wb.) we have to, take this (points to IC box)
065		piece of structure and, ask whether it matches any constraint
066		(points to biplane box), the left hand side of any constraint in
067		the memory.
068	(2.0)	
069	M:	The left hand side of that. (C waves at biplane.) No, what I was
070		going to do (stands, moves toward wb) was just imagine that we
071		have a whole bun – (two-handed wave at biplane box) I mean.
072		(Looks for marker on tray.) Turn this into a procedure (draws
073		box around the biplane box, figure 2b) and we have a whole wad
074		of these things (draws two smaller boxes below biplane box),
075		basically each constraint (1.0)//(inaudible)
076	C:	//corresponds to a constr-, to a procedure.
077	M:	corresponds to a procedure, and just have a set of them. And we
078		just (holds finger of left hand on IC box), start with this context
079		thing and we just go, constraint (taps, with marker, on wb at
080		biplane box), constraint (taps again on new lower box), con-
081		straint (points to but doesn't tap the lower of the three boxes).
082		Fire up- fire them all off. Some of them could just, produce
083		contradictions in which case (2.0) uhhm some of them could
084		produce some contradictions, some of them could, in- the
085		Wednesday mornings are for graduate students one, would ac-
086		tually (picks up eraser) if we have it this way (pointing at right
087		side of biplane box) it says, if you have a meeting on a Wednes-
088		day morning (turns to look at C) with a grad- then assume it's
089		with a graduate student. That's not what we want, we want: then
090		(erases "gs" in right side of biplane fig 2a)
091	C:	//Uh
092	M:	//Actually what we'd is, what we probably want (.) is to have
093		(starts drawing new 3-part box in right side of biplane fig 2b) I
094		mean there's a couple of ways to do this, but we might, um do,

095   if it's a graduate student then do nothing, (filling in parts of
096   3-part box) if it's not a graduate student, then complain (1.0)and
097   if it's unknown, then (.) a- then ask the user (.) I mean then go
098   off to a lisp, (draw arrow pointing out of 3-part box) function
099   which is going to ask user is this, a graduate student. (puts cap
100   on marker) Or something like that//(inaudible)
101 C: //Yeah, but can't we-
102 M: (puts marker on tray) Can we make that=
103 C: =This is going to be very stylized.
104 M: (sits down on table) Yes//so that we want to-
105 C: //Can't we
106 (1.0)
107 C: embed it in the lisp procedure? (.) Rather than in the memory?

C and M are designing the mechanisms by which biplanes and IC
boxes, or rules of action and hypothetical situations, will interact.
M's proposal assumes the medium of the computer, where processes
can be inscribed in a form manipulable by the machine. The whiteboard, however, has no access to, and therefore cannot "run," the
text and graphical objects inscribed there. The graphical formalism
C and M use at the whiteboard is designed for them, in other words,
rather than for the machine. To use the formalism to design the
machine, M must simulate its intended activity. In lines 077–081 he
"animates" the whiteboard objects so as to simulate the behavior of
constraints. Holding a finger of one hand on the IC box, he taps his
marker on three newly inscribed "constraint procedure" boxes to
indicate the manner in which they behave. In this respect, the behavior of the constraints is not inscribed so much as it is performed (see
also Star & Gerson, 1988; Bly, 1988; Tang, 1989). The constitution
of the formalism relies upon a reflexive relation between whiteboard
inscriptions and practices, the inscriptions on the board being produced and used through activities that are not themselves recon-
structible from these "docile records," but whose presence the records presuppose (Garfinkel & Burns, 1979).

   On this occasion, however, the performance is intended not for
the machine but for C. M needs to prescribe a procedure that the
machine would run, but only to the extent that is required to convey
the idea to C. He does this by extending the biplane representation
to capture the three-part conditional, pointing off to an unspecified

mechanism for the interaction with the user. Precisely because the whiteboard is indifferent to these inscriptions, is not "running" over them, it imposes no requirements for completeness beyond their usefulness for the communicative task at hand.

M's proposal arises from the concern that there are different types of constraints, some of which may warrant automatic inference and others of which do not. To be a competent scheduling assistant, the SIE must maintain the social order of "Wednesday mornings are for graduate students." The competence that this rule implies is identified in ethnomethodological studies of social order as the "*ad hoc* elaboration of rules in use*" (Zimmerman & Wieder, 1970). The central observation of those studies is that maintaining any rule of action requires the local elaboration by participants of just what the rule could mean in relation to specific circumstances of its application. The ad hoc constitution of special purpose procedures to handle those contingencies, however, violates C's sense of adequate design. In struggling with this problem of how rules for scheduling should be applied, C and M return to the importance of the tentativeness of the desired meeting with Tore on Wednesday morning.

1:11:12

247	C:	Uhhm. See, I'm pinning my hopes (chuckle)
248	M:	//(chuckle)
249	C:	//here on the notion that, this box that we've made up,
250	M:	right =
251	C:	= isn't yet, a fact that we claim about the world.
252	(1.0)	
253	C:	When I say//schedule
254	M:	//Right,
255	C:	with//Tore
256	M:	//right
257	C:	on Wednesday morning I don't mean, there's a meeting on, I'm
258		having a meeting with T – it's not the same as claiming that
259		there is such a meeting.
260	M:	Right. That's true.
261	C:	Therefore, even if, the SIE didn't make the distinction between,
262		natural law and, nominal constraints and conventional ones,
263	M:	Right =
264	C:	= uhhm, it could, nevertheless, not assume that Tore's a grad-
265		uate student, in good faith. (1.0) Because of the fact that, we

266   haven't yet claimed that there's a meeting with Tore on
267   Wednesday morning, but rather that, we would like there to be
268   one.

In superimposing their formalism onto the world of scheduling, C is able to argue that for the SIE to take a meeting inscribed inside the IC box as actual (and therefore as evidence for Tore's status) rather than hypothetical (leaving Tore's status still in question) would violate a normative order. The notion of "good faith" (line 265) invokes the moral premise that participants in an interaction will neither deliberately mislead each other nor deliberately misread each others' intent. Inscriptions inside the IC box are to be taken as proposals rather than claims, leaving open the question of their adherence to the rules of orderly scheduling. In specifying a procedure whereby the SIE would answer the question of Tore's status, a mapping between hypothetical situations and specific circumstances emerges as the new problem:

1:18:36
364 C: Except that what what's actually been tr- true is that you've been
365   asked, the SIE has been asked to schedule a meeting. There's
366   still isn't a meeting. (.) There's still no claim that there's a
367   meeting on Wednesday morning.
368 (.)
369 M: Right. (.) Right that would be (2.0) Ah. See, I still think that the
370   right way to get the inference here is to imagine there being, a
371   meeting on Wednesday morning and see what the consequences
372   of that would be.
373 C: uh-hmm. So, one of the consequences would be, because of
374   this constraint, (indicates biplane) that Tore is a graduate stu-
375   dent. (.) Right?
376 (1.5)
377 M: Right.
378 C: But so then, the question is how you match up, this: inductively
379   filled out world, that uh, that you have imagined,
380 M: Right
381 C: with what you know of the real world.
382 M: But the problem is that with, the semantics of the memory
383   structure, (.) you already believe that Tore is a graduate student
384   so, stating that Tore is a graduate student inside it, is not, I
385   mean is a//null operation.

386 C: //Why do you already believe this?
387 M: Cause the semantics o:f, nested contexts is that they inherit
388 beliefs. (1.0) That's just (.) a basic property of the memory.
389 (1.0)
390 C: Wait wait wait wait wait.
391 (5.5)
392 C: hhh.
393 (1.5)
394 C: Well, (stands, moves to wb) I mean no no. I mean (picks up
395 marker, points at IC box), if this is the imaginary world now
396 (erases gs box with hand), then it's gonna have to be the case
397 that, you know (writes gs box and wire inside IC box) the, the
398 graduate student gets added in here =
399 M: = Oh ah. Uh right. (.) Right, if graduate student isn't already
400 outside then, okay. So the idea is you would build more struc-
401 ture in (C points to IC box) there.
402 C: Yeah.

M's initial objection to C's proposal in lines 382–388 arises from a misalignment between M and C, corresponding to loss of alignment between the whiteboard inscriptions and their talk. M at line 382 is looking at the whiteboard, on which is inscribed the representation of "gs" outside the IC box, in memory (signifying that Tore's status as a graduate student is already known), while C is looking away from the whiteboard, worrying about the unknown case. C points to the whiteboard while stating, "one of the consequences would be, because of this constraint . . ." But then, while presumably making reference to the IC box ("the question is how you match up this inductively filled out world . . .") he uses his hands to form a closed spherical container in the air in front of him, without referring to or looking toward the whiteboard. M protests that since SIE already "believes" that Tore is a graduate student (presumably, because that is inscribed in memory), restating that fact *inside* the IC box gains nothing. C asks why M "believes this," meaning why does M believe that the SIE already knows that Tore is a graduate student. M hears that as, why would it be a "null operation" to represent Tore's status inside the box, and answers by appealing to the nature of "nested contexts," that is, isolated, insulated boxes and their relations to memory outside. C at that point looks from M over to the whiteboard and sees that indeed, it depicts the very situation that M has described, namely that Tore's status is represented in memory, outside the box. (This inscription occurred over 15 minutes earlier.)

The trouble reveals the extent to which C and M's shared understandings are tied to shared inscriptions on the board. In this case a "garden path" misunderstanding arises from the fact that C and M are not at one moment referring to the same objects. M takes the inscriptions on the board, the residue of their previous work, as the current context, whereas C is referring to a revised representation he has constructed "in the air."

Seeing the source of the confusion, C goes to the whiteboard, erases the gs inscription "outside," and redraws it inside the IC box. This simple action captures the crux of their solution; namely, to assume a consistency between rules of scheduling and requests for meetings, but place any resulting new inferences (e.g., that Tore must be a graduate student) in the same isolated context that contains the meeting. Thus, if processing the constraint "Wednesday mornings are for graduate students" results in the inference that Tore is a graduate student, that piece of structure will have the same *hypothetical* status as the meeting itself.

1:20:34

398	M:	You'd still inherit (inaudible), okay. See, in the case where there
399		was already a graduate student outside (C replaces marker on
400		tray) it wouldn't even build the interior one but that's not a
401		problem.
402	C:	(Steps back from wb.) That's cool, yeah.
403	M:	n'kay. So the- so it's just this case where it builds an outer one.
404		A:nd (C moves in to wb, grabs marker), //so what you're saying
405		is,
406	C:	//Right, there are sort of three cases. One is this (points to gs
407		box outside IC box, not pictured) is empty.
408		One is, this (overwrites "gs" in same box) has graduate student,
409		in which case this (points to new gs box just added to IC box)
410		doesn't happen. And the other this has (starts writing "not" box
411		above gs box) gradua- not graduate student (.) in which case
412		(2.0)
413	M:	It's//gonna contrad-
414	C:	//Well, I don't know.
415	M:	it's gonna generate //a contradiction. (Stands and moves toward
416		wb.)

417 C: //This (points to new gs box inside IC box) isn't gonna get built,
418   the contradiction's gonna, //gonna happen in one sort of (inau-
419   dible).
420 M: //It's gonna, it's gonna [inaudible] this (points to IC box), it's
421   gonna say, right, it's gonna say this context is contradictory,
422 C: Right =
423 M: = which is okay. So (C replaces marker on tray while M grabs
424   marker), on on this other picture (grabs eraser) then, so we
425   would go along (erases gs box outside IC box) we would, fire off
426   all these constraints and it would build structuring here (points
427   to IC box).
428 C: uh hm.
429 M: And then at the end it would go along and go (turns around to
430   face C, back to wb) how about this (.) structure. And actually
431   that sort of fits with the, how about, I mean it's sort of along the
432   same lines of, how about nine-thirty. Cause that's other struc-
433   ture that's being built in here, it runs all the structure. It has all
434   this, I mean it runs all this (.) things it now builds this structure
435   in here.
436 C: Yeah.
437 M: And now it queries you to, agree to essentially all the things it's
438   about to deduce, it seems like.

Although M's concern about the contingency of the scheduling rules still holds, M and C's accomplishment is to design the behavior of the machine so that its internal architecture ignores the distinction, handing judgments of warranted inference off to the user. The solution requires inscribing a consistent set of relations inside the machine and then enlisting the user in reconciling that inscription with the social world. By finessing the problem for social interaction, they satisfy the adequacy requirements of computer science, in that the objects in memory behave in a uniform, consistent manner. The user, moreover, is consulted only once to pass judgment on the adequacy of the resulting structure. Aligning the scenario with the formalism at the time of design, they rely upon the alignment of formalism with circumstances of the social world at the time of use.

Conclusion

This analysis has been concerned with the in situ work of representing human behavior as the skilled, socially and materially organized practice of AI. The sense of "representation" we have developed here is an anthropological one, viewing representation as socially organized activity producing certain publicly available artifacts, used in subsequent interactions with others and with the material world. We have proposed that the work of AI involves a series of transformations or re-representations, originating in researchers' connected experience of the social world, moving from a simplified textual scenario that transforms and stands on behalf of that experience, to a formalism that inscribes the scenario, to the inscription of the formalism as code implemented on a machine, and finally to a reconnection of the machine into the social world through its interaction with a human user. Although certain logical relations hold, this process is not a unilinear progression. Scenarios, abstractions, formalisms, and programs comprise the objects of the work under discussion by AI researchers, objects that mediate between experience on the one hand and machines on the other.

Through the devices of scenarios and formalisms, AI researchers attempt to bring practical activity under the jurisdiction of runnable programs. At the same time, a scenario as written provides only a sketch of what the research problems and their solutions could be.[6] The production of relevant problems and appropriate solutions is itself a practical problem for researchers, solved on specific occasions of technical work. That problem is characterized by a tension between researchers' intuitions about the logic of everyday practice on the one hand, and their allegiance to the logic of AI and computation on the other. In the case at hand, the graphical formalisms inscribed on the board mediate between the two.

Through their skilled work at the board, researchers make scenarios and formalisms relevant to their practical purposes at hand. This work constitutes the "performance" that, according to Star and Gerson (1988), is the necessary companion to inscriptions in use: "Where inscriptions attempt to freeze natural phenomena to make them more manageable, performances 'fiddle' and adjust representations to make them fit local circumstances" (p. 2).

These performances, the "unformulated practices" (Lynch, 1985) of AI design, mediate between the requirements of persons and machines. As a medium for inscribing formalisms, the whiteboard mediates between persons and machines as well. The two-dimensional objects on the board are designed to be manipulated and talked about as representations of persons and schedules that anticipate the requirements of the machine. Their success, however, depends upon the artful practice of researchers as they exploit certain properties of the objects while treating others as irrelevant. As Livingston (1986) has discovered for the practice of mathematics:

If we consider the primordial setting of mathematics to be those occasions when mathematicians, in the presence of one another, work in such a way so as to exhibit to each other the recognizable adequacy of their work, then one of the things that we have seen is that mathematicians work in such a way so as to disengage the mathematical object from the situated work that makes it available and, therein, to disengage that object from the situated work that gives it its naturally accountable properties. Thus, the first major point is that the naturally accountable mathematical object is the local achievement of mathematical provers. (p. 10)

Like any product of skilled practice, the formalism inscribed on the board leaves behind the logic of its own production and use, seen here as collaborative craftwork of hands, eyes, and signs. But analyses of situated practice such as this one point to the contingencies of practical action on which logic-in-use, including the production and use of scenarios and formalisms, inevitably and in every instance relies. In this way such analyses provide an alternative to idealized formulations of reasoning as disembodied mental operations.

In taking AI as a subject of inquiry we are faced with an outstanding issue regarding the representation of human practice. The issue can be formulated, at least initially, as follows: Ethnomethodological studies of the physical and biological sciences eschew any interest in the adequacy of scientific representations as other than a member's concern. The point of such studies is specifically not to find ironies in the relation between analysts' constructions of the phenomenon and those of practitioners (Garfinkel, 1967, p. viii; Woolgar, 1983). Rather, the analyst's task is to take the ways by which practitioners come to an understanding of their phenomenon as the identifying accomplishment of their scientific practice. In turning to AI and cognitive science, however, one is confronted with fields whose phenomenon of interest itself is practice. For cognitive science theorizing, the object is mind and its manifestation in rational action. And in designing so-called intelligent computer systems, representations of practice provide the grounds for achieving rationality in the behavior of the machine.

To the extent that AI is an enterprise dedicated to explicating the social world, it shares with the other social sciences a central question; that is, to what rendering of the phenomenon of interest is the enterprise accountable? In our own case, working from video records presupposes that "it is the embodiment of speech and gesture which provides work with its visibility for practitioners" (Lynch, 1985, p. 7). Moreover, we assume that the identifying problems and solutions of the practice in which we are interested are to be found in the analysis of actual, specific instances of practitioners working together. At the same time, we recognize the produced-and-analyzed character of these video records, as materials with which we are actively engaged rather than as "data" whose sense can be read off directly from the record that the videotape provides.

Without setting up a simple irony, then, in the comparison of AI's enterprise with our own, we wish to open the question of accountability in relation to the project of engineering intelligent machines. AI is interested in reproducing practical reasoning computationally as a means of modeling and thereby understanding it. However, rather than beginning with documented instances of situated inference (e.g., inferring whether someone is a graduate student), researchers begin with what Agre (1990) calls "pseudo-narratives": in this case, postulates and problems handed down by the ancestral communities of computer science, systems engineering, philosophical logic, and the like.[7] Scheduling operates here not as a category of activity in the world but as a pretext for the resolution of problems in constraint-based reasoning. The scenario disciplines and constrains C and M's intuitions in the service of an intellectual enterprise defined not by scheduling activities but by the communities of practice from which the scenario comes and to which it is accountable. C and M's primary concern must be with the accountability of their representations to the scenario and its ancestral communities, rather than with the scenario's relation to the activity it purports to model and for which on this occasion it stands.

The communities of practice of which AI is a part, and from which its resources are drawn, have traditionally taken the production of definitive, decontextualized renderings of a phenomenon of interest as the measure of understanding. In accord with this standard, AI has as a goal to escape from the indeterminacies of argumentation about intelligence through the design of machines that could successfully and definitively reproduce it. The successful design of intelligent machines is to be the proverbial "pudding" that proves the validity of researchers' theories and the efficacy of their methods. However, to the extent that practical reasoning is comprised of the juxtaposition, *bricoleur*-fashion, of disparate elements available in specific, historically and culturally constituted settings, the situated inference of AI research must come to terms with its own irreducibly contingent and ad hoc character.

Lave (1988) has argued that "theoretically charged, unexamined, normative models of thinking lose their descriptive and predictive power when research is moved to everyday settings and relaxes its grip on the structuring of activity" (p. 172) and asks:

What would happen to theorizing about cognition if investigation were moved to the sites of the activity whose interpretation was under debate? What changes in theoretical orientation would be required in order to make such travels seem sensible and of value in the first place? What further theoretical reformulations would follow from a multi-faceted approach to observation and analysis of everyday activity? The argument has been formulated as a journey from the laboratory into the everyday world. (p. 170)

The laboratory Lave has in mind here is the psychology laboratory, but we find her questions equally relevant to the laboratory of AI research. What would happen, we wonder, if the bases for AI's theorizing about everyday activity were not scenarios but actual scenes, captured in some rich medium and inspected in detail for their sense, their local structures, and their relations to other systems of activity? What changes in theoretical orientation would be required for this shift in methods to happen? The design of machines as situated reasoning engines would seem to implicate them in specific sociocultural, historical, temporal, and spatial locations. Yet AI scenarios routinely hold such circumstances in abeyance, implicitly relying upon designer and user to fill in the machine's social location as needed, while systematically neglecting to consider that process itself as an object of research. If, however, as Lave suggests, "thought (embodied and enacted) is situated in socially and culturally structured time and space" (p. 171) the locus of AI theorizing must be opened up to the larger constitutive order of which persons, machines, and activities are invariably and essentially a part.

Notes

1. The work reported here is the result of a collaboration between the authors, an anthropologist, and a computer scientist. The study draws on our combined knowledge and experience of ethnography, ethnomethodology, interaction analysis, computer system design, and AI. The project described here was part of the research program of another division of the laboratory in which we were both members. This provided us with ready access to the researchers we studied and a familiarity with aspects of their work's larger context, both of which contributed to our analysis of the video records.

2. The shortened version used in the meeting may also be a reference to the version, "Wednesday mornings are reserved for graduate students," appearing later in the scenario. Presumably the researchers are familiar with the entire scenario though they only demonstrate their concern here with the first few lines.

3. Figures 6.2a and 6.2b represent the upper left corner of a whiteboard on which various other textual and graphic inscriptions are also lying about as the result of the meeting's first hour. We select this piece of the board and the corresponding episode because they are relatively self-contained, but also because they are perspicuous with respect to the issues of AI in which we have an interest.

4. For the sake of readability in dealing with these technically complex materials, we provide only a standard, nonconversation analytic transcription, though we are sure that these materials would repay careful analysis. In the transcript segments numbers in parentheses indicate elapsed time in seconds. Thus "(3.0)" indicates a pause of three seconds. A dot in parentheses "(.)" indicates an untimed pause, an equals sign " = " indicates "latching," i.e., the beginning of one utterance following directly on the end of the prior with no gap. Double slashes "//" indicate the onset of overlapped talk. Colons ":" indicate prolongation of the immediately preceding sound. Line numbers refer to the place of a segment in the full transcript.

5. The meeting place is left unrepresented during this discussion, as the larger issue of place is a piece of the problem they are holding aside. For the moment, at least, focusing on time and time-related constraints is sufficient for their purposes.

6. The problems posed in the scenario include representing unanticipated information (say, Tore's status), building objects in a machine that track the changing real world (again, Tore's status, which might change from year to year), and

representing indexicals, objects like Wednesday, Speaker, and "I," which depend for their meaning on a situation of use.

7. Agre's point is that these are fictional narratives constructed to resemble "ordinary" narratives read forward from recounted events, whereas in fact they are actually (and covertly) read backward from technical categories and from the need to illustrate, motivate, or exemplify technical proposals cast within those categories. Such "pseudo-narratives" are constructed for the specific purpose of reconstructing commonsense knowledge as something that can be transparently read off of the particular technical representations at hand. For a practitioner's critique of current AI practice and recommendations for an alternative, see Agre (in press).

References

Agre, P. (1990, July). *Portents of planning: A critical reading of the first paragraph of Miller, Galanter and Pribram's* Plans and the Structure of Behavior. Paper presented at the Conference on Narrative in the Human Sciences, Iowa City.

Agre, P. (in press). *Computation and human experience.* Cambridge: Cambridge University Press.

American Heritage Dictionary (1976). Boston: Houghton Mifflin.

Barr, A., & Feigenbaum, E. (1981). Representation of knowledge. In A. Barr & E. Feigenbaum (Eds.), *The handbook of artificial intelligence* (Vol. 1, pp. 141–222). Los Altos, CA: Morgan Kaufmann.

Bly, S. (1988). A use of drawing surfaces in different collaborative settings. *Proceedings of the Second Conference on Computer-Supported Cooperative Work* (pp. 250–256). New York: Association of Computing Machinery.

Brachman, R., & Levesque, H. (1985). Introduction. In R. Brachman & H. Levesque (Eds.), *Readings in knowledge representation* (pp. xiii–xix). Los Altos, CA: Morgan Kaufmann.

Collins, H. M. (1987). Expert systems and the science of knowledge. In W. Bijker, T. Hughes, & T. Pinch (Eds.), *The social construction of technological systems* (pp. 329–348). Cambridge, MA: MIT Press.

CSLI (1987). *Fourth year report of the situated language research program* (CSLI–87–111). Stanford, CA: Center for the Study of Language and Information.

Dreyfus, H. (1979). *What computers can't do.* New York: Harper and Row.

Garfinkel, H. (1967). *Studies in ethnomethodology.* Englewood Cliffs, NJ: Prentice-Hall.

Garfinkel, H., & Burns, S. (1979). *Lecturing's work of talking introductory sociology.* Unpublished manuscript, Department of Sociology, University of California, Los Angeles.

Garfinkel, H., Lynch, M., & Livingston, E. (1981). The work of a discovering science construed with materials from the optically discovered pulsar. *Philosophy of the Social Sciences, 11,* 131–158.

Latour, B. (1986). Visualization and cognition: Thinking with eyes and hands. *Knowledge and Society, 6,* 1–40.

Lave, J. (1988). *Cognition in practice.* Cambridge: Cambridge University Press.

Law, J. (1987). Technology and heterogeneous engineering: The case of Portuguese expansion. In W. Bijker, T. Hughes, & T. Pinch (Eds.), *The social construction of technological systems* (pp. 111–134). Cambridge, MA: MIT Press.

Livingston, E. (1986). *The ethnomethodological foundations of mathematics.* London: Routledge and Kegan Paul.

Lynch, M. (1985). *Art and artifact in laboratory science: A study of shop work and shop talk in a research laboratory.* London: Routledge and Kegan Paul.

Lynch, M., Livingston, E., & Garfinkel, H. (1983). Temporal order in laboratory work. In K. Knorr-Cetina & M. Mulkay (Eds.), *Science observed: Perspectives on the social study of science* (pp. 205–238). Beverly Hills, CA: Sage.

Lynch, M., & Woolgar, S. (1990). Introduction: Sociological orientations to representational practice in science. In M. Lynch & S. Woolgar (Eds.), *Representation in scientific practice* (pp. 1–18). Cambridge, MA: MIT Press.

Schegloff, E. (1972). Notes on a conversational practice: Formulating place. In D. Sudnow (Ed.), *Studies in social interaction* (pp. 75–115). New York: Free Press.

Searle, J. (1980). Minds, brains, and programs. *Behavioral and Brain Sciences, 3,* 417–457.

Star, S. L., & Gerson, E. (1988). *Representation and re-representation in scientific work.* Unpublished manuscript, Tremont Research Institute, San Francisco.

Tang, J. (1989). *Listing, drawing and gesturing in design: A study of the use of shared workspaces by design teams* (Research Center Technical Report SSL–89–3). Palo Alto, CA: Xerox Palo Alto.

Woolgar, S. (1983). Irony in the social study of science. In K. Knorr-Cetina and M. Mulkay (Eds.), *Science observed: Perspectives on the social study of science* (pp. 239–265). Beverly Hills, CA: Sage.

Woolgar, S. (1987). Reconstructing man and machines: A note on sociological critiques of cognitivism. In W. Bijker, T. Hughes, & T. Pinch (Eds.), *The social construction of technological systems* (pp. 311–328). Cambridge, MA: MIT Press.

Zimmerman, D. H., & Wieder, D. L. (1970). Ethnomethodology and the problem of order: Comment on Denzin. In J. D. Douglas (Ed.), *Understanding everyday life: Toward the reconstruction of sociological knowledge* (pp. 285–298). Chicago: Aldine.

7   Behavior setting analysis of situated learning: The case of newcomers

Urs Fuhrer

Many human actions in everyday life occur in settings where actions are highly constrained and organized. Some years ago I started research on how newcomers adapt to such novel, unfamiliar, and coercive settings: The work was done in libraries and university career planning and placement centers (cf. Fuhrer, 1988, 1989a, 1990b). Questions were asked about the experience and behavior of *newcomers* to the settings, about the structure and dynamics of settings when invaded by the uninitiated, and about the reconciliation between the novices as individual persons and the settings as extraindividual systems of activity. These questions are of both practical and theoretical importance: practical, because modern societies expose people to unfamiliar settings very frequently due to technological change, organizational developments, easy migration, and so forth; theoretical because answers to these questions require advancement in our understanding of the regulation of individual or collective actions as part of sociophysical or cultural environments.

A general theme that lies behind the discussion of research in this chapter is that learning (or knowledge acquisition) is inevitably *situated*. Learning takes place in real-life settings, under real performance requirements on actual individuals, and is vulnerable therefore to social influences that may arise at any time. Both retrospective verbal protocols and data of a behavioral path analysis were gathered (among other data; see Fuhrer, 1989a) from newcomers who learned

I thank Lucy Suchman and Hugh Mehan for their encouraging comments on the conference presentation of this manuscript. Also, I am grateful to Roger Barker, Paul Gump, John Levine, Allan Wicker, and Herbert Wright for their suggestions on an earlier version of this chapter. Finally, I would like to thank Jean Lave and Seth Chaiklin for their helpful comments on this manuscript.

179

to prepare a job application in a career planning and placement center.

Here is a *typical situation:* Imagine a freshman who comes into a career planning and placement center to look for a part-time summer job opportunity at a southern Californian public transport company. Here is a verbal protocol that gives some insights into a newcomer's experiences in dealing with this unfamiliar setting:

(S: 3):
When I walked in, I had no idea how I was supposed to solve this task. I didn't know too much about the center and how to use it. I was feeling nervous. I looked around the room and went through most of the room. I figured out where everything was. With some experiences from the high school career center, I knew that I needed to write down necessary information about the company. Right away I spotted the job listings. I went to the job listings and started looking for OCTD. When I got to the board, I was wondering if the girl standing there was looking for the same job. So I kept looking up to see what she was doing. Finally, I thought she was doing another task. It took me a while to find the listing and I was wondering if I was looking in the wrong place. Having made little progress, I felt confused and nervous. I didn't know what to do next and felt embarrassed when I approached the information desk. I asked the guy at the desk what to do. I felt very stressful because I knew other people were watching me. I was embarrassed when I realized that I had to ask more questions. Then when this was happening and I was going back and forth, I realized that I was the "guinea pig" in this place. I had no clue where the job applications were. But I didn't want to look stupid asking questions all the time, since other people were busily working. I felt out of place. Everyone was sitting there and watching me, which made me very self-conscious. I felt intimidated by the things around me and didn't want to be stared at when I didn't know what to do. Maybe the people in the room were thinking I was stupid. People don't bother me at all, but I could see how some people could get apprehensive in there. I felt like a running rat in circles in a maze trying to find the cheese that wasn't there. Again, feeling embarrassed. Mostly, I guess I was anxious about not finding the brochure and probably caused me to be anxious throughout the rest of the task.

At first glance, the verbal protocol indicates that the newcomer's learning activities are hardly reducible to cognitive processes, but rather learning in real-life settings seems to be influenced by both personal and setting-related components. Moreover, emotions such as social embarrassment and social anxiety seem to be a crucial catalyst in the learning process. Thus, theoretical concepts of both cognitive and social psychology will be used to illuminate the psychological processes of newcomers who try to adapt to unfamiliar settings. But unlike theoretical attempts on learning from cognitive and social psychologists who concentrated heavily on processes within persons, both the settings in which newcomers are embedded and person-setting processes will be much more differentiated in the model proposed in this chapter. The theoretical framework builds upon Barker's (1968) ecobehavioral science, which I have sought to expand in significant ways.

The career planning and placement center study

Before the theoretical analysis, it might be useful to present the field study in a bit more detail and then to build the conceptual apparatus out of the presentation of this study.

Knowledge through intervention

Although the laboratory has been the setting most frequently used by psychologists to test their hypotheses, it is, especially for environmental psychologists,[1] not the only setting available. The environmental psychologist who moves outside the laboratory to test a hypothesis is basically concerned with increasing the natural quality of the situation: the naturalness of the behavior, the setting, and the treatment. Often the investigator's role in such a study is simply to observe what occurs, with little or no intervention. However, in the field as in the laboratory, the experimenter has at least some control of both the factors that are arranged by him or her and the random assignment of subjects to conditions. But the investigator who engages in this kind of *quasi-experimental research* does not have full control over the possible sources of variation. Most environmental psychologists are interested in conducting research in the actual setting that concerns them and in preserving the authenticity of that setting than are psychologists from other areas.

According to Barker (1968), in everyday settings particular individual characteristics of people operating settings are not as important for understanding the structure and dynamics of those settings as their collective actions as components of those settings – that is, people in settings interact with each other as role partners. For studying how newcomers adapt to unfamiliar settings one can replace the real staff persons by *confederates* who operate the setting. By doing this one might change the integrity of at least more routinized settings only slightly. This strategy has the advantage that research is still done in a naturalistic milieu with inhabitants (confederates) maintaining the current state of the setting but operating the setting in a controlled way according to the goals of the researchers. Thus, the setting of the present study is a naturally occurring one, which was not created by the researcher but rather by the society. Unlike Barker and his co-workers' (1978) naturalistic approach in which settings were kept untouched, as researcher I am interested to understand the setting by changing at least some of its components, that is, in operating the setting in a controlled way. By changing the structure and dynamic of settings in a controlled way, one can see what happens, that is, one will get some new empirical knowledge by intervention.

Handling prior knowledge in the presence of other people

I studied three variables I thought were relevant to understand the newcomers' learning activities: their *prior setting-specific knowledge* and the presence of other people in the setting, that is, both the number of people and the kind of actions those people are engaged in. Especially critical for a newcomer is how well his or her planned action, despite *the number of people present*, fits into the current setting – that is, the ongoing actions of others already present. This fit between others' actions and the action of a newcomer is hereafter referred to as *congruence of subjects' and others' actions or goals*.

Sixty-four university freshmen who were unfamiliar with the career planning and placement center were recruited as subjects from the social science human subject pool at the University of California, Irvine. Each subject was told that the research was an attempt to understand how people reach particular goals in a realistic setting rather than in a laboratory (see for the details of the procedure Fuhrer, 1989a). The freshmen were confronted with the *task* of completing the application procedure to a part-time summer office job at the Orange County Transport Division (OCTD). The job was announced on a job listing in the career planning and placement center on the University of California, Irvine, campus. The task consists of 13 action steps (AS) as they were usually mentioned by students, who often used the career planning and placement center (see also Figure 7.1). At first, one enters the placement center (AS1), goes to the particular part-time listing (AS2), and copies the information about the particular job one is looking for (AS3). Then one has to find the company brochure in an alphabetized shelf (AS4) to find out both the company's phone number (AS5) and the interview date (AS6). Then one has to copy this information (AS7, AS8). Afterward, the brochure has to be returned on the shelf (AS9) and one has to find the application form (AS10). Because only one application form is available, one has to make a copy of the form (AS11) and to return the form to the binder (AS12). Finally, one can leave the room (AS13). With this information a student is in the position to contact the company (a step that was not part of the study).

During a *preexperimental session* in a room of the social ecology building (2-minutes walking distance to the career planning and placement center), half of the subjects individually learned the order of the action steps. The other half of the subjects had to read a short literature passage and to answer six questions about it. In front of the placement center the subjects were then instructed to obtain the necessary information for preparing the part-time summer job application mentioned already. All subjects were then taken into the placement center and told they could ask questions of the person at the information desk.

Setting-specific prior knowledge (high vs. low; consisting of the 13 action steps) was instructed to half of the subjects. *Social density* (high vs. low) was varied with 2 versus 10 people present in the placement center. *Subject-other goal congruence* was varied in the following way (see Figure 7.1).

In the high-congruence/high-density condition, the confederates were completing certain action steps of the experimental task. Each confederate stayed in a predefined place within the room and conducted a predefined behavior. In the low-congruence and high-density condition, the confederates in the room were sitting on chairs, three persons around each table. In the low-congruence/low-density condition, the confederate was sitting on the chair that was located

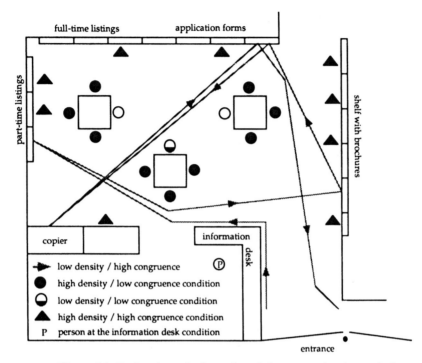

Figure 7.1. Basic schematic floor plan of the career planning and placement center.

in the middle of the room. In the high-congruence/low-density condition, the confederate was going through the action steps of the experimental task (along the broken line in Figure 7.1). The confederate always conducted the action step that the subject had to conduct next.

The behavioral path of each subject was recorded on a floor plan by two hidden observers. Right after the subjects had completed the task, retrospective verbal reports were gathered. That is, the subjects had to verbalize their recorded behavioral path by recalling everything they could remember about their thoughts and feelings while going along the path. The subjects' statements were tape-recorded and transcribed later on. The goal of the protocol analyses was to verify (at least partly) the model of the newcomer's learning activities as it will be presented later in this chapter. The protocols were initially divided into units. Typically, a unit was a sentence, but on

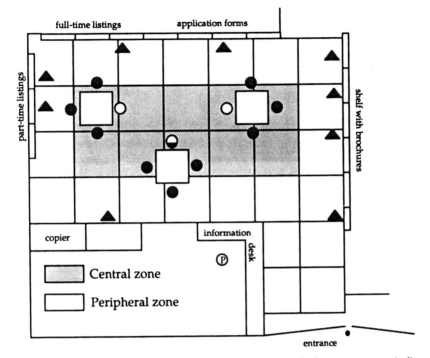

Figure 7.2. Floor plan of the career planning and placement center indicating central and peripheral zones.

occasion it was of clause length or a number of sentences. The interrater reliability of segmenting units was in excess of .90. The intercoder reliability of categorizing was .79.

For the analyses of the newcomers' behavioral path within the center, the floor plan of the center was divided in squares with a size of 1 square meter per square (see Figure 7.2). I then distinguished between squares belonging to a *central zone* encompassing the middle of the room and those belonging to a *peripheral zone* located along the physical boundaries (e.g., walls, shelves, information desk) of the room. Because architectural features of settings moderate people's behavior and their experiences (Evans, 1979; Fuhrer, 1987), I then counted how often a newcomer had entered a square of the central or one of the peripheral zone while dealing with the unfamiliar setting (see for more details Fuhrer, 1990b).

The results of the analyses of both the verbal protocols and the behavioral path will be used throughout this chapter to illustrate the line of theorizing to which I turn now.

The paradigms of cognitive control and ecobehavioral coerciveness

Usually, when psychologists study learning activities, they mostly focus on people's cognitive requirements and rarely on the structures and dynamics of the settings in which learning takes part (cf. Rogoff & Lave, 1984). And in looking at both the cognitive and the environmental dimension in the study of situated learning a third dimension comes into the focus of the researcher: the emotional dimension. To some degree, all individual actions within everyday settings, especially those of newcomers, are somewhat *discrepant* from what is expected; the settings change continuously. Most *emotions within social situations,* such as embarrassment, audience anxiety, shyness, or shame follow such discrepancies, just because these discrepancies produce visceral arousal. And it is the combination of that arousal with an ongoing evaluative cognition that produces the subjective experience of an emotion (cf. Lazarus & Folkman, 1987). Thereby, many social scientists have emphasized the role of others' presence in the generation of social embarrassment (e.g., Heider, 1958; Goffman, 1959). Thus, my major interest here is to present a model that integrates all three dimensions. But, first, I am going to review how the debate has usually been cast.

Much attention has been given in recent years to the principle of cybernetic control in action organization. Basically, these theories assume that human actions reflect an ongoing comparison of present behaviors and underlying *mental representations* against the current situation, and the attempt to bring the one into correspondence with the other (e.g., Miller, Galanter, & Pribram, 1960; Ginsburg, Brenner, & von Cranach, 1985). The view, that individuals' actions are exclusively driven by mental representations, is deeply rooted in the Western human sciences as the correct model of the rational actor (see Suchman, 1987, for a critique of this model).

(S: 60):
When I entered the room, I remembered that the job listings were located on the far

wall. But I was unsure if I was exactly looking at the right place. I felt confused, uneasy, and uncomfortable. But I saw that the resource room was well organized. So, I then started wandering around to scope out the room which guided me to some other listings.

This newcomer's verbal protocol suggests another view. That is, the environment is, itself, organized and coercive and therefore a comprehensive mental representation of the environment is not a sufficient condition of human action. This view characterizes the work done by Barker and his associates (1978). For example, many daily human actions are clustered in a more or less standardized way within certain small-scale places. Barker (1968) named those places *behavior settings*. When Barker looked at these events, he discovered that they had rather permanent and enduring qualities in terms of repeated behavior, time, place, and physical attributes. That is, behavior settings are small-scale social systems composed of people and physical objects configured in such a way as to carry out a routinized program of actions within specifiable time and place boundaries (Wicker, 1983).

Barker then began experimenting with ways to measure these attributes. The primary scale he came up with was called K-21. *The K-21 scale* was developed to answer the problem of whether two putative behavior settings are actually separate or constitute a single setting. The K-21 consists of seven subscales (measuring the interdependence in behavior, leadership, inhabitants, physical space, and so on, between pairs of behavior-milieu parts, called *synomorphs*). A set of synomorphs with k values, inter se, of 20 or less constitutes a single behavior setting; synomorphs with k values of 21 or greater are discrete behavior settings; and scores between 18 and 23 seem to indicate boundary problems. Although most behavior settings such as post offices or school classes are easily identified, it is sometimes difficult to intuit whether, for example, the interlibrary loan desk at a library is a separate behavior setting from the reserve book section.

Research by Barker and his colleagues has shown that behavior settings are important determinants of the molar behavior of children, adolescents, and adults (cf. Barker & Associates, 1978; Schoggen, 1989). The paradigm of ecobehavioral coerciveness, however, tends to be an environmental determinism although Barker (1963) does recognize that people exercise some degrees of freedom in pursuit of their own goals within behavior settings. In his most recent theoretical discussion of person–environment relationships, Barker (1987) suggests that everyday behavior of persons is shaped by two distinct kinds of factors: those that emanate from the person (e.g., cognitions, motivations, emotions) and those that arise from the ecological environment. Barker has investigated both kinds of influences on everyday behavior, and he has explicitly stated several times that each is important (cf. Barker, 1987). Thus, behavior settings as environmental units might be a *possible* meeting ground between the paradigms of cognitive control and of ecobehavioral coerciveness in studying newcomers' learning activities. Up to now, little has been done to combine these efforts (e.g., Lave, Murtaugh, & de la Rocha, 1984; Kruse, 1986; Kaminski, 1986; Fuhrer, 1988, 1990a, 1990b; Schoggen, 1989; Wicker, in press).

Environing schematic actions: The K-21 behavior setting

Behavior settings are parts of communities that are generally recognized by the citizens. These people describe both their daily happenings and their community in terms of behavior settings. Thus, many psychological and behavioral processes in public life domains unfold in the "format" of behavior settings (cf. Schoggen, 1989). In the present study, a newcomer's verbal protocol gives some empirical evidence for this assumption:

(S:35):
I have never been in the career planning and placement center before.

According to the definition of the term behavior settings mentioned previously, a grocery store, a library, or an auction sale are behavior settings, whereas schools or organizations are clusters of behavior settings. Or consider the career planning and placement center as a typical behavior setting. Does the term *behavior setting* indicate the place where the center is located, the staff person's behavior, the assembled users, the arrangement of tables, chairs, shelves, and job listings, or the purpose of the gathering? The answer must inevitably be, All of these together and none of these alone. If the computers break down in the career planning and placement center, brochures and books cannot be checked out, students cannot borrow tapes and books. It is the interdependence of all these parts rather than their similarity that makes a behavior setting a unitary entity.

Furthermore, people's actions within behavior settings are most directly influenced by the setting program (Barker, 1968; Wicker, 1987).

(S: 44):
I really didn't have any idea what's going on here. I kind of knew what to do, but I just wasn't sure. There were no guidelines to follow. I wasn't sure if I was supposed to use the copier. Thus, I had to go back to the information desk to get more information. After a while, I began to understand the logic of the situation.

Thus, many elements of the flow of human actions are "in" or "a part of" behavior settings and take the form of events that are programlike or scriptlike. Such program-bounded routines are the type of activities that Schank and Abelson's (1977) script theory intended to capture from the perspectives of cognitive psychology, social psychology, and artificial intelligence. In some ways, scripts, cognitive schemata, and the like appear to be rediscoveries of behavior setting programs from a social-cognitive approach (cf. Wicker, 1987).

Understanding the whole to understand its parts

For a better understanding of learning in real-life behavior settings, it will be necessary to pay more attention to the details of those behavior settings. If a newcomer (or a psychologist) wished to understand the action of another user of the career planning and placement center, he or she might set about to observe the interactions of a user with his or her surroundings. To do this he or she might view the user through field glasses, so focused that the user would be centered in the field of the glasses with just enough of the career planning and placement center milieu included to encompass all the user's contacts with that milieu: reading the job listings, looking at company brochures, taking an application form, and so on. This first attempt represents a *person-centered approach* to the study of human learning in behavior settings.

The newcomer (and the psychologist as well), however, would learn more about job application procedures by blocking out, at first, the operations of a particular user; then observing the highly stereotyped patterns of behavior around him or her; and finally identifying salient behavioral standards to which he or she must conform. This second attempt represents *Barker's ecobehavioral science approach* (cf. Barker & Associates, 1978). Unfortunately, much of the study of people acting in behavior settings has been the structure and the coercive forces of those behavior settings upon individuals, and of the behavioral aspects of these individuals *en masse*.

The third approach brings the single individual back into the focus of attention. Here, the attempt is to capture both the behavior setting and the individual's actions in one single process. The behavior setting and the individual's actions are not separate elements; rather the behavior setting as the whole is a confluence of inseparable individual and collective actions that depend on one another for their very definition and meaning. The single individual and the behavior setting are in a *transactional relationship* with each other. The term *transactional* (e.g., Stokols & Shumaker, 1981; Altman & Rogoff, 1987), for my purposes, emphasizes the idea that the extraindividual elements of the behavior setting and both the cognitive elements in people's minds and those people's behavior are aspects of a single process, not separate components. Inputs coming from the behavior setting or from the single inhabitant are so intertwined that each contributes to the other and initiates changes in the other (cf. Barker, 1987).

Behavior settings: Sources of goal opportunities and social forces

Behavior settings contain opportunities for goals and actions (Barker, 1968). In a particular behavior setting different people may achieve the same goals. For example, in a career planning and placement center different students are looking for job opportunities and they all behave in the same way. Furthermore, different people may achieve a different cluster of goals in the same behavior setting. One student in the career planning and placement center, for example, is looking for advice from a placement counselor, another student may watch a videotape to get help for preparing his job search, and a third student may be involved in a mock interview which will give her an opportunity to see how she presents herself to an employer. The unity of a particular behavior setting, however, does not arise from the similarity in the goals and motives of the participants. Any behavior setting exists only when it provides its participants with the particular goal opportunities their unique nature requires. Otherwise, the behavior setting will cease (see Wicker & King, 1988).

The changes observed in the behavior of people as they change from one behavior setting to another are obvious. Students visiting the career planning and placement center are engaged, for example, in various kinds of job search activities. When they change from the placement center to the restaurant, one can observe a very different conduct. In the restaurant setting they will be engaged in drinking, eating, or talking with classmates. Despite the great variation in the motives, goals, and skills of the persons participating in this behavior setting, the conformity of their behavior to the particular behavior setting is surprising. What are the sources of this conformity? Well, Barker (1968) listed eight possible sources of the synomorphy of behavioral standards and the nonpsychological milieu. The two of most interest in this chapter are what Barker (1968) called *social forces* and what he named as *learning.*

Social forces indicate one kind of link between people entering into the behavior setting and the standing pattern characteristic of behavior in the particular behavior setting.

(S: 23):
People don't bother me at all but I could see how some people could get apprehensive in there.

These forces imply obligations for setting participants and they can be strongly coercive. The power attaching to the members of behavior settings who occupy responsible positions within those behavior settings, such as the career planning and placement center director, other staff members with immediate authority, or even other users to enforce particular patterns of behavior is well known. For example, if a student enters the career planning and placement center to find a job, his or her behavior is somehow channeled into this behavior setting's specific standing patterns of behavior.

(S: 28):
I kept looking up to see what others were doing. I noticed everybody was writing or copying things down. So, I suspect that they did influence my behavior strongly. I

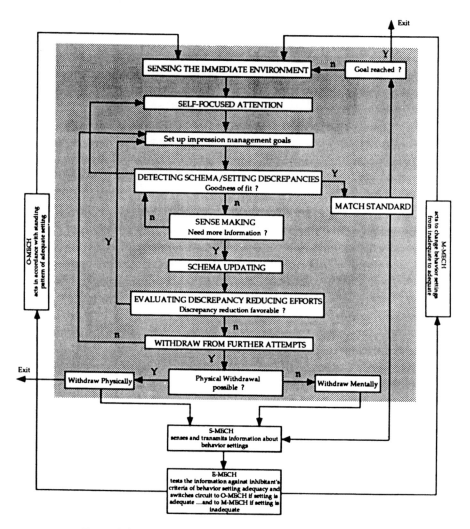

Figure 7.3. A transactional, multiple-acting model of situated learning.

can't explain how. The task wasn't that hard, but it could have been much harder if there wasn't anyone in the center. The other people's behavior played a significant role in guiding me through the center in an easy way.

Barker (1968) believes that the regulation of behavior settings is meaningfully construed in terms of the principles of cybernetic control (see Figure 7.3). Within behavior settings there are routes to goals that are satisfying to the inhabitants. In a career planning and placement center, for example, there are paths for finding jobs or for getting advice on career planning, but there are no paths to goals like buying newspapers, listening to country music, or ordering pizza. Barker hypothesized that some setting participants, mostly staff persons or frequent users who might be identified by the newcomers as insiders or "old-timers," act as if they have a *sensory mechanism (S-MECH)* which receives and transmits information about the behavior setting to an *executive mechanism (E-MECH)*, which tests the information against the participants' criteria of adequacy for the behavior setting.

(S: 3):
That's where I knew for sure that the man at the desk was looking at me. I then was sent to the full-time listings.

If the perceived events are judged adequate, participants employ *operating mechanisms (O-MECH)*, that is, they continue to show the behavior that conforms to both the *goal (G-MECH)* and the *program (P-MECH)* of the behavior setting. If events are judged to be deviant from the behavior setting's main functions, participants will employ *maintenance mechanisms (M-MECH)* to manage the troubles, that is, to bring about changes to restore the behavior setting to a condition that permits their goals to be pursued. Barker proposed two kinds of maintenance mechanisms: *deviation countering (D-MECH)*, by which inhabitants take steps to counteract or alter the interfering conditions, and *vetoing mechanisms (V-MECH)*, by which inhabitants eliminate the interfering conditions.

(S:48):
I went to the copy machine and I stood there for a while because I wasn't sure how to work it. I read the directions on it and got even more confused. Then I realized I was reading the reloading instructions for paper. I found out it was just a regular copy machine. The first copy came out wrong because I didn't put it right. I was embarrassed. The man came over and helped me out.

If the maintenance mechanisms prove successful, occupants switch to operating mechanisms. If the maintenance mechanisms prove unsuccessful, they continue to employ maintenance mechanisms until the potential threat is corrected. These mechanisms regulate the behavior setting in terms of its goal opportunities for inhabitants, which, in turn, reduce the variety of inhabitants' behavioral patterns and maintain it within an acceptable range of standards. Most of the research relevant to Barker's model has dealt with the ways setting participants interact with inadequate states of functioning (e.g., states of over- or underpopulation; see Wicker, 1983; Schoggen, 1989). Almost no research has been focused on the psychological processes within single setting participants with the notable exception of Willems (1964), Gump and Friesen (1964), and more recent research on the person-level processes of setting founders (Wicker & King, 1987; Wicker, in press).

A multiple-acting model of situated learning

Typically, the newcomers' learning activities are not totally directed on carrying out the setting programs. They often attain a variety of other goals, such as engaging in various impression management tactics or developing interpersonal relationships to other setting inhabitants. Thus, the newcomers *simultaneously pursue several goals* and, therefore, they may simultaneously perform different actions. Theoretically, this phenomenon of multiple acting (cf. Fuhrer, 1984) forces us to deal (conceptually) with questions of management and coordinating the various actions that arise from cognitive, social, and environmental demands or goals (cf. Fuhrer, 1990b).

In my presentation of *the model of multiple acting,* I start with a reflection on the characteristics of psychologically new situations. I then focus on both the cognitive requirements for a newcomer's actions such as cognitive schemata or scripts and the function of behavior settings which are external or collective resources of "knowledge." Subsequently, I focus on the social significance of the newcomer's actions. Through impression management, newcomers attempt to construct and maintain particular images of themselves that they project to others. Building on this framework I can be more specific about the hows and whys of the newcomer's emotional experiences because these emotions only occur when a newcomer is felt to have projected an incompatible image of himself or herself before those present.

The nature of new psychological situations

What is the nature of new psychological situations, and what kinds of behavior do they evoke? In answering these questions I refer to an early paper of Barker, Wright, Meyerson, and Gonick (1953), to research on group socialization (e.g., Moreland & Levine, 1987), and to work on organizational socialization (e.g., Louis, 1980; VanMaanen, 1984). In an unfamiliar behavior setting, at least seven situations are possible.

First, the newcomer does not know the sequences of actions that will result in the desired goal (e.g., to get the job application done).

(S: 2):
As I entered the center, my mind was blank and I didn't know what to do.

Second, some newcomers bring to their mind experiences of some corresponding activities in one or more similar behavior settings.

(S: 3):
With some experience from the high school career center, I knew that I needed to write down necessary information about the company.

Third, each act may place the newcomer closer to the goal or move him or her further away from the goal.

(S: 24):
I could see where the job listings were so I walked in that direction, but I wasn't sure how they were arranged so I was a little wary.

Fourth, the newcomer's senses are simultaneously inundated with many unfamiliar cues of the particular behavior setting.

(S: 51):
I can see that there are many job listings on it and it would take a lot of time to look throughout the wall. I was confused about all this information.

Fifth, the newcomer is self-conscious and therefore he or she is socially sensitive to the impression he or she is making upon others.

(S: 47):
I was very conscious of what I was doing because everybody was watching me and I didn't want to mess up.

Sixth, the newcomer avoids the danger of being regarded as a non-member of the particular behavior setting.

(S: 24):
I didn't want to look stupid wandering around when others were busily working. I felt totally out of place. I then tried to do what others were doing.

Seventh, the newcomer's performance deficiencies cause a set of emotional reactions, such as embarrassment and social anxiety.

(S: 49):
I didn't know what to do next and felt nervous and embarrassed.

Prefabricated schemata versus activity in behavior settings

Several researchers have recently asserted the usefulness of schema concepts, such as action schemata or scripts, as cognitive representations of behavior settings, particularly of setting programs (e.g., Kruse, 1986; Wicker, 1987, in press; Schoggen, 1989; Fuhrer, 1990b). *Action schemata* play a double role in behavior settings: There are (1) action schemata as understanding structures, that is, schemata for understanding the behavior setting's standing patterns of behavior; and (2) action schemata as behavioral structures, that is, schemata that guide people in participating in those behavior settings. Schemata as understanding structures guide the interpretation of a given behavior setting in which one is participating. For example, bringing back a particular schema to mind may help the newcomer make sense of what goes on in the behavior setting in which he or she participates. Schemata as behavioral structures should enable the individual to participate in behavior settings. The newcomer's current schemata, however, are not just played out in the course of participation in the behavior setting. According to Suchman (1987), newcomers might act on an ad hoc basis, and schemata are used as internal resources of knowledge for actions-in-behavior settings, but do not in any strong sense determine its course.

(S: 14):
I thought everything was clear in my mind about what to do when I got to the part-time listing. But when I couldn't find what I was looking for, I felt a little lost. I just followed a random path that led me to some brochures. Although I realized that the information I learned in the first part was to be utilized in my task-solving quest. But I was disoriented and couldn't solve the task the way I thought.

Newcomers often abandon their schemata and fall back on whatever embodied skills are available to them (see also the case of beginning skiers; Fuhrer, 1984). Thus, newcomers' actions are improvised insofar as they are designed to cope with surprise, uncertainties, and unforeseeable contingencies of their actions (e.g., Louis, 1980; Suchman, 1987).

Behavior settings: Sociophysical and temporal systems of externalized or collective knowledge

Behavior settings are middle-sized ecological units through which sociophysical and temporal influences are experienced and which people need as orientating contexts (Kaminski, 1986) or as external or collective resources of knowledge (Fuhrer, 1990b). Behavior settings represent "traces" of individual or collective actions or organizational processes. This conceptualization of settings is familiar with the idea of places as external memories of personal or collective experiences (Lang, 1992). Unlike internal knowledge structures as they are represented in the form of cognitive schemata, external knowledge is collective because more than one individual has access to them. Moreover, collective resources of knowledge might be distributed among several setting participants (see Hutchins, this volume) and might be available from instructional material as well, whereas in other behavior settings the knowledge is not distributed but is available from one particular member. In this chapter, I focus on the newcomer's use of one particular collective resource of knowledge, that is, the competence of other participants in the setting.

Behavior settings consist, in part, of standing patterns of behavior. These standards of the behavior settings' appropriate behaviors are important means in guiding the newcomer's actions. The other setting participants' competence facilitates the newcomer's goal attainment in at least two ways: First, setting participants occupying responsible positions usually know the setting program. Therefore, by asking them, one could get them to externalize their schematic knowledge about how the behavior setting operates.

(S: 45):
I began to use the best resource of all – the man at the information desk.

Second, other setting participants enacting ordered sequences of actions with standing patterns of behavior know at least certain parts of the behavior setting's entire program. Thus, newcomers might observe their expressive behavior – that is, try to make sense out of each others' action and try to understand the cognitive schemata in those others' minds.

(S: 28):
I kept looking up to see what others were doing.

The social significance of situated learning

Many social psychological and social anthropological theories assume that people are highly sensitive to the social significance of their conduct (e.g., Festinger, 1954; Goffman, 1959; Latané, 1980) and are motivated to create desired impressions on others. From this view, all behavior settings are potentially threatening for newcomers. Other setting members may focus their attention on the newcomer and the newcomer will be alert to every cue. All of these things may increase the newcomer's level of self-consciousness, that is, the sensitivity to the impression one is making upon others. What matters most to the newcomer is not how he or she views his or her own behavior and its consequences, but rather how others view them. The newcomer must determine the extent to which those others evaluate his or her action as a reasonable action "as part of" the particular behavior setting. Thereby, an important feature is the preexisting knowledge and expectations that those setting participants who are present have about the newcomer. Because other setting participants will interpret the newcomer's behavior in relation to what they already know and expect of him or her (Heider, 1958), it seems likely that a newcomer will normally consider this attributed knowledge when formulating impression management tactics or goals.

(S: 3):
Everyone was sitting there watching me, which made me very self-conscious. Maybe the people in the room were thinking I was stupid. But I didn't want to look stupid.

What is relevant here for learning is that the newcomer will take some goals or actions in the course of learning to conceal his or her identity and to avoid or lessen negative impressions or to enhance positive impressions.

(S: 23):
I saw the other people and I knew what they were thinking about me. I felt like a real idiot.

Thus, a *favorable impression* is defined here in terms of the degree to which a newcomer's actions correspond to the action opportunities of the behavior setting. In relatively routinized situations, social actions proceed without extensive thought about impression management (e.g., Schlenker & Leary, 1982). Newcomers, however, confronted with unfamiliar behavior settings causing puzzlement about how to behave will be more alert in managing the impression they make on others than insiders or "old-timers" among themselves might be.

According to more recent theoretical and empirical work on impression management or self-presentation (cf. Jones & Pittman, 1982; Tedeschi, Lindskold, & Rosenfeld, 1985), it is proposed that there exist both *protective or defensive tactics,* such as concealment, excuses, or self-handicapping that derive from presenters' concerns over engendering disapproval and loss of face rather than from concerns over garnering approval and *acquisitive or assertive tactics,* such as self-enhancement, ingratiation, intimidation, self-promotion, or supplication. These tactics should not be considered as either exhaustive or mutually exclusive, but should be taken merely as a classification that may be useful for the modest goal of dealing with some of the nuances of tactical presentations in situated learning (e.g., Fuhrer, 1989b).

For example, if the newcomer's prior interest is to conceal his or her identity and competence then he or she attempts to "pass through the setting" undetected. For example, newcomers with this impression management goal try to get into the setting and out of the setting as quickly as possible. These newcomers attempt to cover up their competence or try not to be recognized as an outsider among insiders.

(S: 2):
While there, all I thought about was how I could get out as fast as possible. But I didn't really understand what was going on in the center.

Those who pursue this tactic are not primarily motivated to learn how to reach the task-related goal, that is, to elaborate their cognitive schemata; rather they enter the situation with more socially oriented goals, such as concealment and dissimulation. Newcomers with these social goals in mind are involved in some kind of *nonlearning activities.* There is a body of research that points out that many people enter daily settings with such goals (e.g., Garfinkel, 1963; Edgerton, 1967; Mehan & Rueda, 1986).

(S: 47):
I felt funny because I knew I was being watched. But I tried to look as competent as possible. I then tried to escape the attention of the other people and to pass through the task undetected.

Newcomers, however, who are motivated to reach the goal of applying to the particular part-time summer job are engaged in task-related information-seeking activities, such as imitating others or asking questions of knowledgeable setting participants. Some of these newcomers will use less embarrassing modes of information seeking than others. Whether a certain mode of information seeking is embarrassing depends on its appropriateness in the present behavior setting. For example, if no one asks questions, then question asking might be more embarrassing than observing others or reading written instructions.

(S: 8):
I felt embarrassed when I approached the information desk since nobody else was asking questions.

Because newcomers acquire more and more knowledge during the course of learning in the behavior setting, there might be changes in their impression management tactics.

(S: 47):
I felt embarrassed and uncomfortable, at first, because everybody was watching me and I didn't want to mess up. But once I started finding things, I gained confidence and forgot about the people watching me.

Situated learning as coping with social embarrassment

I take this section to illustrate how the proposed multiple-acting model of situated learning is used in practice. Basically, the present model proposes that newcomers attempt to cover up their ineptness because of the embarrassment that they are likely to experience. *Embarrassment* is produced by (1) the presence of others; (2) the awareness that their attention is directed toward oneself; (3) the apprehension about how one supposes others see him or her; and (4) a publicly visible deficient performance (Heider, 1958). Those deficiencies are exactly what characterizes newcomers. *Situated learning*

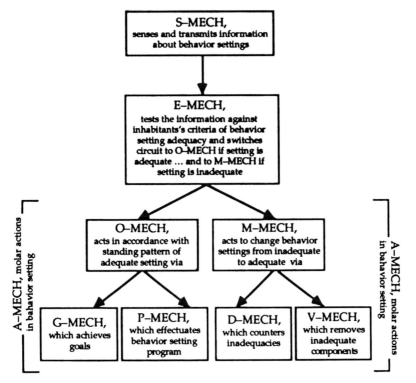

Figure 7.4. A behavior setting's control unit.

goes hand in hand with the psychological effects of these deficiencies, such as embarrassment and social anxiety.

The behavior settings may guide, at least in part, the newcomer's learning activities by providing both collective resources of knowledge and certain physical components (e.g., appropriate furniture, signs, brochures with instructions). All of these resources of knowledge can be important means for coping with embarrassment. For example, rooms can be designed to enhance or to inhibit interpersonal distancing behaviors (e.g., by room barriers or furniture groupings that provide, to varying degrees, some privacy; cf. Evans, 1979). Because the conception of behavior settings includes physical, social, and behavioral components, it allows a comprehensive analysis of situated learning.

In the proposed model (see Figure 7.4), the behavior setting's control unit as described by Barker (see Figure 7.4) is considered only insofar as it provides inputs to the single individual's control unit and as it receives outputs from the individual's control unit. To describe the model in more detail, I start with a first paragraph of the verbal protocol that was presented at the beginning of this chapter.

(S: 3):
When I walked in I had no idea I was supposed to solve this task. I didn't know too much about the center and how to use it. I was feeling nervous. I looked around the room and went through most of the room. I figured out where everything was. With some experiences from the high school career center, I knew that I needed to write down necessary information about the company. Right away I spotted the job listings. I went to the job listings and started looking for OCTD.

Newcomers entering behavior settings act to direct perceptual explorations that sense and transmit information about behavior settings based on cognitive schemata. For example, if the job application schema is activated in memory, this may thereby become available for use as an internal or cognitive resource of knowledge for a discrepancy-reducing feedback model. The newcomer senses and reconstructs the behavior of one or more inhabitants of the behavior setting.

(S: 3):
When I got to the board, I was wondering if the girl standing there was looking for the same job. So I kept looking up to see what she was doing. Finally, I thought she was doing another task. It took me a while to find the listing and I was wondering if I was looking in the wrong place.

The uncertainties in the newcomer's expressive behavior often make him or her highly salient to the rest of the people present, although some of them are trying to pass through the setting undetected.

(S: 3):
I didn't know what to do next and felt embarrassed when I approached the information desk. I asked the guy at the desk what to do. I felt very stressful because I knew other people were watching me.

The fact that other people in the behavior setting often focus their attention on the newcomer increases his or her level of self-attention (Carver & Scheier, 1981), and impression management concerns arising from that increased self-attention are likely to occur to cope with social embarrassment. The newcomer must make attributions about the kinds of attributions others are making about him or her (Heider, 1958). Thus, the newcomer should first notice, perceive, and interpret others' behavior, and then note discrepancies between his or her action performance and performance ideals and should be motivated to reduce those discrepancies.

(S: 3):

I was embarrassed when I realized that I had to ask more questions. Then when this was happening and I was going back and forth, I realized that I was the "guinea pig" in this place. I had no clue where the job applications were. But I didn't want to look stupid asking questions all the time, since other people were busily working. I felt out of place. Everyone was sitting there watching me, which made me self-conscious. Maybe the people in the room were thinking I was stupid. I felt intimidated by the things around me and didn't want to be stared at when I didn't know what to do. People don't bother me at all, but I could see how some people could get apprehensive in there.

Social forces operating through the behavior setting's operating and maintenance mechanisms and mediated by self-attention processes provide inputs to the newcomer's cognitive control unit.

As also shown in Figure 7.4, the activated cognitive schema then operates as a recognition device whose processing is aimed at testing the schema against the behavior setting's behavioral standards. If a person is familiar with the behavior setting, then he or she seems to act in a loosely preprogrammed, sometimes even mindless way. Newcomers who experience a behavioral standard as discrepant from their cognitive schemata may be surprised or even interrupted in their ongoing actions (cf. Louis, 1980), which causes emotional arousal, such as embarrassment and social anxiety (cf. Edelmann, 1987). These discrepancies trigger the newcomers who actively seek information to make sense of what is going on, to revise the activated cognitive schema, and to plan the action accordingly. Sense making is based on observing the distinctive features of actions of others and by inferring from their expressive behavior the underlying cognitive schema by which their behavior is guided or by asking questions to knowledgeable setting participants to externalize someone else's cognitive schema (cf. Fuhrer, 1990b). The behavior of models not only functions as prompts for similar actions, it also draws the newcomer's attention to the particular objects or places that others favored. Once the newcomer comes to understand the situation – that is, when his or her cognitive schema is appropriately updated – the behavior is matched to the behavior setting's behavioral standard.

The verbal data analyses, for example, indicate that low-prior-knowledge newcomers are more engaged in discrepancy-reducing efforts than high-prior-knowledge newcomers. Moreover, low-prior-knowledge newcomers are more engaged in impression management than high-prior-knowledge newcomers. Prior knowledge obviously made these newcomers more resistant to embarrassment in the presence of others than low-prior-knowledge newcomers. Concerns for impression management are particularly likely to occur (1) when low-prior-knowledge newcomers feel crowded, (2) when others' behavior is interpreted as highly evaluative (i.e., when the confederates are just sitting around the tables), and (3) when the confederate is moving through the sequence of action steps in a professional manner. Information seeking with lower concerns for impression management is particularly likely to occur (1) when the number of confederates is small, (2) when others' presence is interpreted as nonevaluative (i.e., when they are involved in the relevant task), and (3) when those others are seen as incompetent relative to the newcomer.

However, newcomers often encounter obstacles in their attempts to attain goals. Some of these obstacles can be dealt with by continuing both sense making and schema updating, but others constitute sufficient impediments that they render further attempts useless.

(S: 3):
I felt like a running rat in circles in a maze trying to find the cheese that wasn't there. Again, feeling embarrassed. Mostly, I guess I was anxious about not finding the brochure and probably caused me to be anxious throughout the rest of the task.

In response to this basic issue, I have assumed the existence of an evaluation process. This evaluation is induced when the current cognitive schema is discrepant from the behavior setting's behavioral standards and, therefore, action is interrupted by such events as useless efforts on the task causing embarrassment. This evaluation process then influences both the goal of elaborating the cognitive schema and the socially oriented goals of impression management and prompts two subsequent behavioral responses for coping with embarrassment. In the first response, the newcomer returns to further information seeking to match his or her behavior to salient standards and to efforts at discrepancy reduction. These attempts are basically motivated by reaching the task-related goal. In the second response, the newcomer is more socially motivated, that is, attempts to cover up his or her incompetence. The newcomer who then infers that he or she appears inept will become embarrassed and socially anxious, which is associated with the tendency to withdraw from any further attempts to reach the goal. Newcomers either disappear, that is, withdraw physically or, when task-specific or situational constraints prevent overt disengagement, withdraw mentally. This may be reflected in task-irrelevant rumination, a decrease in social interaction, or the like. The results of the verbal data analyses indicate that low-prior-knowledge newcomers showed more mental withdrawal than did high-prior-knowledge newcomers. I assume that these newcomers relied more on observing how others completed the task, which seems to be a less embarrassing way of information seeking (see Wicker, 1983).

The behavioral path analyses showed that crowded newcomers are more often found in peripheral squares than uncrowded newcomers. Moreover, newcomers in the presence of others doing another task went more frequently into the peripheral zone and less often into the central zone than did newcomers who dealt with the behavior setting in the presence of congruent others. This effect was most significant for crowded newcomers. These results are in accord with studies by environmental psychologists (e.g., Evans, 1979), which indicate that placement of activities along a wall helps in coping with crowding. On the one hand, by staying in the peripheral zone one can look at the wall and there a newcomer can reduce eye contact with the other people in the room. On the other hand, the visual stimuli within peripheral zones provide an opportunity for newcomers to engage in alternative nonsocially interactive behaviors (e.g., scanning pictures and job listings) not considered inappropriate by others present. These data indicate how physical and social features of the behavior setting interact and how they mediate, for example, perceived crowding. Crowding then affects embarrassment, which, in turn, has an impact on learning. Basically, these emotions can be taken as indicators of the degree of fit between the newcomer's cognitive schemata and the behavior setting's behavioral standard.

(S: 29):
I stopped in front of the bulletin board looking for the job listing. I couldn't see one, which made me nervous and anxious. I felt totally lost.

Emotions may then determine coping responses to which newcomers switch after the evaluation process. Emotions may switch coping responses either to processes that lead to task-oriented goals of information seeking or – in case of frustration, resignation, and embarrassment – to more socially motivated goals of impression management, such as concealment or even withdrawal. Thus, the present model attempts that situated learning is mainly characterized by building up a cognitive schema of the present behavior-setting program under impression management concerns.

The proposed model is certainly expandable to interpret both actions in behavior settings with multiple or even conflicting standards and actions of individuals who try to deviate from the salient behavioral standards. Newcomers who have to adapt to a behavior setting with multiple standards require multiple cognitive schemata, which have to be updated accordingly. Dealing with conflicting standards might lead to more extensive and repetitive efforts to regulate the most significant domains of the accepted public image, whereas deviants may try to match their behavioral patterns that are different from the accepted salient standards, which, in turn, will activate behavior setting's maintenance mechanisms. Moreover, deviants can sometimes be handled successfully when the responsible setting members change somehow the behavioral standards of the behavior setting and, therefore, tolerate a certain degree of deviance. Thus, the newcomers' actions do not leave the present behavior setting unaffected. Both their individual characteristics and the patterns of their interactions with other inhabitants lead newcomers to construct their own meanings and develop their own styles of carrying out setting programs (e.g., Wicker, 1987; Fuhrer, 1990a).

The proposed multiple-acting model of situated learning raises several important questions for future research, including the following: (1) What personal and setting-related factors affect the salience of newcomers' goals? (2) How might a group of newcomers adapt to a novel behavior setting? (3) What are the architectural features that may funnel the newcomers through behavior settings? (4) Under what conditions do newcomers prefer more offensive than defensive impression management tactics? Also, it seems reasonable to assume that *newcomer* is a relative term. For example, when behavior settings are designed "newcomer friendly," then first-time users do not necessarily look like newcomers, whereas behavior settings that are designed "newcomer unfriendly" put many people into the position of newcomers despite their past experiences with settings of the same type.

Concluding remarks

When I put together all these themes, questions can be raised about transactions between a behavior setting's control unit operating through one or more inhabitants' and a single individual's control unit. It has been argued that the primary link between behavior settings and learning activities is via the newcomers' cognitions of the relation between the various goals and the routes the behavior setting provides. Moreover, situated learning is based, at least in part, on a newcomer's knowledge of the setting program, and it is secured by the behavior setting as the immediate environment. The present model attempts to illuminate the fact that situated learning can be understood as the elaboration of cognitive schemata under impression management concerns and, therefore, situated learning is a consequence of successful coping with embarrassment by using both cognitive means and sociophysical means of the particular behavior setting. Thereby, the model makes it possible to "locate" the production of not learning in complex transactional relations among people in real-life encounters.

In closing, I want to reiterate the major points proposed earlier: Looking at newcomers coping with real-life behavior settings demonstrates that situated learning is the joint product of processing cognitive, social, emotional, and environmental goals. Neither cognitive, nor social, nor emotional, nor ecobehavioral models per se would adequately explain situated learning. Instead, situated learning must be viewed as the coordination of multiple actions or goals. The enforced attention to person–environment systems in understanding situated learning will be costly (theoretically and empirically as well), but ultimately it will benefit us all. Whether or not behavior settings prove to be a fruitful approach to the study of situated learning, they serve at least to test Barker's and his co-workers' unique approach to it and to emphasize the crucial importance of the supra- or extraindividual environment as organized in meaningfully regulated environmental units.

Note

1. *Environmental psychology* is the study of transactions between individuals or groups and their physical, i.e., their built and natural environment (cf. Fuhrer, 1983). The term *ecobehavioral science* is used by Barker and Associates (1978) to refer to "extra-individual studies," i.e., for work with behavior settings. Barker recognized the need for an ecobehavioral science, independent of psychology, which would make field studies of a wider range of phenomena and adapt methods from other social sciences.

References

Altman, I., & Rogoff, B. (1987). World views in psychology: Trait, interactional, organismic, and transactional perspectives. In D. Stokols & I. Altman (Eds.), *Handbook of environmental psychology* (pp. 7–40). New York: Wiley.

Barker, R. G. (1963). On the nature of the environment. *Journal of Social Issues, 19*(4), 17–38.

Barker, R. G. (1968). *Ecological psychology.* Stanford, CA: Stanford University Press.

Barker, R. G. (1987). Prospecting in environmental psychology: Oskaloosa revisited. In D. Stokols & I. Altman (Eds.), *Handbook of environmental psychology* (pp. 1413–1432). New York: Wiley.

Barker, R. G., Wright, B. A., Meyerson, L., & Gonick, M. R. (1953). *Adjustment to physical handicap: A survey of the social psychology of physique and disability.* Bulletin no. 55. New York: Social Science Research Council.

Barker, R. G. & Associates (1978). *Habitats, environments, and human behavior.* San Francisco: Jossey-Bass.

Carver, C. S., & Scheier, M. F. (1981). The self-attention-induced feedback loop and social facilitation. *Journal of Personality and Social Psychology, 17,* 545–568.

Edelmann, R. J. (1987). *The psychology of embarrassment.* New York: Wiley.

Edgerton, R. B. (1967). *The cloak of competence.* Berkeley: University of California Press.

Evans, G. W. (1979). Design implications of spatial research. In J. R. Aiello & A.

Baum (Eds.), *Residential crowding and design* (pp. 197–215). New York: Plenum.

Festinger, L. (1954). A theory of social comparison. *Human Relations, 40,* 427–448.

Fuhrer, U. (1983). Oekopsychologie: Some general implications from a particular literature. *Journal of Environmental Psychology, 3,* 239–252.

Fuhrer, U. (1984). *Mehrfachhandeln in dynamischen Umfeldern* [Multiple-acting in dynamic domains]. Göttingen: Hogrefe.

Fuhrer, U. (1987). Effects of social density and pre-knowledge on question asking in a novel setting. *Journal of Environmental Psychology, 7,* 159–168.

Fuhrer, U. (1988). Learning how to act in behavior settings: The case of newcomers. In H. van Hoogdalem, N. L. Park, T. van der Voordt, & H. van Wegen (Eds.), *Looking back to the future* (pp. 92–97). Delft, Netherlands: Delft University Press.

Fuhrer, U. (1989a). Effects of prior knowledge, crowding, and congruence of subjects' and others' goals on question asking in an unfamiliar setting. *Psychological Reports, 64,* 131–145.

Fuhrer, U. (1989b, September). *Social foundations of knowledge acquisition by question asking.* Paper presented at the First Congress of the Swiss Psychological Association, Bern.

Fuhrer, U. (1990a). Bridging the ecological-psychological gap: Behavior settings as interfaces. *Environment and Behavior, 22,* 518–537.

Fuhrer, U. (1990b). *Handeln-Lernen im Alltag: Neulinge auf Informationssuche in institutionalisiertem Alltagsgeschehen* [Learning how to act in unfamiliar everyday settings]. Bern: Huber.

Garfinkel, H. A. (1963). (1963) A conception of and experiments with "trust" as a condition of concerted stable actions. In O. J. Harvey (Ed.), *Motivation and social interactions* (pp. 52–75). New York: Ronald Press.

Ginsburg, G. P., Brenner, M., & Cranach, M. von (Eds.). (1985). *Discovery strategies in the psychology of action.* New York: Academic Press.

Goffman, I. (1959). *The presentation of self in everyday life.* New York: Doubleday Anchor Books.

Gump, P. V., & Friesen, W. V. (1964). Participation in nonclass settings. In R. G. Barker & P. V. Gump (Eds.), *Big school, small school* (pp. 75–93). Stanford, CA: Stanford University Press.

Heider, F. (1958). *The psychology of interpersonal relations.* New York: Wiley.

Jones, E. E., & Pittman, T. (1982). Toward a general theory of strategic self-presentation. In J. Suls (Ed.), *Psychological perspectives on the self* (Vol. 1, pp. 231–262). Hillsdale, NJ: Lawrence Erlbaum.

Kaminski, G. (Ed.). (1986). *Ordnung und Variabilität im Alltagsgeschehen* [Order and variability in everyday happenings]. Göttingen: Hogrefe.

Kruse, L. (1986). Drehbücher für Verhaltensschauplätze oder: Scripts für Settings. In G. Kaminski (Ed.), *Ordnung und Variabilität im Alltagsgeschehen* [Order and variability in everyday happenings] (pp. 135–153). Göttingen: Hogrefe.

Lang, A. (1992). On the knowledge in things and places. In M. von Cranach,

W. Doise, & G. Mugny (Eds.), *Social representations and the social bases of knowledge* (pp. 112–119). Bern: Huber.

Latané, B. (1980). The psychology of social impact. *American Psychologist, 36,* 343–356.

Lave, J., Murtaugh, M., & de la Rocha, O. (1984). The dialectic of arithmetic in grocery shopping. In B. Rogoff & J. Lave (Eds.), *Everyday cognition* (pp. 67–94). Cambridge, MA: Harvard University Press.

Lazarus, R. S., & Folkman, S. (1987). Transactional theory and research on emotions and coping. *European Journal of Personality, 1,* 141–169.

Louis, M. R. (1980). Surprise and sense-making: What newcomers experience in entering unfamiliar organizational settings. *Administrative Science Quarterly, 25,* 226–251.

Mehan, H., & Rueda, R. (1986). Metacognition and passing: Strategic interactions in the life of learning disabled students. *Anthropology and Education Quarterly, 17*(3), 1–21.

Miller, G. A., Galanter, E., & Pribram, K. H. (1960). *Plans and the structure of behavior.* New York: Holt, Rinehart and Winston.

Moreland, R. L., & Levine, J. M. (1987). Group dynamics over time: Development and socialization in small groups. In J. McGrath (Ed.), *The social psychology of time* (pp. 151–181). Beverly Hills, CA: Sage.

Rogoff, B., & Lave, J. (Eds.). (1984). *Everyday cognition.* Cambridge, MA: Harvard University Press.

Schank, R. C., & Abelson, R. P. (1977). *Scripts, plans, goals, and understanding.* Hillsdale, NJ: Lawrence Erlbaum.

Schlenker, B., & Leary, M. R. (1982). Social anxiety and self-presentation. A conceptualization and model. *Psychological Bulletin, 92,* 641–669.

Schoggen, P. (1989). *Behavior settings: A revision of Barker's ecological psychology.* Stanford, CA: Stanford University Press.

Stokols, D., & Shumaker, S. A. (1981). People in places: A transactional view of settings. In J. H. Harvey (Ed.), *Cognition, social behavior, and environment* (pp. 441–480). Hillsdale, NJ: Lawrence Erlbaum.

Suchman, L. (1987). *Plans and situated actions: The problem of human–machine communication.* Cambridge: Cambridge University Press.

Tedeschi, J. T., Lindskold, S., & Rosenfeld, P. (1985). *Introduction to social psychology.* New York: Academic Press.

VanMaanen, J. (1984). Doing new things in old ways: The chains of socialization. In J. L. Bess (Ed.), *College and university organization* (pp. 211–246). New York: New York University Press.

Wicker, A. W. (1983). *Ecological psychology.* Cambridge: Cambridge University Press.

Wicker, A. W. (1987). Behavior settings reconsidered: Temporal stages, resources, internal dynamics, context. In D. Stokols & I. Altman (Eds.), *Handbook of environmental psychology* (pp. 613–654). New York: Wiley.

Wicker, A. W. (in press). Making sense of environments. In W. B. Walsh, K. H. Craik, & R. H. Price (Eds.), *Person environment psychology.* Hillsdale, NJ: Lawrence Erlbaum.

Wicker, A. W., & King, J. C. (1988). Life cycles of behavior settings. In J. McGrath (Ed.), *The social psychology of time* (pp. 182–200). Beverly Hills, CA: Sage.

Willems, E. P. (1964). Forces toward participation in behavior settings. In R. G. Barker & P. V. Gump (Eds.), *Big school, small school* (pp. 29–37). Stanford, CA: Stanford University Press.

Part III

Learning as social production

8 Examinations reexamined: Certification of students or certification of knowledge?

Steinar Kvale

Examinations are a popular object of criticism. In Scandinavia, the yearly examinations in schools and at universities are accompanied by recurrent public debates over their meaning and value. At student protests the examinations are often a target of critique: They may be dismissed as invalid, the grading as subjective and unreliable, the examination situation artificial and oppressive. The attitude of researchers is reflected in the titles of some publications listed in the references to this chapter (Cox, 1967; Stimpel, 1969; Ingenkamp, 1971; Bourdieu & Passeron, 1971; Kvale, 1972; Miyazaki, 1976): "Resistance to change in examining" (Great Britain); "The irrationality of the examination system at German universities"; "The questionable value of grading" (Germany); "The illusion of equal opportunity" (France); "Examinations and power" (Norway); "China's examination hell."

In spite of broad and well-documented critique, examinations and grading procedures generally remain unchanged. The question to be pursued here concerns whether the critiques of examinations as invalid could possibly be based on an invalid understanding of what is evaluated at examinations. Two conceptions of examinations shall be debated: a predictive test of a student's career versus a constitution and a censorship of knowledge.

215

What is evaluated by examinations – students or knowledge?

*Evaluation of students or of knowledge –
a figure–ground reversal*

To evaluate means to establish the value of something. In order to investigate whether an evaluation is valid, it is necessary to ascertain what is evaluated at an examination and why. An examination is an evaluation of a student's knowledge. This formulation of the topic of examination is, however, ambiguous: Is it the individual student who is being evaluated on the basis of his or her presentation of a discipline's knowledge? Or is it the common knowledge of the discipline that is evaluated through the student's presentation of his or her knowledge?

In Figure 8.1, the ambiguous subject matter of examinations is illustrated by Rubin's figure. The ambiguous figure may be seen as two faces – the interaction of two examiners, or of examiner and student. The figure may also be seen as a vase – in the present context, knowledge. The form remains the same, the meaning is different depending upon what is seen as figure and what as background. The meaning of the same examination form becomes entirely different with the two conceptions of what examinations are about – testing individual students or testing common knowledge.

The two conceptions involve different answers as to how to ascertain the *validity* of a given examination. The form of validation depends on what is investigated and why (cf. Kvale, 1989). In a test context, the what of evaluation is the individual student and the why is the efficient prediction of his future career. In contrast, in the knowledge context, the what of evaluation is the discipline's knowledge, and the why is the constitution of a common true knowledge. The appropriate theoretical contexts for investigating differ correspondingly: test theory and learning theory versus epistemology and sociology of knowledge.

In the present understanding, examinations involve both a selection and certification of students into a profession and the selection and certification of the knowledge of a discipline. The nature of the relation between the two conceptions remains to be analyzed. This

Figure 8.1. A figure–ground understanding of evaluation of student or of knowledge.

involves as well an institutional perspective on the certification of students and knowledge within different professions, as the more general relation of an examination system to the historical development of the contradictions of a society.

The purpose of this chapter is to investigate the explanatory power of a knowledge conception of examination. The necessary qualifications – as validity to different disciplines and educational levels as well as for different national systems of examinations – will not be pursued in the present context. The selection of individual students has received ample emphasis in the examination literature, but a constitution of knowledge through examinations has hardly been mentioned. After a brief overview of research of examinations as tests of individual students, the remaining part of the essay will be confined to a knowledge understanding of examinations.

Examination as a test of individual students

Examination research has, in line with common sense, investigated examinations as tests of individual students (see the references given in the introduction as well as my own earlier discussions of examinations – Kvale, 1972, 1977, 1980 – of which a brief summary follows). Research has focused on the examination understood as a *psychometric* test concerning the legitimate selection of students and the efficient prediction of their careers. Many studies have demonstrated a rather low intersubjective *reliability* for the grading of essays and oral examinations, around 0.60 and 0.30, respectively, whereas the computerized multiple-choice test approaches a perfect reliability of 1.00. There have been fewer investigations of the *validity* of examinations. The predictive validity of grades for later achievements is relatively low: around 0.40 within the educational system, and 0.00–0.10 between final grades and later job success.

The *educational influence* of examinations in guiding and motivating learning has been little investigated. Some studies suggest that the multiple-choice tests may further superficial learning and that learning for grades may lead away from an intrinsically motivated learning to a less efficient, instrumental, motivation (Becker, Geer, & Hughes, 1968; Frederiksen, 1984).

Investigators have attributed the manifest weaknesses of examinations as tests and as educational aids to the weight of tradition, to conservatism, and to resistance to change among teachers. I earlier interpreted the manifest test and educational weaknesses of examinations by more latent *social power functions*. Examinations are a bureaucratic stroke of genius, providing a simple and legitimate selection for privileged educational and occupational positions. While in fact involving a class bias, the sorting by examinations grants an "illusion of chance equality." The importance of selection by grades lends a pressure to the social influence of examinations: a disciplining in school and a socialization to the qualification requirements of the labor market. The learning for grades in school socializes the students to working for wages in occupational life. The historical changes of examinations is related to their social context. The development of ritual through bureaucratic to technological forms of examinations may be traced to the development of a feudal society into a competitive and a monopoly capitalist society (Kvale, 1977).

Relations between the different forms, functions, and contexts of examinations are complex and variable. In the 2,000-year-old Chinese examination system, the minute ranking of the candidates was used in the strict selection of candidates for the higher levels of the educational and governmental hierarchies. In contrast, for the Jesuits – who in the 16th century introduced the 1–6 grading system in European schools – the selection function of grades was mainly symbolical, to honorary positions within the class, as ranking of seat order. The Jesuits used grading explicitly to enhance discipline and diligence through competition for grades.

Different as the functions of examinations may appear, they have one common assumption – they focus on what the examinations do to the individual students.

Examinations as a test of common knowledge

The alternative approach focuses on how examinations may contribute to the constitution of what is the valid knowledge of a discipline. The individual students are here "bracketed" as mere carriers of the knowledge to be evaluated. The focus is on the knowledge evaluated, tested, graded, and certified by the examination as the legitimate knowledge of the discipline.

Constitution of knowledge. An examination is an evaluation of a student's knowledge of a discipline. The common knowledge of a discipline is evaluated by means of the student's pesentation of the knowledge at the examination. In a literal sense, an examination is a test of knowledge, an examination of the value and validity of the discipline's knowledge. In this sense, examinations are a continual assessment of the knowledge of a discipline, a yearly testing and confirmation of the value of the knowledge taught and acquired in a field. A discipline's knowledge is not only transmitted in teaching and checked at examinations; the examination itself contributes to establish the valid knowledge of a discipline. The generally vague definitions of goals of learning and the lack of explicit criteria for evaluation leave large margins for interpretation by the examiners and censors; through their concrete evaluative decisions, they operationally define what is the valid knowledge of a discipline. From the viewpoint of the sociology of knowledge and of cultural reproduction, and of anthropology with its study of rites of passage, examinations may be seen as contributing to "the social construction of reality" (Berger & Luckmann, 1967). The present focus is on the processes by which the institution of examinations contributes to the development, transmission, and maintenance of a discipline's knowledge.

In a knowledge conception of examinations, it is the value of the individual student's knowledge with respect to the discipline that is evaluated, and not with respect to the student's individual career. Validity is no longer established by the statistical correspondence between students' present and future achievements but concerns the truth of the knowledge presented at an examination. The frame of reference for ascertaining validity is the nature of the knowledge of a discipline and of how well an examination measures and furthers true knowledge of the field.

Censorship of meaning. The establishment of what is valid knowledge in a field involves taking a position on what is true or false, right or wrong, and what knowledge is valuable enough to be furthered. A clear position taking on knowledge may, in a liberal society, be rejected as a censorship of meaning. An official religious or political censorship was common in earlier centuries but has with the Enlightenment generally been abolished during peacetime in liberal states. The present issue concerns whether examinations today may function as a form of religious, political, and ideological censorship: Are examinations an official institution controlling what knowledge and opinions are acceptable and which may obtain an official authorization as legitimate knowledge in a discipline?

A linguistic link of examinations and censorship is found in the use of the two terms in the Scandinavian and German languages. In the Scandinavian languages one speaks of *eksamenscensur*, an external examiner is called a *censor*, and examining *censur*. In German the word *Zensur* also means a grade, and *zensieren* the activity of grading.

There exist some reports of examinations functioning as direct censorship of political and religious knowledge. In describing his own study of philosophy, Sartre refers to Marx's statement that the ideas of the ruling class are the dominant ideas. The "Communist students were very careful not to appeal to Marxism or even to mention it in their examinations; had they done so, they would have failed" (1963, p. 17). In the same vein, a Danish theologian, Lindhart, has described how the religious establishment in Denmark and Norway in the late 19th century used examinations as a weapon against the feared radical religious movement of Grundtvig. The examination questions were cleverly formulated and the students who revealed Grundtvigian sympathies were failed. The faculty did not conceal that the motive was dogmatic. And one proceeded in a similar fashion by the "examination" before the appointment of a bishop (see Kvale, 1972).

Today, however, reports of a censorship of knowledge tend to be disclaimed as extreme, atypical cases, and as a misuse of the examination institution. Whereas a censorship of knowledge was legitimate in feudal times, it is today disclaimed as illegitimate in liberal societies adhering to the principle of freedom in speech and thought. Concerning examinations, a first empirical question is whether the freedom of thought expounded in lectures may be undermined by a censorship of meaning at the examination, thus invoking an "illusion of free thought." A second value question concerns whether university censorship of knowledge is necessary and desirable for the transmission of knowledge.

The issue of censorship has received little attention in examination research. In the past few decades there has been a trend to replace the old and somewhat negative terms of *examination, grading,* and *censoring* by the modern concept *evaluation.* As indicated by the word root, the issue of values remains.

Examinations as a test of students and of knowledge

Two conceptions of the subject matter and the purpose of examinations have been presented – a test of individual students versus a constitution of a discipline's common knowledge. The precise nature of their relationship remains to be worked out; here a possible analogy may be found in the older form of the Protestant confirmation ceremony. The young confirmands were examined by the pastor in church and had to document their knowledge of the sacred text and confirm their adherence to the values of the faith. They were then, in turn, confirmed as adult members of society, with the right to work and enter into marriage. The confirmation ritual thus involves both the selection and confirmation of the new recruits to adult status, and their confirmation of the common faith of the community.

An internal relation between personal status and knowledge is indicated by Marx in his somewhat cryptic remarks about examinations in the critique of Hegel's philosophy of law. An examination is a legal recognition of the official knowledge as a privilege; the examination is the objective link between the official position and the individual. "The examination is nothing but the bureaucratic baptism of knowledge, the official recognition of the transubstantiation of profane knowledge into sacred knowledge" (*Marx-Engels Werke*, 1961 I, p. 253).

How is a valid evaluation of knowledge obtained?

The examination committee

The use of examination committees in Scandinavia serves here as a case study of the knowledge-validating function of examinations, with the focus on examination at university levels and mainly within the social sciences and humanities. In the present context the main theme is the interaction between examiners; the examiner–student interaction at examinations requires a separate analysis.

At the Scandinavian universities, the results of several years of study can be evaluated at a single examination, often consisting of 2 days of essays and an ensuing oral examination. The grade level obtained may be the single decisive criterion for entry to more advanced studies. Earlier the oral examination had also been a ceremonial affair, with the candidates expected to appear in a black suit or dress and the situatio being characterized by solemnity and anxiety.

The examination committee consists of one or two faculty members and an external examiner or *censor* who comes from another university or from professional practice. The examiners read and evaluate the papers independently and then meet to make a joint evaluation. Only the final grade is public. This form of committee examination resembles the evaluation committees for dissertations, appointments, and tenure.

The spontaneous comments of examiners and censors after arriving at a common grade may give some indications of the form and the purpose of the proceedings. The following descriptions are based on informal observations and reports, with approximate reconstructions of "typical" remarks. Videotapes of the conversations within an examination committee and systematic interviews with the examiners about the meaning of their work are, to my knowledge, lacking.

First phase – in the examination situation. A comment may be made immediately after arriving at a consensus about a grade: "It was astonishing how much we were in agreement," sometimes with the addition, "and despite the fact that we come from widely different theoretical approaches to the field." The consensus is further confirmed when the censor, not infrequently delayed and slightly agitated, announces the final grades to the waiting students: "We were very much in agreement about the given grades."

Second phase – at the party after the examination. The students may in their teachers' lectures have heard rather conflicting opinions about what is the true scientific knowledge of the discipline. At the examination party some may have gathered courage to question the alleged consensus of the committee. The official facade of consensus may then crack somewhat: "There were, though, a few cases with a certain disagreement; we met with slightly different proposals for a grade, but after some discussion we arrived at full agreement about the final grade."

Third phase – after some drinks. Later in the evening, after a few more glasses, the evaluative consensus may become utterly demolished – "Well, there was once a case. . . ." The examiner then may come up with a long and emotional account of an examination with marked disagreements about the final grade. Such cases tend to be at another institution and some years old. The disagreements may be attributed to a narrowness and stubbornness of a colleague, which may have been so pronounced that the committee had to compute the arithmetic means of the different grade proposals.

A break of confidentiality. If internal disagreements in a committee are made public, there may be issued an official reprimand. At the University of Oslo a grade scale from 1 to 6 is used, with 4–6 as failing grades. Some 20 years ago, an examination committee in the social sciences had the same essay evaluated as 1.3, 2.9, and 3.5 by the three examiners. The disagreement concerned in particular whether the given essay question had been answered at all. After long discussions, with the inclusion of a second essay, the most extreme grades were moderated. In order to reach one common grade the arithmetic mean was computed to 2.4, just barely enough for the minimal requirement of 2.5 for entry into the graduate study.

The internal disagreements, which particularly concerned the position of experimental psychology versus social and clinical psychology, were made public by one of the examiners as a protest against what he considered a gravely unjust evaluation. Together with a related case, this led to the following decree by the Academic Senate:

Discussions within an examination committee are confidential. When a grade has been arrived at, it is not permissible that a member of the committee informs the student that he did not agree with the grade given, or in other ways refers to controversial views which may have been expressed in connection with the censorship.

A teacher must not agree to censure an examination essay unofficially and in a way that the student comes into a legitimate opposition to the official examination committee. It must be quite clear that it cannot be proved that an examination is 100% "just." The examination committee has, though, been charged with the responsibility for the grading and carries out this task according to its best judgment and conviction, taking all aspects into consideration, including a comparison with the achievements of the other candidates. (see Kvale, 1972, p. 114)

An inside view. When questioned in a relaxed setting about the work of the examination committee, an examiner may describe his work as follows. In the censoring meeting, the examiners give their descriptions and evaluations of an essay, suggest a grade, and provide the reasons for their evaluation. There may, in some instances, occur different evaluations of the same essay; one examiner may emphasize aspects of a paper to which the others have given little attention; two examiners may have weighted the dimensions of the answers differently, as, for example, the relative importance of breadth of knowledge versus logic of argumentation. Even if the examiners may have proposed diverging grades, the discussion on the committee involves a reciprocal correction and adjustment of the criteria for evaluation; and the final grade is the result of a genuine consensus about the quality of the knowledge evaluated.

The comments and reactions to differences in evaluations point to the attainment of *a rational consensus among colleagues* as a main goal of an examination committee. It is essential that there is a genuine consensus about the final evaluation of a student's knowledge. The consensus is to be arrived at through a rational discourse about the quality of the knowledge presented; a mechanical computation of an arithmetic means testifies to a breakdown of a rational discourse of the value of the knowledge. The examiners should be loyal colleagues, and internal disagreements should not be made public; they should in union publicly represent the true common knowledge of their discipline.

The tensions between the different views of the work of the examination committees will now be related to a more general tension between the ideal of an uncoerced discourse and a social coercion to consensus.

The uncoerced discourse

Examinations as discourse. The inside view of the evaluation of essays in a committee approaches the hermeneutic interpretation of meaning in the humanities. The purpose is here through a dialogue to arrive at a correct understanding of the meaning of a text and to evaluate the quality of a text within the interpretative tradition of a discipline. The internal description of the evaluation in a committee may approach the ideal description of a discourse given by Habermas (see Bernstein, 1983; Løvlie, 1984). A discourse is characterized by a rational argumentation. The participants are obliged to test statements about truth and falsity of propositions on the basis of argued points of view, and where the best argument wins. The discourse is a form of argumentation where no social exertion of power takes place; the only form of power is the force of the better argument. In this Socratic ideal of a dialogue, all motives beyond a cooperative search for truth are excluded. Habermas's discourse theory of truth implies a continual discourse aiming at universal valid truths as an ideal. Habermas's theory is related to a pragmatic philosophy as developed by Peirce. The emphasis is here on the communal efforts of constituting the social reality, the negotiation of truth within the interpretative community (cf. Polkinghorne, 1983).

The work of an examination committee may be seen as a negotiation of true knowledge in a discipline. The committee serves as representative of the interpretative community, continually assessing the validity of a discipline's knowledge. The committees are faced with the task of maintaining and renewing the traditional body of knowledge, deciding what new lines of thought are to be included in the discipline and what is to be rejected.

The description of an examination committee as negotiating what is true knowledge in a field may appear somewhat exaggerated. The routine of evaluation appears more commonplace, as a check of whether the basic concepts, methods, and data of the discipline are presented convincingly in the examination paper. Fundamental epistemological disputes are not typically considered part of the standard evaluation activities.

Evaluation, metaevaluation, and censorship. A distinction between evaluation and metaevaluation may here be appropriate. *Evaluation* is used to refer to the process of ascertaining the worth of a student's knowledge in relation to a given frame of reference and common value context. *Metaevaluation* refers to the evaluation of the frame of reference itself, when the concept of valid knowledge in a discipline is at stake. In other words: How is the validity of those values that provide the common frame of reference for evaluating students' knowledge established?

The negotiation about new and valid knowledge usually takes place indirectly in the discussion of the value of the candidate's presentation of the new knowledge. Concurrent with the direct evaluation of the individual students, there takes place a metaevaluation of the discipline's common knowledge. In normal stable periods of a discipline, the metaevaluative aspect of an examination is hardly visible. In times of radical, paradigmatic changes in knowledge, when the traditional values of a discipline are challenged, a metaevaluative function of examinations may become visible, because of the necessity of defining the limits of a discipline, of establishing the core concepts, methods, and data. During periods when a discipline simultaneously contains incommensurate frames of reference, a set of common standards has to be worked out anew in order to obtain unitary evaluations of the students' knowledge.

In recent decades, within the *discipline of psychology* in Scandinavia, there have been controversies over whether psychoanalytic, critical, and Marxist thought may be included in a scientific psychology. In given periods and departments, students who believed the works of Freud, Habermas, and Marx were relevant for psychology may have refrained from mentioning it in their examination papers, and some were failed when they tried to integrate these outside theories into psychology. It is sometimes independent students with previous excellent levels of achievement who suddenly fail when bringing new conceptions into the discipline in their examination papers. The examiners' comments to these examinations that extend the field by bringing in new interpretations may be "The essay falls outside the given task," or "The meaning of the essay question has been misunderstood."

In such cases where the examiner's metaevaluation of the discipline is apparent, there may be accusations of a censorship of meaning, sometimes accompanied by strong emotional and personal conflicts – between students and examiners, or between examiners. The basic issue is experienced as an attempt to invalidate the true knowledge standards of one's field rather than the particular grade assigned to a student. A few years later it may happen that the previously unacceptable theories become incorporated into the mainstream of the field. In Denmark, psychoanalysis, critical theory, and Marxism were controversial before 1968 but have since marched the long way through the examination system, now to be generally accepted as legitimate ways of understanding in the social sciences.

Not every candidate who fails is politically persecuted or an unrecognized genius. The controversial censorship cases are statistical exceptions; from the present viewpoint, however, they are the deviant cases, the crisis in communication, that make visible the ordinarily overlooked knowledge-constituting functions of examinations, the marking of the boundaries of a discipline's territory. The censorship cases invoke a metaevaluation, where the value frames for evaluating an essay are at stake. It should, though, not be overlooked that the many routine evaluations also involve a metaevaluation – here an implicit acceptance and certification of the knowledge passed at the examinations.

The coercion to consensus

A scientific discourse is, in principle, indefinite. There is no requirement of immediate action. There may always come new arguments that may alter or invalidate earlier knowledge. The examination discourse is, on the contrary, subject to the force of action – a definite decision about the value of an essay has to be made within a given time limit, and once given, the grade is irreversible.

The force of the better argument is not always sufficient to obtain a genuine consensus about the value of an examination essay. External social constraints may be necessary to arrive at a final consensus. The formal rules require unanimous consensus when signing the examination protocol; there is no room for a minority opinion about the grade given. The examination meeting is usually conducted with a time pressure; agreement about the grades for a number of candidates has to be reached within a given time limit, and the pressure may be augmented by the anxious candidates waiting outside the door to hear the final grade verdict. There is also subtle pressure toward being a good colleague: It is not well to be seen as one-sided and stubborn.

Going beyond the ideal discourse of rational arguments, the social context may lead to drawing in extraneous factors and entering into social bargains. When in doubt about whether to let a candidate pass, a final argument may take the following form: "Well, his understanding of the basic concepts of the field leaves much to be desired, and retaking the exam will hardly lead anywhere – he may though become a good practitioner, so let him pass." Such an inclusion of the predictive dimension by a final evaluation is, however, not considered an officially legitimate argument. A recourse to arithmetic means of the grade proposals when the discourse breaks down is only a last refuge. Implicit or explicit compromises across candidates may take place – "You had your way with the grade of the last candidate; now it should be you who gives in." Deliberate bargaining tactics to get one's own students through with a high grade may take place but are disapproved of as foul play. Although tactical bargaining is part of the game in the political and economic sphere, for example, by labor unions' and employers' deals on wage increases, a deliberate bargaining is illegitimate when evaluating the truth of a knowledge claim at an examination. Truth is negotiated, not bargained.

The discussion in an examination committee may be a blend of two forms of arguments, or of two language games: an ideal discourse aiming at truth and a social bargaining toward consensus and/or of enforcing one's own viewpoint. The discussions may involve a delicate balance of a rational discourse and a socially determined rhetoric. There is the tension between a principally open and endless scientific discourse about true knowledge, and the practical necessity of action, of reaching a definite and irrevocable shared consensus about the value of an essay – the grade. The social coercion of examinations to arrive at a working consensus about what is valid knowledge may contribute to a disciplinary unity in a field. The examinations of knowledge counteract a social and intellectual anarchy where all conceptions are considered equally valid.

Examination issues reexamined

Some consequences of a reinterpretation of the subject matter and purpose of examinations – from individual student prediction to common knowledge constitution – can now be spelled out. Thus, some of the many disputes about form and procedures of examinations and grading, which may appear bizarre from a psychometric point of view, may become understandable when examinations are seen as an institution of knowledge constitution.

The examination candidates as sacrificial lambs

Within a conception of examinations as knowledge constituting and meaning censoring, the individual student recedes into the background. The candidates are merely side figures, the supporting cast of the play, who bring forth knowledge for the yearly testing and confirmation of what is the valid knowledge of the discipline. The purpose of the examination is to maintain the traditional knowledge of the discipline, to delimit its boundaries, and, less often noticed, to incorporate new developments into the authorized body of knowledge.

A parallel to a restitutive understanding of the practice of law may be suggested. Here, the criminal and his trial are seen as necessary to maintain the respect for the law; the purpose of the trial is to protect the law against any challenge or offense. The validity of the verdict of the individual criminal being guilty or not guilty recedes in the background. What matters is to uphold and maintain the law as a defense against anarchy and chaos.

In the continual task of knowledge maintenance and meaning stabilization, the individual candidates are mere pawns. They are sometimes sacrificed in the faculty's socially necessary trial of maintaining and renewing the definition of the valid knowledge of the interpretative community. In internal faculty disputes about the true valid scientific knowledge of the discipline, the students are the ones to be offered. The candidates for the examinations are the yearly lambs, some of whom have to be sacrificed at the examination table, in order to maintain the socially necessary common knowledge.

Grades as predictors or as rewards

The selection of students for educational and occupational privileges is generally assumed to rest on an assumption of the efficiency of grades as predictors of future achievements. When grades, despite their documented low predictive efficiency, continue to be used as selection criteria, this may be due to their earlier mentioned bureaucratic simplicity and legitimacy.

In a knowledge-constituting conception of examinations, high grades are rewards for those students who have given the most true and valid presentations of the discipline's knowledge. The grades are then not predictors, but rewarding devices, a reward for those students who have best succeeded in approximating the true absolute knowledge of the discipline. Correspondingly, low grades are punishments for not presenting the true knowledge, of not giving it due respect. The access by grades to educational and occupational privileges may function as "back up reinforcers" of the "token grades"; the main issue is rewarding the desired examination behavior most closely approximating, and confirming allegiance to, the true knowledge.

The use of grades by selection to higher privileges does not then take place due to predictive efficiency, but as rewards for – and a pressure to give – due service to the scholarly community in fostering the ideals of true knowledge. The bottleneck of selection provides the impetus for enforcing the correct knowledge of the discipline.

The artificiality of examinations

A common complaint about examinations is that the examination situation is artificial – that is, the content and form of the examination tasks have little relevance for future work performance. To apply a recent concept: Examinations have little ecological validity.

In a knowledge-constitutive understanding of examinations, this critique is beside the point. The similarity of the examination situation to later job situations is irrelevant when the function of the examination is the constitution of a consensually valid understanding of the discipline's knowledge.

Consensus – a starting point or a goal?

Examination research has documented an often low reliability of grading. Within a *positivist* conception, knowledge consists of objective facts, and a low intersubjective reliability in grading is then due to subjectivity and error by the examiners.

Within a *hermeneutic* understanding, knowledge is manifold and its meaning must be interpreted. The goal is, through a rational discourse, to arrive at a consensus about the meaning of a text. Initial differences among examiners about the value of an essay need then not be something subjective and negative. It is rather a positive accomplishment that an examination committee is able to, with the subtleties and ambiguities of knowledge, to arrive at a final consensus about the value of an essay. Different evaluations of an essay are not something to be lamented, but a challenge to be overcome.

Although discrepant evaluations tend to be downplayed by examinations, they are generally recognized and considered more legitimate in the evaluation of dissertations, appointments, and tenure decisions. Here it may appear absurd to compute correlations of interrater reliability; the task more visibly also involves taking a position on what is valuable knowledge that should be promoted in a field.

Curriculum plans, taxonomies of knowledge, and the teaching process may clarify the goals of learning and the valid knowledge in a field. It is, however, the examiners through their evaluation decisions who make the decisive operational definitions of the valid knowledge of the discipline.

Differentiation of grades and preciseness of knowledge

Given the often low reliability of grading, a final evaluation of an essay on a one-dimensional scale, even with decimals, may involve a pseudoexactness.

From a conception of evaluation as a constitution of knowledge, a finely differentiated grading scale may contribute to a preciseness of knowledge. If the task of an examination committee is merely to make a pass – fail decision, the conception of the knowledge at the basis of the evaluative decision need not be particularly precise. If the task is, however, to arrive at a consensus about the position of an essay on a finely differentiated scale of quality, this requires precise and intersubjective concepts of valid knowledge. A finely differentiated grading scale may contribute to the development of precise and consensually valid knowledge in a discipline.

The legal profession has generally strict and differentiated evaluation procedures. This has earlier been interpreted as indicating a necessity of establishing discipline, loyalty, and rank order within the legal profession (see Kvale, 1972). From the present knowledge conception, the strict evaluative differentiation by the examinations of law involves a coercion toward establishing precise and consensual interpretations of the legal texts.

Power is knowledge

In lectures, students are taught that knowledge is power. At examinations they learn that power is knowledge. The examination committee defines for the students what is valid and legitimate knowledge in a field. The examinations provide an operational definition of valid understanding of the social reality, a definition that may be dangerous to contest for a student. He may be tempted to rephrase a Socratic question for the examination: Do the examiners represent a given conception of knowledge because it is true, or is the knowledge true because it is represented by the examiners?

The knowledge of a discipline is not constituted solely by examinations. The production and verification of knowledge takes place in scientific research, professional practice, and public debates. The earth will not become flat, nor stand still, if an examination committee should decide so. It is, however, the examiners who decide the locally valid and legitimate knowledge, the understanding of science the students will pledge allegiance to before they are allowed, through the examination, to enter the profession.

The exertion of power through examinations thus goes beyond the social selection and disciplining of students to also encompass selection and certification of a discipline's knowledge. The latter again involves the tension between a quest for true knowledge and an ideological mystification of a subject matter with socially oppressive consequences.

The question of alternatives

A critique of examinations is often met with a question, What is the alternative? The counterquestion is, Alternative to what? The present figure–ground reversal of the what and why of examinations – from individual career prediction to a common knowledge constitution – implies rather different answers to the alternative question. The practical consequences of the two conceptions can be illustrated by some extreme versions.

Refinement of examinations as a psychometric test. The reliability of grading may be improved by introducing mandatory courses in evaluation techniques and measurement scales for the examiners, and by monitoring statistically their grade means and dispersions. If the purpose is to increase the predictive efficiency of selection to future education, different psychological tests may be added to the grades, to a composite battery, to be developed in a similar way as the test batteries constructed for predicting the success of airplane pilots. And according to research on selection (Bowles & Gintis, 1976), an inclusion of the parents' level of income in the battery would increase the predictive efficiency for success in higher education. An increase in the efficiency of selection through such an open class bias would here clash with the legitimacy of a selection based on the notion of chance equality.

Refinement of examinations as a censorship of meaning. Drastic alternatives to a censorship function of examinations in defining legitimate knowledge would be the religious inquisition and processes against heretics and witches in earlier centuries and the processes against political heresy in recent times. In modern liberal societies a repressive tolerance with sophisticated ideological control has replaced open censorship of meaning (cf. Chomsky, 1977). Within education indirect techniques such as differential financial support and psychological counseling are less visible and resistance-provoking forms of knowledge control than an open censorship of meaning.

The answer to the question of alternatives to the present forms of examinations will thus be rather different for a career prediction and for a knowledge-constituting purpose of examination.

Changes in knowledge and examinations

In this section the explanatory potential of a knowledge conception of examinations is investigated in a sociohistorical context. Some current reforms of examinations are discussed on the basis of an understanding of examinations as reflecting and constituting valid knowledge in a discipline. It is thus possible that the opposition of some teachers to the current technological and humanist reforms of examinations may be based on a knowledge conception of examinations, which has been unrecognized by the psychometric and humanist reformers themselves. They may, therefore, be mistaken in attributing such opposition to a mere traditionalism or irrational resistance.

Crisis of legitimation

In current society, knowledge and values are subject to a crisis of legitimacy; the validity and authority of traditional standards are dissolving. This concerns social knowledge and values at large, and in many university disciplines there is a lack of consensus about what constitutes valid and basic knowledge. The traditional body of knowledge – the basic concepts, methods, and data – is no longer taken for granted.

With a crisis in values and knowledge, and with some disciplines being a mixture of relativism and local dogmatism, it becomes difficult to maintain a common rational discourse. A reciprocal argumentation about true and false knowledge is irrelevant in the milieu of both a relativist indifference to the issue of truth and falsity and a dogmatic clinging to a truth beyond questioning.

Examination reforms and knowledge crisis

Evaluation of knowledge is difficult when the legitimacy of common values and standards has become critical. In Figure 8.2 three forms of examinations are depicted as reactions to a general crisis of establishing valid knowledge – authoritarian, technological, and humanistic. Common to the formally rather different examinations is a lack of discourse; they do not further a discourse about knowledge, neither in the horizontal dimension between examiners nor in the vertical dimension between examiners and candidates. A brief, simplified, description of the three forms of examinations is given here, highlighting their relationship to the conception and constitution of the knowledge of a discipline.

The authoritarian examinations. One reaction toward a crisis in knowledge is turning back to tradition. The "back to the basics" may involve the enforcement of strict traditional forms of examination. A rational discourse between examiners, and ideally between examiners and candidates such as the public dissertation dispute, may relapse into a purely formal exercise of authority. And when the knowledge examined is no longer accepted as legitimate and author-

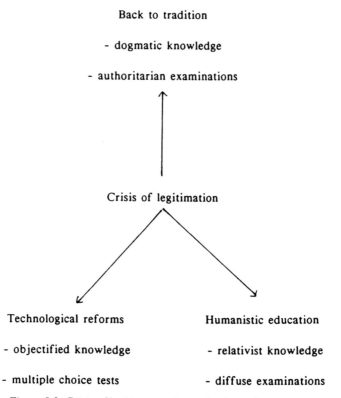

Figure 8.2. Crisis of legitimacy and examination reforms.

itative, the exercise of authority at the examination becomes authoritarian.

The knowledge constituted by the authoritarian examinations is dogmatic. It is true because it stems from tradition and is taught by an authority. A critical examination of the knowledge taught is irrelevant or undesirable. A discourse on what is true and false, a philosophical questioning of the validity of the foundation of a discipline is replaced by an enforcement, and a loyal acceptance, of the knowledge authorized by tradition.

Technological multiple-choice tests. The validity of the knowledge tested also appears unproblematic for the reforms of examinations. The tests assume that knowledge consists of isolated facts and logical rules for combining the facts. This conception reflects a logical empiricist philosophy of knowledge and it is well suited to the current computerization of knowledge. The question of valid examinations has become a question of measuring techniques, of reliable and efficient techniques for measuring the existing objective body of knowledge.

The multiple-choice test is a central device. Knowledge tends to become decontextualized into atomistic data and formal rules of combination. The questions are to be answered as true or false, not allowing for the complexity and ambiguity of knowledge. The formulation of the questions and of the true and false answers is generally made by distant experts in test bureaus; they alone decide what is valid knowledge, with little possibility of questioning or discussion. The evaluation is computerized, again leaving out any possibility of discourse. There is a growing empirical evidence that the emphasis on multiple-choice examinations may lead to a superficialization of the knowledge taught and acquired, emphasizing memory of factual knowledge rather than more complex cognitive processes (Frederiksen, 1984).

The conception of knowledge furthered by the standardized multiple-choice examinations is objectivistic; knowledge is either true or false. Knowledge consists of answering the questions of others, not of questioning the knowledge itself.

The humanistic open evaluation. In the "humanized" open and often diffuse examinations, the quest for valid knowledge has also been diminished. The diffuse examinations are legitimated by a humanistic and a therapeutic psychology, where the students' personal development and self-realization is central. Teaching and evaluation are based on a therapeutically conceived dialogue, characterized by positive emotions and freedom from anxiety. Formal examinations are regarded as externally required bureaucratic formalities, with no intrinsic educational value.

The humanistic diffuse evaluation has a variety of forms. The topic and the question for the examination may be chosen by the student himself, sometimes also the examiner. The essay may be written at home, both preparation of a paper and the oral examinations may take place in groups, and the grading on a scale is replaced by a pass–fail decision. Evaluation of the knowledge product of a student's learning is deemphasized to the advantage of an evaluation of the learning process, and with a change from teacher's evaluation to a self-evaluation as an ideal. The importance of the formal examination situation is downplayed and replaced by informal counseling and supervision during the learning process. The requirements of formally appointed external examiners, or censors, are relaxed, whereby the likelihood of open disputes over the validity of knowledge is reduced.

The knowledge constituted by the humanistic diffuse examinations is subjectivistic – the search for true knowledge is subordinated to the development of the person; knowledge is a means for the self-realization of the individual student. The question of valid knowledge has become irrelevant, knowledge is relativistic, the world consists of multiple realities with no necessity of finding out whether one reality is truer than another.

A discourse ideal of examinations. Three current trends of examination reforms have been depicted as involving dogmatic, objectivist, and relativist conceptions of knowledge. For limited areas the described reforms may be valid tests of knowledge, as the technological forms of testing factual information and logical relations, and the humanistic examinations as testing professional–client interaction. They do, though, not allow an open discourse on the validity of the knowledge tested.

In contrast, the examination committees described earlier entail in principle the possibility of approximating the ideal of a discourse on valid knowledge. The public defense of a dissertation is, despite the obvious power relations and the ritual form, probably the closest that an examination comes to an ideal discourse, aiming at a convincing consensus about valid knowledge. There is an open dispute about the truth value of the candidate's thesis, and the candidate argues and defends his knowledge claims in the public dispute, answering the critical claims of his official opponents and also of possible "ex auditory" opponents from the public. The often tough public argumentation at the defense of a dissertation approaches the ideal of a discourse where the only force is that of the better argument.

Examination as a public discourse on the validity of the knowledge taught and tested is obviously a border case. It may though serve as a guiding ideal for the educational evaluation of knowledge. In addition to the many practical constraints of a discourse conception of educational evaluation, there is the issue of whether it is possible in a society permeated by a crisis of legitimacy of knowledge and values to maintain educational evaluation of knowledge as a public discourse.

Conclusion

Understanding and changing the forms of evaluation require an understanding of what is evaluated at examinations. Two conceptions of the subject matter of examinations have been put forth here – certification of individual students versus certification of a discipline's common knowledge. The emphasis in the present essay has been – in contrast to the common view – upon examinations as an institution contributing to the constitution of the knowledge of a discipline. The explanatory power of a knowledge conception of examinations was tested in a reinterpretation of some of the many apparent contradictions and paradoxes of examinations; the knowledge conception was further applied in an interpretation of current changes in evaluation – authoritarian, technological, and humanistic – as reactions to a crisis in the legitimation of knowledge. An ideal of examination as a public discourse on valid knowledge was introduced.

According to the present analysis, the forms of examination reflect the conception of knowledge to be promoted in different societies. And current changes of examinations reflect broader historical changes in conception of knowledge. Theory of knowledge and of value is basic to a theory of evaluation. The kind of knowledge to be promoted becomes the criterion for judging specific forms of examinations, of how they sample and further the knowledge goals of education. The knowledge-constitution conception of examinations has here been presented in general form, its explanatory potential needs to be tested out specifically with respect to different disciplines. On a theoretical level the relation of examinations as both a certification of individual students and of common knowledge needs to be worked out, as well as the knowledge-constituting role of examination in relation to other forms of constituting the knowledge of a discipline, such as scientific research, professional practice, and public discourse.

References

Becker, H., Geer, B., & Hughes, F. (1968). *Making the grade.* New York: Wiley.

Berger, P. L., & Luckmann, T. (1967). *The social construction of reality.* New York: Doubleday.

Bernstein, R. J. (1983). *Beyond objectivism and relativism.* Philadelphia: University of Pennsylvania Press.

Bourdieu P., & Passeron, J.-C. (1971). *Die Illusion der Chancengleickeit* [The illusion of equal opportunity]. Stuttgart: Ernst Klett.

Bowles, S., & Gintis, H. (1976). *Schooling in capitalist America.* London: Routledge and Kegan Paul.

Chomsky, N. (1977). *Language and responsibility.* New York: Pantheon.

Cox, R. (1967). Resistance to change in examining. *Universities Quarterly, 21,* 352–358.

Frederiksen, N. (1984). The real test bias: Influences on teaching and learning. *American Psychologist, 39,* 193–202.

Ingenkamp, H. (Ed.). (1971). *Die Fragwürdigkeit der Zensurengebung* [The questionable value of grading]. Weinheim: Beltz.

Kvale, S. (1972). *Prüfung und Herrschaft* [Examinations and power]. Weinheim: Beltz.

Kvale, S. (1977). Examinations: From ritual through bureaucracy to technology. *Social Praxis, 3,* 197–206.

Kvale, S. (1980). *Spillet om karakterer i gymnasiet – elevinterviews om bivirkninger af adgangsbegrænsning* [The grading game in high school – Interviews with pupils on the side effects of grading]. Copenhagen: Munksgaard.

Kvale, S. (1989). To validate is to question. In S. Kvale (Ed.), *Issues of validity in qualitative research* (pp. 73–92). Lund: Studentlitteratur.

Løvlie, L. (1984). *Det pedagogiske argument* [The pedagogical argument]. Oslo: Cappelen.

Marx-Engels Werke (Vol. 1). (1961). Berlin: Dietz Verlag.

Miyazaki, I. (1976). *China's examination hell.* New York: Weatherhill.

Polkinghorne, D. E. (1983). *Methodology for the human sciences.* Albany: State University of New York Press.

Sartre, J.-P. (1963). *The problem of method.* London: Methuen.

Stimpel, H.-M. (1969). Die Unvernunft des Prüfungswesens an deutschen Hochschulen [The irrationality of the examination system at German universities]. *Blickpunkt-Hockschuldidaktik, 1,* 67–73.

9   Beneath the skin and between the ears: A case study in the politics of representation

Hugh Mehan

Constructing social facts: Clarity from ambiguity

Events in the world are ambiguous. We struggle to understand these events, to embue them with meaning. The choice of a particular way of representing events gives them a particular meaning. There is often a competition over the correct, appropriate, or preferred way of representing objects, events, or people. In fact, although there are many possible modes of representing the world and communicating them to people, the course of history can be envisioned as successive attempts to impose one mode of representation upon another.

Proponents of various positions in conflicts waged in and through discourse attempt to capture or dominate modes of representation. They do so in a variety of ways, including inviting or persuading others to join their side, or silencing opponents by attacking their positions. If successful, a hierarchy is formed, in which one mode of representing the world (its objects, events, people, etc.) gains primacy over others, transforming modes of representation from an array on a horizontal plane to a ranking on a vertical plane. This competition over the meaning of ambiguous events, people, and objects in the world has been called the "politics of representation" (Holquist, 1983; Shapiro, 1987; Mehan & Wills, 1988; Mehan, 1989).

For example, there are many ways in which nonresident laborers can be represented: "guest workers," "potential citizens," "illegal aliens," "undocumented workers." Each formulation or way of representing this group of people does not simply reflect its characteris-

The comments Candace West, Jean Lave, and Seth Chaiklin made on an earlier draft were very helpful and improved the quality of the chapter considerably.

tics. Each mode of representation defines the person making the representation and constitutes the group of people, and does so in a different way. To be a GUEST worker is to be an invited person, someone who is welcome and in a positive relationship to the employer; to be a guest WORKER is to be someone who is contributing to the economy, productively, by laboring. The formulation: POTENTIAL CITIZEN invokes similar positive connotations. It does so within the realm of citizenship and politics, however, rather than in the realm of market economics, as the guest worker formulation does. The "potential citizen" is not yet a complete citizen, but is on the path of full participation in the society. The ILLEGAL ALIEN designation invokes many opposite ways of thinking. "Illegal" is simple and clear: a person outside of society, an idea reinforced by the "alien" designation – foreign, repulsive, threatening. Finally, representing this group as UNDOCUMENTED WORKERS implies a person or persons who contribute economically, but do so in an extralegal capacity.

So, too, a recent "surrogate mother case" illustrates that a newborn baby is subject to multiple and competing interpretations. The case turned on the issue of whether the baby's mother had the right to retain her after she had agreed to give her over to the (artificially inseminating) father. Those who favored her right to do so resisted the use of the "surrogate mother" term in favor of the "natural mother" designation. They drew the analogy between the surrogate mother case and disputes over adoption or custody after divorce. This language portrays custody as an issue involving interpersonal relationships and commitments involving parents and children. Those who favored the (artificially inseminating) father's claim to the child (and therefore opposed the "surrogate" mother) invoked language associated with contracts and legally binding arguments. This mode of representation led one commentator to say "it made the Baby M case bear an uncanny resemblance to 'the all sales final style of the used car lot' " (Pollitt, 1987, p. 682).

A similar competition over the meaning of a group is played out in schools every day when educators try to decide whether a certain child is "normal" or "deviant," belongs in a "regular educational program" or in a "special education program." Deciding whether students are "normal" or "special" is a practical project that occurs routinely in U.S. schools. Although this activity is as old as schools themselves, in response to recently enacted state and federal legislation this classification and sorting activity has become more formalized. There are now procedures mandated by law, especially PL 94-142, "The Education for All Handicapped Students Act," concerning the referral of students to special education. This law, established to provide an equitable education to handicapped youngsters in the least restrictive environment possible, imposes time limits for the assessment of students and specifies the participants involved in decision making. For example, final placement decisions are to be made by a committee composed of the student's teacher, a school psychologist, a representative from the district office, the child's parents, and, in some cases, a medical official.

In general, I am interested in how the clarity of social facts such as "intelligence," "deviance," "health," or "illness" are produced from the ambiguity of everyday life. In the work described in this chapter, I concentrate on a particular instantiation of that general interest – the production of student identities. In short, I am asking: How are student identities produced? How does a student become a "special education" or a "regular education" student?

This line of questioning places my investigation in the "social constructionist" tradition of research, which is concerned with the ways in which the stable and enduring features of our everyday world are assembled through historical processes and in concrete social settings. The constructivist is interested in how the stable features of social institutions such as schooling (e.g., Mehan, Hertweck, & Meihls, 1986; McDermott et al., 1978, and this volume; Erickson & Shultz, 1982; Levine, this volume), science (e.g., Latour & Woolgar, 1986; Knorr-Cetina, 1981), medicine (e.g., Cicourel, 1981; Fisher & Todd, 1983; West, 1984), politics (e.g., Nathanson, 1984, 1987; Mehan & Wills, 1988), and the family (e.g., Laing, 1967; Pollner & McDonald-Wikler, 1985; Gordon, 1988) are both generated in and revealed by the language of the institution's participants.

In this line of work, people's everyday practices are examined for the way in which they exhibit, indeed, generate, the social structures of the relevant domain. The notion of structures is meant in a Durkheimian sense, that is, they are "external to and constraining upon" the immediate social situation (Durkheim, 1895/1950). In addition, they are not subject to change as an act of will or volition by individuals (Garfinkel & Sacks, 1970). Furthermore, the structures must be more than an analytic device of the researcher. Inferences about social structure are permissible only when the workings of the structure can be located in people's interaction.

A social fact of the school system: Handicapped students

In order to understand the process by which students are considered for placement in one of a number of special education programs or are retained in regular classrooms, we (Mehan et al., 1986) followed the progress of students' cases through the special education referral process mandated by federal law (PL 94-142). During the 1978–1979 school year in which my colleagues and I observed this sorting and classification process in a midsize school district in southern California, 141 students out of a total school population of 2,700 students were referred for "special education"; 53 of these cases were considered by the committee with responsibility for final placement decisions. Most (38) of the students considered by the "eligibility and placement" (E&P) committees were placed into the "learning disabilities" (LD) program (a "pullout" education program in which students spend a part of their school day in their regular classroom and the other part of the day in a special classroom), and 7 were placed in the "educationally handicapped" (EH) program (a program in which students spend all of their school day in a special classroom). Notably, no students were placed in special programs outside the district and only 1 student considered by the committee was retained in his regular classroom.

These figures, which represent the aggregate number of students placed into educational programs, would conventionally be accepted as an example of a "social fact." Furthermore, each number represents a point in a student's educational career, that is, his or her identity as a "special education" or a "regular education" student. Hence, we have two senses of social structure here: one represented as aggregate data, the other represented as social identities.

Given this statistical distribution, I am asking: What practices produce this array, these careers, these identities? In answering this question, I propose to show that these "social facts" of the school system are constructed in the practical work of educators in their person-to-person and person-to-text interaction. In the analysis that follows, I explore a way of showing how the routine practices of educators as they carry out their daily work construct a "handicapped" student by tracing one student's case through the special education referral process. The major steps in this process are "referral," "educational testing," and "placement decision."

In order to uncover the discursive and organizational arrangements that create descriptions of students as handicapped, my colleagues and I employed an interconnected set of research methods. In addition to observing in classrooms, teachers' lounges, testing rooms, and committee meetings, we interviewed educators and parents, reviewed students' records, and videotaped events that were crucial in the construction of students' identities. Students' records provided such baseline data as the age, sex, and grade of students, the official reason for referral, the name of the person making the referral, the date of referral, psychological assessment information, and final disposition of cases. Information available from school records was checked against information that became available to us through observation, videotaping, informal discussions, and more formal interviews with educators in the district.

Observations in classrooms and analysis of lessons videotaped there gave us insight into the reasons teachers referred students and the relationship between teachers' accounts of student behavior and students' classroom behavior. Videotape of educational testing sessions and Eligibility and Placement Committee meetings served as the behavioral record we examined for the educators' sorting and classifying practices. It also served as a multipurpose document for interviews with participants in these key events in the referral process.

Constructing an LD student: The case of Shane

We discovered, upon the analysis of the materials gathered by these diverse research techniques, that the student classification process in the Coast District had a number of components. The schools' work of sorting students most frequently started in the

classroom, continued through psychological assessment, and culmi-
nated in evaluation by the E&P Committee. Thus, as Collins (1981)
suggested, a "social structure" – the aggregate number of students
in various educational programs or their identity as "special" or
"regular" students – was generated in a sequence of organizationally
predictable interactional events (classroom, testing session, meetings).

An important feature of this process is the transformation of discourse into texts. Discourse from one setting in the sequence of
events in the referral process becomes the text used for discussion in
the next session. So, for example, after a teacher and students interact in the classroom (discourse), the teacher fills out a form (text).
That text is introduced into the discourse of the School Appraisal
Team (SAT) meeting. From the discourse of the participants in that
meeting, another piece of text is generated, this time a "summary of
recommendation," which instructs the school psychologist to begin
educational testing. The administration of the educational test tran-
spires as face-to-face interaction between tester and student. Based
on that discourse, the tester writes a report. That text is sent to the
placement committee, where it becomes part of the file, which,
representing the child, becomes the basis of the final placement
decision. Such texts, generated from a particular event in the se-
quential process (e.g., a testing encounter), become the basis of the
interaction in the next step in the sequence (e.g., a placement committee meeting). These texts become divorced from the social interaction that created them as they move through the system, institutionally isolated from the interactional practices that generated them
in the preceding events.

Step 1: Calling for help

The process by which a child becomes "educationally handicapped" usually begins in the classroom when, for whatever reasons,
a teacher refers a child by completing a referral form. Completing
the form and making the referral do not automatically make the child
LD or educationally handicapped; but unless that bureaucratic step
is taken, the child cannot be eligible to achieve that status. On
October 10, approximately 1 month after the start of school, the

fourth-grade teacher at the Desert Vista School referred "Shane" for possible placement in special education for his "low academic performance" and his "difficulty in applying himself to his daily class work."[1]

In order to gain more insight into the teachers' reasons for referring students than was available on official referral forms, we videotaped classroom lessons and viewed them with the teachers. Following guidelines concerning these "viewing sessions" that have proved productive in the past (e.g., Cicourel et al., 1974; Erickson & Shultz, 1982), teachers were asked to "stop the tape any time they found anything interesting happening." While watching a videotape of a math lesson in which Shane and others were participating, the teacher stopped the tape just after Shane said "no way" while assembling a pattern with geometric shapes called tangrams:

130　　Teacher: Yeah, he, he starts out like that on a lot of things. It's like, I can't do it. He's just glancing at it. . . . He's very apprehensive about approaching anything. But once he gets into it, and finishes something he's just so pleased with himself. And I'll say, hey I thought you said "No way." "Well?"

Later in the interview, the teacher stopped the tape again and commented:

406　　Teacher: I mentioned before, yeah, that whenever he's given some new task to do it's always like, too hard, no way I can do it, until we, oh, come on, you just get into it and try it. When he finishes, I mean its like fantastic, you know that he did it.[2]

These comments reinforced the teacher's representation of the child as one who has trouble applying himself to his school work. It is interesting to note, however, that all the other students in the lesson expressed similar consternation with the difficulty of the task. Nevertheless, the teacher did not treat the comments by the other students as instances of the concern over work difficulty; she did, however, treat the comments by Shane as exemplifying this reason for referring him. This gap between referral reason and students' behavior was a general pattern in our study (Mehan et al., 1986, pp. 69–97), which implicates the problematic nature of the behavioral record beneath special education referrals and the important role

that teachers' expectations and conceptions play in forming judgments about students' behavior.

Step 2: Refining the definition

The referral was forwarded to the next step in the referral
system, the School Appraisal Team, a committee composed of educators at the Desert Vista School. At its first meeting in October, the
school psychologist was instructed to assess Shane. For a variety of
practical reasons that plague bureaucratic processes such as this
referral system, including a large backlog of cases, difficulty in obtaining parental permission, and necessary records from another
school district, the recommended assessment did not take place until
December and January – 2 months after the original referral.

The school psychologist administered a battery of tests to Shane
on December 6, including an informal assessment called the "Three
Wishes," the Goodenough Draw A Man Test, and portions of the
Wechsler Intelligence Scale For Children – Revised (WISC-R). The
SAT met again on January 4. After hearing the results of the first
round of assessment, the committee recommended that the psychologist complete testing. In response to that instruction, the school
psychologist completed the WISC-R and administered the California
Assessment Test (CAT) and the Bender Gestalt. On February 2, the
committee heard the psychologist's report of testing. The psychologist reported that Shane had a verbal IQ of 115. He was reading at a
fourth-grade level. His arithmetic and spelling tested at 3.0 and 3.5,
which "put him below grade level." His test age on the Bender
Gestalt was 7.0–7.5, while his actual age (at the time) was 9.0, which
put him "considerably below his age level." Based on this assessment, the SAT recommended that Shane be considered by the
"Eligibility and Placement" (E&P) Committee for possible placement into a program for the learning disabled.[3]

We see illustrated here the process by which general calls for help
from a classroom teacher become refined and specified in official
language. The teacher had said Shane "has difficulty in applying
himself to classwork." That vague observation is now transformed
into a technical assessment: Shane's academic skill is expressed in
numerical terms (IQ of 115, test age of 7.5). He is compared with a

normative standard: He is "behind grade level." No longer is he a child "who needs help"; now he is a candidate "learning disabled child."

This refining is fundamental to the way in which the diagnostic process creates handicapped students and handicapped students' careers. Students' identities are sharpened as they move from regular education classrooms to testing rooms and finally to meeting rooms.

Step 3: Resolving competing representations of the student

When the E&P Committee met on February 16 to discuss Shane's case, the following dialogue took place:

92   Psychologist: does the uh, committee agree that the, uh learning disability placement is one that might benefit him?
93   Principal: I think we agree.
94   Psychologist: We're not considering then a special day class at all for him?
95   Special Education Teacher: I wouldn't at this point//
96   Many: = No.

The committee decided to place Shane into an LD group, a pullout educational program in which students spend a part of the school day in the regular classroom and the other part of the day in a special program. The "special day class" indexed by the psychologist (line 94) is the EH program in which students spend the entire school day in a special classroom.

When we observed these E&P meetings, we were struck by a prominent feature of the interaction. Although committee members came to meetings with a variety of opinions about the appropriate placement of students, by meeting's end one view of the children, that one recommended by the district, prevailed. Furthermore, this agreement was reached without debate or disagreement. For example, before the E&P meeting reviewed in this chapter, the classroom teacher, reflecting on the changes in the student she referred in October, was no longer convinced that Shane needed special education. The mother, worried about the stigmatizing effect of even a mild placement such as an LD group, did not want any special education for her child. Although definite and vocal before the meeting, they were silent during the meeting. In trying to understand how committee members (including parents) lost their voices while routinely coming to agreement with the school's recommendation, we turned our attention to the discourse of the placement committee meetings prior to the "decision to place" students occurred (see transcript lines 92–96).

During the course of the meeting, four reports were made to the committee, one by the school psychologist, one by the child's teacher, one by the school nurse, and one by the child's mother. These reports varied along three dimensions: (1) the manner in which they presented information, (2) the manner in which they grounded their assertions, and (3) the manner in which they represented the child. By arraying the reports along these dimensions, I found three "languages" being spoken in the meeting: a psychological language, a sociological language, and a historical language. Competing versions of the child are presented in these "languages" or idioms, but only one, the version of the child presented in the psychological language, prevails.

Mode of presentation. The information that the committee obtained from the classroom teacher and the mother appeared in a different form than the information made available by the school psychologist. The information that the psychologist had about the student was presented to the committee in a single uninterrupted report whereas information was elicited from both the classroom teacher and the mother. Here is the psychologist's opening statement to the committee:

1   Psychologist: Um. What we're going to do is, I'm going to have a brief, an overview of the testing because the rest of, of the, the committee has not, uh, has not an, uh, been aware of that yet. And uh, then each of us will share whatever, whatever we feel we need to share.
2   Principal: Right.
3   Psychologist: And then we will make a decision on what we feel is a good, oh (3) placement (2) for an, Shane.

The school psychologist then provided the committee members with the information she had about the student:

3   Psychologist: Shane is ah nine years old, and he's in fourth grade.
       Uh, he, uh, was referred because of low academic performance
       and he has difficulty applying himself to his daily class work. Um,
       Shane attended the Montessori School in kindergarten and first
       grade, and then he entered Carlsberg-bad in, um, September of
       1976 and, uh, entered our district in, uh, '78. He seems to have
       very good peer relationships but, uh, the teachers, uh, continually
       say that he has difficulty with handwriting. 'kay. He enjoys music
       and sports. I gave him a complete battery and, um, I found that,
       uh, he had a verbal IQ of 115, performance of 111, and a full scale
       of 115, so he's a bright child. Uh, he had very high scores in, uh,
       information which is his long-term memory. Ah, vocabulary, was,
       ah, also, ah, considerably over average, good detail awareness and
       his, um, picture arrangement scores, he had a seventeen which is
       very high//

4   Special Education Teacher: = Mmmm//
5   Psychologist: = very superior rating, so he, his visual sequencing
       seems to be good and also he has a good grasp of anticipation and
       awareness of social situations. Um, he (5) (she is scanning her
       notes) scored in reading at 4.1, spelling 3.5, and arithmetic 3.0,
       which gave him a standard score of 100 in, uh, reading, 95 in
       spelling, and 90 in arithmetic. When compared with his [overall]
       score, it does put him somewhat ah below his, you know, his
       capabilities. I gave him the Bender Gestalt (clears throat) and he
       had six errors. And his test age was 7.0 to 7.5 and his actual age is
       nine, so it, uh, he was considerably beneath his, uh, his uh, age
       level. (2) His, I gave him the, uh VADS and his, um (5 or 6)
       (looking through notes) both the oral-aural and the visual-written
       modes of communication were high but the visual oral and the oral
       written are low, so he, uh, cannot switch channels. His expressive
       vocabulary was in the superior range (6). Uh, visual perception falls
       above age level, so he's fine in that area (6). And fine motor skills
       appear to be slightly lower than, uh, average, (voice trails off slightly),
       I saw them. (3) He read words very quickly when he was doing the
       academics but I didn't see any reversals in his written work. Uh, I
       gave him several projective tests and, um, the things that I picked
       up there is that, um he [does] possibly have some fears and anxie-
       ties, uh, (5). So I had felt ah, that perhaps he might, uh, uh, benefit,
       um, (3) from special help. He also was tested, um, in 1976 and at
       that time he was given the WISC-R and his IQ was slightly lower,
       full scale of a 93 (3 or 4). His, um, summary of that evaluation, uh,

was, uh, he was given the ITPA and he had high auditory reception, auditory association, auditory memory. (2) So his auditory
skills are good. (3) He was given another psychol- psychological
evaluation in 1977. He was given the Leiter and he had an IQ of
96 (6). And, um (3 or 4) they concluded that he had a poor mediate
recall (2) but they felt that was due to an emotional overlay and
they felt that some emotional conflicts were, uh, interfering with
his ability to concentrate.

At the end of this presentation, the psychologist asked the student's teacher to provide information:

5   Psychologist: Kate, would you like to share with u:s?
6   Classroom Teacher: What, the problems I see ( ) Um. . .
7   Psychologist: Yes.
8   Classroom Teacher: Um. Probably basically the fine motor types
     of things are difficult for him. He's got a very creative mi:ind and
     expresses himself well ( ) orally and verbally and he's pretty alert to
     what's going on. (2) Maybe a little bit [too] much, watching
     EVERYthing that's (hh) going (hh) on, and finds it hard to stick to
     one task. And [mostly] I've been noticing that it's just his writing
     and things that he has a, a block with. And he can rea:ad and
     comprehend some things when I talk to him, [but] doing indepen-
     dent type work is hard for him.
9   Principal: mhmmm, putting it down on paper . . .
10   Classroom Teacher: Yeah::, and sticking to a task//
11   Principal: = mmhmmm//
12   Classroom Teacher: = and getting
     it done, without being distracted by (hehhehheh)
13   Special Education Teacher: How does he relate with what the
     other kids do?
14   Classroom Teacher: Uh, very well. He's got a lot of frie:ends, and,
     uh, especially, even out on the playground he's, um (3), wants to
     get in on the games, get on things and is well accepted. So:o, I
     don't see too many problems there.

In this sequence, we have the classroom teacher beginning to
present some of the conditions under which Shane has trouble (8),
being interrupted by the principal (9), then the special education
teacher took the floor (13). From that point on, the special education
teacher asked the classroom teacher a series of questions about

Shane's peer relations, reading level, and performance in spelling and math.

After the school psychologist asked how Shane handled failure, the questioning shifted to the mother, who was asked about her son's fine motor control at home:

46 Special Education Teacher: How do you find him at [home] in terms of using his fingers and fine motor kinds of things? Does he do//

47 Mother: =He will, as a small child, he didn't at all. He was never interested in it, he wasn't interested in sitting in my lap and having a book read to him, any things like that//

48 Special Education Teacher: =mhmmm//

49 Mother: =which I think is part of it you know. His, his older brother was just the opposite, and learned to write real early. [Now] Shane, at night, lots of times he comes home and he'll write or draw. He's really doing a lot//

50 Special Education Teacher: ( )

51 Mother: =he sits down and is writing love notes to his girl friend (hehheh). He went in our bedroom last night and turned on the TV and got out some colored pencils and started writing. So he, really likes to, and of course he brings it all in to us to see//

52 Special Education Teacher: =mhmmm//

53 Mother: =and comment on, so I think, you know, he's not [NEGAtive] about//

54 Special Education Teacher: =no//

55 Mother: =that any more//

56 Special Education Teacher: =uh huh

57 Mother: He was before, but I think his attitude's changed a lot.

These transcript excerpts show that the information that the psychologist had about the student was presented to the committee in a single, uninterrupted report, while the mother's and classroom teacher's information was elicited by other members of the committee. The school psychologist's presentation of the case of the committee was augmented by officially sanctioned props, including the case file itself (a bulky manila folder on display in front of the psychologist), test results, carefully prepared notes. When she spoke, she read from notes. By contrast, neither the mother nor the teacher had such props. They spoke from memory, not from notes.

Grounds of assertions. The members of the committee supported their claims about the child in different ways. The psychologist provided a summary of the results of a given test or subtest in a standard format. She named the subtest, reported the student's score, and gave her interpretations of the results. For example:

I gave him a complete battery, and I found that, uh, he had a verbal IQ of 115, performance of 111, and a full scale of 115, so he's a bright child.

He had very high scores in, uh, information, which is his long-term memory.

His, um, picture arrangement scores, he had a seventeen, which is very high, very superior rating.

While the psychologist reported information about the student gained from the use of quasi-scientific tools, the classroom teacher and mother based their reports on firsthand observations. For example, the teacher provided general statements, "he's got a very creative mind and expresses himself well" (8), as well as some more specific assertions: "he can read and comprehend some things when I talk to him, but doing independent type work is hard for him" (8). While the psychologist's observations were confined to a relatively short period of time (hours of testing) and a circumscribed setting, the classroom teacher's and mother's observations were based on a longer period of time and a less circumscribed spatial and social arrangement. For the teacher, this period was a school year and the space was the classroom, while the mother's observations concerned the child's actions in a wide variety of situations spanning a lifetime.

Thus, information gathered by systematic, albeit indirect, observations (i.e., that from specialized tests) *was presented to* the committee, whereas information gathered by direct, albeit unguided or unstructured, observation (which included information about classroom experiences and home life) *was elicited from* participants. Furthermore, the mode in which information was presented to the committee varied according to the status and official expertise of the participants in the meeting. The most highly technical information (that from tests) was made available by the most highly trained and highest-ranking people in attendance at the meeting, whereas the personal observations were made available by the participants with the least technical expertise and lowest ranking. Speakers of officially higher rank and who spoke with their authority grounded in technical expertise presented their information, whereas speakers of lower rank, who spoke with authority based on firsthand observations, had information elicited from them.

Mode of representation. Shane's mother, his teacher, the school psychologist, and the school nurse discussed the student and his academic performance differently. The student was characterized by the psychologist as having "troubles" and "problems." This mode of representation is constituted by her syntax and her vocabulary: "he has difficulty applying himself to his daily work" (3), "he cannot switch channels" (5), "he has some fears and anxieties" (5). The verbs "have" and "is" make the "troubles" and "problems" Shane's; they are beneath his skin, between his ears. The classroom teacher characterized the problem in a similar way: "the fine motor types of things are difficult for him" (8), "doing independent type work is hard for him" (8).

While the student's problem is the focus of attention for the entire committee, the mother and teacher discussed the student in a different language than did the psychologist and the nurse. Notable in this regard are comments about the student's motivation: "he enjoys math" (28), "he enjoys handwriting and wants to learn it" (30), "he seems to enjoy handwriting and wants to learn it" (30), "he really tries at it hard and seems to wanna learn it better" (34). She also introduced a number of contingencies that influenced the student's performance: First, his performance varies as a function of preparation: "If he studies his spelling and concentrates on it he can do pretty well" (22). Second, his performance varies according to the kinds of materials and tasks: "It's hard for him to copy down [math] problems . . . if he's given a sheet where he can fill in answers and work them out he does much better" (28); he does better on group tasks, "but doing independent type work is hard for him" (8). If the tasks at hand are a means to some other end desired by the student, then his performance improves: "if there's something else he wants to do and knows he needs to do and knows he needs to get through that before he can get on to something else, he'll work a little more diligently at it" (45).

The mother's language contrasts even more sharply with the psychologist's than does the teacher's. The mother spoke about changes through time, continually contrasting her son as he was at an earlier age with how he is now. In each of these contrasts, she emphasized improvements and changes for the better. Although she seems to acknowledge the official committee position about Shane's problem, she provided an alternative explanation about the source of the problem. For her, the locus of difficulty was not within him ("it's not physical," "it's not functional"), but it was to be found in his past experience and the situations he had been in.

In short, the teacher, like the psychologist, characterized the issue before the committee as "Shane's problem." The teacher's characterization, unlike the psychologist's, however, had a contingent quality. She spoke sociologically, providing contextual information of a locally situated sort. The mother's language, by contrast, has a historical dimension; she spoke in terms that implied changes through time.

Stratifying languages of representation

Committee members often came to E&P meetings with differing views of the student's case and attitudes about the student's placement. During this meeting, the various members of this committee perceived Shane differently. The psychologist located the child's problem beneath his skin and between his ears, whereas the classroom teacher saw the student's problem varying from one classroom situation to another, and the mother saw the child's problem changing through time. That is, the teacher and the mother provided accounts about the student's performance in languages that were different than the psychologist's version of the student's academic difficulties.

This discussion, if left here, would be at best an interesting example of perspectival differences in representation that occur in face-to-face interaction. That is, psychologists, teachers, and parents have different languages for talking about children because of their different experiences and backgrounds. Although the perspectival dimension of representation is certainly an important aspect of the social construction of this child's identity, closing the discussion at this point would leave out a crucial ingredient: These modes of representation are not equal. By meeting's end, one mode of representation, that voiced in a psychological language, prevailed. The psychological representation of the student supplanted both the sociological and historical representations of the student.

So, the question that must be asked is: How did the psychologist control the discourse, dominating the other voices in the conversation? Or, asking this question in another way: How does this mode of representation achieve its privileged status?

In order to determine how the stratification of these modes of representation is accomplished discursively, it is instructive to look at the manner in which the committee treated the descriptions of the child offered by the committee members. The reports by the psychologist and the nurse were accepted without question or challenge, while those of the mother and the teacher were interrupted continuously by questions. This differential treatment is at first surprising, especially in light of the differences in the manifest content of the three descriptions. The psychologist's description is replete with technical terms ("VADS," "Bender," "detail awareness," "ITPA," "WISC-R") and numerical scales ("IQ of 96," "full scale of 93," "test age was 7.0 to 7.5"), while both the mother and the teacher describe the student in lay terms ("he has a creative mind," "doing independent work is hard for him," "he wasn't interested in sitting in my lap and having a book read to him").

Thus, the speaker who includes technical terms in her language *is not asked* to clarify terms, whereas the speakers of a vernacular *are asked* to clarify their terms. No one in the meeting asked the psychologist for more details or further information. In fact, the mother only requested clarification once during the course of the entire meeting and that was just as the formal business was being concluded. Her question was about "PE":

422   Special Education Teacher: check over ((( ))) (5–6) I don't think
      I addressed PE
423   Psychologist: I don't think we uh, [oh], ok, we do not need that,
      okay, he does not need physical edu//
424   Mother: =(I want to ask something about that while
      you mentioned PE. You mean physical education)
425   ???: mmhmmm

426 Mother: Does the school have a soccer program or is that just totally separate from um, you know, part of the boys' club o::r//
427 Principal:　　　　　　　　= Right. It's a parent organized, um, association//
428 Mother: = Is there something (one?) at the school that would have information on it if it comes up in the season, because Shane really has expressed an interest in that

Here we see the mother ask her only question in the session, about a nontechnical topic, at the end of the meeting, after the placement decision had been reached.

The differences in the way in which the three reports were treated, especially the requests for clarification of technical terms during the committee meeting, help us understand why the psychologist's representation was accorded privileged status by the committee. The psychologist's report gains its authority by the very nature of its construction. The psychologist's language obtains its privileged status *because* it is ambiguous, because it is full of technical terms, *because* it is difficult to understand. The parents and the other committee members do not challenge the ambiguity of the psychologist's report because the grounds to do so are removed by the manner in which the psychologist presents information, grounds assertions, and represents the child in discourse.

Meaning is said to be negotiated in everyday discourse. Speakers and hearers are both responsible for the construction of understanding. According to observers from a wide variety of perspectives, a first maxim of conversation is that speakers intend to make sense and be understood (Merleau-Ponty, 1964; Sacks, Schegloff, & Jefferson, 1974; Grice, 1975; Searle, 1969; Gumperz, 1982). Hearers contribute to meaning in discourse by making inferences from the conversational string of utterances. They display their understanding actively through "back channel work" (Duncan, 1972), which includes eye contact, head nods, and vocalics such as uh huhs and lexical items like "I see," or "I understand." When the hearer does not understand, "a request for clarification" is in order. The manifest purpose of such requests is to obtain more information. The request for clarification is generated by hearers when they do not think that the speaker is speaking clearly.

The grounds for this kind of negotiation of meaning are removed from the committee by the way in which language is used by the psychologist. When the psychologist speaks, it is from an institutionally designated position of authority. Furthermore, the psychologist's representation of the child is based on her professional expertise. The privileged status of the psychologist's expertise, in turn, is displayed in the technical language of her report.

There is a certain mystique in the use of technical vocabulary, as evidenced by the high status that the specialized language of doctors, lawyers, and scientists is given in our society (West, 1984; Philips, 1977; Shuy & Larkin, 1978; Latour & Woolgar, 1986; Wertsch, 1986; Cohn, 1987). The use of technical language indicates a superior status and a special knowledge based on long training and specialized qualifications.

A certain amount of this mystique is evident in the psychologist's language and is apparent in the committee's treatment of it. When technical language is used and embedded in the institutional trappings of the formal proceedings of a meeting, the grounds for negotiating meaning are removed from under the conversation. Because the speaker and hearers do not share the conventions of a common language, hearers do not have the expertise to question, or even to interrupt the speaker. To request a clarification of the psychologist, then, is to challenge the authority of a clinically certified expert. The other members of the committee are placed in the position of assuming the psychologist is speaking knowledgeably and the hearer does not have the competence to understand.

When technical language is used, even though the possibility for active negotiation of meaning is removed, the guise of understanding remains. To be sure, the understanding is a passively achieved one, not the active one associated with everyday discourse. Instead of signaling a lack of understanding via such implicit devices as backchannel work and explicit ones like requests for clarification, the committee members (including the parents) remain silent, thereby tacitly contributing to the guise that common understanding has been achieved.

Conclusions

In addition to making some specific points about the research I have been conducting on the institutional construction of identities, I conclude by making some more general points about the constitu-

tive model of discourse that is implied by this work and then specu-
lating on the reason that the psychological language is so powerful in
educational decision making.

The institutional construction of identities

By looking at the language of groups of educators as they
engage in the work of sorting students, I have tried to demonstrate
the situated relevance of social structures in the practical work activities performed by people in social interaction. Educators carry out
the routine work of conducting lessons, assigning students to ability
groups or special programs, administering tests, and attending meetings. The notion of *work* stresses the constructive aspect of institutional practice. Educators' work is repetitive and routine. Its mundane character should not overshadow the drama of its importance,
however, because steps on students' career ladders are assembled
from such practice. The enactment of routine bureaucratic practices
structures students' educational careers by opening or closing their
access to particular educational opportunities.

Essentially, the teacher is calling for help. Her call is cast in
general not specific terms. This call starts the process that constructs
students' institutional identities. These often undifferentiated appeals become refined and specified in official language as they move
from regular education classrooms to testing rooms and finally to
meeting rooms. Through this process, the child becomes an object.
The members of the committee do not have access to the teacher–
student interaction; only the residue of that interaction is represented
in a file, a decentered text. At the outset, the child was a participant
in discourse with his teacher and his classmates. But, from that point
on, the child's contribution to his own career status drops out. The
child becomes represented in text. The only way we gain access to
the child is in textual representations of his interactions. Thus, the
child becomes objectified as the case moves from the classroom to
testing to committee meeting.

I found three languages spoken in the committee meeting, which
is the last step in this identity construction process: a psychological,
a sociological, and a historical language. The psychological language
included absolute and categorical statements about the student's

abilities. On the basis of information from systematic, albeit indirect, techniques of observation, the locus of the problem was placed within Shane. The result was a "context-free" view of the child, one who had a general disability that cuts across situations. The classroom teacher spoke in a sociological idiom; she tempered her report with contingent factors of a situational sort. According to information from unsystematic, albeit direct, observation, she said that the student's performance was influenced by his state of motivation, kinds of classroom tasks, and types of materials. The result was a "context-bound" view of the child, one who had specific problems, which appeared in certain academic situations, but who operated more than adequately in other situations. The mother's language was historical. Based on years of direct observation, she provided particulars about the biography and history of her son and noted changes and improvements across time as well as situational circumstances as the source of his difficulties.

The psychologist's recommendations were accepted without challenge or question, while the sociological and historical recommendations were routinely interrupted with requests for clarification and further information. I propose that the resolution of competing versions of the child can be understood in terms of the authority that reports gain by their manner of presentation, method of grounding truth claims, and modes of representation.

The psychological language gained its authority from the mastery and control of a technical vocabulary, grounded in a quasi-scientific idiom. Because of the fact that the psychologist's report was obscure, difficult to understand, and ambiguous, not in spite of it, the grounds for questioning or challenging were removed from the conversation. It is this technical, quasi-scientific authority that contributes to the stratification of languages of representation and thereby the construction of children's identities.

When people have competing versions of ambiguous events that transpire in the world, they often try to negotiate a commonly agreed upon definition of the situation. Often, consensus is achieved when one or another of the protagonists relinquishes his or her representation of the world as the preferred version, after having heard superior information or having been convinced of the efficacy of an argument. In the case considered here, the resolution of competing modes of representation was not negotiated. The members of the committee resolved the disjuncture between sociological, historical, and psychological versions by credentialing the psychological version as the official version of this student. Thus, an institutionally sanctioned version of experience is superimposed upon multiple and competing versions of experience.

Language as constitutive activity

The constructivist view of social life poses mutually constitutive relations between modes of thought, modes of discourse, and modes of action. Discourse does not passively reflect or merely describe the world. Because language is action, different uses of language constitute the world differently. Events in the world do not exist for people independently of the language people use to make sense of them. Instead, objects are defined through elaborate enactments of cultural conventions, which lead to the establishment of such well-documented "institutional facts" (Searle, 1969) as "touchdowns," "marriages," "insults," "banishments," "property rights" (D'Andrade, 1984), and, as I have proposed, "learning disabilities" and "educational handicaps." When the constitutive rules of discourse are in effect, behavior becomes action, and actions become "touchdowns," "marriages," "illness," "schizophrenia," "deviance," "intelligence," and "educational handicaps."

Modes of representation. When discourse is viewed as activity that culturally constructs clarity out of ambiguity, then we should not be surprised to find multiple modes of representation. Marriage, schizophrenia, and learning disabilities are constructed by cultural conventions in much the same way that touchdowns are constructed by the constitutive rules of football. Just as crossing the goal line only counts as a touchdown if the appropriate players are present and has been duly constituted by the referee, so, too, a student's behavior only counts as a learning disability if the appropriate institutional officials apply the appropriate institutional machinery (educational testing, parent conferences, placement meetings, etc.). Without the application of that institutional machinery, educational handicaps do not exist.[4]

In the case we have considered, there were many ways in which Shane could have been formulated: "normal student," "educationally handicapped student," "gifted student," "learning disabled student." Each formulation or way of representing Shane does not simply reflect or merely describe his characteristics; each mode of representation constitutes him, and does so in a different way. A "normal student" is constituted as fitting within the parameters or norms of intelligence; a "gifted student" is constituted as having exceptional talents. An "educationally handicapped" or "learning disabled" student is constituted to have an inherent disorder. Importantly, each of these formulations characterizes intelligence or talent in terms that place it inside the student. Intelligence, whether normal, exceptional, or lacking, is treated as a personal and private property of the individual. This way of characterizing people exemplifies the use of dispositional properties in the explanation of people's behavior. Each of these modes of representation naturalizes the child, thereby masking the social construction work that generated the designation in the first place.

In short, we know the world through the representations we make of it (Bakhtin, 1981). A particular way of representing events in language influences, first, the way we think about the events represented, and, second, the way we act toward the events.

The politics of representation. Modes of representing events vary according to the perspective from which a representation is constructed. Perspective here refers to the standpoint from which a person is participating in discourse. One dimension of perspective is the person's physical location in the here-and-now of face-to-face situations (Gurwitsch, 1966). Another is the person's location in social institutions, cultural arrangements, and sociohistorical space–time (Bakhtin, 1981).

We have found that professional educators (i.e., school psychologists), for a variety of biographical, historical, and cultural reasons, described students in dispositional terms, whereas parents and, to a lesser extent, classroom teachers formulated students in more contextual terms (Mehan et al., 1986, pp. 109–157). Although there are many possible modes of representing the world and communicating them to others constructed from particular biographical, historical, and social-cultural perspectives, the course of history can be envisioned as successive attempts to impose one mode of representation upon another. Proponents of various political positions attempt to capture or dominate modes of representation. If successful, a hierarchy is formed, in which one mode of representing the world (its objects, events, people) gains primacy over others, transforming modes of representation from an array on a horizontal plane to a ranking on a vertical plane.

It is not accidental in this "politics of representation" (Holquist, 1983; Shapiro, 1987; Mehan & Wills, 1988; Mehan, 1989) that institutionally grounded representations predominate, for example, psychiatrists' representations prevail over patients', professional educators' representations override parents' formulations. Institutional officials speak with a technical vocabulary grounded in professional expertise. Ordinary people speak in a common vernacular grounded in personal experience. More and more often in our increasingly technological society, when a voice speaking in formalized, rationalistic, and mathematical terms confronts a voice grounded in personal, commonsense, or localized particulars, the technical prevails over the vernacular.

When categorizing a student, these educators reproduced the status relations among the different discourses that exist in society. A universalizing language that is given higher status in the meeting and whose variables are read into the child, thereby decontextualizing the child, is the same language we see gaining power and authority in recent times. Thus, the concrete face-to-face encounters that generate an instance of a category are constitutive moments and reproduce the relations among categories that we see gaining ascendancy historically.

The prevalence of the psychological idiom

As a closing note to this chapter, I would like to speculate on the reason why the psychological language is privileged over the other languages in educational decision making. The privileging of the psychological language speaks to the prevalence of the psychological idiom in our society. This psychological idiom has two important dimensions: one, a focus on the individual and, two, a base in the technological.

Since Tocqueville, observers of American society (e.g., Williams, 1960; Bellah, Madsen, Sullivan, Swidler, & Tipton, 1985) have identified individualism as a core value in American society. We see the causes of human behavior in terms of states and traits (D'Andrade, 1984). These states and traits are in the heads and between the ears of people. We say that people are successful or unsuccessful because of their personal effort and hard work – which are rabidly individualistic terms (Bellah et al., 1985).

Commentators such as Gould (1981) and Noble (1977) have identified a second politically relevant theme in American society: the increasing reliance on technical solutions to the problems facing our mass, democratic society. We turn to instruments such as the IQ test to sort students for political, educational, and medical programs. We turn to medical, legal, and scientific experts for guidance on a wide variety of problems in American society. We employ missiles, rockets, and computer-based command and control systems to ward off foreign aggressors. The inventor is a cultural hero – as embodied in the myths of Benjamin Franklin and Thomas Edison. Mastery over nature is a way to progress (Williams, 1960).

Individualism and technical knowledge constitute two of the most important dimensions of a psychological account of human behavior. Both of these dimensions are readily apparent in the discourse that dominates special education selections. Thus, there is a strong affinity between the idiom that predominates educational discourse and a dominant metaphor in American society. Both cite personal and individual characteristics as the basis of success and failure. Both rely on technical knowledge and expertise in decision making.

This power of the individualistic and technological dimensions of the psychological account of human behavior in the dominant idiom in a decision-making situation suggests there is a linkage between what happens in a mundane, everyday social situation (e.g., a meeting within a school) and an important albeit ephemeral aspect of social structure (i.e., American core values or ideology). The linkage is expressed in the psychologist's language. The psychologist is speaking with a voice that unites the concerns and activities of a particular time and place with those of the wider cultural belief system.

To do more than speculate about this linkage, of course, it is necessary to ground any such claims about the workings of ideology in discourse. The approach taken in this study (an ethnographically grounded study of the modes of representation in everyday discourse) is suggestive of a way to proceed to connect social discourse with social structure and ideology without reducing one to the other.

Notes

1. Source: referral form in student's school record.
2. Source: interview of teacher conducted by Alma Hertweck. A number of conventions have been used in the transcripts reproduced in this chapter: ( ) = unclear talk; EVERYbody = emphasis; (heheh) = laughter; rea:ad = stretched talk; // = overlapping utterances; (3) = pause measured in seconds.
3. Source: School Psychologist's Assessment Summary. This report was also read to the E&P Committee on February 16 (see my discussion of this report in the context of the E&P meeting).
4. See Searle (1969, pp. 34–35) for an important discussion of the "count as" relationship, i.e., how behavior becomes instances of cultural categories.

References

Bahktin, M. M. (1981). *The dialogic imagination.* Austin: University of Texas Press.

Bellah, R. N., Madsen, R., Sullivan, W. M., Swidler, A., & Tipton, S. M. (1985). *Habits of the heart.* Berkeley: University of California Press.

Cicourel, A. V. (1981). Language and medicine. In C. A. Ferguson & S. B. Heath (Eds.), *Language in the USA* (pp. 347–367). Cambridge: Cambridge University Press.

Cicourel, A. V., Jennings, K., Jennings, S., Leiter, K., MacKay, H., Mehan, H., & Roth, D. (1974). *Language use and school performance.* New York: Academic Press.

Cohn, C. (1987). Sex and death in the rational world of defense intellectuals. *Signs, 12,* 687–718.

Collins, R. (1981). On the microfoundations of macrosociology. *American Journal of Sociology, 86,* 984–1004.

D'Andrade, R. G. (1984). Cultural meaning systems. In R. A. Shweder & R. A. LeVine (Eds.), *Culture theory: Essays on mind, self, and emotion* (pp. 88–119). Cambridge: Cambridge University Press.

Duncan, S. (1972). Some signals and rules for taking speaking turns in conversation. *Journal of Personality and Social Psychology, 23,* 283–292.

Durkheim, E. (1950). *The rules of sociological method.* Glencoe, IL: Free Press. (Original work published 1895)

Erickson, F., & Shultz, J. (1982). *The counselor as gatekeeper: Social interactions in interviews.* New York: Academic Press.

Fisher, S., & Todd, A. (1983). *The social organization of doctor–patient communication.* Washington, DC: Center for Applied Linguistics.

Garfinkel, H., & Sacks, H. (1970). On formal structures of practical actions. In J. C. McKinney & E. A. Tiryakian (Eds.), *Theoretical sociology* (pp. 337–366). New York: Appleton–Century–Crofts.

Gordon, L. (1988). *Heroes of their own lives.* New York: Viking.

Gould, S. J. (1981). *The mismeasure of man.* New York: W. W. Norton.

Grice, H. P. (1975). Logic and conversation. In P. Cole & J. Morgan (Eds.), *Syntax and semantics:* Vol. 3. *Speech acts* (pp. 41–58). New York: Academic Press.

Gumperz, J. (1982). *Strategies of discourse.* Cambridge: Cambridge University Press.

Gurwitsch, A, (1966). *Studies* in phenomenology and psychology. Evanston, IL: Northwestern University Press.

Holquist, M. (1983). The politics of representation. *Quarterly Newsletter of the Laboratory of Comparative Human Cognition, 5* (1), 2–9.

Knorr-Cetina, K. (1981). *The manufacture of knowledge: An essay on the constructivist and contextualized nature of science.* Oxford: Pergamon Press.

Laing, R. D. (1967). *The politics of experience.* New York: Pantheon.

Latour, B., & Woolgar, S. (1986). *Laboratory life: The construction of scientific facts.* Princeton: Princeton University Press.

McDermott, R. P., Gospodinoff, K., & Aron, J. (1978). Criteria for an ethnographically adequate description of concerted activities in context. *Semiotica, 24,* 245–275.

Mehan, H. (1989). Oracular reasoning in a psychiatric setting: The resolution of conflict in language. In A. D. Grimshaw (Ed.), *Conflict talk* (pp. 160–177). Cambridge: Cambridge University Press.

Mehan, H., Hertweck, A., & Meihls, J. L. (1986). *Handicapping the handicapped: Decision making in students' careers.* Stanford, CA: Stanford University Press.

Mehan, H., & Wills, J. (1988). MEND: A nurturing voice in the nuclear arms debate. *Social Problems, 35,* 363–383.

Merleau-Ponty, M. (1964). *Signs.* Evanston, IL: Northwestern University Press.

Nathanson, C. E. (1984, August). *The social construction of the Soviet threat.* Paper presented at the meeting of the American Sociological Association, San Antonio, TX.

Nathanson, C. E. (1989). *In sympathy with labor.* New Haven: Yale University Press.

Noble, D. (1977). *America by design.* Oxford: Oxford University Press.

Philips, S. (1977). *The role of spatial positioning and alignment in defining interactional units: The American courtroom as a case in point.* Paper presented at the meeting of the American Anthropological Association, Huston, TX.

Pollitt, K. (1987, May 23). The strange case of Baby M. *Nation, 667,* 682–688.

Pollner, M., & Mc Donald-Wilkler, M. (1985) The social construction of unreality: A case study of a family's attribution of competence to a severly retarded child. *Family Process, 24,* 241–254.

Sacks, H., Schegloff, E. A., & Jefferson, G. (1974). A simplest systematics for the organization of turn-taking in conversation. *Language, 50,* 696–735.

Searle, J. (1969). *Speech acts.* Cambridge: Cambridge University Press.

Shapiro, M. (1987). *The politics of representation.* Madison: University of Wisconsin Press.

Shuy, R., & Larkin, D. L. (1978). Linguistic considerations in the simplification/ clarification of insurance policy language. *Discourse Processes, 1*, 305–321.

Wertsch, J. (1986). Modes of discourse in the nuclear arms debate. *Current Research on Peace and Violence, 10*, 102–112.

West, C. (1984). *Routine complications: Troubles in talk between doctors and patients.* Bloomington: Indiana University Press.

Williams, R. (1960). *American society.* New York: Knopf.

10 The acquisition of a child by a learning disability

R. P. McDermott

Conceived as a deficiency in capacity, feeblemindedness *isolates* the subject by virtue of that deficiency. In seeking a definite cause of feeblemindedness one is denying that it can have any *meaning* – that is, a history – or that it may correspond to a *situation*.

(Maud Mannoni, 1972, p. 44)

The interiority of pains, afterimages and spots before the eyes cannot impugn the overt, public character of cognitive skills, or the external aims of practical moral decisions. It is only when mental activity regains its place within everyday life, therefore that its outer directness becomes finally clear.

(Stephen Toulmin, 1985, p. 17)

The emergence of institutionalized education is accompanied by a crisis in diffuse education, which goes directly from practice to practice without passing through discourse. Excellence has ceased to exist once people start asking whether it can be taught, i.e., as soon as the objective confrontation of different styles of excellence makes it necessary to say what goes without saying, justify what is taken for granted, make an ought-to-be and an ought-to-do out of what had up to then been regarded as the only way to be and do.

(Pierre Bourdieu, 1977, p. 200)

Sometimes if you try harder and harder, it just gets worser and worser.

(Adam, 1977, third grade)

From 1976 to 1978, Michael Cole, Lois Hood, and I gathered a series of videotapes from one classroom of eight- and nine-year-old

Richard Blot, Eric Bredo, Robbie Case, David Charnow, Michael Cole, and Jean Lave offered helpful comments on a previous draft. John Broughton helped greatly with the Appendix, Renu Gupta with the Appendix chart, and Mimi Cotter with the occasional Gestalt flavor. This paper is dedicated to the late Robert F. Murphy who understood well how a culture can disable. I owe him a letter.

children in various settings. Our effort at the time was to locate the children "thinking" aloud in the hope that we could identify naturally occurring examples of some mental activities that seemed so well defined in experimental settings. Our concern was that activities like attending, remembering, problem solving, and the like, although often invoked in formal institutional descriptions of our children, in fact had few referents in their daily lives. It wasn't just that no one had ever seen a memory, for various unseen things (electrons, gods, missing stars that fill out a navigator's imagination) have had a useful theoretical career without being seen; it was rather that we had no way to gauge the usefulness of the theories we had available about memory, attention, or problem solving. If experimental psychology was to be useful in the description of individual learners, as different perhaps from the task of modeling how "minds" might work, then a tighter and more systematic fit would have to be achieved between experimental tasks and the demands on people as they lived their lives and plied their learning.

Our suspicion, and ultimately our conclusion, was that little such fit could be expected to the extent that psychology relied theoretically and methodologically on predefined tasks to probe the minds of individual persons. The problem was that in everyday life persons and tasks never quite stand still; the gap between subject and object, between stimulus and response, could not be filled by positing models of what was happening inside the organism, for the reason that neither subject nor object, neither stimulus nor response, was available for analysis as it was sequenced in the experience of persons in the lived world. In everyday life, tasks could be ongoingly altered, reframed, and pushed aside in ways that made it impossible for an experimenter to anticipate or to take systematically into account. Experimental cognitive psychology, we concluded, was condemned to a life of ecological invalidity; there was no systematic way of reasoning from experimental results to a description of individuals living out their institutional lives together (Cole, Hood, & McDermott, 1978). On the basis of experimental data, guesses could be made about how to handle our children, but it was not clear just what informed the guessing or how we might judge its adequacy.[1]

As an offshoot of our main concern, we became fascinated by how we might describe the learning biographies of different children.

There was Nadine, who seemed to know most things and to learn quickly whatever she did not already know; there was Reggie, who seemed to know a great deal about everything but how to get along with his peers; there was Matt, who hid out for the year and seemingly never engaged in any official, school-learning task; and there was Adam, who suffered as an officially described Learning Disabled (LD) child, but who seemed always eager to try. It was this last child who most captured our focus. As soon as we went to tell his story of course, we were immersed once again in the problems of how to do an ecologically valid description. His head did not seem to work very well on isolated cognitive tasks, either on standardized tests given by the school reading specialist or on the more theoretically sensitive tasks we gave him. Did we really want to describe what went on in his head? Just what was the phenomenon under investigation anyway? Where is LD to be found? Is it to be "found" at all? Is it anything more than a way of talking about some children and available for analysis only as a kind of rhetoric? Might it not best be described as a political label, a resource for keeping people in their place, a "display board" for the contradictions of our school system? We tried to consider all the options (Cole & Traupmann, 1981; Hood, McDermott, & Cole, 1980). The present chapter revives Adam's story in order to raise some questions about various approaches to the explanation of learning failures and to provide a focus for an account of notions of context and learning.

The argument

The title displays the theoretical edge of the chapter.[2] LD is usually assumed to be acquired by children due to some lapse in their development. By the normal line of reasoning, the child is the unit of analysis, and the disability is a mishap that scars a child's road to competence. This chapter suggests an alternative way of thinking about the problem. LD exists as a category in our culture, and it will acquire a certain proportion of our children as long as it is given life in the organization of tasks, skills, and evaluations in our schools. In the daily construction of settings called educative in American culture, moments are put aside for the discovery, description, and remediation of certain children who display particular traits (Mehan,

1992, this volume; Mehan, Hertwick, & Meihls, 1986; Sarason & Doris, 1979). Although the folk theory has it that the traits (an inability to pay attention, an occasional lapse in word access, trouble with phonics, etc.) belong to the child and are the source of both the disordered behavior and the subsequent label, it is possible to argue that it is the labels that precede any child's entry into the world and that these labels, well-established resting places in adult conversations, stand poised to take their share from each new generation. What Goffman (1979) claimed for gender identity is no less true for LD:

> What the human nature of males and females really consists of, then is a capacity to learn to provide and to read depictions of masculinity and femininity and a willingness to adhere to a schedule for presenting these pictures. . . . One might just as well say there is no gender identity. There is only a schedule for the portrayal of gender. . . . There is only evidence of the practice between the sexes of choreographing behaviorally a portrait of relationship. (p. 8)

We might just as well say there is no such thing as LD, only a social practice of displaying, noticing, documenting, remediating, and explaining it. This theoretical shift makes LD no less real to the participants of life in schools where occasions for displaying LD are so frequent, but it should at least make us wonder what we all do that makes LD so commonly sensible and ubiquitous in our experiences with institutionalized learning. *Notice that the claim here is not that we have no children who for whatever reason learn much slower or in different ways than others. It is only that without social arrangements for making something of differential rates of learning, there is no such thing as LD.* In America, we make something of differential rates of learning to the point that the rate of learning rather than the learning is the total measure of the learner. In another culture, or in our own if one is rich enough to receive an appropriately protective education, learning problems might slow a person down, but they do not have to destroy the learner.[3] Not all cultures make a fuss over different ways of learning. We seem to be extreme in this regard. There are great constraints on how childhood can be constructed in any given culture (Belmonte, 1989; Chamboredon & Prevot, 1975; Poster, 1980; Ramirez, 1990; Wartofsky, 1983). In allowing schools to become the site of sorting for recruitment into the wider social structure, we may have gone too far for the collective good. We may have made it necessary to invent occasions – millions of them – to make learning disabilities institutionally and unnecessarily consequential.

The good sense of a social structural and cultural account of LD can emerge from questions about the institutional arrangements served by having so many children designated LD. By institutional arrangements, we must consider everything from the most local level of the classroom to the more inclusive level of inequities throughout the political economy (preferably from both ends of the continuum at the same time). After following Adam for 18 months, we gave up on specifying his traits as the explanation of his behavior and began talking instead about what happened around him daily that seemed to organize his moments as an LD person. Even at this most local level, we could find that many people were involved in Adam's problem. On any occasion of his looking inattentive, for example, it took Adam to look away at just the right time, but it took many others to construct the right time for Adam to look away; it took others to look away from his looking away, and still more to discover his looking away, to make something of it, to diagnose it, to document it, and to remediate it. Whatever was Adam's problem inside his head, we had forced on us the recognition that Adam had plenty of problems all around him, in every person on the scene, in most every scene called educative. Analytically, the inside of his head became less interesting to us. The work that the participants did around Adam's disability and the sequencing of that work with other conversations required of persons in education became the phenomena of interest. It is in this vein that we claimed that Adam's disability was not just visible in the sense that the world was a neutral medium for what he could not do, but that the world was precisely organized for making his disability apparent, that he was the negative achievement of a school system that insisted that everyone do better than everyone else (Hood, McDermott, & Cole, 1980).

Context

To gain support for such an account, a description would have to focus less on the traits of the children labeled and more on the contexts for the interactional display and management of the traits at just the right moments for all to notice. Context becomes a key term, not just in the common sense of the named organizational "thing" in which a "disability" becomes visible, but in the more demanding sense of the analytic device by which members' activities are shown to be constitutive of both the named organizational setting and the disability in ways that make them a function of each other and subject to erasure as units of analysis at any moment in which they cannot be shown to be mutually constitutive (Byers, 1985; McDermott, Gospodinoff, & Aron, 1978; Scheflen, 1973). This is a difficult notion, which has been given a nice image by Birdwhistell (in McDermott, 1980):

I like to think of it as a rope. The fibers that make up the rope are discontinuous; when you twist them together, you don't make *them* continuous, you make the *thread* continuous. . . . The thread has no fibers in it, but, if you break up the thread, you can find the fibers again. So that, even though it may look in a thread as though each of those particles is going all through it, that isn't the case. That's essentially the descriptive model. (p. 4)

In school, Adam is a fiber, or many fibers, if you like. So are those about him. Together, they make up a rope. The category LD can be one way to name the rope, and, at the level of the rope, it might make sense to talk of Adam as disabled. If he spends his day arranging, with the help of his friends, not getting caught not knowing how to do some school task, he might well, however substantial his mind, finish school without having learned much in the way of received knowledge and having been made, in effect, for such tasks under such conditions, LD. But notice that the disability in this case does not belong to Adam. A fiber cannot make a rope, and the very existence of a rope arranges for the fibers to disappear as units of analysis.[4] Adam is a fiber, which, when joined by other fibers, helps to make the rope, or in this case the category LD, into the unit of analysis. It is not so much that Adam is disabled as that he participates in a scene well organized for the institutional designation of someone as LD. In their concerted activities, people arrange LD as a context for the management of persons in situ. People mutually constitute contexts for each other by erasing themselves, by giving themselves over to a new level of organization, which, in turn, acquires them and keeps them informed of what they are doing together. It is in this sense that LD is a context that acquires children.

It is possible to add a visual image to Birdwhistell's insight with the "twisted-cord illusion" (see Figure 10.1a; from Fraser, 1908). It is a set of concentric circles, which, when placed against a particular background, gives the appearance of a spiral (or, alternatively phrased, it is a spiral, which, when not placed against a particular background, give the appearance of a set of concentric circles). The effect is strong enough that, if one is asked to follow any of the circles, one's finger easily follows the eye into the center of the circle; only by a more careful tracing do the concentric circles become apparent. With only a slightly different background, Fraser was able to alter the apparent shape of another set of concentric circles into a set of round-angled squares (Figure 10.1b). The easy point is that the context or background overwhelms the text or foreground. For purposes of an analogy for the human sciences, the more interesting point is that text and context, foreground and background, shape each other. There are only two kinds of fiber in these twisted ropes. The concentric circles are made of alternating streaks of black and its apparent absence, the latter made clear by its contrast to both the black streaks and the black squares in the background. It is not just that the fibers are analytically unavailable when one is focusing on the rope, it is that half the fibers do not exist except in contrast to other fibers and other parts of the background. All parts of the system define all the other parts of the system. Without the background, there are neither ropes nor fibers.[5]

Learning

The argument put forth about Adam's disability requires not just a shift away from our commonsense notion of context, but a disruption of our most cherished notions about learning. Again we can turn to Birdwhistell (in McDermott, 1980) for a formulation. Note that he uses the terms *teaching* and *learning* interchangeably.

We've always assumed that teaching is a special activity which necessarily goes on in special contexts in which certain orders of learning also occur. In my opinion in

Figure 10.1a and 1b. From Fraser (1908). Reprinted with permission from Cambridge University Press.

organizing such as activity, you are dealing with a calibration in which the behavior is at least as parallel as it is complementary and in which there are acted out, patterned participations, systematic dances which take place.

I've been concerned with the difference between that model of teaching which is seen to come out of a dyadic (the so-called teacher–student) relationship and that model of teaching which comes from a contextually well-defined relationship in which the critical issue is the maintenance of the appropriate contact at the appropriate level. What I am concerned with are the conditions that maintain the contact in which the information not yet stored in specific instructions moves into the system and becomes a part of it so that "learning" can take place. (p. 16)[6]

In order to describe Adam, or better, in order to figure out what we had described after we spent a year trying to describe Adam, we needed a theory of learning that could take into account that learning is not an individual possession. The term *learning* simply glosses that some persons have achieved a particular relationship with each other, and it is in terms of these relations that information necessary to everyone's participation gets made available in ways that give people enough time on task to get good at what they do. If that happens enough, it can be said that learning happens. It probably makes more sense to talk about how learning acquires people more than it makes sense to talk about how people acquire learning. Individually we may spend our time trying to learn things, but this phenomenon pales before the fact that, however hard we try, we can only learn what is around to be learned. If a particular kind of learning is not made socially available to us, there will be no learning to do. This is a primary fact that we have made little use of theoretically. If we can stop focusing on who learns more or less of particular, culturally well-defined fragments of knowledge, and ask questions instead about what is around to be learned, in what circumstances, and to what end, learning achievements would become statements about the points of contact available to persons in various social settings (Lave, 1988a, b). What could LD be in such a world?

Before extending the arguments about context and learning in a discussion of various approaches we have available for the description of children like Adam, it is necessary to introduce Adam in the various settings in which we came to know him.

<u>The Phenomenon</u>

| Everyday | Cooking | Classroom | Testing |
| Life | Clubs | Lessons | Sessions |

- - - - - - - - - > - >

Adam's Visibility as a Problem

- - - - - - - - - > - >

School-like Demands and Constraints

Figure 10.2. The phenomenon.

Adam, Adam, Adam, and Adam

Because we were interested in the social organization of learning and thinking, we followed the children in Adam's class across a number of settings. When the class went away to a farm for a few days, we went with them. We used school holidays to take individual children around the city. We videotaped all the children in their classrooms, in some one-to-one testing settings, and, most extensively, in afternoon activity clubs that we set up for them two days a week. We were often struck with how much some children varied across the different settings. Adam stood out as the child who varied the most, and we can use the order in that variation to organize our discussion.

There were four settings in which we knew Adam fairly well: Everyday Life, Cooking Club, Classroom Lessons, and Testing Sessions. We can roughly gloss them along a continuum displaying either Adam's visibility as a problem (from invisible to a source of constant embarrassment), or schoollike demands (from fairly loose to very constrained). Figure 10.2 tries to capture that Adam was least visible as a problem in Everyday Life situations. He appeared in every way competent, and, more than most of the children, he could be wonderfully charming, particularly if there was a good story to tell. In the Cooking Club, Adam was only a little more visible as a problem. When he worked with his friend Peter, he got his cake made without any trouble. When he had to work with someone else, there were often some arguments, some tears, and some taunting from others before he could get his work done. Classroom Lessons presented the same story, although troubles were more frequent, and the adults seemed to be drawn more obviously into his problem in the sense that they would try to reframe the task he was facing or they would chastise him for his misbehavior. Finally in the Testing Sessions, Adam stood out from his peers not just by his dismal performance but by the wild guesswork he tried to do.

As the settings differed in the degree to which Adam stood out as a problem, so they differed along a continuum to the extent that they were schoollike in their constraints and their demands. Our question about how to describe Adam turned into a question about how to describe the settings in which the different Adams could emerge. Our initial efforts focused on identifying how these different settings could call the different Adams forth, and to that end we transcribed our tapes and worried about the details of the conversations that were made available for Adam's different displays of competence. For the purposes of this chapter we need to ask a subsequent, and yet more primitive question that, although having emerged from much data analysis, demands much less in the way of data display. Our effort in this chapter is to identify some of the approaches one could take to the description of the continuum, to point to some of the pretheoretical assumptions each makes about the nature of context and learning, and to extract what might be the most useful notions for our own purposes. The first approach focuses on the inadequacy in Adam's head, the second on the arbitrariness of the tasks Adam is asked to work on, and the third on the interactional dilemmas thrown in Adam's way as he moves through school.

The continuum of difficulty and deficit

The approach most immediately available to common sense describes the continuum from Everyday Life to Testing Sessions in terms of difficulty. Everyday life is popularly understood to be the least demanding of the various settings we occupy during the course of our days. There is the argument from Bartlett (1958), rarely challenged, that in Everyday Life one can get away with all sorts of sloppy reasoning, forgetting, and losing track in a way that schools, and other institutional settings similarly constrained (courtrooms, accounting offices, etc.), would never allow. By this way of theorizing, Testing Sessions stand at the opposite end of the continuum from Everyday Life, because they demand so much precision in calculation and clarity in argument. There is no "ya know" clause possible on a test; the reader cannot be expected to fill in the blank spaces or to make sense of what the test taker does not make clear. Testing Sessions are hard. Classroom Lessons only sometimes less so. Cooking Clubs generally less so. And Everyday Life generally undemanding. In comparison to tests, it takes fewer mental steps to get through our daily chores; we do not have to keep as much in mind. So it is argued.[7]

By our most popular line of folk reasoning, Adam becomes more visible as we move across the continuum because he is performing less well in the face of increasing demands. Under the loose constraints of Everyday Life, Adam can blend into the crowd and do what he has to do without anyone worrying about the quality of his mind. In the Cooking Club, this is equally true when he can work with Peter, who can read the recipe and oversee the step-by-step planning of the cake. When he cannot work with Peter, he has to work hard to arrange for someone else's cooperation, and, if that is not forthcoming, he begins to stand out. In Classroom Lessons, the tasks can be even more demanding, and Adam appears even less adequate to meeting the challenge. A close inspection of the classroom tapes showed Adam acting out on those occasions when he could be called on to perform. For example, while the teacher was asking the class questions and calling on children for answers, Adam could be found crawling under his work table, giving the finger to a friend, and so on; when the teacher switched to the next part of the lesson and called the children forward to see a demonstration, Adam would join the crowd. When the going gets cognitively demanding, Adam stands out; otherwise, he is part of the crowd.

This approach has its attractions. It is coherent enough to support the bulk of professional interpretations of our children's learning troubles in and out of school. Adam had not been spared professional labels. His LD was well documented not just by the school, but by a university reading clinic that he attended for tutoring. As much as he seemed fine in Everyday Life, school work seemed terribly hard for him. Although Adam's case was extreme, this is an experience that we all recognize. That Everyday Life seems easier than Testing Sessions is a basic fact of life for us all, and tying it to cognitive difficulties makes great intuitive sense. In addition, once questions about children are framed in these terms, once our inquiry is narrowed down to the question of what is wrong with this or that child, support for a deficit theory can be found wherever one looks. If we go to our tapes of Adam and his friends, they constantly behaved as if they avoided tasks that were too difficult for them, and they worried about looking like they could have a deficit of some kind. If they did get caught not knowing something important, they offered excuses. In the Testing Sessions, Adam hardly seems to address the tasks at hand. Given that they are so hard, he simply uses what extratask information he can get to guess at the answer. If he has to choose between cup and spoon for the answer, he says, "Cu- um-spoon" slowly enough to pick the answer that the tester seems to respond to; it is easier to use Everyday Life cues than to think out the questions. In the Cooking Club, if isolated from Peter and faced with thinking demands, he goes off to play with a friend; if there is no choice but to confront the task, he can feign crying or an allergy attack until someone comes to his aid. He can also be quite clear about his troubles; in a Classroom Lesson, he throws down his pencil and says that he can't do it – "It's too hard." Cognitive difficulties separate those who can from those who cannot and make the deficits obvious.

The deficit approach rests on a number of assumptions of questionable validity, however. Although it is true that Everyday Life *seems* easier than life in school, there is no reason to assume that the difference has only to do with increased cognitive demands. The tasks do not have to be cognitively more complex for us to experience them as harder. The trouble could lie along other dimensions; for example, school tasks could be harder simply because they are more arbitrarily constructed, or because an inadequate performance on school tasks could lead to a degradation ceremony. Experience is a good beginning place for an analysis, but we cannot risk the assumption that our experience can deliver the categories we need to complete an analysis. Apparent cognitive difficulty could be a cover for other realities, a fact that could make deficit and disability inappropriate words for describing Adam.

If we examine the notions of context and learning inherent in the deficit approach, we can gain a little more insight into what we are getting ourselves into when we describe someone as LD. In the deficit theory, as in all commonsense uses of the term, context refers to an empty slot, a container, into which other things are placed. It is the "con" that contains the "text," the bowl that contains the soup. As such, it shapes the contours of its contents; it has its effects only at the borders of the phenomenon under analysis. Notice how different this image is from Birdwhistell's image of the fibers and rope. In the static sense of context, the fibers remain fibers, each unto itself, no matter what their relations with the other fibers or how they are used in a rope. Adam is Adam, and, though different contexts might shape his behavior with different demands, he is what he is. Behind the moment-to-moment relations between things, there are the things, and it is the things that count. The soup does not shape the bowl, and the bowl most certainly does not alter the substance of the soup. Text and context, soup and bowl, fiber and rope, Adam and the various learning scenes, all can be analytically separated and studied on their own without doing violence to the complexity of their situation. A static sense of context delivers a stable world.

Accompanying this sense of context is a static theory of learning. By this account, knowledge and skill enter heads, where they wait passively for situations in which they might prove useful. School-derived knowledge and skill are supposed to generalize and to make children ready for a wide range of adaptive behaviors. The learner is a passive container, filled up by his efforts in school, slowly gathering up the skills purportedly essential to some jobs that will eventually have to be tackled. The problem with LD children is that they enter school without some rudimentary skills for paying attention and processing information. They are hard to fill. Some school situations are easier on them than some others, but in the long run their inability to keep pace with their peers forces them to stand out and fall even further behind. They are what they are; learner and environment are separable, and they do not greatly alter each other.

These static assumptions about context and learning are supported by static notions of both language and culture. The deficit theory assumes that language and culture are storehouses from which children acquire their competence. Some children get more and some get less. These are assertions about which we should be most uncomfortable. Language it seems is not available to the species just for purposes of expression, but for purposes of social alignment, for purposes of getting people into the necessary configurations for certain cultural jobs to get done (Bilmes, 1986; McDermott & Tylbor, 1986; Volosinov, 1929/1973; Wieder, 1974). When language is systematically unavailable to some, it is important that we not limit our explanation to the traits of the persons involved; it is equally essential that we take into account the interactional circumstances that position the people in the world with a differential access to the common tongue (McDermott, 1988). Similarly, it has become increasingly clear that any seeming lack of culture on the parts of some represents a systematic position within a cultural continuum of display only; that is, one way to be a perfectly normal member of a culture is to be a person who seemingly lacks what other members of the culture claim to have (Drummond, 1980; Varenne, 1983; Varenne & McDermott, 1986). Language and culture are not a gold-standard currency with only so much to go around; they are more like phonologies, in which each sound, each position in the mouth, is significant only as it is defined by the other sounds, and no sound is any more real, any more rich, or any more privileged than any other.

The social policy that flows from these static notions of context, learning, language, and culture are easily recognizable to us. Those who do not get enough knowledge from home or school need to be encouraged to get some more. They need to acquire more language and culture in order to be ready for more situations. They cannot afford to learn on the job; they cannot afford to assume that they will be shaped by new contexts, or that the language and culture that they need will be available to them in situ. They need to get more things in their heads to cut down their deficits in the face of difficult demands.

When we line up for consideration the assumptions about context, learning, language, and culture, we have to wonder whether we have available in the deficit theory a way of describing anything that is alive. Certainly, these static models have given us some predictive powers; for example, children called LD early in school generally continue to do badly. But we must remember here Gramsci's (1971) warning that we are not seeking a science of people that only predicts behavior; if things are not good today, there is little use for a science that simply tells us that they will be the same tomorrow.[8] Science should not assume that people are dead; nor should it help to choke them to death with categories that do not reveal the rich lives and struggles of all who appear left behind. In choosing an approach to Adam, we must be careful that we do not trust our common sense too much; if it were as sturdy a guide as we would like, why are we and many of our children in so much trouble. The same facts that we have suggested as support for a deficit approach to Adam's problem can be understood in other ways, and possibly with better results.

The continuum of arbitrary demands and left-out participants

The second way of looking at the range in Adam's performances has us focusing less on Adam and more on the tasks he is asked to perform. In Everyday Life, Adam can use any resources to get a job done. If he has to remember a telephone number, he can memorize it, write it down, call information, or ask a friend. School tasks are different from this in that a person is often restricted in what he can make use of; procedure is of the essence. On tests, this trend is exaggerated. What else is a test but an occasion on which you cannot use any of the resources normally available for solving some problem; memory notes or helping friends are now called cheating. Is it possible that Adam is better understood as a child who is faced not by increasingly more difficult tasks, but increasingly more arbitrary tasks? We were quite sensitive to this possibility at the time when we first looked at Adam. At the very least, cross-cultural psychology had been extraordinarily clear in showing how various kinds of smartness could be reduced to apparent ignorance in the face of culturally arbitrary and cross-culturally foolish tasks (Cole & Means, 1981). We were interested in the possibility that the same problem existed in our own schools, most obviously for children from culturally and linguistically different minority groups, and more generally for us all at different times in our school career.

In Everyday Life, Adam found the resources at his disposal more than adequate. In the Cooking Club, he had an equivalent freedom if he was working with a friend. If, however, he was working with someone who was not willing to help, or if the people around him were trying to outdo him, then the task of cooking suddenly became more difficult. It is not just the case that Cooking Club can be made easy by someone helping Adam to do what he cannot; it is rather that, under the gentle circumstances of working with the friend to make a cake together, he can do what he cannot do if the task is both to make a cake and not to get caught not knowing how to read a recipe. In the Cooking Club, we quite by accident organized some confusing circumstances for children of this age: for example, a two-cup cup, teaspoon and tablespoon, baking soda and baking powder, ingredients on one side of the page and instructions on the other side. Adam's friend Peter is one of the children who could sort out these problems; when working with Peter, Adam not only followed the directions Peter reads to him, he sometimes reads the recipe himself. When working under less gentle circumstances, he will rarely look at the page. The task is obscured by the social work he must do to arrange not looking incompetent. In this way, reading "teaspoon" for "tablespoon" becomes more likely, not because Adam's head does not work, but because he barely looks at the page and ordinary resources for the solution to the problem are disallowed. In the Testing Session, Adam is so preoccupied with getting the answer that it is not clear he even hears many of the questions. He might be handling more mental steps avoiding the questions than he would have to handle if he addressed the questions. Arbitrary demands make him stand out. There may be more to LD than disability.

Understanding Adam by way of the arbitrariness of the demands placed on him represents an advance over the blind ascription of the deficit approach. It encourages, for example, a more careful look at the child and his circumstances and insists that we be more sensitive to what might be going on in the child's surround. However, to the extent that it leaves our commonsense assumptions of the relation between learner, task, and setting undisturbed, it quickly falls back into a deficit theory. Why is it, one could ask, that Peter can handle all the arbitrariness and Adam cannot? It is understandable why immigrants to the country run into these troubles for a few years, or even for a generation or two. But everyone should be able to adjust. Now consider that Peter is black and from a poor, tough neighborhood and Adam is from a wealthy, white family from the right part of town. It still comes down to one head against the world a few times a day, and Adam's head does not measure up. What are arbitrary demands anyway? What aren't arbitrary demands?

Upon careful examination, the continuum of arbitrariness leaves us with the same sense of context, learning, language, and culture as the deficit account. The conceptual assumptions remain the same. Contexts and their demands are still static, although there are more of them than allowed by the deficit approach. Adam is still Adam, and tests are tests. Contexts and their members are still separable. Learning still sits inside the student waiting to be called forth, although now in the form of specific sets of skills that must be used in situationally specific ways. Language and culture are still the sorts of things one can have more or less of, as if those who had less were not a systematic version of the culture everyone else had.

A continuum of degradation and labeled children

A third approach to Adam's behavior focuses on how much and on what grounds a person is liable to degradation in the different settings. What is at stake here is an appreciation of how much each setting organizes the search for and location of differential performances and how much that search further organizes the degradation of those found at the bottom of the pile. Garfinkel (1956; Pollner, 1978; see also Pollner & McDonald-Wikler, 1985, for a stunning reverse case) has shown how degradation is always a ceremony in which public agreement on what one can be degraded for is displayed and directed against the total identity of others. This means that it takes much work across persons to make an individual liable for some part of their behavior; a person must not only do the wrong thing, but exactly the wrong thing that everyone is looking for someone to do and then at just the right time.

By this line of reasoning, Adam is a problem in Everyday Life, primarily because everyday life is well organized for the systematic location of problems (Scott, 1985). Cooking Club is mostly about cooking, and only occasionally a source for a learning-related degradation ceremony. On one occasion, Adam and a friend made a green cranberry bread (a physical possibility, we are told, in an aluminum bowl with ingredients inserted in just the wrong order). When the others gathered around to see and laugh, he simply said, "So I made a goddamn mistake, so what." The issue passed. Other occasions for degradation do not move along so easily, no matter Adam's response. Classroom Lessons, for example, can be so well organized for putting the spotlight on those who are doing less well than the others that hiding becomes a sensible strategy for all of the kids some of the time and for some of the kids all the time. Adam seemed to suffer in the classroom, and this is in part how he became visible to us. During one small-group reading lesson, Adam was having a difficult time matching words with accompanying pictures. Reading "fake" for "face," he became tangled in a complex conversation with the teacher as she walked in and out of his group with occasional tips for the kids. It took us days of looking even to guess at the ways they seemed to be not understanding each other. What kept us curious was the attention paid to Adam's disability by the other children in his group. Adam's LD generally played to a packed house. Everyone knew how to look for, recognize, stimulate, make visible, and, depending upon the circumstances, keep quiet about or expose Adam's problem. Occasionally, they tried to explain it; "cause it's hard for him," explained Peter to the other kids. Occasionally, they wondered aloud about it; while walking behind him on a day when things were not going well, René shook her whole body, stamped her foot, and yelled after him, "Ohh. Why can't you read?" Testing Sessions, of course, exacerbate these problems, and Adam was at his least functional under these conditions.

There may be more to LD than disability. There may be many other people involved: certainly everyone in Adam's classroom, in various ways everyone in the school, everyone in the schooling business, all of us. This fact hit us hard the day Adam was asked to make banana bread in the Cooking Club. The adult showed them how to do it, and the pairs of children were then to do it on their own. Adam and Peter stayed close to each other as was their pattern when they entered the room. They then played ball on the side of the room as the adult did the demonstration bread. When they came to do it on their own, Peter announced he was allergic to bananas. Adam would have to go it alone or with someone else. Adam worked on getting others to help, but, to make a long and fascinating story unfortunately short, it came down to Adam against the recipe, his head against the world. The adult was annoyed with Adam for not watching the demonstration and was actively unhelpful. The other children were either making their own cakes or busy exposing Adam's not being able to work on his. In the first 10 minutes, from the time he first picked up the recipe, he asked for information from others 12 times, but each time came away unsure of what he needed to know. He looks at the recipe a few times, but it is not clear that he ever reads it; either way, it is perfectly clear that whatever he picks up from whatever source, he tries to double check it with those around him. After these 12 requests for information, he makes a crucial error. He is putting the ingredients into the bowl as they are listed in the ingredients section, and not in the order specified in the directions. This has him putting in yogurt second instead of fourth, and before the more efficient workers finish with their third entry, namely, bananas. Quite aside from using the list of ingredients as instructions, his error was in seemingly going faster than Nadine's group. Nadine liked to finish her cake first. Adam might be ahead of them, or he might be wrong. Either way, his disability might be a good way to focus on the problem. It might be time to spotlight Adam. It might be time for LD to make it into the room. For anyone needing to know who is doing what, how fast, and how well, the ascription of LD might offer an appropriate guide to perception. Let's listen to how a moment is organized for a conversational display of LD:

(The girls are screaming and Adam whimpering. The double vowels in Lucy's talk are chosen to show that she is reading to Adam as one would read to a child in a phonics lesson. The scene opens with Adam returning from the adult with the sense that he knows what to do next.)

Adam:	Finally!
	Where's the yogurt. Oh.
Nadine:	You're *up* to yogurt already.
Adam:	Yeah.
Nadine:	Where's the bananas.
Adam:	We, uhm, they didn't give us bananas yet.
Nadine:	Well, go get 'em.
Adult:	The bananas are here on the shelf.

Adam:	But this is our second page.
Lucy:	That is a teaspoon. That is a tablespoon.
Adam:	This is a teaspoon, and it says
Lucy:	It says tablespoons, twoo taablespooons.
Adam:	We're right here, Lawana. Lawana, we're right here.
Lucy:	That's
Nadine:	That's the ingredients, not the instructions.
Lucy:	That's baakiing powowder.
Adam:	What do you mean, baking powder?
Nadine:	You go in this order.
Adam:	(Oh my God). What do you mean, in what order?
Nadine:	Look! This is the instructions. That's what you need to do all this.
Adam:	Ai yai yai.
	One . . . Cup . . . Mashed . . . Fresh

(Everyone looks away, and Adam returns to the adult for more advice.)

When Adam takes the recipe back to his bowl, he holds the paper in front of his face, and offers a public, but mock reading (with the actual words from the ingredients list): "One . . . Cup . . . Mashed . . . Fresh." Then he is off to the adult for some questions and a little crying. Walking back into the group, he cries out, "I was right, stupid" to no one in particular and then calls his nominal partner, "Ah, c'mon, Reggie. Wouldjya." Reggie attends to the tears, "Crying?" and, after a few seconds, says, "Here, I'll help ya."

How many people are involved in Adam's visibility? Reggie, Nadine, Lucy, the adult, of course. In addition to all the people in the room, did it make a difference that we set up the club to see what the kids could do with a minimum of help, or that we were all getting paid on government grants to figure out the nature of school failure? More of course. Could Adam be disabled on his own? Only if he could work on a task that was not culturally defined and had no consequences for his life with others; that not being a possibility, he can only be disabled through his interactions with others. Culture is a sine qua non of disability. Could he be disabled without LD being a part of the communicative resources available to the Cooking Club members in their dealings with each other? Why couldn't he be wrong just about how he was making the banana bread? There was something else in the air. There was the issue of his skill and how it measured up to the skills of others. Was he up to yogurt already? There are basic questions asked in all scenes called educative in America: Who can do it? Who can't? Who is smart? Who is dumb? These are not the dominant questions that are asked in all scenes in America; they can leak by way of school into homes and onto some jobs, much less in school yards, and not at all in singles bars, but they are ubiquitous in schools. How is it, Goffman (1979) once asked, that a young man cannot know a word in school and feel dumb and not know a word in a car garage and have not his intelligence but his masculinity put on the line? An identical cognitive absence can be interpreted different ways depending on the scene. For Adam, school scenes often result in everyone's recognition that he can't, that he has "got it all wrong," that he may never be able, that he will always "can't." These questions acquire their answers, and in the process, with the help of tests, diagnoses, specialists, and government-sponsored budgets, LD acquires its share of the children.

The degradation account of Adam's behavior along the continuum of scenes relies on a different sense of context, learning, language, and culture than the previous approaches. If the assumptions of this approach are a little better tuned with our experiences, and possibly a little less lethal to our children, then we may have grounds to prefer a degradation approach to the others.

Context

Context is not a fixed entity to Adam, for it shifts with the interactional winds. Each new second produces new possibilities along with severe constraints on what is possible. So it is with the rest of the people in Adam's world. Everyday Life, Cooking Club, Classroom Lessons, and Testing Sessions all come stacked with limits on what can be accomplished together, while at the same time each scene is constantly on the verge of being something else. Generally, each scene turns out to have been approximately what it started out to be, but only because everyone worked to help each other to such an ending. Along the way, they followed each other's instructions and constructed a new day like the one before. In this sense, context is not so much something into which someone is put, but an order of behavior of which one is a part. In this same sense, fibers are not so much put into ropes as they participate in an organization of fibers that makes their every move relevant only to the extent that they play out the life of a rope. Similarly, Adam was a contributing member of various organizations that made his behavior relevant to the life of LD; this happened more often in Testing Sessions and Classroom Lessons than it did in Cooking Club or Everyday Life, and this was made possible by people, including Adam, organizing these scenes in ways that made LD differentially available in the different scenes.

Adam's LD is made available for all to see, because everyone was looking for it. In the Cooking Club, it is not so much the difficulty of the material as that Adam cannot address the material without worrying about whether he can get it straight or whether anyone will notice if he does not. This is not paranoia; everyone is often ready to notice, and, depending on the situation, ready also to look away or to make Adam's problem even more public. In the quoted transcript, Adam's LD is made public. Looking for Adam's LD has become something of a sport in Adam's class, a subset of the wider sport of finding each other not knowing things. In the Cooking Club, many kids get things wrong without too much worry; their wrong moves speak only to not knowing how to follow a badly organized recipe. The same mistakes are for Adam a source of degradation. They speak to his LD. Adam spends his day arranging not to get caught not having information that he could get from print. His every move is designed not to have LD again ascribed to him, and, as such, his every move confirms and recreates the possibility that the label of LD will be available in the classroom for anyone to ascribe to Adam. "Where is the LD?" Behaviorally, the answer is clear. It is all over the classroom as an interactional possibility. Everyone stands in some relation to it. Everyone is part of the choreography that produces moments for its public appearance. LD is distributed across persons, across the moment, as part of the contextual work members do in the different scenes. Neither Adam, nor his disability, can be separated from the contexts in which they emerge.

Learning

By taking such a radical stand on context, the degradation approach relies exclusively on the description of the *organization* of behavior for subject matter. Neither Adam nor his disability are analytically available as entities; they are only intelligible as relations, and then only moments in relations.[9] What then of learning? Learning traditionally gets measured on the assumption that it is a possession of individuals that can be found inside their heads. By the degradation approach, learning is not in heads, but in the relations between people. Learning is in the conditions that bring people together and organize a point of contact that allows for particular pieces of information to take on relevance; without the points of contact, without the system of relevancies, there is no learning, and there is little memory. Learning does not belong to individual persons, but to the various conversations of which they are a part. What we call learning, warns Birdwhistell, is simply the other side of an institutionalized dance called teaching. We all know how to do it, to look like either learners or teachers, but the actual relation between taking on roles in the teacher–learner dance and the contexts in which we do learning seems obscure at best. Birdwhistell, in fact, hints that they might be mutually exclusive, that it takes so much attention to do the teacher–learner dance, there is little room for new information to enter the system.

When Adam works in the cooking club with Peter, he gets his cake made, and he reads the recipe. Conditions were ripe for new information to be made available to Adam, information that had him taking language from a printed page. When he has to work on his own, under the possibly degrading eyes of others, a quite different kind of information enters the system. Under these latter conditions, he gets no time to read, but he gets constant instruction on how to look LD. The instructions stored in the system are not simply about how to read. Reading to get the cake made is not Adam's only point of contact with the other members of the class. The instructions stored in the system are also about who is to finish first, with the best banana bread, with the recognition that they are the most competent. Given this more inclusive agenda, information about how to read can get lost easily, and Adam can get acquired by LD. It is the business of degradation and not education that seems to organize selected moments in the Cooking Club, even more moments in Classroom Lessons, and more still in the Testing Sessions.

Language and culture

The language and culture that Adam encounters in his daily round may not be what most of us assume them to be. Language is easily understood as a neutral tool of expression that helps us to say and write what we like and to interpret what others have said and written for us. On these grounds, Adam needs more language. Like most children called LD, he loses his words at various important times, and reading and writing are pure torture for him. More language for sure. By the degradation stand, however, Adam's language may be quite complete. Language is not a neutral medium; it comes to us loaded with social structure. It comes to us loaded with sensitivities to the circumstances under which it was born and maintained in previous encounters. It comes to us biased with the social agendas of a school system that pits all children against all children in a battle for success. What is true of the contexts in which Adam finds himself called LD is no less true of the English language that we use in schools and in our interpretation of children in schools; they are well organized for the systematic creation of behavioral absences, which are carefully monitored by all in the system for use in their accounts of how the world works. Indeed, all of American culture seems well poised to have Adam and millions of others failing in school. By this standard, Adam has exactly the language required of his position. Culturally, he is taking one of two perfectly normal pathways through school: He is failing. There is a language waiting in every classroom in America for anyone who might take that road, and Adam has done his job well. He acquired and was acquired by a culturally recognized and mandated absence. He had achieved school failure. Adam had been acquired by the language of LD that was in place before he was born.

Languages help us to build the scales along which we calculate our pluses and minuses. So it is with culture. The poet John Montague grew up without a mother and was taunted by the members of his culture for not having what was prescribed for all children. Bad enough not to have a mother, but to be taunted for it as well is a double loss. "There is an absence," he warns, "real as presence" (Montague, 1983, p. 29). Cultures do not just promise mothers; they require them, or worse, they require just one, your own. Nothing less than your own mother is acceptable, and nothing less than a perfectly normal cognitive development is acceptable either. To grow up unable to learn as fast as others is a loss in a school system that emphasizes and measures comparative development, and to be taunted for it is a double loss.

These are important distinctions. Mothers precede their children like languages precede their next generation of speakers. Cultures and languages fill the world before any given child's arrival, and they define what must be present and what must be noticed as absent. Montague had to go it without a mother, and, as a stutterer, he had to go without a full compliment of English for some time, "until the sweet oils of poetry eased it, let the light in." That was tough on Montague, but the overall cultural system sounds gentle enough, particularly if we supply proper services for the orphaned and the inarticulate. Culture and language define what each of us needs, force us to attend to those of us who are left short, and ideally equip us to help them over their disabilities. Unfortunately, cultures are never so magnanimous, nor can they be. As a series of ideal types, *cultures are defined most essentially by the inability of all to live up to their directives.* Cultures offer only "collective illusions," prescriptions that give us a way to talk about how we should live together in exchange for an inarticulateness about how we actually do live together (Murphy, 1971, 1987). Cultures cannot supply the resources members need in order to live in them without exposing the arbitrariness of their particular way of life. They exist by their promises, and they feed off each of us to the extent that we try to follow them and fail.[10] They give us mothers and fathers without letting us think that mothers and fathers have to be many other things as well (e.g., spouses, siblings, workers, lovers, and in each of these roles possibly neurotic, pained, bored, oppressed, and even dead); and they give us language to express ourselves without letting us know the limits of expression, without telling us that inarticulateness is endemic to the human condition. And so too they give us LD.

Mothers acquire their children. Languages acquire their speakers. So disabilities acquire their learners. Who is there first? Long before Adam was born, we had LD – or an equivalent: strethosymbolia, for example, or just plain stupidity. It is an absence we know how to look for. American culture makes the absence of learning real as presence.

Before any teachers of children enter the schools every September, failure is in every room in America. There is never a question of whether everyone is going to succeed or fail, only of who is going to fail. Because everyone cannot do better than everyone else, failure is an absence real as presence, and it acquires its share of the children. Failure and success define each other into separate corners, and the children are evenly divided as if by a normal curve, into successful and failing. Among those who fail are those who fail in ways that the system knows how to identify with tests, and these children are called special names. LD acquires its share of the children.

The degradation approach alters considerably our commonsense resources for understanding our problems. Context and learning no longer have individual subjects as variables, but refer instead to the organizing devices people have available for dealing with each other. Similarly, language and culture are no longer scripts to be acquired, as much as they are conversations in which people can participate. The question of who is learning what and how much is essentially a question of what conversations they are a part of, and this question is a subset of the more powerful question of what conversations are around to be had in a given culture (Goodwin, 1991). To answer these questions, we must give up our preoccupation with individual performance and examine instead the structure of resources and disappointments made available to people in various institutions. To do this job, we may not need a theory of individual learning, and, given its use in our current educational system, we may not be able to afford one.

Appendix

The problem of ecological validity: A summary in 1990 of Cole, Hood, & McDermott (1978)

Our effort was to specify the relation between tasks well defined in experimental settings and apparently similar tasks as they appear in everyday life. What might the literature on models of memory or attention be about if one cannot find some way of applying the models to people remembering and attending in their daily activities?

We tackled our question with four bodies of evidence, each displaying different assumptions about the world and forcing different methods of analysis. First, we went to the literature to look for speculations about how thinking is done in everyday life. Throughout psychology, we found a strong bias that everyday-life thinking is an impoverished version of what can be elicited in special and more demanding settings such as tests and experiments. This makes great common sense, but leaves unspecified just how tests and experiments demand more mental steps of us or just how everyday life can proceed without logical precision.

Our second body of evidence came from the efforts of experimental psychologists to use experimental data to reach conclusions about minds at work outside the laboratory. Their results seem to show that people thinking in everyday life have many supports on their side; the world is well structured and redundant in a way that eases the demands on their thinking. Individual thinkers can be sloppy, but the world will carry them. In experimental settings, they have less support, and their thinking processes become both more efficient and more visible.

For our third and fourth bodies of evidence, we turned to videotapes of children and adults engaging in complex activities together, for example, making cakes, setting up a nature laboratory, or giving and taking intelligence tests. The difference between the third and fourth approach turned on how each organized a description. For our third case, we looked at the videotapes through the descriptive categories of experimental psychology. When we saw what we thought might be an example of remembering, we wrote it down. The same for attending and problem solving. By restricting our language and insights to the rules of experimental psychology, that is, by assuming that the people were offered tasks that could be reasonably well defined and stable enough to last through the duration of the problem solver's effort, we found considerable evidence for the good sense of both the speculations and the experimental evidence for the characterization of everyday life as easier in its demands on thinking.

For our fourth body of evidence, we used the same behavior, but looked at it in a different way. Instead of deciding beforehand what we were looking for, we looked at the tapes to see how the participants were organizing each other. Whether or not a person was trying to remember something was not our immediate concern, for we wanted to stay open to the possibility that any apparent act of remembering could well be a subordinate part of another activity (instances of people really trying to remember something actually being rare outside of school); we were also interested in the possibility that much of what passes for remembering in everyday life is nothing but a display of memory, that is, a socially well orchestrated interaction in which looking like one is remembering is socially consequential, but with likely little relevance to actual psychological processes glossed in the literature on memory. Looking in this way, we saw little that looked like psychological events and little that would require the description of the ghost in the machine for an explanation of how the behavior of the participants was organized.

In Figure 10.3, under the four columns listing our four bodies of evidence, are three positions about the difficulty of thinking in everyday life and the possibility of specifying thinking in laboratory settings in any way that would be relevant to the lives of people in their institutional worlds. The first story has it that thinking in everyday life is almost too easy to be interesting, and it is only by challenging people with the rigors of careful laboratory experimentation that one can capture minds at work. The second story has it that everyday-life thinking is well supported by the world, which makes thought processes invisible enough that can only be apprehended in the less supportive world of the laboratory. The third story has it that thinking in everyday life is likely more complicated than any category system we can impose on its study, and, given the reflexive nature of all task environments, any science that relies on predetermined tasks for analysis is necessarily distorting the description of people's thinking in ways that render such descriptions systematically invalid in ecological, historical, or institutional terms. In the chart, each of the three stories is put against each of our four bodies of evidence for support.

The result is a hopefully useful snapshot of the range of claims that can be worked on and verified by different methods. To the extent that the field relies on predefined tasks against which to measure people's performances, experimental cognitive psychology can only detail the lack of complexity in the thinking people do in everyday life; nor is there any way for it to take into account the

	Speculations	Experimental Evidence	Observational Evidence	Natural History Analyses
Story 1	Simple and sloppy	Simple and sloppy	Simple and sloppy	Indeterminate on many levels
Story 2	Redundant, structured, and socially organized	Redundant, structured, and socially organized	Redundant, structured, and socially organized	Structured by the work people do; indeterminate and possibly difficult
Story 3	Difficult to do or to specify	Unverifiable by experimental procedures	Unverifiable by experimental procedures	Endlessly complex; hard for participants and specifiable only with rigor and respect

Figure 10.3. Ways of theorizing and studying psychological tasks, their appearance in everyday life, and their relative complexity.

ecological, historical, or institutional situations in which and with which people do their thinking (and further constitute and reflexively organize those same situations). A more contextually sensitive description of people's behavior would deliver us a much more complex and lifelike dramatis personae, but would offer us little reason to continue the study of memory, attention, and problem solving as that study is presently phrased. We have a choice between the precision study of well-established topics with little relevance to the ongoing world or the rigorous study of the as yet undefined things people do with each other in their collective lives. This chapter urges that we choose the people over the topics, rigor and respect over misplaced precision. Others may choose otherwise, but we cannot forget Wittgenstein's (1958, p. 232; see also Skupien, 1990) warning that in psychology "the existence of the experimental method makes us think that we have the means of solving the problems which trouble us; though problem and method pass one another by." We have reached the point that this mistake has been institutionalized. Ecological invalidity has become a requirement of most available interpretations of our own children. It is part of how children are acquired by learning disabilities.

Story I: Everyday life is sloppy and easy. Educational professionals know better

Everyday-life tasks are generally assumed to be simple in the sense that they require fewer mental steps than laboratory tasks. Participants are allowed a wide range of mistakes and are not held accountable for errors and oversights. Everyday-life tasks are not usually studied by psychologists, but the general assumption of simplicity can be found in various speculations, and can be supported, tangentially, by experimental studies and by observational studies restricted to the analytic language of experimental cognitive psychology. Once the world is studied with full attention to the complexities of people's lives, tasks become hard to define and the speculations and their verification seem to be precarious.

Story II: Everyday life is complex but well organized.
Educational professionals understand how to make the most of
an environment

Everyday-life tasks are complex, but easy to perform because they are embedded in the structure of discourse and the stuff of social interaction; for example, free recall of isolated items may be hard, but items structured in narrative seem to enhance memory skills. Inside the assumptions of experimental cognitive psychology, everyday life and its inhabitants are analytically available as more or less efficient structures for moving through the world attending, remembering, planning, and problem solving in experimentally interesting ways. Outside the logic of predefined tasks, actors become capable of acting in much more complex ways that can be predecided by psychologists; everyday-life tasks become analytically indeterminate and everyday life exhausting.

Story III: Everyday life is an adventure. The people know more
than we can yet imagine about what they are doing

In everyday life, tasks are reflexively defined and constituted from one moment to the next. There is great risk in assuming that the world will stand still long enough for us to analyze it; if it were that easy, we would not need to study it. Appropriating tasks from ongoing activities for purposes of analysis must be justified in terms of the ecological, historical, and institutional validity of the analysis. Conclusions about how people think and with what degree of efficiency are unverifiable without a supportive institutional analysis. By this standard, most contemporary psychology is invalid. Experimental methods can only document variation in what people cannot do in relation to supposedly well-defined, frozen tasks. That may be useful for delineating how the mind in some general sense might work. It is not useful, and cannot be useful, to the description of our children as they live complex institutional lives. Theoretically, at least, our children can be freed from being acquired by disabilities.

Notes

1. See the Appendix summarizing the arguments of the earlier work. We were to finish a book on the topic, but our lives have diverged enough to make the task impossible. The working paper we circulated in 1978 has enjoyed some notoriety and is still cited in the literature. Only excerpts have been published so far, and in the Appendix, I offer a summary of that paper's overall intentions and results.

2. The title is adapted with appreciation from Cicourel (1970) and Sankoff and Laberge (1973).

3. We should never forget Margaret Rawson's (1968) account of the remarkable accomplishments of dyslexic boys who receive an education directed to their strengths rather than weaknesses.

4. Because the conference focused on context, it makes sense to use Birdwhistell (1970; McDermott, 1980) for a key formulation. The tradition of which he is a part, including the work of Bateson (1972), Scheflen (1973), and Kendon (1982, 1990), has been principled in the use of the term. Compatible ideas (cited throughout this volume) are available in Soviet activity theory and American ethnomethodology and cognitive anthropology. For example, compare the similarities in Birdwhistell's formulation of context with the following quote from Schegloff (1984, p. 52):

   > Taking sentences in isolation is not just a matter of taking such sentences that might appear *in* a context *out* of a context; but that the very composition, construction, assemblage of the sentences is predicated by their speakers on the place in which it is being produced, and it is through *that* that a sentence is context-bound, rather than possibly independent sentences being different intact objects in and out of context.

   What is true here of sentences is true of any behavior we might want to use as a unit of analysis.

5. For a psychology founded on the possibility that such "illusions" are in fact the key to the ways we perceive the most mundane aspects of the world, see Kohler (1969); in the same mold, Lewin's (1933/1935) paper on the feebleminded makes a number of points relevant to the argument of this chapter.

6. There is an obvious similarity between Birdwhistell's "conditions that maintain the contact" in terms of which new information (learning) enters the interactional arena and Vygotsky's "zone of proximal development" (1978, 1934/1986; Engeström, 1986; Minick, 1985, this volume; Newman, Griffin, & Cole, 1989). By distancing his formulation from ordinary, dyadic theories of teaching and learning, Birdwhistell makes essential what is often not appreciated in Vygotsky, namely, that one person cannot *do* a zone of proximal development to another; at their pedagogical best, people can only *participate* together in a zone of proximal development. Cole and Griffin (1986) offer one stunning example and Lave and Wenger (1991) an exciting overview of the issue.

7. There is of course no descriptive foundation to the assumption that everyday

life is "easier." No one who has ever looked carefully at films of human behavior could claim that. The question of comparative difficulty, as different from comparative usefulness, for example, will hopefully become uninteresting. Assumptions about comparative ease play a dominant role in contemporary psychological theory and are called into question in the Appendix.

8. The following lines show that Gramsci is making both an epistemological and a political complaint about prediction as a criterion of excellence in social science description:

> But the fact has not been properly emphasised that statistical laws can be employed in the science and art of politics only so long as the great masses of the population remain (or at least are reputed to remain) essentially passive, in relation to the questions which interest historians and politicians . . . in politics the assumption of the law of statistics as an essential law operating of necessity is not only a scientific error, but becomes a practical error in action. (1971, pp. 428–429)

The inappropriateness of prediction as a goal in ethnography is well claimed in the essays of Frake (1980).

9. Much the same point is offered in the tradition of Soviet activity theory (Cole & Griffin, 1986, p. 127):

> We should be trying to instantiate a basic *activity* when teaching reading and not get blinded by the basic *skills*. Skills are always part of activities and settings, but they only take on meaning in terms of how they are organized. So instead of basic skills, a sociohistorical approach talks about basic activities and instantiates those that are necessary and sufficient to carry out the whole process of reading, given the general conditions for learning.

10. Another formulation to the same point is available in Suchman (1987). The dialectics of life in a culture with particularly empty promises will perhaps never be captured better than in Beckett's (1938) *Murphy*, a near relative to Murphy's (1975, 1987) Murphy. In Beckett's *Murphy*, Neary is finding life without Miss Counihan unbearable, and Wiley explains our world to him (1938, pp. 58–59):

> "From all of which I am to infer," said Neary, "correct me if I am wrong, that the possession – Deus det! – of angel Counihan will create an aching void to the same amount."
>
> "Humanity is a well with two buckets," said Wiley, "one going down to be filled, the other coming up to be emptied."
>
> "What I make on the swings of Miss Counihan," said Neary, "if I understand you, I lose on the roundabouts of the non-Miss Counihan."
>
> "Very prettily put," said Wiley.
>
> "There is no non-Miss Counihan," said Neary.
>
> "There will be," said Wiley.
>
> "Help there to be," cried Neary, clasping his hands, "in this Coney Eastern Island that is Neary, some Chinese abstractions other than Miss Counihan."
>
> "Now you are talking," said Wiley. "When you ask for heal-all you are not talking. But when you ask for a single symptom to be superseded, then I am bound to admit that you are talking."

References

Bartlett, F. (1958). *Thinking.* New York: Basic Books.

Bateson, G. (1972). *Steps to an ecology of mind.* New York: Ballantine.

Beckett, F. (1938). *Murphy.* New York: Evergreen.

Belmonte, T. (1989). *Broken fountain* (2nd ed.). New York: Columbia University Press.

Bilmes, J. (1986). *Discourse and behavior.* New York: Plenum.

Birdwhistell, R. (1970). *Kinesics and context.* Philadelphia: University of Pennsylvania Press.

Bourdieu, P. (1977). *Outline of a theory of practice* (R. Nice, Trans.). Cambridge: Cambridge University Press. (Original work published 1972)

Byers, P. (1985). Conversation: A context for communication. *Nagoya Gakuin Daigaku, Gaikokugo Kyoiku Kiyo, 13,* 26–40.

Chamboredon, J., & Prevot, J. (1975). Changes in the social definition of early childhood and the new forms of symbolic violence. *Theory and Society, 2,* 331–350.

Cicourel, A. V. (1970). The acquisition of social structure: Toward a developmental sociology of language and meaning. In J. D. Douglas (Ed.), *Understanding everyday life* (pp. 136–168). Chicago: Aldine.

Cole, M., & Griffin, P. (1986). A sociohistorical approach to remediation. In S. deCastell, A. Luke, & K. Egan (Eds.), *Literacy, schooling, and society.* Cambridge: Cambridge University Press.

Cole, M., Hood, L., & McDermott, R. P. (1978). *Ecological niche picking: Ecological invalidity as an axiom of current experimental cognitive psychology* (Working paper no. 14). New York: Laboratory of Comparative Human Cognition, Rockefeller University.

Cole, M., & Means, B. (1981). *Comparative studies of how people think.* Cambridge, MA: Harvard University Press.

Cole, M., & Traupmann, K. (1981). Comparative cognitive research: Learning from a learning disabled child. In W. A. Collins (Ed.), *Aspects of the development of competence* (Minnesota symposium on child psychology, Vol. 14, pp. 125–154). Hillsdale, NJ: Lawrence Erlbaum.

Drummond, L. (1980). The cultural continuum. *Man, 14,* 352–374.

Engeström, Y. (1986). The zone of proximal development as the basic category of educational psychology. *Quarterly Newsletter of the Laboratory of Comparative Human Cognition, 8*(1), 23–42.

Frake, C. (1980). *Language and cultural description.* Stanford, CA: Stanford University Press.

Fraser, J. (1908). A new visual illusion of direction. *British Journal of Psychology, 2,* 307–320.

Garfinkel, H. (1956). Conditions for a successful degradation ceremony. *American Journal of Sociology, 61,* 420–424.

Goffman, E. (1979). *Gender advertisements.* London: Macmillan.

Goodwin, M. (1991). *He-Said-She-Said.* Bloomington: Indiana University Press.

Gramsci, A. (1971). *Selections from the prison notebooks*. New York: International Publishers. (Original work written between 1929 and 1935 and published between 1949 and 1951)

Hood, L., McDermott, R. P., & Cole, M. (1980). "Let's try to make it a good day" – Some not so simple ways. *Discourse Processes, 3*, 155–168.

Kendon, A. (1982). The organization of behavior in face to face interaction: Observations on the development of a methodology. In K. Scherer & P. Ekman (Eds.), *Handbook of methods in nonverbal behavior research* (pp. 440–505). Cambridge: Cambridge University Press.

Kendon, A. (1990). *Conducting interaction*. Cambridge: Cambridge University Press.

Kohler, W. (1969). *The task of gestalt psychology*. Princeton: Princeton University Press.

Lave, J. (1988a). *Cognition in practice*. Cambridge: Cambridge University Press.

Lave, J. (1988b). *The culture of acquisition and the practice of understanding* (Report IRL88-0007). Palo Alto, CA: Institute for Research on Learning.

Lave, J., & Wenger, E. (1991). *Situated learning: Legitimate peripheral participation*. Cambridge: Cambridge University Press.

Lewin, K. (1935). A dynamic theory of the feeble-minded. In *Dynamic theory of personality* (D. K. Adams & K. E. Zener, Trans.; pp. 194–238). New York: McGraw-Hill. (Original work published 1933)

McDermott, R. P. (1980). Profile: Ray L. Birdwhistell. *Kinesis Report, 2*(3), 1–4, 14–16.

McDermott, R. P. (1988). Inarticulateness. In D. Tannen (Ed.), *Linguistics in context* (pp. 37–68). Norwood, NJ: Ablex.

McDermott, R. P., Gospodinoff, K., & Aron, J. (1978). Criteria for an ethnographically adequate description of the activities and their contexts. *Semiotica, 24*, 245–275.

McDermott, R. P., & Tylbor, H. (1986). On the necessity of collusion in conversation. In S. Fisher & A. Todd (Eds.), *Discourse and institutional authority* (pp. 123–139). Norwood, NJ: Ablex.

Mannoni, M. (1972). *The backward child and his mother* (A. M. Sheridan, Trans.). New York: Random House. (Original work published 1964)

Mehan, H. (1992). Understanding inequality in schools: The contribution of interpretive studies. *Sociology of Education, 65*, 1–20.

Mehan, H., Hertweck, A., & Meihls, J. L. (1986). *Handicapping the handicapped*. Stanford, CA: Stanford University Press.

Minick, N. (1985). *L. S. Vygotsky and Soviet activity theory*. Unpublished doctoral dissertation, Northwestern University.

Montague, J. (1983). A flowering absence. *Irish Literary Supplement, 1*(3), 29.

Murphy, R. F. (1971). *Dialectics of social life*. New York: Basic Books.

Murphy, R. F. (1975). The quest for cultural reality: Adventures in Irish social anthropology. *Michigan Discussions in Anthropology, 1*, 48–64.

Murphy, R. F. (1987). *The body silent*. New York: Holt.

Newman, D., Griffin, P., & Cole, M. (1989). *The construction zone*. Cambridge: Cambridge University Press.

Pollner, M. (1978). Constitutive and mundane versions of labeling theory. *Human Studies, 1,* 269–288.

Pollner, M., & McDonald-Wikler, L. (1985). The social construction of unreality. *Family Process, 24,* 241–257.

Poster, M. (1980). *Critical theory of the family.* New York: Continuum.

Ramirez, F. O. (1990). Reconstituting children: Extension of personhood and citizenship. In D. Kertzer & K. Schaie (Eds.), *Age structuring in comparative perspective* (pp. 143–165). Hillsdale, NJ: Lawrence Erlbaum.

Rawson, M. (1968). *Developmental language disabilities: Adult accomplishments of dyslexic boys.* Baltimore: Johns Hopkins Press.

Sankoff, G., & Laberge, S. (1973). On the acquisition of native speakers by a language. *Kivung, 6,* 32–47.

Sarason, S., & Doris, J. (1979). *Educational handicap, public policy, and social change.* New York: Free Press.

Scheflen, A. E. (1973). *Communicational structure.* Bloomington: Indiana University Press.

Schegloff, E. (1984). On some questions and ambiguities in conversation. In J. M. Atkinson & J. Heritage (Eds.), *Structures of social action: Studies in conversation analysis* (pp. 28–52). Cambridge: Cambridge University Press.

Scott, J. (1985). *Weapons of the weak.* New Haven: Yale University Press.

Skupien, J. (1990). *Aspects of mind: Rationality and understanding in Wittgenstein's philosophical investigations.* Unpublished doctoral dissertation, Columbia University.

Suchman, L. (1987). *Plans and situated actions.* Cambridge: Cambridge University Press.

Toulmin, S. (1985). *The inner life: The outer mind* (1984 Heinz Werner Lecture Series, Vol. 15). Worchester, MA: Clark University Press.

Varenne, H. (1983). *American school language.* New York: Irvington.

Varenne, H., & McDermott, R. P. (1986). "Why" Sheila can read: Structure and indeterminacy in the reproduction of familial literacy. In B. B. Schieffelin & P. Gilmore (Eds.), *The acquisition of literacy: Ethnographic perspectives* (pp. 188–210). Norwood, NJ: Ablex.

Volosinov, V. N. (1973). *Marxism and the philosophy of language.* New York: Academic Press. (Original work published 1929)

Vygotsky, L. S. (1978). *Mind in society: The development of higher psychological processes* (M. Cole, V. John-Steiner, S. Scribner, & E. Souberman, Eds.). Cambridge, MA: Harvard University Press.

Vygotsky, L. S. (1986). *Thought and language* (A. Kozulin, Ed. and Trans.). Cambridge, MA: MIT Press. (Original work published 1934)

Wartofsky, M. (1983). The child's construction of the world and the world's construction of the child: From historical epistemology to historical psychology. In F. S. Kessel & A. W. Siegel (Eds.), *The child and other cultural inventions* (pp. 188–215). New York: Praeger.

Wieder, D. L. (1974). *Language and social reality.* The Hague: Mouton.

Wittgenstein, L. (1958). *Philosophical investigations* (3rd ed.). London: Macmillan.

11 Context and scaffolding in developmental studies of mother–child problem-solving dyads

Harold G. Levine

The issue of how adults help children to perform and learn has received a great deal of recent attention. Much of this research stems from the sociohistorical ideas of the late Russian psychologist L. S. Vygotsky (1978, 1934/1986, 1987), especially his conception of the zone of proximal development (zpd). In essence, the zpd represents the child's susceptibility to influence, that is, the difference between what a child can do with assistance and what he or she is able to do without it. It is assumed that most capable adults are able to target appropriately their strategic interactions with children within the latter's zpd, thereby facilitating learning. However, the actual empirical evidence for the relationship between strategic assistance (or *scaffolding*) and learning is currently somewhat limited and not altogether telling (Levine, Schneider, Pelland, & Hall, 1987).

There are two major problems for those who would interpret the findings from mother–child studies. The first is that there is little consensus about what to look for in the mother–child dyad that would constitute evidence for scaffolding. That is, theory would dictate that some aspect of the joint *doing* of a task, or verbal (and nonverbal) interaction about and for it, would be what is internalized by the child. The most immediate, and visible, expression of effective scaffolding would be the child's improved performance on the task at hand and/or on a near-transfer task. However, beyond these generalities there is nothing inherent to the theory that would predict

The research on which this chapter is based was supported by NICHD Program Project Grant #HD11944-06. I would like to thank the following individuals for their constructive comments on an earlier version of the manuscript: Seth Chaiklin, Ronald Gallimore, Elizabeth Hall, Steinar Kvale, Jean Lave, Ann Mastergeorge, Lucy Suchman, and Thomas Weisner.

306

just what about the doing of the task, or the talking about it, would lead to learning.

A second interpretive problem has more to do with the way in which inquiry into issues of scaffolded performance has typically been conducted. I wish to argue that we have been adopting the wrong logic in thinking about how scaffolding occurs, and that this incorrect logic stems from how we conceptualize the interactional context for a child's (or mother's) performance.

Although we have become quite fond of the word *context*, its too frequent use has resulted, perhaps inevitably, in its having different meanings for different developmental researchers. For some, context is a *facilitative* phenomenon. That is, it is something that preexists and has a determinative (or facilitative) effect on child performance, mother scaffolding, and the like. Under these circumstances, investigators look for main effects of single (or small sets of) interactional variables on aspects of child problem-solving performance. For others, context is constructed by the parties interacting and therefore is *constitutive* of child performance and mother scaffolding. Taking this latter point of view seriously, I believe, forces a change in recent interpretations of the dynamics of interaction within the zpd. In current constructions, scaffolding behaviors are uncritically assumed to proceed from mother to child and to stem from some inherent (but undefined) virtue in the strategies themselves. Rather, use of a genuinely constitutive context forces us to examine the contingent nature of maternal helping behaviors during moment-by-moment interaction.

In this chapter I will examine the constitutive nature of interaction between language-limited, developmentally delayed children and their mothers. Interactions by adults with delayed, or mentally retarded, children were of particular theoretical interest for Vygotsky who argued that, whatever the biological substratum of delay, the consequences of developmental "defects" were predominantly social: "All contact with people, all situations which define a ['mentally defective'] person's place in the social sphere, his role and fate as a participant in life, all the social functions of daily life are reordered" (Vygotsky, 1987, p. 12). For Vygotsky, this "reordered fate" of the retarded child played itself out through the child's zpd. He argued that adults characteristically focused only on the child's actual level of development. In so doing, they regularly failed to provide the kind of well-timed, verbally mediated assistance that would facilitate higher levels of achievement and, ultimately, the development of higher-order psychological processes.

The question, then, of whether dyads of developmentally delayed children and their mothers are somehow deficient in key aspects of verbal mediation becomes central to the present study. To address this issue, I will closely examine the interactions of mothers and their developmentally delayed children while performing an everyday task analogue: the pairing and putting away of shoes. My central argument is that, in spite of the highly individualized nature of interaction and participation for the mother–child dyads studied, the data show that there are patterns of interaction common to many of these dyads. These patterns suggest that mothers inadvertently constrain both the language and the joint performance of problem solving with their developmentally delayed children.

Developmental delay in its sociocultural context

Developmental delay is a general term for substandard performance on language or cognitive measures. However, the concept of substandard performance is itself somewhat problematic. Some children have consistently low scores when tested with a variety of psychometric measures, whereas others are much more variable. In fact, for this latter group of children, scores on some scales or subscales may even be in the normal range. While recent research indicates that the scores of delayed children are remarkably stable over time (Bernheimer & Keogh, 1988), there is some evidence that the performance scores of children who test at a relatively high level at an early age are more variable when they are older. A social component seems to be at work here because children who are doing well tend to come from families who have taken a broader view of developmental delay, preferring to evaluate their children on broad social and everyday skills, not merely on the more restrictive cognitive and IQ measures (B. K. Keogh & L. P. Bernheimer, personal communication).

The etiology for developmental delay may be due to organic factors or perinatal trauma. More often, and for the sample of children studied here, the cause of delay is simply unknown. For children under the age of 6 years, one characteristic of developmental delay is its ambiguity, and parents of delayed children frequently find themselves shunted back and forth between professionals as they, and the professionals, search for a firm diagnosis. For most parents this is a highly frustrating and anxiety-producing time in their lives.

We suspect that this search for *a* diagnosis, with its ups and downs of hope and despair, has important consequences for how parents ultimately come to define their children's competencies and the expectations they have of them. These expectations, in turn, may have a dramatic impact on daily interactions with their children, particularly in terms of the frequency with which parents create tasks for them to accomplish and the techniques by which they scaffold task-related problem solving.

The majority of these *ambiguous* delayed children will eventually be diagnosed as mildly mentally retarded. Research with mildly retarded adults using retrospective interviewing and life history techniques suggests that parental attitudes are crucial in determining the retarded individual's attitude toward his or her delay and general emotional well-being (Turner, 1982). This research with adults also suggests that they were systematically denied important cultural experiences and knowledge while children (Levine & Langness, 1985, 1986). The cumulative effect of such denial is the creation of individuals who often are incompetent in the world at large and seen as deviant or "funny." Because the vast majority of individuals who are mildly retarded merge into the general population after leaving school (Edgerton, 1967) in mid to late adolescence, indicating that there is nothing inherent to mental retardation that prevents everyday functioning, one must assume that a different life course has resulted for those who remain identified by the system as *retarded.* The process of labeling – and its indirect production of retarded performance – is therefore a social process.

We now have a great deal of knowledge about the lives of mildly retarded adults, especially the ways in which they cope with everyday demands. We also have their retrospective accounts of their childhood, with strong indications that they were treated differently. What we are lacking are longitudinal studies of developmentally delayed children to study if, and how, these primary social forces are at work.

With regard to cognitive functioning, we need to know the details of parent–child interactions. In particular, we need to know how everyday tasks are presented and accomplished and what factors impact a mother's approach to problem solving with her developmentally delayed child.

Sample children and their families

Subjects for this study were 30 developmentally delayed children (16 male, 14 female) and their families. The children were between 31 and 44 months of age (mean = 37.9; *SD* = 3.3). The Gesell developmental quotient varied between 45 and 105 (mean = 72.2; *SD* = 15.6). All children were from middle-class and lower-middle-class Anglo families where English was the primary language spoken. Children whose delay was attributable to a specific medical and/or genetic diagnosis were omitted from the study.

Research procedures

Each family was assigned a trained project fieldworker who spent at least 10 hours in the home over a 3-day period collecting a variety of observational data. After a minimum of 6 hours in the home, the fieldworker asked the mother to participate with her child in a variety of task activities, including the shoe-sorting task discussed here.

The object of the shoe task was for the child to put away four pairs of shoes, including sneakers, dress shoes, house slippers, and sandals. When possible, the child's own shoes were used; and they were put away, when feasible, in their normal place. The instructions to the mother were simply to have her get her child to put the shoes away in pairs. She was encouraged to use any verbal or nonverbal strategies she deemed appropriate.

Mother–child interaction was videotaped and transcribed. The transcriptions were then examined for recurring features of verbal and nonverbal interaction, turn taking, and contingent production of task solution behaviors and strategies. The main features of this analysis follow.

Varieties of maternal scaffolding and the joint production of interaction about problem solving

Verbal tactics

Mothers in the sample are quite varied in the diversity of their linguistic repertoires. Some mothers use a very limited number of differing verbal strategies, whereas others often shift their language to engage the child and acknowledge his or her actions. An example of the contingent nature of these verbal tactics follows:

Dyad 314

(1)   C(hild): Shoes {hands slipper to M}.
(2)   M(other): Shoes {takes slipper}.
(3)   M: Shoes {holds slipper up in front of C}.
(4)   M: One.
(5)   C: {Reaches out for shoe}.
(6)   M: Gimme the other one {momentarily takes one of C's hands; with her other hand she waves the shoe up and down}.
(7)   M: Where's the other one {M signs apparently for *the same*}?
(8)   C: {Reaches for shoe in M's hand}.
(9)   M: No.
(10)   M: Where's the other shoe?
(11)   M: That matches {repeatedly points to slipper in her hand}?
(12)   M: {Signs *shoe* apparently}.
(13)   M: They're the same {signs *same*}.
(14)   C: {Looks around quickly, then tries to grab slipper in M's hand}.
(15)   M: No.
(16)   M: Where's the same {signs *same*}?
(17)   M: Shoes {signs *shoe*}.
(18)   C: {Looks at slipper in M's hand} Shoes {takes slipper from M}.
(19)   M: Shoes {signs *shoe*}.
(20)   M: Same {signs *same*}.
(21)   C: {Is examining the slipper he is now holding in his lap}.
(22)   M: They're the same.
(23)   M: Where's the other one {takes slipper from C}?
(24)   M: Where's the other one?

After an additional 32 maternal utterances the child finally pairs the slippers successfully. The transcript is replete with changing verbal strategies. In line 2 the mother repeats what her child has said, repeats herself in 5, and introduces new verbal content in 4 and 6. Line 7 ("Where's the other shoe?") is similar to line 6 except that there has been a syntactic shift from a statement to a question. In line 9 the mother gives feedback to the child about his action to reach for the shoe in her hand, and then virtually repeats her statement of line 7. In line 11 she introduces the new term "matches," and in line 13 the new term "same." The child is still quite active, but unresponsive to specific maternal directives, and the mother provides negative feedback again in line 15. In line 16 she again repeats herself from line 13, but shifts syntactically. In the remaining lines 17 through 24, in the face of very few task-appropriate responses from her son, the mother tries a variety of repetitions of verbal gambits she has already used.

This mother uses a series of verbal tactics to engage her child. She alternates semantic repetition, repetition with syntactic shifts, and the introduction of new semantic information. As to the latter, her referential speech progresses from "shoes" to "one" to "the other one" to "the other shoe" to "that matches" to "the same" and then back to terms she has already used. This mother employs other verbal tactics such as feedback and, later in the interaction, semantic expansions on what she has already said and semantic simplications as well. Unlike other mothers in our sample she seldom uses verbalizations meant to orient the child or get his attention (e.g., "Look here" or "Come sit by me").

Other mothers in our study are much less inventive in how they use language to engage, or respond to, their children. Some mothers seem almost to have limited language repertoires in terms of their ability to alter the semantic or syntactic content. Thus, they may typically spend a great deal of interactional time orienting the child, giving feedback, or merely repeating the content of earlier utterances. Interestingly, our earlier research shows that using a variety of semantic and syntactic strategies is not only relatively unusual, but also that this is not necessarily linked with successful child performance on the pairing demands. Mothers who use more straightforward feedback (whether positive or negative) and orientations are more likely to have children successfully pairing shoes in this task (Hall, Levine, & Hecht, 1988).

Nonverbal tactics

In addition to a variety of verbal tactics, mothers of developmentally delayed children vary in the degree to which, and ways in which, they conduct interaction using nonverbal prompts. The following excerpt, from the same mother–child dyad, shows the multiplicity of nonverbal interactional gambits:

(1) M: {Grabs C} Come here.
(2) M: Put them on the table side by side {pulls C to her and points him in the direction of the table}.
(3) M: Put one {slaps the table with one hand}.
(4) M: Two shoes {slaps the table with the other hand}.
(5) C: {Looks down at table and puts both slippers down but about 8 inches apart}.
(6) M: Put them together.
(7) M: Put them together {brings C's hands together}.
(8) M: Put them together {brings C's hands together}.
(9) M: {Lets go of C's hands and holds him up by putting her hands around his ribs}.
(10) M: Pick this one up {takes C's left hand and moves it to touch slipper on C's left}.
(11) M: Can you get this {takes C's right hand and moves it toward slipper on C's right}?
(12) M: Ah {pushes the slippers together with C's hands}, together.
(13) C: {Smiles}.
(14) M: They're the same {brings C's hands together in the sign for *same*}.

Thus, in 11 of the 12 turns taken by the mother she employs some form of nonverbal cuing to her child. In line 1 she pairs her verbal command ("Come here") with the physical action of actually holding onto the child. She then indicates that she wants the shoes on the table side by side and points her son in the direction of the table (line 2). Lines 3 and 4 are further demonstrations of her verbal output. In lines 7 and 8 she provides a form of redundancy to her verbal instructions by literally bringing the child's hands together while asking him to put the shoes together. In lines 10, 11, and 12 she motors her child through the actions she has labeled verbally, and in line 14 helps her child sign the word for *same*. Throughout this entire sequence the child is essentially unresponsive except at one key juncture (line 5) when he demonstrates not only that he is attending but also able to generally follow directions. The mother's subsequent actions (lines 6 through 14) are efforts to refine further the child's demonstrated level of performance.

Other researchers (e.g., Greenfield, 1984; Rogoff & Gardner, 1984) have suggested that redundancy in communicative modes may be an important feature of maternal scaffolding for the inexperienced child. Our own data from a previous study of 20 mother–child dyads shows-that, in almost one-half of all mother turn-taking, some form of nonverbal prompting (including simple prompts, motoring the child, or signing) occurs, either as a stand-alone prompt or paired with a verbalization. Our mothers in this study, however, vary from approximately 15% of their turns including these nonverbal prompts to nearly 80% with them.

Context markers

Earlier work with mothers of normally developing children interacting during the course of supermarket shopping indicated how frequently mothers embedded marketing tasks, for example, select-ing yogurt, in ongoing, family-based, social activities (Levine, 1984). In a study of four mother–child dyads, the act of selecting yogurt was always related to some experience the child had previously had, or to some other social meaning of the act (e.g., as something that you take to school in your lunch pail). Everyday objects are thus imbued with mutual experience and the meaning of the objects is socially me-diated.

I looked for similar contextualizing by these mothers of develop-mentally delayed children in this shoe-pairing task. There are ex-amples of mothers personalizing the task by associating the child's name with the shoes (e.g., "Becca's pretty shoes"), inquiring into personal preferences (e.g., "You like shiny shoes, huh?"), likening them to a sibling's shoes (e.g., "Like Alice's shoes"), or reminding the child of similar actions the child has done before (e.g., "Just like you put your own shoes away?"). Occasionally, the mothers also provide a new context for the task, as one mother who asks her child to line up the shoes because "We're going to make a train." Mothers would also occasionally physically redesign the environment of shoes, putting them in pairs in front of the child or placing the shoe they wished paired directly within eyesight of the child.

The frequency with which mothers provide a new context for the child's actions is strikingly low, a mere 4% of all possible maternal interactions. This limited evidence supports the idea that, faced with a child with more limited responsive and initiatory repertoires, these mothers in turn respond by concentrating only on the mechanics of the task at hand. What they omit in their active problem solving, at least with regard to the kind of task studied here, are tactics that link the current problem with other similar experiences the child has had. Part of the argument for the social construction of mental retardation hinges on just such limited bridging experiences.

Voice of reason

Mothers in the sample occasionally make efforts to help their children reflect on the task. Specifically, they try to have the child understand that the shoe-sorting task is not a random activity, but a set of discrete operations logically organized and linked together. The implied message to the child is that the strategies for completing the task are subject to reason and that the mother's verbalizations are the linguistic representation of that reasoning.

In general, this *voice of reason* in use by the mother takes the form of a dialogue in which higher-order questions about doing the task are embedded. The actual dialogues that the mothers use take a variety of forms. In some cases the mother engages in the dialogue but takes both parts, consistent with the child's limited language production abilities. Thus, she asks the child a question about the task or how to do it, and answers the question herself out loud while making sure that the child is listening. The following example is characteristic:

Dyad 328

(1) M: Oh, does that look like that one {holds the dress shoe out next to the sneaker C is holding}?
(2) C: {Puts sneaker down on floor still grasping it}.
(3) M: No.

At other times the mother uses a dialogue with her child to list the sequences necessary to complete the task, or a subpart of it, almost as a kind of advanced organizer:

Dyad 309

(1) M: Know what we need to do, though {pulls chair aside}?
(2) M: We need to put them [i.e., the shoes] up on your shelf.
(3) C: {Picks up one of the sneakers and begins to examine it}.
(4) M: Here {touches shelf}.
(5) C: Oh, this is xx[1] {holds sneaker up}!
(6) M: xx xxx shoe {looks at C's activity}.
(7) M: OK, can we put all the ones that are the same together?
(8) M: Two by two?

In another type of dialogue the mother asks a question of the child that explicitly raises an issue about pairing, matching, or putting the shoes away in the correct place. As an example, one mother held her child by the arm and, while doing so, also held up one sandal and one sneaker which the child had paired. She said, "Do these go together? Are these the same? Can you make them match?"

Sometimes mothers demonstrate correct pairings or steps in the sequence for completing the pairing task, as in the following example:

Dyad 325

(1) M: OK, now see how they all match?
(2) M: See {moves over to chair}, two tennis shoes that's the same {picks up pair of tennis shoes}.
(3) M: We have two high tops, those are the same {picks up dress shoes}.
(4) M: Two sandals, the same, and two slippers, the same {picks up pairs of sandals and slippers as she names them}.
(5) M: They're the same {looks into C's face}.
(6) M: They match {still looking into C's face}.

The transcripts reveal two other versions of the dialogue. In the first the mother states (or implies) that there is a next step to the task and that the child should be thinking about this. This is a higher-order suggestion and includes such statements as "You know, you can get up and find it" or "Slow down and listen." In the second, the mother labels or describes a correct (or incorrect) pairing action by the child as a way of getting him or her to reflect linguistically on what the latter has done by these actions. Examples include "Yes, that's a match" or "No, that's different."

In spite of the hypothesized importance of the one-party dialogue to subsequent child performance, the transcripts show relatively little of this interaction strategy. Less than 10% of all maternal turns include such dialogues. This finding accords with the relative lack of broader experiential linkages to the task at hand noted previously. It also is in marked contrast with mothers of nondelayed children: In a study by another member of our research team (Mastergeorge, n.d.) on a puzzle piece placement task, mothers of nondelayed were more likely ($p < .05$) to use voice of reasoning strategies than a matched sample of mothers of delayed children.

Task definition and task shifting

An important feature about everyday cognition is that a seemingly simple, straightforward task such as putting away shoes can be defined in a variety of ways. This may be seen in the following:

Dyad 304

(1) M: (What is) what kind of shoe {leans toward C as she speaks}?
(2) C: A brown {fiddles with sandal as she speaks}.
(3) M: A brown shoe {looks down on shoe pile as she speaks}.
(4) M: Where's the other one {looks from shoe pile to C as she speaks}?

This mother begins (line 1) by asking the child to identify what kind of shoe she has in her hands, and then confirms (line 3) that it is a brown shoe. With confirmation that her child is attending and correctly answering her question, the mother shifts to a more abstract task request by asking her indirectly (line 4) to use the shoe she has as a visual referent and to find the match for it. Thus, even within four lines of discourse this mother has presented two different tasks to her child, an identification task and a matching task. Review of all transcripts reveals five major ways (and a residual category) in which this group of mothers redefines the task for their children (see Table 11.1).

These separate redefinitions of the shoe sorting task can be ordered into a simple hierarchy based on the amount of knowledge that

Table 11.1. *Task definitions, frequencies, and examples in mother–child discourse about a shoe-sorting task*

Task Definition	Frequency (%)	Examples
A. Shoe sorting	3.7	"Let's put these shoes away."
B. Pairing without a visual referent, matching to a visual referent	30.1	"Get another pair of shoes." "Get the other one." "Get another shoe that looks like this one."
C. Identification, retrieval, placement	30.5	"What's that?" "Is that a shoe?" "Go get that shoe over there." "Put the shoe in your hand in the closet."
D. Play–task related	4.8	"Those shoes won't fit you, but try them on if you want."
E. Attention getting and focusing	26.4	"Johnnie." "Look here." "Come on."
F. Other	4.5	Interaction about off-task actions

the child would be assumed to have to complete the task. Thus, at the most abstract level (*shoe sorting*), a directive such as "Let's put these shoes away" assumes that the child understands pairing, retrieval, placement, and the overarching goal of the task (pairing of shoes and their proper placement) since information of these types is not provided. At a somewhat less abstract level (*matching to a visual referent*), an utterance such as "Get another shoe that looks like this one" assumes that the child can understand the concept of matching, though not be able to spontaneously generate a matching strategy in the current circumstance nor understand the overall goal of the task. In other instances, such as *play-task related* and *attention getting and focusing*, the mother tries to engage her child in other ways with the hope of leading him or her back to the sorting task.

Another feature of task presentation is how frequently mothers shift back and forth between task definitions, contingent upon the child's actions. They may shift upward or downward in task complexity and abstraction. Sometimes they shift upward in task complexity and abstraction. Sometimes they shift upward after a child has successfully completed a task demand, or downward when he or she has failed. When mothers shift in either of these two ways, we refer to this as appropriate scaffolding because the mother is attempting to adjust her task demand to the child's level of performance and competence. In cases in which the mother shifts to a more complex task after the child has failed at an easier one, or the mother shifts to a less complex task following a successful child performance, this was considered as maternal scaffolding insensitive to the child's performance level.

For the 30 dyads studied here, mothers shift appropriately 15.1% of the time and inappropriately 5.8% of the time. Of the shifts by the mothers 56% are repetitions of the same level of task abstraction. This latter percentage may reflect either the mothers' inability to gauge their children's level of performance, or difficulties they may have in producing contingent scaffolding. In some cases, it undoubtedly also reflects maternal frustrations in engaging an inattentive child.

Interaction games

The mother–child interactional tactics discussed thus far occur at the level of the utterance. The data from the transcripts also reveal that mothers and their children may construct overarching games within which the problem solving and the interaction about it are embedded. Thus, the actual utterances become subservient to the language, or interaction, game that is being played. An example of this follows:

Dyad 338

(1) M: Are we going to put your shoes away now {M comes and sits in front of C on her knees and looks at C}?

(2) C: No {C turns around to look at M and moves so that she is sitting directly in front of M, holds onto baby shoe from the shoe pile with one hand and her right foot with the other}.

(3) M: Well, they don't fit you {M is looking at C, then leans forward toward C}.

(4) C: {Lets go of right foot, still holds baby shoe in left hand, looks to shoes on floor}.

(5) M: OK, let's do this {M places her hands down in front of her and leans closer to C}.

(6) M: Let's see which pair fits you {looks directly into C's face as she talks to her}.

(7) C: {As M speaks, looks down at baby shoe; plays with it}.

(8) M: You want to try that on {continues to look at C as she speaks to her}?

(9) C: {Looks at the baby shoe and then puts it back down in the shoe pile; grabs tennis shoe from pile and puts it up in the air so that M can see it}.

(10) M: Oh, you know which pair fits you {nods head in affirmation as C holds up tennis shoe in front of her face} because they're yours {M looks at C}.

(11) C: {As M speaks, C puts tennis shoe back down and picks up the baby/dress shoe and shows it to M}.

(12) M: Let's see; do they fit you {M looks at baby/dress shoe, then looks at, and leans more toward, C}?

(13) C: Yes {still holding the baby shoe in front of her}.

(14) C: {Tries to place baby/dress shoe on her right foot by raising her right foot into the air; her foot slips}.

(15) M: {Watches}.

(16) C: {Again tries to fit right foot into dress shoe; foot slips again}.

(17) M: Nope, doesn't fit {M shakes her head sideways to reinforce her words}.

(18) M: Well, let's put it away then {looks directly into C's face, establishes eye contact}.

(19) M: Okay {continues to look directly into C's face}?

In this sequence the child begins by being defiant (line 2) in the face of the mother's attempt to orient the child to the task at hand (line 1). From the child's action in line 2, the mother decides that her daughter wants to play with the shoes. In response, the mother (line 3) tries to dissuade her daughter from playing with the shoes; but, by lines 5 and 6, decides to engage her in a game about whether the shoe fits. The mother's overarching strategy becomes clear in line 18: Because the shoe doesn't fit, they should put it away. Initially this strategy fails and there follows another 26 lines of interaction in which the child pursues her own agenda of trying on the shoe while the mother reacts to the child's increasingly defiant stance. Finally, they reach an accord:

(20) M: Let's put them away, okay {M pushes C's glasses back onto her face and the hair out of C's face}.
(21) C: {As M completes this action, C looks at her}.
(22) C: {Grunts; looks down at the floor}.
(23) M: Put these away first and then we'll try on another pair {M puts the two baby shoes together in front of C on left side of her, then moves hand toward shoe pile}.
(24) C: {C looks at shoes and gets up and takes shoes over to her dresser drawers}.
(25) C: {Opens dresser drawers} Shoes {throws dress shoes inside second drawer; shuts drawer slightly and then turns around and comes back toward M}.

This mother–child sequence becomes increasingly routinized over the next three shoe pairings, with the mother offering to let the child try on the pair of shoes, observing that they do not fit, and then putting them away in the drawer. That the child is still very much in control of this game, and her actions, can be seen in the last pairing episode. In this episode the mother makes her usual offer to have the child try on the shoe and the child complies. However, the child is resistant to putting the shoe away, even when the mother commands her to "Put it away." Rather, the child continues to put the shoe on her foot. Finally, the child says "All done now," pairs the tennis shoes in front of her, walks over to the dresser, opens the drawer, deposits the shoes, and returns to her mother's side.

Although interactional games are not common to the group of mother–child dyads studied here, their existence in a small number of dyads is important. Games such as these demonstrate the active stance which even developmentally delayed children take to engage their mothers in interaction, and ways in which mothers can, and do, use this engagement to structure problem solving for their children.

Conclusions: Contextualizing mother and developmentally delayed child interactions in problem-solving tasks

This chapter provides examples of how mothers and their developmentally delayed children interact to complete the demands of an everyday task analogue, the pairing and putting away of shoes.

These examples highlight how both mother and child participate in interactions, and thereby jointly construct a context for their problem solving.

Of course, neither mother nor child arrives at the problem-solving setting as an experienced participant. Each, for example, has a relatively long history with the other in settings requiring joint problem solving where behaviors and interaction strategies have been tried and tested. In addition, each may have a different understanding about the specific purpose of the current activity. Finally, mothers respond not merely to the task at hand but, in complex ways, to both their short- and long-term goals for their children, to important family routines, and to the child's ability level and their perceptions of it (Levine & Mastergeorge, 1989; McGillicuddy-DeLisi, 1982; Miller, 1988; Nerlove & Snipper, 1981; Sigel, 1986).

The construction of the context for problem solving also occurs in the moment, during interaction within the task setting itself. Mothers and children spontaneously call upon, use, and recreate a variety of tactics, or mechanics, for doing the work of problem solving. A critical element of this is the mother's verbal mediation of both her own and her child's involvement. In the mother–child interactions described here, the mechanics of verbal mediation and problem solving are accomplished in seven ways. They are verbal tactics, nonverbal tactics, context markers, the voice of reason, task definition, task shifting, and interaction games.

The specifics of these interactional mechanics shed light on the nature of verbally mediated problem solving and scaffolded performance for developmentally delayed children. As discussed earlier, these mothers seldom use a variety of semantic and syntactic strategies to engage their children in problem solving. Of the verbal tactics that are frequently used, only a few such as feedback and attention getting are significantly correlated with aspects of successful child performance. In terms of nonverbal tactics the mothers in this study are quite variable in the frequency with which they are used. Although other research has indicated the importance of redundancy in lines of communication (i.e., pairing verbal and nonverbal cues), the current findings show no distinct trend regarding nonverbal tactics.

An additional feature of the interaction between mothers and developmentally delayed children is that mothers' use of context markers is limited. They focus only on the specific problems associated with accomplishing the immediate shoe-pairing task, with little clear bridging to other child experiences or problem domains. Similarly, mothers' use of the voice of reason is rare. Children are not, therefore, engaged in dialogic thinking, nor are they often presented with higher-order questions or problems related to the shoe-pairing task. Thus, there are few bridges to a larger set of problem-solving strategies.

Mothers in this study typically do not define the task at the most abstract level (i.e., shoe sorting), but rely on lower-order tasks including pairing, matching, identification, retrieval, and placement. When they shift among these tasks, they are three times as likely to shift appropriately as inappropriately. However, more than half of the time they repeat the same level of task definition. Finally, there are some instances of interaction games, indicating that some mother–child dyads, at least, are able to embed the shoe-sorting task into another frame (e.g., play, everyday chores). The relative absence of such games, however, again points to the lack of bridging strategies used by mothers to place this simple task into a larger task framework, whether this framework be that of other instructional tasks, of the work of the everyday world, or of the simple association with other experiences.

Correlations of the individual interactional mechanics used by mothers with aspects of child performance indicate that, while a few are significantly correlated, the majority are not. This latter finding attests, at least in part, to the individualized character of specific mother–child dyads. However, another conclusion also seems warranted: In spite of their individualized character, dyads involving mothers and developmentally delayed children generally seem to be constrained by the language use of mothers. The mothers studied here limit their use of a variety of semantic and syntactic tactics; they keep task definitions at relatively low levels; they fail to engage in interactional games; and, most important, they infrequently bridge from the shoe-sorting task itself to other experiences, domains, or problem-solving strategies. Thus, they fail to embed the particular problem, and the process of problem solving itself, in an extended context. These findings, then, would appear to support the argument that mild mental retardation may be associated with the denial or limitation of certain basic experiences in childhood. In this case, the experiences are potentially far-reaching ones because they involve the *doing* and *thinking* of basic, everyday tasks, namely, cognition.

Much has been made in the literature about whether mothers of developmentally delayed children are deficient in parenting strategies or are actually adapting to their children appropriately (Crawley & Spiker, 1983; Schneider & Gearhart, 1988). Do these mothers, in other words, effectively engage their children within the latter's zpd?

The data presented here suggest that there are two likely answers to this question, each of which is, in some measure, correct: (1) the child's behavior is sufficiently erratic that the concept of a stable zpd is not a tenable one with these children, and therefore not targetable by mothers in joint interaction; and (2) these mothers and their children have found ways, over time, to create functional contexts for interaction, yet the contexts themselves are limited by constrained maternal language use and problem-solving assistance. In particular, mothers fail to provide the dialogical and experiential bridges necessary to enhance their children's further development.

Further data are essential to understand completely whether there is an essential relationship between the interactional context that parents and their developmentally delayed children create and the later atypical cognitive development of these children. In particular, the study of interaction in other kinds of problem-solving situations seems critical, as does the longitudinal study of mother–child interaction. What also seems clear, however, is that the study of scaffolded behavior must be more than the search for simple maternal interaction variables and their effects on child behavior, as the facilitative model of context would indicate. To study scaffolding independently of the complexity of the interaction itself is to locate the social processes of cognitive development in the wrong kind of context.

Note

1. xx and xxx indicate words that were unintelligible on the video recording.

References

Bernheimer, L. P., & Keogh, B. K. (1988). Stability of cognitive performance of children with developmental delays. *American Journal on Mental Retardation, 92*, 539–542.

Crawley, S. B., & Spiker, D. (1983). Mother–child interactions involving two-year-olds with Down Syndrome: A look at individual differences. *Child Development, 54,* 1312–1323.

Edgerton, R. B. (1967). *The cloak of competence: Stigma in the lives of the mentally retarded.* Berkeley: University of California Press.

Greenfield, P. M. (1984). A theory of the teacher in the learning activities of everyday life. In B. Rogoff & J. Lave (Eds.), *Everyday cognition: Its development in social context* (pp. 117–138). Cambridge, MA: Harvard University Press.

Hall, E. A., Levine, H. G., & Hecht, B. F. (1988). *Redundant communication channels in mothers' assistance of developmentally delayed child performance.* Paper presented at the meeting of the American Educational Research Association, New Orleans, LA.

Levine, H. G. (1984). *Maternal instruction in everyday cognition: A micro–ethnographic study of interaction about cognition.* Paper presented at the meeting of the American Anthropological Association, Denver, CO.

Levine, H. G., & Langness, L. L. (1985). Everyday cognition among mentally retarded adults: An ethnographic approach. *American Journal of Mental Deficiency, 90,* 18–26.

Levine, H. G., & Langness, L. L. (1986). Conclusions: Themes in an anthropology of mild mental retardation. In L. L. Langness & H. G. Levine (Eds.), *Culture and retardation: Life histories of mildly mentally retarded persons in American society* (pp. 191–206). Dordrecht: Reidel.

Levine, H. G., & Mastergeorge, A. M. (1989). *Mother–developmentally delayed child interactions in socio-cultural context.* Paper presented at the biennial meeting of the Society for Research on Child Development, Kansas City, MO.

Levine, H. G., Schneider, P., Pelland, M., & Hall, E. A. (1987). *Maternal scaffolding, child ability, and performance of developmentally delayed children on an everyday task analog.* Paper presented at the biennial meeting of the Society for Research on Child Development, Baltimore, MD.

McGillicuddy-DeLisi, A. V. (1982). The relationship between parents' beliefs about development and family constellation, socioeconomic status, and parents' teaching strategies. In L. M. Laosa & I. E. Sigel (Eds.), *Families as learning environments for children* (pp. 261–299). New York: Plenum.

Mastergeorge, A. M. (n.d.). *The relationship between maternal tutorial beliefs and maternal tutorial interactions: A comparison of mothers of developmentally delayed and non-delayed children.* Graduate School of Education, University of California, Los Angeles. Unpublished manuscript.

Miller, S. A. (1988). Parents' beliefs about children's cognitive development. *Child Development, 59,* 259–285.

Nerlove, S. B., & Snipper, A. S. (1981). Cognitive consequences of cultural opportunity. In R. H. Munroe, R. L. Munroe, & B. B. Whiting (Eds.), *Handbook of cross-cultural human development* (pp. 423–474). New York: Garland STPM Press.

Rogoff, B., & Gardner, W. (1984). Adult guidance of cognitive development. In B.

Rogoff & J. Lave (Eds.), *Everyday cognition: Its development in social context* (pp. 95–116). Cambridge, MA: Harvard University Press.

Schneider, P., & Gearhart, M. (1988). The ecocultural niche of families with mentally retarded children: Evidence from mother–child interaction studies. *Journal of Applied Developmental Psychology, 9,* 85–106.

Sigel, I. E. (1986). Reflections on the belief–behavior connection: Lessons learned from a research program on parental belief systems and teaching strategies. In R. D. Ashmore & D. M. Brodzinsky (Eds.), *Thinking about the family: Views of parents and children* (pp. 35–65). Hillsdale, NJ: Lawrence Erlbaum.

Turner, J. L. (1982). *Workshop society: Ethnographic observations in a work setting for retarded adults* (Socio-Behavioral Group working paper no. 20). Mental Retardation Research Center, University of California, Los Angeles.

Vygotsky, L. S. (1978). *Mind in society: The development of higher psychological processes* (M. Cole, V. John-Steiner, S. Scribner, & E. Souberman, Eds.). Cambridge, MA: Harvard University Press.

Vygotsky, L. S. (1986). *Thought and language* (A. Kozulin, Ed. and Trans.). Cambridge, MA: MIT Press. (Original work published 1934)

Vygotsky, L. S. (1987). *The collected works of L. S. Vygotsky: Vol. 1. General problems of psychology* (R. W. Rieber & A. Carton, Eds.; N. Minick, Trans.). New York: Plenum.

12 Solving everyday problems in the formal setting: An empirical study of the school as context for thought

Roger Säljö and Jan Wyndhamn

In everyday life "thought is," as Rogoff (1984, p. 7) puts it, "in the service of action." Cognitive activities are thus inseparable aspects of the many concrete and abstract activities and projects that people engage in in their day-to-day affairs. The Cartesian legacy of maintaining a strict line of division between the mental and the practical in characterizing research has, however, fostered the assumption that "the only true domain of psychological study is internal mental activity" and, consequently, to regard "the problem of how social and physical context influences individuals' mental processes as unimportant or secondary" (Wertsch & Stone, 1985; cf. e.g., Kvale, 1977). In recent years, there has been a noticeable trend toward attempting to reestablish the links in research between the abstract and the concrete aspects of human activity. Carraher, Carraher, and Schliemann (1985) and Lave, Murtaugh, and de la Rocha (1984), to mention just two examples relevant to the study to be presented here, have shown how elementary arithmetic tasks are dealt with in everyday settings on the one hand and in formal contexts on the other. The results are revealing; Lave, Murtaugh, and de la Rocha (1984) observed "virtually error-free arithmetic performance" by people when acting as shoppers, but "frequent errors in parallel problems in the formal testing situation" (p. 83; cf., e.g., Marková, 1982; Rogoff, 1982).

As an epistemological project, the conscious attempt to bridge the gap between the practical and the abstract is at the heart of the Vygotskian tradition (Vygotsky, 1934/1987, 1978; cf. Wertsch, 1985).

The research reported here was financed by the Swedish Council for Research in the Humanities and Social Sciences.

327

In order to understand "the *humanization* of the *child's* mind" (Brushlinskii, 1979, p. 39), we should – following the Vygotskian spirit – "seek the origins of conscious activity and 'categorical' behavior not in the recesses of the human brain or in the depths of the spirit, but in the external conditions of life" (Luria, 1982, p. 25).

In modern societies cultivation of cognitive skills to a considerable extent takes place in formal settings, especially in schools. In terms of the theory of activity, this means that institutions of formal learning have established themselves as yet another "system of activity" (Leont'ev, 1972/1981), which to a certain extent has developed autonomous rules and traditions for communication and for the definition of phenomena such as learning and competence. Schools thus provide external conditions for learning activities that differ from those that exist when these activities are embedded in the routines of activities in other social settings (cf. Minick, 1985). Expressed differently, the actions of individuals become subordinated to the "premises for communication" (Rommetveit, 1974) that people assume to be relevant for the particular context of schooling (cf. Säljö & Wyndhamn, 1987).

The purpose of the present study is to contribute to the understanding of the social nature of human cognition and to illustrate how within one such system of activity such as schools, concrete conditions for solving problems are provided that determine how they are attended to. To continue in the language of activity psychology, our focus will be on studying how the *actions* and *operations* that individuals perform when dealing with one specific, everyday problem differ when the *sense* of the task as people see it differs (cf. Wertsch, Minick, & Arns, 1984, pp. 154ff.; Cole, 1985, pp. 151ff.; Säljö & Wyndhamn, 1988).

Empirical study

The aim of studying how the "framing" (Goffman, 1974) of a task in a formal setting determines cognitive actions was studied empirically by having students work on the everyday problem of establishing what it would cost to send a letter by using the official table of postage rates of the Swedish post office. Thus, the students had at their disposal a photocopied excerpt of the first page of the postage rates (Figure 12.1). The task given to students to be focused

LETTERS
Domestic

Regular letters (and picture postcards)

Maximum weight grams	Postage SEK
20	2.10
100	4.00
250	7.50
500	11.50
1000	14.50

Figure 12.1. Excerpt from postage rates of the Swedish post office.

on here was formulated as follows: What would it cost to send a letter that weighs 120 grams within Sweden? At one level, the task must be described as fairly easy. It can be solved directly by consulting the table (correct answer: 7.50 Swedish kronor [SEK]) and many of the participants would have had experience with this commonly available table, as well as other similar ones. At another level – and as will be shown – reading this table under these circumstances can obviously be viewed as an abstract problem. The students were not supposed to perform the authentic action of sending a letter. Rather, they were attending to a hypothetical instance of an everyday action and the major motive for attending to this problem was one of *learning* (and not sending letters) as defined in a certain formal setting. Thus, there is, we argue, an initial, intricate step of rendering the problem meaningful in the particular context of the classroom.

The attempts to provide this task with different senses were achieved through two types of variations. In the first case, the variation was the type of lesson in which the task was presented, where in one instance it appeared within the context of a mathematics lesson and in the other within the context of a social studies lesson. The other type of variation concerned whether the task appeared in isolation or as part of the more extensive undertaking of establishing postage rates for a series of seven letters weighing from 10 to 1,200 grams.

Participants

In all, 214 students aged 15 or 16 in the eighth and ninth grades of the Swedish comprehensive school took part in the study.

Reading off

Calculating

Example 1

Example 3

The postage is 7.50 SEK because it costs 7.50 from 100 grams and up to 250 grams.

The postage is 6.10 SEK because a letter that weighs 20 grams costs 20.10 SEK and a letter that weighs 100 grams costs 4. Then it will be 2.10 + 4 = 6.10 SEK.

Example 2

Example 4

The postage is 7.50 SEK because it weighs more than 100 and so it shouldn't be there but rather in next price category (250 g).

The postage is 12.60 because I take 20 grams x 6 = 120 and then 2.10 x 6 = 12.60.

Figure 12.2. Types of solutions presented by students *reading off* the table and *calculating* to establish postage rates.

Three participants did not complete the task and the analysis will be based on the answers given by the 211 students. The tasks were distributed by the regular teacher within the context of a normal lesson. The participants solved the problem individually as a paper-and-pencil task, and the analyses are based on the written solutions and explanations presented by students.

Results

At the functional level the task of establishing the postage rate for sending a letter weighing 120 grams leads to two fundamentally different kinds of cognitive actions. One way of approaching the task is to consult the table, reading off the postage rate that is assumed to be correct. The other solution is to use a strategy that implies calculating the postage rate. Examples of these two modes of handling the task are given in Figure 12.2.

Disregarding the variation in the settings (i.e., lessons) in which the task was introduced and the design of the task given (i.e., whether it involved finding one postage rate or several), these two types of solutions to the problem appear in roughly the same proportions as can be seen from Table 12.1. There is a somewhat higher proportion

Table 12.1. *Frequencies and percentages of participants estimating postage rates through* reading off *and* calculating

Action	Grade 8 n (%)	Grade 9 n (%)	Total n (%)
Reading off	53 (48.6)	60 (58.8)	113 (53.6)
Calculating	56 (51.4)	42 (41.2)	98 (46.4)
	109	102	211

Table 12.2. *Actions performed to solve task of establishing postage rates in a mathematics and social studies lesson respectively*

Action	Mathematics class n (%)	Social studies class n (%)	Total n (%)
Reading off	55 (42.6)	58 (70.7)	113 (53.6)
Calculating	74 (57.4)	24 (29.3)	98 (46.4)
	129	82	211

of answers in the reading-off category among the grade-nine students, although the proportions in this group deviate only moderately from those found among the grade-eight students. However, for the present study, this general description of the outcome is primarily of interest as a general indicator of the finding that in the group of participants as a whole, the two ways of using the table were represented.

In analyzing the outcome when the task was introduced in a mathematics and social studies lesson respectively clear differences can be noted (Table 12.2). When given the task of establishing the postage rates for letters in the context of a mathematics class, 57.4% of the students interpreted this as a mathematical task, thus engaging in some kinds of calculations in order to come up with an answer. When dealing with the same problem in the social studies class, only 29.3% used mathematical operations to arrive at an answer. This difference between lessons is statistically significant ($\chi^2 = 15.91$, $df = 1$, p $<.001$).

To go into further detail, there were two types of mathematical operations that were used among the participants who attempted to establish the postage rate by means of some kind of calculation. One type of solution was to use the principle presented in example 3 in Figure 12.2 of adding the postage rates for 100 grams (SEK 4.00) and 20 grams (SEK 2.10) to arrive at the answer of SEK 6.10. The other type of mathematical solution of the task implies an interpolation between the postage rates for letters between 100 and 250 grams. This interpolation was done on intuitive grounds as a general estimation or, more often, as a formal mathematical operation. A special variant of this latter mode of procedure is illustrated by example 4 in Figure 12.2. In this case, the student – after having established that 20 grams is a multiple of 120 grams – multiplies the postage rates for 20 grams (which can be found in the table) by 6. With respect to the overall problem of finding the correct postage rate for the letter, both these types of solutions are ineffective, because the postage rate is not related to the weight of the letter in the way that is assumed in either of these suggested solutions. Among the students who used either of these two ways of solving the problem, the strategy of adding the postage rates for letters weighing 20 and 100 grams is the most common one (82.7%).

With respect to the group of participants reading the table to establish the postage rates, two different solutions appeared. The variation in this case related to whether one, after having found the interval between 100 and 250 grams (which all those did who read the table to find the postage rate), pointed to the lower value, SEK 4.00, or the higher value, SEK 7.50, as the correct answer. In passing it can be mentioned that 39.7% of the total group of participants managed to arrive at the correct postage rate.

These results, then, indicate that the overall context in which the participants find themselves tends to determine their interpretation of the task. Dealing with postage rates as part of a mathematics lesson has a tendency to lead to students perceiving the task as mathematical in nature and, conversely, when the task is embedded in the context of a social studies class, there is a tendency to read the table and to abstain from calculating. In the design of our study, however, a different variation was also introduced – namely the one between solving one problem (120-gram letter) and the more general

Table 12.3. *Comparison of results of tasks requiring establishing postage rates for one (120 grams) and seven letters (from 10 to 1,200 grams) respectively*

Action	One letter n (%)	Seven letters n (%)	Total n (%)
Reading off	39 (44.3)	74 (60.2)	113 (53.6)
Calculating	49 (55.7)	49 (39.8)	98 (46.4)
	88	123	211

task of deciding on postage rates for several letters varying in weight. The outcome with respect to the variations in actions in these two types of situations is shown in Table 12.3.

As can be seen, the tendency to interpret the task as mathematical in nature is more common when the participants are presented with the problem of establishing the postage rate for one letter than when they are given the more extensive task of finding the postages for a series of letters ($\chi^2 = 5.18$, $df = 1$, p $<.05$). It would seem as if reading off the postage rates directly from the table provided was a more natural mode of proceeding when the number of letters became so large that it was unpractical and possibly too time-consuming to use calculations. Here the use of the table was perceived – we might hypothesize – as a functionally appropriate tool that made the problem of finding the correct postage rates for the series of letters possible to handle in a reasonably efficient way within the constraints of the classroom setting.

Furthermore, the design of this task made it more difficult to keep to either of the mathematical solutions used by the participants. The most common strategy of adding postages for a particular letter resulted in some cases in postage rates that were higher than that of the interval in the table, and the detection of inconsistencies of this kind may have served as an impetus for considering the logic of the table and how it should be used. Also, the use of a letter weighing 10 grams as the first item on the list of seven letters should have been suggestive of using a different strategy for establishing the postage rate, because many of the participants would know that the postage

Table 12.4. *Outcome on task of finding postage rate for a letter weighing 120 grams*

| Action | Mathematics class | | Social studies class | |
	One letter n (%)	Seven letters n (%)	One letter n (%)	Seven letters n (%)
Reading off	12 (25.5)	43 (52.4)	27 (65.9)	31 (75.6)
Calculating	35 (74.5)	39 (47.6)	14 (34.1)	10 (24.4)
	47	82	41	41

rate for a letter is SEK 2.10 (and not SEK 1.05, which is the value one would arrive at by using a strategy of interpolating).

Combining the results already described, we find that the activities that the participants engage in to find the postage rate for the letter weighing 120 grams are codetermined by the context in which this task is set. The types of solutions suggested may thus be read as responses to the setting as well as to the problem per se. In Table 12.4, the information in Tables 12.2 and 12.3 is combined to give a comprehensive presentation of the variation in whether participants read the table in order to find the postage rate or whether they solved it through some kind of mathematical operation.

While three of four participants in the mathematics class solving the problem with one letter use what we have referred to as a mathematical approach and calculate the answer, the picture is exactly the reverse as regards the students in the social studies class. In other words, the participants' interpretations of how to solve a problem seem to relate closely to their implicit and explicit assumptions about what is a natural mode of proceeding in a certain situation and given a certain type of task.

To take the analysis of how people deal with this type of everyday problem in a formal setting one step further, it might be worthwhile to take a closer look at the group of participants who used the table in the way intended and who thus, potentially, could arrive at the correct answer. As has been mentioned already, all of the students who attempted to read the table to arrive at the postage rate found the correct interval, the one between 100 and 250 grams. However,

Table 12.5. *Suggested postage rates among participants who read the table of postage rates*

Suggested postage	Mathematics class n (%)	Social studies class n (%)	Total n (%)
SEK 4.00	18 (32.7)	10 (17.2)	28 (24.8)
SEK 7.50	37 (67.3)	48 (82.8)	85 (75.2)
	55	58	113

with respect to the answer preferred there were two options; SEK 4.00, which is the postage rate for a letter weighing a maximum of 100 grams, and SEK 7.50, which is the correct value. In Table 12.5, the distribution of answers among the 113 students who read the table to find the postage rate can be seen.

What is interesting about this table is that it also indicates an obvious difference between the two contexts among the group of participants who read the table to find the postage rate. The proportion of students who chose the lower value, SEK 4.00, is considerably higher than is the case among those who dealt with this task in the social studies class. Although this difference just fails to reach statistical significance ($\chi^2_{obs} = 3.63$, $\chi^2_{crit\ .05} = 3.84$, $df = 1$), it can be seen as indicating that different principles of seeking the correct value seem to be operating in the two contexts. Our interpretation of this would be that the logic that tends to lead to the choice of the lower value, SEK 4.00, more frequently in the mathematics class is the mathematical principle of rounding off to the closest figure, which, in this case, is the lower value. Thus, even here the mistake made may – when considered "from within the context of the discourse situation" (Rommetveit, 1988, p. 33) – turn out to be the consequence of the specific communicative premises under which the students attempted to find the postage rate.

The framing of cognitive problems

The point of our study has not been to illustrate the extent to which participants had the general competence to find out the postage rate for a letter. Had the problem appeared in a different setting as part of a genuine decision of what it would cost to send a letter to a friend, other strategies of seeking the relevant information would have been available, including the most natural one of asking someone who knows. The range of information-seeking alternatives is thus different, as are the criteria for making a wise decision on how to act. In the authentic case of sending a letter, it would, for instance, in many cases be a commendable strategy to put on some extra stamps, because it is better to be on the safe side rather than running the risk of embarrassing the person receiving the letter, who would have to pay extra and maybe even collect the letter at the post office. Very often one would, of course, also be uncertain of the exact weight of the letter one is about to send and, rather than going through the trouble of attempting to find out the precise weight, one would add stamps. In the world of formal schooling, such modes of reasoning that are sensitive to the social meaning of the act of sending letters would probably be regarded as attempts of evading the problem given.

Rather, our knowledge interest has been a heuristic one of illustrating by means of a prototypical instance that the meaning of a task cannot be defined independently of the context in which this problem is attended to and the individual's assumptions of what are the relevant premises for his or her actions. The activities developed by the participants provide evidence that they hold strong implicit predefinitions of what it means to take part in mathematics and social studies lessons that lead them to treat the problem given in specific ways. To refrain from doing calculations in the mathematics class may be just as difficult as it is unlikely that one would resort to this strategy when at the post office. (For a recent, in-depth analysis of how context and problem create each other, see Lave, 1988.)

Thus, to broaden the perspective the observations reported should not be interpreted as being indications of a passive subordination of problem-solving actions to the "premises for communication" present in either a mathematics or social studies class. At a more fundamental level, it seems as if a more accurate account of what the actions imply is that they do not merely reflect contextual definitions of appropriate modes of handling the problem. Rather, the participants construe wider contexts in terms of which their solutions of the problem of establishing the postage rate appear rational. To illustrate this, we shall borrow some illustrative excerpts from the larger study, from which the present results derive, in which there were additional sources of data (interactional data from participants engaged in collective problem solving and interviews) (cf. Säljö & Wyndhamn, 1990). When being asked to explain the logic behind the postage rate they suggest, the participants taking a mathematical approach typically attempt to provide a rational account by pointing to the fact that it should cost about the same per gram to send a letter irrespective of its weight. Consider the following excerpt from a group of three students working together on the same problem.

Dana: Maybe we can take 4 crowns[1] and divide it by 100, then we'll find out what 1 gram would cost.
Dave: That'll be 4 öre.
Erik: 4.80 in that case {multiplies 120 by 4}
Dave: How do you work that out?
Erik: Watch this. {calculates using paper and pencil}
(three turns left out)
Dave: Check what 2.10 divided by 20 is! {calculates on paper}
Erik: If you do that you get . . . 1 gram costs 1.05. No, it can't be!
Dave: Work it out! {calculates}
Dana: 0.105
Erik: Here, 1 gram costs 4 öre . . . and here it costs 1 öre and a little more . . .
Dave: I think it costs 4.80.

In thinking about this kind of problem, the need to find an explicit criterion that makes the postage rate appear as rational is evident. Many find it "unfair" that the same postage rate should apply for letters weighing 120 grams and, for example, 240 grams; and this line of reasoning, then, is a strong impetus for interpolating in the table, thus reducing the postage rate for the letter weighing 120 grams in our study.

The postage rate table in this case can be viewed as a tool that reflects the general idea of a quantitative relationship between weight and postage rate. For practical reasons, however, this relationship is not strictly linear and this has to be realized in this context and accepted as a premise for establishing the postage rate. In other words, a successful interaction with the table entails knowing that there are certain conventions in a society that imply that linear relationships are not considered relevant in certain situations. However, if we continue further in the transcript from the dialogue quoted, we find that the students' adherence to the logic of assuming that the price per gram should be the same irrespective of the weight reflects an assumption that the table presented to the public is a less detailed version of the one used at the post office. The following passage is an excerpt that appears after the suggestions of establishing the postage rate per gram and then multiplying by 120.

Interviewer:	Do they work like this at the post office?
Erik:	No, at the post office they have a more detailed table: 20, 21, 22, 23 (grams) and so on.
Dave:	No, they can't sit like this.
Dana:	They have a machine that works out the postage rate.
Dave:	If they don't have a machine, they read in a table 20, 25, 30, 35 . . . and round off, sort of.

Situated learning in this context thus seems to imply that one establishes a frame of reference in terms of which one learns that strictly quantitative relationships are often not suitable to have as working algorithms in everyday settings such as the one of establishing postage rates. The pragmatic interest in having a limited class of postage rates and a corresponding limited number of stamps invalidates the purely quantifying approach given precedence by many of the participants.

When the postage rate is determined by reading the table, typical explanations given of the postage rates, the intervals and the design of the table, point out that such matters are the result of decisions taken by people. In the written explanations given by the students in the social studies classes in this particular study, several statements imply such a perspective: "The government has decided to have it that way" or "The prime minister has decided." Being in this position of seeing the postage rates as products of social negotiation, it is – we would argue – much easier to cope with the "arbitrariness" of the table than if one expects exactness, or "fairness," in the sense previously hinted at. Knowledge of the world and the usefulness of conventions in everyday life thus seems to imply that one has less difficulty in accepting outcomes that may seem "unfair" from a strictly formal, quantitative perspective. And taking this perspective was obviously much easier if one assumed that one was doing social studies rather than "maths."

Concluding comments

For the individual, the problem of establishing postage rates in the school setting is thus not identical with the problem of dealing with this issue in an everyday situation. The very meaning of the action as a communicative and psychological event varies as contexts vary. In the school setting the individual operates in a paper-and-pencil world and her or his actions are "energized" (Leont'ev, 1972/1981) by a different set of motives. The knowledge valued is generally of the abstract, literate type and students – qua students – orient themselves in their activities in accordance with their assumptions of what counts as valid definitions of situations and problems. This means that the competencies developed may have only limited applicability in other sectors – or "provinces of meaning" (Berger & Luckmann, 1966) – of socially and technologically complex societies. Thus, in our view, the growth of communicative enclaves in modern societies per se constitutes a challenge for research on human thinking in the sense that parallel, and maybe even competing, ways of construing reality develop and provide the basis for new forms of knowledge and problem-solving skills. The assumed superiority of the abstract type of knowledge and the accompanying "literate bias of schooling" (Olson, 1977) may therefore be more a matter of faith and tradition than a rational mode of expanding human intellectual repertoires.

In our view, studies of human cognition should be based on an epistemology recognizing that the world is inherently complex, multifaceted, and open to interpretation. The Cartesian heritage – the reductionism inherent in "abstract objectivism," to use Volosinov's (1930/1973) terminology – has provided us with the epistemological perspectives through which it has become natural to avoid seeing actions in context as the basic object of inquiry for bringing about genuine insights into human cognition. Continuing along these lines, we are doomed perhaps to repeated discoveries of the findings that have been made since the early childhood of research on cognition (cf., e.g., Wilkins, 1928; Bartlett, 1932), through its adolescence (e.g., Katona, 1940/1967; Wertheimer, 1945/1966), and well into maturity (e.g., Wason & Johnson-Laird, 1972; Flavell, 1977; Ramsden, 1984) – namely, that humans live and act in a world of meanings. The challenge for research is to create theoretical constructs – rather than abstractions – that build on this organic relationship between thinking and the world in which human projects take place. In this way we will learn what is specifically human about human cognition.

Note

1. Swedish currency (SEK) is divided into kronor (crowns) and öre (100 to the crown).

References

Bartlett, F. C. (1932). *Remembering*. Cambridge: Cambridge University Press.

Berger, P., & Luckmann, T. (1966). *The social construction of reality*. New York: Anchor.

Brushlinskii, A. V. (1979). The interrelationship of the natural and the social in human mental development. *Soviet Psychology, 17*, 36–52.

Carraher, T. Z., Carraher, D. W., & Schliemann, A. D. (1985). Mathematics in the streets and in schools. *British Journal of Developmental Psychology, 3*, 21–29.

Cole, M. (1985). The zone of proximal development: Where culture and cognition create each other. In J. V. Wertsch (Ed.), *Culture, communication, and cognition: Vygotskian perspectives* (pp. 146–161). Cambridge: Cambridge University Press.

Flavell, J. (1977). *Cognitive development*. Englewood Cliffs, NJ: Prentice-Hall.

Goffman, E. (1974). *Frame analysis*. New York: Harper and Row.

Katona, G. (1967). *Organizing and memorizing*. New York: Hafner. (Original work published 1940)

Kvale, S. (1977). Dialectics and research on remembering. In N. Datan & H. W. Reese (Eds.), *Life-span developmental psychology* (pp. 165–189). New York: Academic Press.

Lave, J. (1988). *Cognition in practice*. Cambridge: Cambridge University Press.

Lave, J., Murtaugh, M., & de la Rocha, O. (1984). The dialectic of arithmetic in grocery shopping. In B. Rogoff & J. Lave (Eds.), *Everyday cognition: Its development in social context* (pp. 67–94). Cambridge, MA: Harvard University Press.

Leont'ev, A. N. (1981). The problem of activity in psychology. In J. V. Wertsch (Ed.

and Trans.), *The concept of activity in Soviet psychology* (pp. 37–71). Armonk, NY: M. E. Sharpe. (Reprinted from *Voprosy Filosofi,* 1972, *9,* 95–108)

Luria, A. N. (1982). *Language and cognition.* New York: Wiley.

Marková. I. (1982). *Paradigms, thought, and language.* Chichester: Wiley.

Minick, N. (1985). *L. S. Vygotsky and Soviet activity theory: New perspectives on the relationship between mind and society.* Unpublished doctoral dissertation, Northwestern University, Evanston, IL.

Olson, D. (1977). From utterance to text: The bias of language in speech and writing. *Harvard Educational Review, 47,* 257–281.

Ramsden, P. (1984). The context of learning. In F. Marton, D. Hounsell, & N. Entwistle (Eds.), *The experience of learning* (pp. 144–164). Edinburgh: Scottish Academic Press.

Rogoff, B. (1982). Integrating context and cognitive development. In M. E. Lamb & A. L. Brown (Eds.), *Advances in developmental psychology* (Vol. 2, pp. 125–170). Hillsdale, NJ: Lawrence Erlbaum.

Rogoff, B. (1984). Introduction: Thinking and learning in social context. In B. Rogoff & J. Lave (Eds.), *Everyday cognition: Its development in social context* (pp. 1–8). Cambridge, MA: Harvard University Press.

Rommetveit, R. (1974). *On message structure.* London: Wiley.

Rommetveit, R. (1988). On literacy and the myth of literal meaning. In R. Säljö (Ed.), *The written world* (pp. 13–40). Heidelberg: Springer-Verlag.

Säljö, R., & Wyndhamn, J. (1987). The formal setting as a context for cognitive activities: An empirical study of arithmetic operations under conflicting premises for communication. *European Journal of Psychology of Education, 2,* 233–245.

Säljö, R., & Wyndhamn, J. (1988). A week has seven days. Or does it? On bridging linguistic openness and mathematical precision. *For the Learning of Mathematics, 8,* 16–19.

Säljö, R., & Wyndhamn, J. (1990). Problem-solving, academic performance and situated reasoning: A study of joint cognitive activity in the formal setting. *British Journal of Educational Psychology, 60,* 245–254.

Volosinov, V. N. (1973). *Marxism and the philosophy of language* (L. Matejka & I. R. Titunik, Trans.). New York: Seminar Press. (Original work published 1930)

Vygotsky, L. S. (1978). *Mind in society: The development of higher psychological processes* (M. Cole, V. John-Steiner, S. Scribner, & E. Souberman, Eds.). Cambridge, MA: Harvard University Press.

Vygotsky, L. S. (1987). *Thought and language* (A. Kozulin, Trans.) Cambridge, MA: MIT Press. (Original work published 1934)

Wason, P. C., & Johnson-Laird, P. N. (1972). *Psychology of reasoning: Structure and content.* London: Batsford.

Wertheimer, M. (1966). *Productive thinking.* London: Tavistock. (Original work published 1945)

Wertsch, J. (1985). *Vygotsky and the social formation of mind.* Cambridge, MA: Harvard University Press.

Wertsch, J., Minick, N., & Arns, F. J. (1984). The creation of context in joint problem-solving. In B. Rogoff & J. Lave (Eds.), *Everyday cognition: Its development in social context* (pp. 151–171). Cambridge, MA: Harvard University Press.

Wertsch, J., & Stone, C. A. (1985). The concept of internalization in Vygotsky's account of the genesis of higher mental functions. In J. V. Wertsch (Ed.), *Culture, communication and cognition: Vygotskian perspectives* (pp. 162–179). Cambridge: Cambridge University Press.

Wilkins, M. C. (1928). The effect of changed material on the ability to do formal syllogistic reasoning. *Archives of Psychology, 102,* 5–83.

13 Teacher's directives: The social construction of "literal meanings" and "real worlds" in classroom discourse

Norris Minick

Hamlet:	Who's grave's this sirrah?
Clown:	Mine sir.
Hamlet:	What man dost thou dig it for?
Clown:	For no man sir.
Hamlet:	What woman then?
Clown:	For none neither.
Hamlet:	Who is to be buried in it?
Clown:	One that was a woman, sir; but rest her soul she's dead.
Hamlet:	How absolute the knave is! We must speak by the card or equivocation will undo us. By the Lord, Horatio, this three years the age has grown so picked that the toe of the peasant comes so near the heel of the courtier he galls his kibe.

(Shakespeare, 1969, pp. 967–968)

While videotaping first-grade classrooms some time ago, I happened to observe two teachers reading a children's poem in strikingly different ways. The poem, entitled "Surprises," is by Jean Conder Soule.

This research is being carried out by the author and James V. Wertsch (Clark University) with financial assistance from the Spencer Foundation. Support for early phases of the research effort was provided by the Center for Psychosocial Studies (Chicago) and by a postdoctoral fellowship grant (HD07307-01) from the Department of Health and Human Services to the University of Chicago. The data presented, the statements made, and the views expressed are the author's.

My sincere thanks go to all the participants at the conferences on which this volume is based for discussions and comments that contributed substantially to this chapter. Special thanks go to Ed Hutchins, Roger Säljö, Hugh Mehan, Jean Lave, and Seth Chaiklin for their detailed comments on the paper at various stages of its development. Special thanks are also due to Ragnar Rommetveit for a recent paper (Rommetveit, 1988) that made it possible for me to see – if somewhat belatedly – the connection between "literal meaning" and "objective" representations of reality.

(1) Surprises are round or long and tallish.
(2) Surprises are square or flat and smallish.
(3) Surprises are wrapped with paper and bow,
(4) And hidden in closets where secrets don't show.
(5) Surprises are often good things to eat,
(6) A get-well toy or a birthday treat.
(7) Surprises come in such interesting sizes.
(8) I LIKE SURPRISES.

In one case, the teacher read the poem as a means of introducing me to her pupils as they were entering the classroom in the morning. After reading the poem, the teacher explained why I was there with my video camera. The poem was used to convey the idea that surprises can come in an infinite variety of forms (including bald men in tweed jackets operating video equipment) and that they can often be fun, exciting, and quite positive things.

In a second classroom, the poem was included in the work of a reading group alongside exercises involving the substitution of adjectives in sentences and the decoding of words that differed only in their initial consonants. Here, the teacher introduced the poem in the following way:

T: Now. I am going to read you a little poem called "Surprises" and I want you to tell me ONE THING in that poem about surprises that you can tell me about surprises. You have to listen to know about it.

After the teacher had read the poem, the following interchange occurred:

T: Now I want you to tell me something about surprises you heard in that poem. The last person I ask is going to have the hardest job. Mike?
C: I like surprises.
T: I like surprises. Ok. What are surprises like?
C: Big and small.
T: [nods head yes] Big and small. Millie?
C: Large and small.
T: Same thing he said. I need a new one. Come back to you. It's harder as it goes along. Mandy?
C: It could be toys or something to eat.
T: Good. Toys or something to eat. Good. Becky?

C: Square and circle.

T: Good. Circles or squares.

C: It could be . . uhmmm . . . color.

T: Colors. [Looks to written text.] Ok. Let's see if there's anything in there that talked about colors. It didn't say in the poem about colors. They COULD be colors though. I'm going to read it again, and I bet we get some more people that can tell this time. [Teacher rereads poem with exaggerated enunciation and slower speed. Hands of two pupils go up after "flat and smallish," and teacher says "Hands down."]

T: Josh, tell me another thing that we didn't . . .

C: Surprises are interesting.

T: Interesting. Ok. Good. Mary?

C: Flat and . . .

T: Flat and . . .

C: [Inaudible]

T: What.

C: Flat and little.

T: Flat and little. We already said little. Little is right but we already said it. Julie.

C: They can be clothes. They can be clothes.

T: They can be. . . ?

C: Clothes.

T: Clothes? [Looks to the written text.] They can be clothes? Well? I don't think it said they could be clothes. They certainly could be clothes, you're right. Sandy?

C: Treats.

T: Treats? We already said "something to eat." We already said they could be toys or something to eat. Beth?

C: Wrapped in bow and paper?

T: Good. We got something new there. Wrapped in bows and papers. How about where they were hidden. Kelly, where did we hide them?

C: Closets.

T: Yes. You remembered that now. They could be hid in a closet. You have to be a very good listener and think when you hear words.

There are obvious differences in the way that these two teachers incorporated this text into the activity of the classroom; they used the text in different ways toward different ends. Presumably, the first reading led to an interpretation that corresponded more closely to what the author intended to convey in writing and publishing this poem. It is also more typical of what teachers do in facilitating comprehension of literary prose and poetry.

The second reading, however, is neither an aberration nor an accident. It is part of a family of social practices that the child encounters in school in which task motives and goals, participants' social positions and relationships, and ideologies, technologies, and customs of language use give rise to attempts to construct close relationships between what is meant and what is said, between what is made known through an utterance and what is explicitly represented in language. The development of this family of speech practices – which I will refer to here as *representational speech* – is one of the foci of our current research.

If there is a single "feature" that differentiates "representational" from "nonrepresentational" forms of speech, it is a concern that the meaning of an utterance must correspond to what is actually represented in words. This concern is reflected at a rather elementary level in the second reading of the poem on surprises. On this reading, what we can learn about surprises from the text is restricted to what is actually said about surprises in that text; what the poem "tells us" about surprises is restricted to what is explicitly stated in the language of the text itself. The teacher gives a variety of cues to the children indicating that this is the kind of "reading" that she wants and the children demonstrate through their responses that they understand this. The teacher does not reject claims that "colors" or "clothes" *could be* surprises, but she returns to the text, examines it, and insists that there is nothing in the language of the text that "says" that they are. Correspondingly, the children demonstrate their developing understanding of "representational" readings of text in their careful attention to what is actually "said" in the language of the poem (e.g., surprises are "flat and little" and are "wrapped in bow and paper") (Donaldson, 1978).

This concern that the meaning of an utterance must correspond with what is actually represented in language does not itself *constitute* "representational" speech. On the one hand, this "concern" with the representation of meaning does not arise spontaneously in the mind of the individual; it is rooted in the role that language assumes in the mediation of specific forms of social practice. Clanchy's (1979) historical analysis of the role of written records in English law, for example, indicates that this concern with a clear and complete representation of meaning in language only emerged as the role of the written record shifted from that of a symbolic token representing the existence of an orally constituted contractual agreement to that of a "definitive" statement of the content of the agreement. On the other hand, representational forms of speech can no more be reduced to a concern with the representation of meaning than modern industry can be reduced to a concern with shelter, food, and transportation. Representational speech involves technologies (e.g., formal definitions) and activities (e.g., reviewing text to assure consistent use of terms) that have developed in connection with specific social practices in order to facilitate the representation of meaning in language. Of course, from a psychological perspective, representational speech also involves the development of human skills in using these technologies and carrying out these practices.

Searle (1979, pp. 117–136) and others have argued – correctly I think – that it is impossible to construct linguistic representations that correspond fully and unambiguously with a single "intended meaning." In the process of carrying out a wide range of social practices, however, there are many contexts in which considerable effort is devoted to the achievement of precisely this end. This concern with explicit and unambiguous representation of intended meaning in language plays a limited but important role in the lawyer's attempt to represent an agreement between clients in written contract, in the legislator's work in drafting legislation, in the bureaucrat's effort to construct administrative rules and regulations, and in the scientist's struggles to explicate systematic theory, to describe experimental conditions and results, or to construct "operational definitions." Technologies and activities such as the formal definition of technical terms (e.g., Lyons, 1977) and the analysis of the language used in the expression of ideas (e.g., Eskridge & Frickey, 1988) play a critical role in the representational use of language in these practices.

For the past several years, we have been studying the processes through which the technologies, practices, and ideologies that constitute representational speech are introduced to the child in the early years of formal schooling. The present chapter draws on preliminary analyses of videotape records of approximately 300 hours of class-room activity in six early primary classrooms, two each at the kinder-garten, first-grade, and second-grade levels. Taping was carried out in a single suburban middle-class school district over the course of a school year. In this chapter, I limit my discussion to a form of representational speech that we are currently calling "representa-tional directives."

Our research on representational forms of speech was stimulated by two closely related concerns. First, there is evidence from "cross-cultural" research indicating that 2 to 3 years of schooling leads to dramatic increases in performance levels on many tasks commonly used to assess cognitive development (Rogoff, 1981; Scribner & Cole, 1981). We are concerned with understanding what it is about the child's experience in the classroom that leads to these perfor-mance differences and what their significance is for understanding cognitive development. Second, Vygotsky's early work on the devel-opment of "scientific concepts" in school-age children (Shif, 1935; Vygotsky, 1934/1988, chap. 6) suggested connections between social practices, modes of discourse, and modes of thinking that we felt should be pursued (Minick & Wertsch, 1986; Wertsch & Minick, 1990). More broadly, we believed this research program might be a useful way to develop and extend Vygotsky's perspectives on the integral connections between social practice, discourse, and psycho-logical development (Minick, 1988, 1989a, 1989b; Vygotsky, 1971, 1978, 1934/1988; Wertsch, 1985).

Representational speech and the bracketing of situational sense

Near the end of my eldest son's kindergarten year, the family was seated at the dinner table when my wife noticed that Eric's milk was located precariously near the table's edge. Anticipating imminent disaster, my wife said, "Eric, you're going to spill your milk; MOVE YOUR GLASS." After a moment's pause – with a twinkle in his eye and a satisfied grin – Eric slid his glass to the corner of the table, carefully balancing it there so that the slightest movement would cause it to fall. In this response, it is my claim that Eric differentiated what was "said" from what was "meant," transforming what had been uttered as a nonrepresentational directive into a representational directive. He then played with the discrepancy between these two kinds of meaning, performing an action that corresponded with represented meaning while flouting nonrepresentational meaning. I will also claim that Eric had to make three interdependent cognitive-metalinguistic moves in order to accomplish this.

The first and most obvious involved turning his attention to the words used to express intended meaning. Eric had to focus on the words "move your cup" and explore some subset of the range of possible actions that might correspond with them. Had my wife used the words, "Move your cup *away from the edge of the table*," Eric could have played a similar game, but he would have had to play it under a quite different set of constraints (see Minick & Wiebking, 1989; Wiebking, 1990). Attention to the actual wording of an utterance – attention to what is actually "said" – is critical to the construction of representational meaning.

The second move Eric made here is less obvious but no less important. In addition to a focus on the wording of an utterance, the construction of representational meaning also requires what I will call the "bracketing of situational sense." Rommetveit (1974, 1979, 1988), among others, has argued that the subjective understandings of the interests and concerns that define a given context of social practice and discourse play a central role in the attribution of meaning to what we are calling nonrepresentational utterances. In the episode just outlined, for example, the appropriate nonrepresentational reading of "move your glass" or "move your glass away from the edge of the table" derives from the immediate concern with not spilling the milk and from many other more implicit interests and concerns that define the social context (e.g., the child must be able to reach the glass – and the milk must remain in it – so that the child can drink from it). The construction of a representational reading of an utterance demands that these kinds of the human interests and concerns be "bracketed out" in the process of construing utterance meaning.

The third factor underlying Eric's representational interpretation of the utterance is still less obvious but has extensive – perhaps profound – implications. I have suggested that the construction of representational meaning depends on a "bracketing" of the human interests and concerns that define a social reality temporarily shared by interlocutors. Representational uses of language also depend on a "joint commitment to a shared social reality" of the kind Rommetveit discusses in his work, but here this "joint commitment" is to a qualitatively different kind of social reality. Understanding Eric's representational construal of the phrase "move the cup" requires a temporary commitment to an "objective" and "monistic" world that is defined in isolation from the world of human concerns and interests (Rommetveit, 1988). It is in our mutual commitment to this kind of world that we understand any intentional movement of the cup – whatever its relationship to the anticipated movement – to correspond to a representational interpretation of the directive. Within this world, "movement" and "the table's edge" exist not in connection with local concerns of milk and family harmony, but as a separate world whose characteristics and qualities can be described and understood in isolation from any human interests and concerns. Part of my goal in this chapter is to suggest that the child's introduction to representational forms of speech is also both simultaneously and necessarily an introduction to this mode of conceptualizing the world, a represented world that is basic to forms of cognition, discourse, and practice that underly Western forms of science and rationality.[1]

Given related work on "decontextualized" modes of language use (e.g., Olson, 1977; Snow, 1983; and Wertsch, 1985), it is worth noting that what I am referring to here as "representational" forms of speech do not necessarily imply a "decontextualized" interpretation of "word" or "sentence" meaning, a "decontextualized" interpretation of the meaning of "the words themselves."

First, in the example discussed here and in the representational directives that we encounter in the classroom, the interpretation of representational meaning depends heavily on links between utterances and the "context" they refer to. In the episode just outlined, the meaning of phrases such as "your glass" and "the edge of the table" are clearly defined by the context within which the utterance was made. What is "bracketed out" in the construction of representational meaning seems to be quite limited and specific. What is "bracketed" is not the relationship between the phrase "the edge of the table" and it's referent in a specific speech context, but the constellation of interests and concerns that makes the referent humanly meaningful in a situationally defined way – that makes the "edge of the table" a danger to the milk, the tranquility of the meal, and family harmony.[2]

Second, fundamental to the construction of representational meaning is the social constitution and recognition of "contexts" in which this "speech genre" or "voice" is appropriate. Reading a request for "a 500-word, double-spaced summary of the paper" in a list of paper submission requirements for an academic conference, for example, I rely on my understanding of the reviewers' concerns and interests in understanding that they probably expect between 400 and 500 words in the summary. The fact that "technically" or "literally" the language seems to specify a summary of 500 words – no more and no less – is something that most readers will not and should not notice. On the other hand, there are contexts in the reading or writing of certain legal documents where this more technical or literal interpretation of language may be demanded. The claimholders in the case of *The United States v. Locke* discovered this when they "misread" a statute requiring the filing of mining claims "prior to December 31," assuming this meant simply "by the end of the year" – with December 31 included. The recognition or constitution of contexts in which representational or technical readings of text may be appropriate or advantageous is an integral part of the construction of representational meaning.

Directives in the classroom

An extensive and growing body of research indicates that skills in manipulating what we are calling representational meaning develop in rather striking ways during the first several years of the child's exposure to formal schooling (for a recent review, see Bonitatibus, 1988). Our own experimental work (Minick & Wiebking, 1989; Wiebking, 1990) provides rather clear evidence that this differentiation and development of representational speech is a product of the child's experiences in the classroom. In our analyses of the uses of language in classroom activities and discourse, we have identified a wide range of speech practices that may contribute to the child's differentiation of representational speech as a distinct genre and that may support the child's development of skills in using language representationally (Minick, 1987; Wertsch & Minick, 1990).

We are currently referring to one of these forms of speech as "representational directives." Teachers in primary-school classrooms spend a great deal of time telling their pupils what to do and how to do it. These directives are mostly nonrepresentational. Appropriate interpretation depends heavily on situational sense. Still, all the teachers we have observed demand representational interpretations of some directives. In this section, I review three types of classroom events in which directives are defined – or redefined – as representational directives.

Conflicts between representational and nonrepresentational meaning

In the dinner table scene discussed earlier, my son created a direct conflict between representational and nonrepresentational interpretations of the phrase, "move your cup." In classroom discourse, children are exposed to similar conflicts of interpretation. In some cases, these conflicts are created quite consciously in a teacher's effort to insist that a child represent intended meaning more fully in language, an end that many teachers equate with that of developing better communication skills. In discussing her pupils' failure to consistently "capitalize" the names of holidays, for example, a second-grade teacher wrote "thanksgiving day" on the board in lower case letters and asked what needed to be done. When a boy responded that she needed to "capitalize the letters," she echoed this phrase – thereby drawing attention to what the child had said – and began writing "THANKSGIVING DAY" in upper case letters on the board. That is, she began to do "what he had said" in capitalizing all the letters. The boy responded immediately, saying that the teacher needed to "capitalize the first letter of each word." This response required a more elaborate linguistic representation of intended meaning and was accepted as "clarifying" what was meant.

Similar conflicts of interpretation emerge when teachers are giving directives to their pupils. In the following episode, a kindergarten teacher is attempting to regulate her pupils' activity while they are doing worksheets at their desks. In her attempts to control and direct classroom activity, the teacher shifts from an emphasis on "situational sense" to an emphasis on what has been "said," creating a conflict in the accepted mode of interpreting the original utterance.

In this episode, the children are working on the first of two worksheets, though the teacher has not yet told them that there will be a second. This latter point is important, because it contributes to the creation of a differential in understanding of situational sense – and utterance meaning – between the teacher and some of her pupils. In response to a child who asks what they are to do when they are finished with the worksheet they are working on, the teacher says, "I'm going to tell you the signal to show me you're done. It's put your pencil down. It's not raise your hand, it is just put your pencil down and then I'll know you're finished." The directive in this utterance, a directive that plays a central role in the remainder of the episode, is the phrase, "put your pencil down." Here, at the beginning of the episode, the teacher does not direct attention to the phrase itself, but tries to clarify its meaning by defining it as a signal that indicates her pupils are finished working, a signal comparable with that of raising their hands.

Following this utterance, two of the three children sitting at the table on which our camera was focused put their pencils down on the table, but a third (Bradley) reached across the table to return his pencil to a mug (serving as a pencil holder) that was located in the middle of the table. Apparently in response to this – and to other children (off camera) who are doing the same thing – the teacher says, "We're going to do another paper, so as soon as I see people sitting ... keep your pencil." At this point, there is an energetic exchange between Bradley and a girl at his table who has put her pencil down on the desk, with Bradley apparently trying to convince the girl that her pencil should be returned to the mug. Bradley seems to have understood the phrase "put your pencil down" to mean "put your pencil away." This is certainly a legitimate interpretation of the utterance. The action of "putting their pencils down" was to have functioned as a signal that they had *completed their work.* Within the context of this kindergarten classroom – where pencils are used rather infrequently and are kept in their holders – this reading of utterance meaning and situational sense seems quite appropriate.

As noted in the preceding paragraph, the teacher initially responded to "misinterpretations" of this directive by trying to establish greater correspondence in understanding of situational sense. By saying that, "we're going to do another paper," for example, she was trying to exclude an interpretation that would lead the children to put their pencils away. She also attempted to exclude this interpretation by issuing a second directive – "keep your pencil" – that explicitly contradicted it.

This second directive marks a shift in the teacher's communicative strategy. In her next utterance, she abandons the attempt to establish a common understanding of situational sense and shifts to the explicit representation of meaning in language. Her first move is to elaborate her initial directive by trying to specify WHERE the pencil is to be put: "Just put it down *next to your . . . next to your paper.*" At this point, Bradley abandons his attempt to convince his tablemate to return her pencil to the mug and moves the mug nearer to his own worksheet. The teacher then addresses Bradley directly, drawing his attention to the wording of her directive and to the lack of correspondence between her words and his actions: "A few people are still working . . . when I see all the pencils down. . . . Where is your pencil Bradley?" After Bradley points to his pencil in the mug, the teacher says, "Where did I say? Didn't I say just put it DOWN . . . by your paper? Put it DOWN, not back in your mug." This episode is followed immediately by an exchange between the teacher and another child off camera who has also "misinterpreted" the initial directive. "Where did I say to put the pencils Sarush?" [Child: (Inaudible).] "Where did I say to put it?" [Child: (Inaudible).] "I'm talking to Sarush, Sarah. Where did I say to put it? Can't hear you." [Child: "Down."] "Next to your paper, not back."

The communicative and social dynamics of an episode of this kind are obviously quite complex. In her effort to communicate a directive to her pupils, however, there is a clear shift in the teacher's strategy. Initially, she attempts to clarify meaning by elaborating and drawing attention to the appropriate "situational sense" to be used in interpreting her utterances. By the end of the episode, she is elaborating her linguistic representation of the directive and insisting that if her pupils will only attend carefully to *what she has said* they will understand *what she wants them to do.*

As we have suggested, this ideology that meaning can be fully encoded in language forms and that understanding is possible through a focus on this represented meaning is a common feature of representational uses of speech. In important respects, the teacher here has redefined her initial utterance. What she initially treated as a nonrepresentational utterance – to be understood against the backdrop of situational sense – is redefined as a representational directive that was to be interpreted by focusing on what is actually represented in "the words themselves."

A similar process is played out in a rather different way in the following episode, an episode in which a second-grade teacher is working with four pupils at a table during "reading group." This episode begins as the teacher attempts to shift from a discussion of library books that are on the table in front of the children to work on a story in the basal readers that are under the children's chairs. The teacher initiates this shift by clearing away several notebooks that lie atop her copy of the reader while saying, "Now. We are going to read a story. Please put your books under your chair. And, we are going to read a story which you are going to enjoy."

As in the preceding episode, the teacher's initial utterance contains a directive (i.e., "please put your books under your chair") as well as statements that would seem to be intended to contribute to a shared understanding of situational sense (i.e., "we are going to read a story"). The children respond to this utterance in different ways. One boy (Todd) puts his library book under his chair and then takes out his reader, placing it on the table in front of him. When he sees the teacher begin to turn the pages of her reader, Todd begins to look through his. Framed by the suggestion that "we are going to read a story" and the teacher's subsequent actions, Todd has apparently taken the teacher's directive as a marker indicating that they are to prepare to do that reading. This task begins with putting the library books away, but also includes taking the reader out and locating the new story. In marked contrast, a boy seated to Todd's right bends over and puts his library book under his chair – leaving his reader there – and sits bolt upright with his hands on the table. As he notices Todd looking through his reader, he begins to look nervously back and forth from Todd to the teacher, but does nothing more. Finally, two girls sitting to Todd's left reach to put their books under their chairs and then hesitate, looking from Todd to the teacher without sitting back up. Apparently concluding from the teacher's indifference that Todd must be doing the right thing, they then pull their readers out from under their chairs and begin looking through them.

In their responses to the teacher's initial utterance in this episode, the children in this reading group reflect the tension between two distinct interpretations of the directive, "Put your books under your chair." Todd unhesitatingly attributes a nonrepresentational meaning to this language, taking it as a directive to move on to work in the reader. With similar confidence, at least initially, the boy to his right seems to attribute a representational meaning to the directive. Ignoring the teacher's suggestion that they should move on to work in the reader, he puts his book under his chair and does nothing more. The girls to Todd's left seem unsure of how they should interpret the directive, looking to the teacher's response to Todd's action as a means of clarifying the issue. It is not surprising that this tension between these readings of the teacher's directive emerges here, because this teacher frequently insists on a strict interpretation of represented meaning both in giving directives and in other aspects of classroom activity.

At this point in the interaction, the teacher notices that several of the children are looking through their books. Her response is immediate. There is a studied tone of irritation in her voice as she says: "Todd, did Mrs. W. say, 'Open your book to . . .' Did she?" [Todd shakes his head, "No."] "No, she did not," the teacher continues. Todd and the two girls respond by closing their readers, while the second boy – who has been displaying considerable tension up to this point – relaxes in his seat.

In contrast to the episode we discussed earlier, this teacher does not immediately refer back to the initial directive (i.e., "put your books under your chair") and focus attention on the wording of that utterance. Taking a somewhat different approach, she asks whether she has said anything that explicitly authorized her pupils to "open their books." While she does not insist that they comply with the initial directive – by returning their readers to their place under their chairs – she makes it very clear that their actions are to correspond with what she actually represents in language. This message is reinforced moments later when the teacher finds once again that several of the children are furtively peeking into their readers: "Excuse me. I have not good listeners today. Now, put your hands on your books. [The "guilty" three immediately place their hands on their books.] Put your books under your chairs. [The three immediately put their books under their chairs.]"

Here, the teacher makes several nested moves that make it clear that she is demanding a representational interpretation of directives. First, she begins with a directive that has a clear representational meaning but a rather opaque situational significance (i.e., "put your hands on your books"), encouraging a shift to representational interpretation. She follows this with a directive that is identical to that which initiated the episode, returning them to the position they would have been in had they followed a representational interpretation of her first directive (i.e., "put your books under your chairs"). All of this is introduced with the statement about "good listeners," driving the message home clearly. Good listening requires a focus on what is said and behavior that corresponds with the actions represented in such directives.

Before moving on to a discussion of other types of "representational directives" that commonly occur in classroom discourse, several comments are in order. First, the tension between representational and nonrepresentational meaning that emerges in these kinds of episodes is at least partially a function of shifts in the teacher's definition of the nature of the utterance. In neither of these episodes is it clear that the teacher "intended" her utterance to be interpreted as a representational directive at the time it was made. In the second episode, the teacher did not object to the children's "misinterpretation" of her utterance until it became apparent that their looking through their readers might interfere with her effort to review new vocabulary before beginning to read. Even here, she did not initially object to their having their readers on the table. It was only after the children began looking through their readers a second time that she insisted that her initial utterance had not "warranted" taking their readers out from under their chairs. In the first episode, both the way that it unfolded and our subsequent discussions with the teacher indicate that she did want the children to put their pencils down next to their papers when she uttered the initial directive. Still, it was only after she saw children failing to do this – and only after her efforts to clarify situational sense had failed – that she began to treat her directive as "representational." Only at this point did she attempt to represent her meaning in language more fully and to direct her pupils' attention to that language.

Second, in both of these episodes, the insistence on a representational interpretation of directives appears to be driven by the teachers' efforts to maintain strict control over their pupils' activities in order to maximize effectiveness or efficiency of classroom activity. In the second episode, it was only when the children's actions threatened to interfere with the teacher's plans that she began to insist on a representational interpretation of her directives. In the first episode, it was the teacher's recognition that the children were doing things that would interfere with the process of efficiently shifting the class to work on the next worksheet that led to her insistence on a representational construction of the phrase "put your pencil down."

Formal training in following representational directives

In the preceding discussion, I refrained from using the phrase "representational directive" because it was unclear that the teachers involved had intended a representational interpretation of their directives at the time they made them. In this respect, although a representational directive is eventually constructed, we do not find the established approaches to organizing activity and discourse that are characteristic of representational directives as a distinct "genre" of speech and practice.

Although teachers vary significantly in the extent to which they use representational directives as a means of organizing classroom activity, this form of directive appears as a distinguishable speech genre in all the classrooms we have observed. Indeed, formal training in following what we are calling representational directives is a recognized part of the school curriculum, beginning with the introduction of what are commonly referred to as "listening exercises" at the kindergarten level.[3]

Formal training in following representational directives is an interesting phenomenon for several reasons, but it is particularly significant in connection with the problem of the "bracketing of situational sense." These classroom exercises are designed in such a way that actions designated by teacher's directives serve no purpose in a broader task situation. As a consequence, the activity setting itself creates the "bracketing of situational sense" that is such a difficult aspect of the psychological differentiation of representational from nonrepresentational meaning. In this respect, this training provides a "scaffold" for developing skills in operating on representational meanings.

The following episode provides a useful illustration of the dynamics involved in formal training in following representational directives. Here, a first-grade teacher is working with a small reading group on an exercise that has been outlined in the basal reader.

Now this is a little bit harder, so watch this. [The teacher writes the letters "G" and "H" on the blackboard.] Put your finger on the first letter, Lia, the first one. [The child points to the letter "G" – which is on the left – holding her index finger on the letter.] Good. Now stay there. Draw a line under the next letter. [The teacher hands chalk to child as she says this. The child makes a horizontal line under the "H," beginning on the right and moving to the left.] Uh. But you did it. . . . Wait a minute, now I want you . . . always draw your line from left to right. [The teacher erases the original line, illustrates proper orientation of line with finger motion, and the child makes the line.] Good. OK. Very good. OK. You did it all on that one. Now this is the last one like this. [The teacher writes "M," "N," and "O" on the board.] OK. Amanda. Draw a line around the first letter; that means make a circle around the first letter. [The child draws circle around the "M."] Good girl. Give the chalk to Justin. Put your finger on the next letter – not the chalk but your finger – on the next letter. Now, draw a circle un . . . no . . . draw a line under the last letter. [Child: "This one?" Pointing to the "O."] Is that the last one? [Child: Yes?] Um-hmm. [The child draws horizontal line from left to right.] Good. Boy, you're very good at directions. I'm proud of you.

This excerpt illustrates important characteristics of the discourse involved in formal training in following representational directives, characteristics that are found in many other forms of representational speech. I'll address two points here.

First, as I suggested earlier, there is no cooperative task here beyond that of properly enacting actions represented in directives; there is no "situational sense" that might create an interpretation of intended meaning that would go beyond what is represented in a particular sentence or phrase. If the participants were engaged in a task concerned with the order of letters in the alphabet, a request to "put your finger on the first letter" might be interpreted as meaning: (1) *to indicate in some way*, (2) *the letter that comes earlier with respect to alphabetical order*. In this training episode, the teacher makes it clear that phrases such as "put your finger on" are to be interpreted as meaning precisely that and nothing more. This is communicated, for example, in the teacher's emphasis on strict accordance with directives in comments like, "not the chalk but your finger." Moreover, even though the "objects" used in the task are letters arranged in alphabetical order, several of these children demonstrate confusion about what is meant by terms such as first and last in this context. It is not that they do not know the order of the letters in the alphabet. They certainly do. The problem is that there is no task that would define situational sense such that the meaning of terms such as "first" and "last" – or phrases such as "put your finger on" – could be disambiguated. Perhaps more appropriately stated, the bracketing of situational sense creates forms of semantic ambiguity – ambiguity in represented meaning – that do not exist in nonrepresentational uses of language.

Second, this construction of representational ambiguity gives rise to compensatory mechanisms essential to the construction of useful representational speech. Three of these mechanisms might be mentioned in this context. First, there is an increase in the amount of "information" actually represented in language. Rather than say "point to" the teacher says "put your finger on." This narrows the range of actions that correspond with the directive, by demanding actual contact between the finger and the object, for example. Second, there is a shift toward a more descriptive mode of expression. The teacher does not use terms such as *point, circle,* or *underline,* which are bound up with the socially meaningful activity of "indicating" in many contexts of classroom discourse, terms that would therefore "draw in" – or "debracket" – situational sense. Rather, she uses a more neutral descriptive language, reflected in directives such as "put your finger on" or "draw a line around." This facilitates the maintenance of the joint commitment to an "objective" or "disinterested" mode of representing the world that we discussed earlier. Finally, this representational ambiguity is associated with the need to "define" terms as they are used in directives. In this episode, for example, the teacher insists that when she says "draw a line under," this means to draw a line from left to right; that when she says "draw a line around" this means to draw a circle around.

Representational directives in the mediation of classroom practice

As I have suggested, episodes involving the redefinition of directives and episodes involving formal training in following representational directives occur in a classroom environment in which the use of the latter plays an important role in the organization of classroom activity. Our observations indicate that there are two situations in which teachers commonly use representational directives in managing classroom activity. In both, teachers are usually trying to move their pupils through a comparatively mechanical task that has little immediate pedagogical significance. One situation in which representational directives are commonly used is where a teacher has failed to communicate situational sense and shifts to the use of representational directives as an alternate means of guiding her pupils through tasks that they do not adequately understand. A second occurs where a teacher withholds any explanation of task, insisting that her pupils act on the basis of representational directives rather than on the basis of their understanding of task or situational sense. In both cases, representational directives are used as a technology of classroom management and control.

Failure to communicate situational sense. As noted, representational directives are often used to direct and control classroom activity when a teacher fails to communicate her definition of "situational sense" in introducing a task. Here, the teacher's attempt to explain a task begins with a focus on what must be done, why it is being done, and what is – as a consequence – important and unimportant. Failing to communicate this understanding of situational sense, the teacher is forced to shift to the use of representational directives, guiding and controlling classroom activity by representing each of the actions her pupils are to perform in language. By restricting activities to those explicitly represented in language, the teacher is able to lead her class through a task even though they may have an inadequate understanding of the social concerns and interests that define it. In the end, this often helps children understand the task logic – or situational sense – that the teacher attempted to communicate at the outset.

The following episode provides a useful illustration. Here, a second-grade teacher has devoted 5 minutes to explaining a task that involves "number families" (e.g., 3, 4, and 7) and the four "number sentences" that these number families can generate through the operations of addition and subtraction (i.e., $7-3=4$, $7-4=3$, $3+4=7$, $4+3=7$). The task involves writing number families and number sentences in graphic forms presented on a worksheet so that they can then be cut out and fit into slots in a line drawing of a house. The resulting product is to be used as a puzzle to develop and assess knowledge of number families and arithmetic facts.

As she introduces the task, the teacher talks about number families and the way that the "puzzle" will be used when completed, pointing repeatedly to the worksheet and to the drawing in an attempt to establish a common understanding of task situation. As evidenced by raised hands, questions, and pained facial expressions, however, it becomes increasingly apparent that the teacher is not succeeding in her efforts to explain what is to be done. The following excerpt marks the teacher's final effort to explain the task and her shift to a classroom management strategy that relies on representational directives.

Then, you will cut this out, so that you can put the slots in there. They will fit exactly in there. . . . Right behind it. We don't glue it because we want to be able to move it back and forth. Do you understand? And then in this square you will cut that out and you will have an answer in there and somebody is going to have to figure out what number sentence they are going to have to use to get that answer. So you understand what we're doing? . . . OK . . . LET'S TRY THIS TOGETHER. Paper passers. Let's do this first. No one is going to cut or do anything. The first thing we're going to do is pass out the house.

The teacher's effort to establish common situational understanding is reflected in the initial portions of this excerpt, in phrases such as "we want to be able to move it back and forth" and "somebody is going to have to figure out what number sentence they are going to have to use to get that answer." This explanation of the task, its elements, and its product are intended to provide a frame within which to interpret directives for action or inaction (e.g., "you can put the slots in there" or "don't glue it"). It is meant to establish common understanding of what the slots are (i.e., means of covering and displaying problems and answers) and what is meant by "don't glue it" (i.e., "don't do anything to attach the number sentences to the 'house' that will prevent you from moving them back and forth").

The words "OK . . . LET'S TRY THIS TOGETHER" – uttered slowly and with exaggerated emphasis – mark the teacher's transition to the use of representational directives as a means of leading the class through the task one step at a time. This process involved extensive interaction lasting over a period of 30 minutes. Throughout this process, the teacher made a consistent effort to represent in language the actions she wanted carried out (with the extensive use of gestures and objects to clarify the referent of a given word or phrase). She also insisted that the children's actions correspond to those authorized by what she had said.

The ground rules of this phase of the interaction are indicated in its introduction. In statements like, "no one is going to cut or do anything," and, "the first thing we're going to do is pass out the house," the teacher makes it clear that no one is to perform any action that is not explicitly authorized in her directives. The following utterances illustrate the nature of the verbal directives that were used to control classroom activity over the next 30 minutes.

The next thing you're going to do is . . . I want you to take the ten and cut that out and put it . . . off to the side. Cut out the ten . . . ONLY the ten.

All right. Next thing you're going to do is to cut out the entire first number family. Right now! Cut out the whole thing, all the way around [moving finger along rectangular line that encloses equations representing the first number family], in ONE BIG RECTANGLE.

Now. After you have done that first number family . . . I want you to take your scissors and go across the first one . . . go across the first one [pointing to the line that separates the first number sentence from the others].

Several characteristic features of representational directives are apparent here. First, a variety of markers are used to differentiate directives for distinct actions from one another. Phrases such as "the next thing you're going to do is," "all right – next thing," or "now – after you have done" reinforce the message that the children are to do only what they are told to do when they are told to do it. Second, this implication that actions are to be restricted to those that are explicitly authorized is reinforced by overt reminders. In saying, "cut out the ten ... *ONLY the ten*," for example, the teacher makes it clear that this directive is not to be taken as a general authorization to begin cutting out the many numbers and number sentences that have been constructed on the worksheet. If their developing understanding of task and situation suggests this reading of the directive, it is to be "bracketed." Finally, the teacher makes use of extensive – and sometimes exaggerated – verbal and nonverbal elaboration of directives that make it possible for her pupils to follow her directives without depending on their understanding of the goals and constraints that define this particular task situation. In directing the class to "cut out the entire first number family," for example, the teacher quickly defines what she means by this in both language and gesture: "Cut out the whole thing, all the way around [moving finger along rectangular line around the number family], in ONE BIG RECTANGLE." This elaboration makes it possible to carry out the task – to understand directives – without reference to what we have called situational sense.

Indeed, in an important sense, it is a misstatement to say that this speech style makes it *possible* to carry out the task without reference to situational sense. In fact, the way that this teacher organizes this activity makes it *necessary* to bracket situational sense in the interpretation of directives. In guiding her class through this task, the teacher selects one of a multitude of possible action sequences that could lead to successful task performance and demands that her pupils follow precisely that sequence. Other approaches to the task – which might be equally effective in completing the task – are forbidden.

For example, the worksheet used in this episode contained four number sentences, each marked off in an elongated rectangle. All four, "stacked" on one another, formed the large rectangle that the teacher referred to as the "whole number family." In giving directives, the teacher insisted that the large rectangle be cut out first, with the number sentences subsequently being cut free one at a time, beginning with the one at the top. Pupils who carried out actions that did not correspond with these directives were reprimanded even where these actions corresponded with the goals or needs of the broader task. Indeed, it is difficult to distinguish these reprimands from those elicited by students' actions that coincided with neither directives nor task goals. In both cases, attention was directed to the lack of correspondence between what had been explicitly stated in a directive and what had been done. For example, in response to a child who began by cutting out the top number sentence, the teacher said, "You did NOT follow my instructions. I said to cut out the ENTIRE number family. Cut this WHOLE THING OUT." Similarly, in response to a child who had cut out all four number families following directives to cut out "one big rectangle" and the "first number family," the teacher said, "YOU are not following my instructions. Did I say to cut out ALL the number families? What did I SAY? Cut out the very FIRST number sentence."

Measured against the logic of the task itself – against situational sense – neither child had done anything wrong. In both cases, they had merely anticipated actions that the teacher subsequently authorized in directives. What they had done wrong was to carry out actions defined by an emerging understanding of the task that did not correspond with explicit directives from the teacher.

Thus, as a means of helping her pupils understand a task and how it was to be carried out, this teacher shifted from the explanation of situational sense to the verbal representation of actions required to carry out the task. To accomplish this, she: (1) selected a sequence of actions that would lead to the successful completion of the task, (2) attempted to represent these actions as fully and clearly as possible in directives, and (3) insisted that her pupils act carefully and exclusively in accordance with these directives, minimizing reliance on their understanding of situational sense.

In effect, the teacher created a context for the interpretation of directives that approximated that characteristic of formal training in following representational directives. There is certainly a task situation here that would permit a nonrepresentational interpretation of directives. By introducing an essentially arbitrary relationship between acceptable actions and the task goals they realize, however, the teacher places her pupils in a position where the interpretation of meaning becomes heavily dependent on what is actually represented in directives; she demands that they bracket their emerging understanding of situational sense in interpreting directives. In contrast to contexts involving formal training in following representational directives, however, the child is forced to assume extensive cognitive responsibility for the task of bracketing situational sense in interpreting directives. In this respect, the teacher's reprimands that insist on adherence to a representational reading of directives provide a scaffold for the child's developing skills in bracketing situational sense.

Withholding explanations of situational sense. The second situation in which we have commonly observed the use of representational directives is also characterized by a "failure" to share the teacher's understanding of situational sense. Here, however, this "failure" is artificially introduced by the teacher, who makes no attempt to explain the goals or rationale of the task that she is guiding her students through. Here, the teacher withholds any explanation that would lead to a shared understanding of situational sense and makes it clear that the children are not to act on the basis of their own hypotheses concerning it. Here again, the teacher constructs a situation comparable with that which characterizes formal training in following representational directives. The children must attend carefully to verbalized directives and act in correspondence with them. This device provides the teacher with a degree of control over classroom activity that is difficult to attain if children are allowed to act in accordance with their often widely varied and discordant understandings of situational sense, making it possible for the teacher to manage efficiently pedagogically insignificant activities.

Consider the following episode involving a first-grade class working on a science lesson concerned with mirrors and the principles of reflection. The apparent purpose of the lesson was to illustrate that if one cuts a symmetrical two-dimensional object along the line of symmetry and places half the object against a mirror one can reproduce an image of the whole object (i.e., as composed by half the object and its reflection). We will focus on a task – best characterized as preparation for this lesson – in which representational directives were used to guide the class through a process of cutting geometric shapes in half along the line of symmetry.

In introducing this lesson, the teacher began by asking her pupils to tell her things that they had learned in earlier lessons about mirrors and reflection. Among many responses the teacher received, one child said that if you put a triangle against a mirror you will see a diamond. The teacher responded with positive reinforcement that seemed subtly stronger than that which she gave other answers. She also rephrased this answer so that it corresponded more closely with the conceptual focus of the upcoming lesson: "AHH. If you have half a thing and you show it in the mirror you get the other half showing too. Good for you, Tina." The teacher did not, however, mention any connection between this answer and the upcoming lesson. Indeed, as this phase of the lesson ended, another child noted that if you show a half circle in the mirror you'll see a full circle, but the teacher responded quite negatively: "Uh-huh. That's just like we said. The symmetrical things." Once again, no effort was made to explicitly connect this comment with the preparatory phase of the lesson in which the geometrical shapes were cut in half, a phase that began with the teacher's next word.

In the preparatory phase of the lesson, the teacher used representational directives to lead the class through the construction of the "halved" geometric shapes (i.e., circles, rectangles, and triangles) that would be used in the upcoming lesson. In contrast to what we saw in the previous episode, the teacher withheld any explanation of why she was asking the class to produce these shapes until the process was completed. She introduced the preparatory phase in the following way.

Now. Mrs. B. has three shapes. Uh. Raise your hand if you know what you call this shape [Holding up circle]. Katie? [Child: Circle.] OK. What would you call this shape? [Holding up the rectangle.] Brian? [Child: Um. Um.] . . . It begins with an "r." [Children in background raising hands and saying: "Oh! Oooh!" Child: "Rectangle."] OK. What would you call this shape? Jordan? [Child: Triangle.] OK. Now, Benji's going to pass yellow triangles. Give everybody one. Don't do anything with them until we get them . . . all. Juan, I'm going to ask you to pass the red rectangles. And Lauren, I'm going to ask you to pass the green circles.

This introduction is itself composed of two phases. In the first, the teacher attempted to define the word – referent relationships of key terms she subsequently used in her directives (i.e., circle, square, and rectangle). In the second, she began to shift to the process of organizing activity through representational directives, using a common phrase to suggest that the children were to act only in correspondence with her directives (e.g., "Don't do anything with them until . . .").

The following excerpts illustrate the characteristics of the speech that constitute the remainder of the episode:

OK. Let's start with the circle. And I want you to fold the circle once so it is the same on both sides. That means, fold it in half. [Child: Which way?] Doesn't matter . . . circles . . . [Child: Circle. Circle doesn't matter. (largely inaudible brief discussion among children)] OK. OK. When you've folded your circle in half, I want you to take out your scissors, and I want you to cut – your circle – ON THAT FOLD.

Now, take your two parts and lay them near your name tag. And pick up your red rectangle. Fold it so it is the same on both sides. That means – fold in half. But you could fold it two different ways. You could fold it the long way [teacher demonstrates] or the fat way [teacher demonstrates]. It doesn't matter. It just has to . . . has to be the SAME on both sides. Then, open it. Cut on the line of symmetry.

A great deal could be said about this language, but three comments will have to suffice. First, it is important to stress that the specific directives that the teacher gives here are motivated by the concerns of the broader lesson – they derive their meaning and significance from it. It is the broader task situation that demands that they cut the objects in half *along the line of symmetry* and determines that it doesn't matter which way the rectangle is folded and cut as long as it is "the same on both sides." In this respect, each of these operations – and their connections with one another – would probably be more easily comprehended by the children if they were told why they were doing what they were doing. Nonetheless, information that would facilitate this understanding of task logic or situational sense is systematically withheld.

Second, even within the episode itself, the teacher withholds information that might facilitate understanding – or confidence in understanding – of situational sense. Note, for example, how the teacher works through the process of folding the circle without letting the children know that they are doing this in order to create a "fold" or "line of symmetry" along which they will then cut. They are not even asked to take their scissors out of their desks until the folding has been completed. This "bracketing" of situational sense from the discourse encourages the children to rely heavily on linguistically represented directives in carrying out their activities.

Third, note the exaggerated use of representational directives reflected in phrases such as, "take out your scissors," and "then open it." Surely most children would be able to infer that it would be best to take out their scissors to "cut the circle" or that they should "open" the folded rectangle to cut it on the line of symmetry. In the use of representational directives, however, where the teacher withholds explanations of situational sense and reprimands children who move ahead of – or away from – her explicit directives by relying on their own understandings of task logic, this exaggerated explicitness serves simultaneously to move the class through the task and to convey the message that they are to operate solely within the bounds specified by explicitly represented directives.

Closing

I have tried to do two things in this chapter. First, I have tried to show that something like "literal meaning" – what I am calling "representational meaning" – does in fact exist and that it has a real place in the social, linguistic, and mental life of children and teachers in school. In doing this, I appear to be fighting upstream against a virtual flood of scholars who are rightly moving away from a central assumption of what has been "mainstream" semantics and language philosophy – the assumption that the place to begin the study of meaning in language is in the analysis of the "meaning" of words and sentences abstracted from particular contexts of use. In taking "representational meaning" as the focus of our research, however, we are not rejecting the notion that language only assumes meaning in particular contexts of usage, that linguistic meaning is determined by the physical setting, the assumptions of interlocutors, the purposes of interlocutors, and so on. To the contrary, we are arguing that the construction of "representational meaning" is dependent upon very particular kinds of social settings, social relationships, and social practices.

Second, I have tried to illustrate local aspects of the relationship between social practice and the construction of representational meaning as they appear in the case of "representational directives" in the classroom. On the one hand, I have suggested that representational meaning has an important social function in the organization of classroom activity. Teachers seem to "use" or "construct" representational directives as a means of controlling and organizing classroom activity in contexts: (1) where differences in teacher–pupil perceptions of situational sense are likely to cause disparate interpretations of nonrepresentational directives, and (2) where the difficulties in overcoming these differences are thought to outweigh the value of overcoming them. On the other hand, I have tried to make it clear that representational meaning should not be thought of as a device located in the teacher's head or in language itself, a device that can be rolled out like a movie projector to achieve particular ends within the classroom. To the contrary, representational meaning emerges in classroom discourse only when activity – and the language that mediates it – is organized in particular ways for particular purposes.

There is a great deal to be learned in exploring these local connections between social practice and cognition as they are reflected in the concrete face-to-face encounters of teachers and pupils in the classroom. On the other hand, it has become increasingly clear to us that any real understanding of the connections between social practice and the emergence of representational meaning in language demands that we take a much broader view of the social systems in which representational forms of speech function and develop.

One way to move toward such a broader view is to begin asking why the activities that we see in the classroom are there and why they are being carried out in the way that they are. For example, the teacher in one of the classrooms we have studied uses representational directives relatively rarely. One of the things that distinguishes this teacher from others in our sample is that she delegates to her pupils a great deal of responsibility for defining the purposes, means, and products of classroom activities; she delegates to her pupils much of the responsibility for defining "situational sense." Because she does not assume "ownership of meaning" in organizing classroom activities, this teacher is not constantly faced with the task of conveying *her definition* of situational sense to her class, a task that demands either a nonrepresentational communication of this definition or a resort to the use of representational directives. This draws our attention to the fact that the emergence of representational speech is not merely a function of a teacher's attempts to communicate with a class of 20 to 30 pupils. It is not a direct product of the local dynamics of interaction between teacher and pupil within the classroom. On the contrary, the ubiquity of representational directives in the classroom stems from the fact that the activities that are to be carried out there are defined by social realities such as curriculum, standardized testing, and teaching materials that have their roots in social systems that extend substantially beyond the classroom walls.

Although it may be both useful and necessary to take this kind of approach in moving our analysis beyond the classroom, our attempts to develop a coherent perspective on the many manifestations of representational speech have convinced us that it will never be sufficient. Representational uses of speech emerge in a bewildering variety of ways and in a multitude of different contexts both inside and outside the classroom. Still, there are common features in the technologies, practices, and ideologies that define these various manifestations – and there seem to be functional links between them that demand a broader perspective on their common roots in the broader social system.

As I suggested earlier, I suspect that a useful clue in this search for a broader perspective on the links between the psychological and the social in the study of representational speech may be found in Rommetveit's recent critique of the "myth of literal meaning" (Rommetveit, 1988). Rommetveit argues that the myth of literal meaning is merely one face of a broader myth that posits a "monistic" and "objective" real world that can be discussed, described, referred to, and indeed lived in. Just as the myth of literal meaning posits a language that has meaning independent of local concerns, interests, and perspectives – independent of the formation of "temporary mutual commitments to shared perspectives" – the myth of the "monistic real world" posits a world that can be described and comprehended in isolation from such local concerns, perspectives, and commitments.

As I suggested earlier, the "bracketing of situational sense" that underlies the construction of "representational meaning" is at the same time the bracketing of the local concerns, interests, and perspectives that is required if one is to comprehend or participate in the myth or illusion of Rommetveit's "monistic" or "objective" real world. This socially constituted and temporarily shared "bracketing of situational sense" is an essential element in the social construction of this "monistic real world." Understood in this way, our study of the introduction of representational forms of speech to primary school children is recast as a study of their introduction to social and mental activities that take place in this "mythical" monistic real world. My son's response to the request to move his milk – and his parents' understanding of it – not only demanded a shared commitment to a represented real world in which the "edge of the table" exists not as a danger to milk or family harmony, but simply as a position within – a part of – this objective, dehumanized, and monistic world. Many of the contexts in which we see "representational speech" being introduced to the child in the primary-school classroom – in science, social studies, or classroom regulations – are linked with social practices and social institutions outside the school that also depend on this "myth" of a monistic real world. I suspect, then, that it is to concepts concerned with the social function and historical development of this "monistic real world" – to concepts such as Max Weber's "rationalization of society" or Bruno Latour's "centers of calculation" – that we will ultimately have to look in our effort to develop coherent perspectives on why school children are introduced to these forms of social practice, speech, and thinking and what significance this may have for their development as psychological and social beings.

Notes

1. An adequate review of the issues that could – and probably should – be addressed here would require a major treatise on the history of Western thought and 20th-century philosophies of language and cognition, an undertaking that would take me far beyond the limits of this chapter and my own competence. The interested reader might look to Popper (1971), Habermas (1981/1984), and Baker and Hacker (1984).
2. The concept of "object meaning," as defined by Leont'ev (1978) within the tradition of the Vygotskian sociohistorical school, underlies this discussion of situationally defined meaning.
3. We are not suggesting, of course, that there is a conscious effort on the part of teachers to develop skills in handling what we are calling "representational speech," that they consciously differentiate representational from nonrepresentational speech in the way that we do here. To the contrary, teachers often assume that the development of good listening skills in any context demands careful attention to the meaning explicitly represented in language.

References

Baker, G. P., & Hacker, P. M. S. (1984). *Language, sense, and nonsense: A critical investigation into modern theories of language.* Oxford: Basil Blackwell.

Bonitatibus, G. (1988). Comprehension monitoring and the apprehension of literal meaning. *Child Development, 59,* 60–70.

Clanchy, M. T. (1979). *From memory to written record: England, 1066–1307.* Cambridge, MA: Harvard University Press.

Donaldson, M. (1978). *Children's minds.* New York: W. W. Norton.

Eskridge, W. N., & Frickey, P. P. (1988). *Legislation, statutes, and the creation of public policy.* St. Paul, MN: West Publishing.

Habermas, J. (1984). *The theory of communicative action: Vol. 1. Reason and the rationalization of society* (T. McCarthy, Trans.). Boston: Beacon Press. (Original work published 1981)

Leont'ev, A. N. (1978). *Activity, consciousness, and personality* (M. J. Hall, Trans.). Englewood Cliffs, NJ: Prentice-Hall.

Lyons, J. (1977). *Semantics* (Vol. 1). Cambridge: Cambridge University Press.

Minick, N. (1987, August). *Mind in action: Representational speech in classroom discourse.* Paper presented at the conference on Context, Cognition, and Activity, University of Linköping, Sweden.

Minick, N. (1988). The development of Vygotsky's thought: An introduction. In R. W. Rieber & A. S. Carton (Eds.), *The collected works of L. S. Vygotsky: Vol. 1. Problems of general psychology* (pp. 17–36). New York: Plenum.

Minick, N. (1989a). *L. S. Vygotsky and Soviet activity theory: Perspectives on the relationship between mind and society* (Literacies Institute Technical Reports Special Monographs, no. 1). Newton, MA: Educational Development Center.

Minick, N. (1989b). Mind and activity in Vygotsky's work: An expanded frame of reference. *Cultural Dynamics, 2,* 162–187.

Minick, N., & Wertsch, J. V. (1986, October). *Formal school instruction and the function of words in thought.* Paper presented at the First International Congress on Activity Theory, Berlin.

Minick, N., & Wiebking, S. (1989, March). *School experience as a factor in mastering "literal" or "decontextualized" meaning: An experimental study.* Paper presented at the meetings of the Society for Research in Child Development, Kansas City.

Olson, D. R. (1977). From utterance to text: The bias of language in speech and writing. *Harvard Educational Review, 47,* 257–281.

Popper, K. R. (1971). *Objective knowledge: An evolutionary approach.* Oxford: Clarendon Press.

Rogoff, B. (1981). Schooling and the development of cognitive skills. In H. C. Triandis & A. Heron (Eds.), *Handbook of cross-cultural psychology: Vol. 4. Developmental psychology* (pp. 233–294). Boston: Allyn and Bacon.

Rommetveit, R. (1974). *On message structure: A framework for the study of language and communication.* London: Wiley.

Rommetveit, R. (1979). On "meanings" of acts and what is meant by what is said in a pluralistic social world. In M. Brenner (Ed.), *The structure of action* (pp. 108–149). Oxford: Blackwell and Mott.

Rommetveit, R. (1988). On literacy and the myth of literal meaning. In R. Säljö (Ed.), *The written world: Studies in literate thought and action* (pp. 13–40). Berlin: Springer-Verlag.

Scribner, S., & Cole, M. (1981). *The psychology of literacy.* Cambridge, MA: Harvard University Press.

Searle, J. R. (1979). *Expression and meaning: Studies in the theory of speech acts.* Cambridge: Cambridge University Press.

Shakespeare, W. (1969). Hamlet, Prince of Denmark. In A. Harbage (Ed.), *William Shakespeare: The complete works.* Baltimore: Penguin.

Shif, Zh. I. (1935). *Razvitie zhiteiskikh i nauchnykh poniatii* [The development of everyday and scientific concepts]. Moscow: Uchpedgiz.

Snow, C. (1983). Literacy and language: Relationships during the preschool years. *Harvard Educational Review, 53,* 165–189.

Vygotsky, L. S. (1971). *The psychology of art.* Cambridge, MA: MIT Press.

Vygotsky, L. S. (1978). *Mind in society: The development of higher psychological processes* (M. Cole, V. John-Steiner, S. Scribner, & E. Souberman, Eds.). Cambridge, MA: Harvard University Press.

Vygotsky, L. S. (1988). Thinking and speech. In R. W. Rieber & A. S. Carton (Eds.), *The collected works of L. S. Vygotsky: Vol. 1. Problems of general psychology* (N. Minick, Trans.). New York: Plenum. (Original work published 1934)

Wertsch, J. V. (1985). *Vygotsky and the social formation of mind.* Cambridge, MA: Harvard University Press.

Wertsch, J. V., & Minick, N. (1990). Negotiating sense in the zone of proximal development. In M. Schwebel, C. Maher, & N. S. Fagley (Eds.), *Promoting cognitive growth over the life span.* New York: Lawrence Erlbaum.

Wiebking, S. (1990, April). *Developing skills in differentiating sentence meaning from utterance meaning in the early primary grades: An experimental investigation.* Paper presented at the meeting of the American Educational Research Association, Boston.

Part IV

Conclusion

14 Understanding the social scientific practice of *Understanding practice*

Seth Chaiklin

The chapters in this volume are the result of a conscious effort by the editors to identify researchers from a wide range of disciplines and theoretical traditions who were trying to understand individual practice by using a social or societal analysis.[1] The task of this concluding chapter is to reflect about the chapters in this volume in order to formulate some ideas about future directions for developing a social scientific study of individual practice. In other words: Where do we, as researchers concerned about understanding human practices located in social and societal interactions, go from here?

Not many researchers were working with this perspective in the mid-1980s when the authors in this volume came together, and those who did felt isolated. Our premise was that because so few people were actively trying to develop this perspective it would be more important to try to learn from each other than to promote or defend a single approach.

The editors encouraged the chapter authors to write their chapters by starting from their positive content, instead of defending their views against or criticizing dominant traditions. We wanted to avoid an all-too-common situation in which advocates for an uncommon research approach write mostly about what is wrong or limited with dominant views, and only present their positive ideas at the end of a chapter or article, usually developed thinly and too often defined as a

I thank Harris Chaiklin, Ole Dreier, Mariane Hedegaard, Steinar Kvale, and Jean Lave for their comments on various drafts of this chapter. I thank Jean Lave for her willingness to act on the idea that it was important for researchers to come together to develop positive directions rather than always stand in a reactive mode, for her hard work to organize these meetings and edit this volume, and for her open spirit and restless commitment to articulating a social science worth practicing.

negation of the dominant views they were discussing. The resulting chapters show the excellent results.

For the most part these chapters focus on human practices at the level of concrete interactions of individuals acting in a meaningful social context. Each chapter is motivated by a premise that individual actions must be understood by issues and factors that are not immediately present in the situation, nor contained only in the persons acting in these situations. In particular, the authors have sought to understand human practices as socially (and/or historically or societally) situated, and their chapters illustrate how to make such analyses in the context of specific concrete problems. An important theme that emerges individually and collectively from these chapters is that scientific understanding of individuals engaged in a practice must include some analysis of the sociohistorical context in which the practice developed and proceeds.

The present chapter continues in that spirit by using structural and historical methods to analyze the chapters in this volume as examples of social scientific practice. The first half of the chapter makes a comparative overview of the chapters in this volume from three different reference frames. The first frame considers the chapters in relation to each other, and emphasizes their considerable diversity. The second frame considers the chapters in relation to some existing theoretical traditions in the social sciences and then more generally to a Western scientific tradition. This view emphasizes a continuity with these traditions. The third frame considers some common characteristics of these chapters, some of which distinguish them from currently dominant theoretical traditions within the social sciences. This serves to formulate the concept of "societally significant practices" as an area of study of individual practices. The second half of the chapter uses structural and historical analyses to explicate the significance of such an approach, and introduces the concept of *theory/practice* as a way to conceptualize this social science. Two strategies are discussed for working in this tradition, and the role of political and moral aspects are discussed.

What do we have here?

Not one voice

In relation to each other, the chapters in this volume have many differences. Their authors were trained originally in anthropology, sociology, or psychology, and several different theoretical traditions can be found: cognitive anthropology, ethnomethodology, cultural-historical psychology, phenomenological psychology, critical psychology, and ecological psychology.

Many of the chapters are formulated in relation to a particular research tradition, and their contents are often directed to current research questions in those traditions. For example, Levine asks, What does the concept of scaffolding mean in a Vygotskian tradition? Minick asks how Vygotsky's analysis of concept development can be used to analyze the interactions between a teacher and his class. Suchman and Trigg develop the use of the concept of representational devices within an ethnomethodological study of a cognitive science.

The practices investigated in these chapters cover a wide range of phenomena. Framed in abstract terms, one group of practices involved highly sophisticated professional tasks that require years of preparation and training: ship navigating (Hutchins), medical treatment (Engeström), psychotherapeutic treatment (Dreier), blacksmithing (Keller & Keller), artificial intelligence research (Suchman & Trigg), and grading university examinations (Kvale). Another group of practices reflected tasks that most of us could encounter at one time or another and for which special preparation or training is not usually given: using a new setting (Fuhrer), handling of "learning-disabled" children by parents (Levine), peers (McDermott), or institutions (Mehan), and schoolchildren trying to handle tasks given in a school classroom (Minick; Säljö & Wyndhamn). And one could list many other kinds of differences among these chapters in terms of the age and social position of the people engaged in the practices under investigation, and so forth.

A variety of empirical methods were used including observations based on experimental manipulations (Fuhrer; Levine; Säljö & Wyndhamn), observations of individuals acting in typical situations

(Dreier; Engeström; Fuhrer; Hutchins; Keller & Keller; Levine; McDermott; Mehan; Minick; Suchman & Trigg), interviews (Dreier; Engeström; Fuhrer), stimulated recall (Engeström; Mehan) and participant observation (Dreier; Kvale; Keller & Keller).

The chapters had different tactical goals. For example, some chapters could be characterized as expanding and clarifying specific theoretical concepts. Fuhrer investigated the individual psychological processes when a person is in a particular behavior setting; Levine tried to clarify the meaning of "zone of proximal development"; Säljö and Wyndhamn operationalized Leont'ev's concepts of *action* and *operation* and their interactions as a function of the framing of a task. Other chapters gave rich description of the elements of a practice that should be understood theoretically. Dreier described a set of analytic categories to be used to analyze psychotherapeutic sessions; Engeström described doctor–patient interactions in relation to a communication framework and historical traditions; Hutchins described the performance of individual tasks in terms of the developmental history of the persons who are performing them and in the larger coordination that takes place between the tasks; Keller and Keller described the variety of considerations that a blacksmith uses to produce a spoon; Minick takes a typical interaction between a teacher and a first-grade class to characterize some consequences of the communication that may go beyond the teacher's conscious intentions. Other chapters can be characterized as trying to explain the origins of "social facts." Both Mehan and McDermott examine, respectively, the institutional and social processes by which a child is labeled as educationally handicapped. Suchman and Trigg describe how artificial intelligence work is produced. Kvale describes the knowledge-constituting function of university examinations.

Despite the common concern for including social and societal concepts in analyzing practices, there was not a homogeneous view about how to handle this problem theoretically. There are some real and difficult issues that divide these traditions. For example, dialectical traditions take it for granted that it is necessary to take societal relations as a starting point for understanding individual actions as seen in the chapters by Dreier and Engeström. Other chapters (e.g., Mehan) present a more tentative view that questions the relation between the two. Yet other chapters focused more on the social interaction among individuals in a setting without directly considering the influence of the societal roles of these persons (Fuhrer; Levine).

Another issue is the relation between research practices and the social practices being investigated. Some authors are explicit in their chapters that they want their analyses to contribute to the reformulation of the practices they are describing (Dreier; Engeström; McDermott). Others do not comment on this question, or in private conversation are not so sanguine about the necessity or importance of this connection.

I emphasize the diversity within these chapters to suggest that it will not be possible to evaluate (and dismiss) the work (and research traditions) represented here simply on the grounds of their inclusion of a social or societal dimension to their analysis. At the same time, the diversity does not preclude the possibility of finding common grounds of discussion. There are some important commonalities that cut across the work reported in these chapters.

Unities in the diversity: "The more things change . . ."

The chapters in this volume were authored by people who chose to work outside currently dominant theoretical traditions in their respective social sciences. However, the content of the work reported here does not represent a significant historical break. All the chapters in this volume use concepts that come from traditions of thought that have relatively long histories in the social sciences. These chapters represent a blossoming or continuation of some long-standing traditions – cognitive anthropology, ethnomethodology, cultural-historical psychology, phenomenology, critical psychology, and ecological psychology – rather than a departure or new turn from the predominant approaches in the social sciences.

Cognitive anthropology, with a focus on understanding individual actions in a social context, is at least 30 years old. Ethnomethodology, with a focus on understanding how people's statements serve to organize and sustain an action setting, started in the late 1950s (e.g., Garfinkel, 1967). The empirical beginnings of the cultural-historical tradition, with a focus on the contributions of social interaction and societal demands on the process of psychic development, are usually marked with the work of Vygotsky, Leont'ev, and Luria in the 1930s, who in turn drew upon a philosophical tradition of dialectical logic that is traditionally marked by developments introduced by Hegel in the first third of the 1800s, and subsequently by Marx, Ilyenkov, and others (e.g., Ilyenkov, 1974/1977; Levitin, 1982). Phenomenological research traditions, generally concerned with a qualitative description and interpretation of experiences in historical and social context, can trace their philosophical roots to Husserl, Heidegger, Merleau-Ponty, Sartre in the 20th century and to Bretano and Dilthey in the 19th century (e.g., Spiegelberg, 1978). Critical psychology started in the late 1960s, drawing inspiration from the cultural-historical tradition, and more generally from a materialist dialectic and historical materialism (e.g., Holzkamp, 1983). Ecological psychology, with its emphasis on describing settings for behavior rather than the focusing on personal characteristics, started in the late 1940s with the work of Roger Barker and Herbert Wright (e.g., Barker, 1968).

In short, these chapters are grounded in specific theoretical and empirical traditions that are at least 20 to 60 years old (and even older if you include the philosophical traditions that inspired some of these empirical traditions). They are not defined in relation to dominant trends in the social sciences. They are not ruptures in thought that have emerged de novo from a crisis in currently dominant intellectual traditions. If they are receiving more attention now, it may reflect the inability of currently dominant or popular traditions to resolve their own objectives in satisfactory ways.

More generally, these chapters and the traditions they represent reflect the continuation of a scientific tradition of thought that first found full expression in the 17th century with Francis Bacon, René Descartes, and Galileo Galilei, and extended slowly to an idea of social sciences in the 18th century. To be sure, these chapters do not accept all the presuppositions of the writers from these time periods, nor can they be understood as the result of a simple progression of the intellectual concerns of these periods. However, there are three common characteristics worth noting.

First, these chapters reflect a belief in a rational tradition of scientific investigation as having the potential to contribute to our understanding of human action. They do not propose or illustrate an overthrow of reason or a turn to individualist, irrationalist religious belief. The authors do not claim that all attempts at scientific analysis of human practices are doomed to failure because of unanalyzable effects of context or society. Instead, they demonstrate a variety of approaches for formulating and addressing problems of social and societal context in their studies and their writing.

Second, a characteristic found in Bacon and many other philosophical writers that has carried through to the present day, and is found in all approaches to the social sciences, is the belief in the need for theoretical methods to produce valuable results. There is no expectation that data accumulation alone will be of any value. The ultimate aim is to discover or develop general principles that can be used to understand specific phenomena.

Third, everyone whose work appears in this volume is concerned with canons of rigorous scientific methods that have traditionally motivated the sciences: intersubjectivity, replicability, and the use of empirical evidence. For example, at the end of the two-part conference from which these chapters came, the closing discussion spontaneously turned to methodological issues involved in advancing the work further. Some of the questions raised were common to existing methodological concerns in the social sciences. For example, how should one interpret interview data? What kinds of data should be considered reliable and what not? Are self-reports that interpret behavior acceptable? In short, researchers who are working with social, societal, and historical concepts as part of their scientific explanation are not broadening their focus in order to be released from the traditional demands of scientific rigor. The expanded scope of theoretical interest, compared with other social scientific traditions, does not require that all methodological problems must be also different. What may be different are the criteria used for deciding what kinds of data to collect and how to interpret them. At various times, social scientific traditions have emphasized general epistemological principles (e.g., experimental control is always necessary, only observable behavior can be analyzed). The traditions found in this volume have emphasized finding methods and theoretical concepts that can be used to collect information about social and societal factors that could help to understand the practice under investigation. Consequently, one may find that existing methods and data sources may be systematically interpreted in new ways, in addition to new methodological developments. The chapters by Hutchins and by Keller and Keller discuss some of the methodological problems that arise when one tries to manage the expanded scope of analysis introduced by a societal or historical analysis.

These three common points with a modern scientific or Enlightenment tradition are important to note given recent proclamations of many writers, especially philosophical ones (e.g., Rorty), that we live in a postmodern era. Although these chapters were originally collected because they represent alternatives to predominant approaches in the social sciences, one does not find any explicit appeal to postmodern themes as the central motivation. Instead, the chapters in this volume continue in some long-standing scientific values that have motivated scientific work. However this common ground with other social sciences does not mean that the specific theoretical traditions represented in this volume can be understood entirely in terms of the interests that have motivated other theoretical traditions in the social sciences that have investigated individual behavior. The expanded focus on social, societal, and historical factors as part of understanding individual practice leads to characteristics that tend to distinguish the work in this volume from other social scientific traditions.

Investigating individuals in societally significant practices

The chapters in this volume have five common characteristics that can (almost) be summarized in the following statement: They are concerned with the theoretical description of the practices of individuals in societally significant institutions.

First and foremost, all the studies reported in these chapters, even the more theoretical ones, take concrete, meaningful societal practices as a *direct object* of study. That is, each chapter describes an investigation of a human practice in the setting where it would normally occur, even if it had not been the object of study. Even the studies that used more controlled, experimental procedures took explicit care to arrange tasks, settings, and participants that were as close to the typical practice as possible (Fuhrer; Levine; Säljö & Wyndhamn).

Second, most of these practices take place either within or in relation to societal institutions: children in public school (Minick; Säljö & Wyndhamn; McDermott), school administration (Mehan; Kvale), treatment of patients in a medical clinic (Engeström) or by a therapist (Dreier), a blacksmith making a spoon for a museum (Keller & Keller), the military (Hutchins), and a research institution (Suchman & Trigg).

Third, each chapter has a definite theoretical interest. These studies of practice did not simply argue that because it was a human practice, it should be studied and described in its own right. In each case, there was an effort to start with or develop theoretical concepts from a theoretical tradition and to try to describe the practice being investigated in relation to those concepts. In other words, the practices are important, but so is the development of scientific methods and concepts to investigate these practices.

Fourth, in studying a human practice, it is not enough to look only at the actions performed or the knowledge directly required for the task. Many of the chapters wrestle with the idea that not all knowledge belongs to the individual. For example, Hutchins described how knowledge could be distributed across a social system, and Kvale discussed how a definition of what is to be known can be a societally formed process, continually being re-created through local decisions about acceptable examinations. Similarly, most of the chapters included an analysis of the societal role of actors in the practice. Engeström discussed the political and economic forces that impinge on doctor–patient interactions; Minick described the teacher as participating in a social institution that is trying to develop particular cognitive abilities of its participants; Keller and Keller described how the work of a blacksmith responds to several societal constraints, namely, the tradition and standards of smithing, the style of a period, and the needs of a museum. In addition to a societal perspective, the social interactions among the participants in a practice are important to examine, even if the goal is to understand the characteristics of an individual. For example, both McDermott and Levine described social interactions between an individual child and others as a way to understand their existing and potential development.

Fifth, the particular practices selected for study were ones that have significant consequences for the people participating in these practices. This point is a further specification of the third point that it is not practice alone that is the goal of these studies. Although the chapter authors were not specifically asked to address practices that make a meaningful difference in the life of the participants of the practice, that was often the case. Consider that Mehan could have easily studied the interactions between the cafeteria workers and the children in the school instead of the interactions between the teacher, parent, psychologist, and principal in deciding the future classroom placement of a child. Fuhrer could have studied people coming to use a new video arcade. Hutchins could have studied a weekend sailor learning to navigate a two-person sailboat. Similarly, the case described by Keller and Keller takes some of its significance from the fact that it provides a concrete example of a more general area of handicraft work, encompassing glassblowers, ceramics workers, cabinetmakers, and so forth.

Taken as a whole, the chapters in this volume could be characterized as examples of research in a yet-to-be-embodied tradition that I will designate as *societally significant practices*. Studies in this area try to develop a theoretical account of the actions (or possibilities for actions) of individuals participating in a societally significant practice, while it is occurring, by an analysis that locates the practice in a social, societal and/or historical perspective. Many different theoretical perspectives and methods might contribute to the development of such a research tradition, including the research perspectives illustrated in this volume.

The focus of this hypothetical research tradition is not characteristic of social science traditions that have typically studied individuals. To understand some consequences of this view, the remainder of the chapter continues with structural and historical analyses of social science practice. The analyses are necessarily sketchy, but they help illustrate what is meant by such analyses and thereby highlight some general problems for future development of this perspective.

Structural and historical traces of social science

The thesis that motivates this section is that social science arose, partly, because we believe it will contribute to the improvement of our institutional and social practices. This "we" in this thesis can be understood from three reference points: a society, a group of scientists working in a research tradition, or a single scientist. The primary interests and motivations of these referents are worth differentiating, as well as their interactions and divergences. From this structural analysis, I will conclude that the question is most sensibly addressed at the level of research traditions, because it shifts the emphasis away from trying to account for the behavior of individual scientists or any particular study within a tradition.

Collective and individual interests: What can we expect from social science research?

Societal perspective. From a societal perspective, "we" refers to the collective objectives of a society, as reflected by its support or suppression of various kinds of inquiry. Historically, public and private funding of scientific research has been supported and justified for its potential to improve the public good. In many contemporary societies, there are institutions, often supported with considerable public funds, to enable people to conduct social scientific research. This would not be possible if there was not some belief that these activities would contribute, in some unspecified way, to the improvement of our conditions of life.

This idea was first articulated in the 17th century by Francis Bacon who is usually credited, along with Galileo and Descartes, with initiating (or formulating) modern scientific method. Bacon emphasized the collective or societal aspects of both the process of searching for knowledge and the goals that the search tries to achieve. In his view, the extension of man's power over nature is never the work of a single investigator, but the fruit of an organized collectivity of researchers financed by the state or public bodies. Bacon argued that science had a definite role in the conduct of human life, serving as an instrument constructed by man to realize values of fraternity and progress, aiming to improve the condition of humanity (Rossi, 1968).

Research-tradition perspective. When the "we" refers to a social scientific discipline or research traditions within a social scientific discipline, then the relevant perspective is the long-term program of the discipline or tradition.

All theoretical traditions in the social sciences must eventually face the same question: What does the tradition expect to accomplish? An important aspect of any research tradition is the expectation that with sufficient time and effort, it will be possible to resolve basic problems that researchers within the tradition have co-formulated. Solutions to basic problems in a research tradition are usually seen as fundamental or at least valuable to the improvement of human conditions and possibilities. In other words, research within a theoretical tradition will eventually accrue to the public good. To some extent, it is necessary for all research traditions to hold this view if they are going to secure the material resources (e.g., money, institutional support) needed to continue their work. But this view is not forced entirely from a desire to get these societal resources. A research tradition always has some intellectual claim that its approach will prove more useful for achieving specified ends than other approaches in the same discipline.

Individual perspective. When the "we" in the thesis refers to individual social scientists, then this motivation is clearly one among several. Wolf-Deiter Narr (1983) offered a list of indicators of the scientific process for social sciences. The end result of this process is "(a) to gain a reputation, (b) to achieve a political program enlightening critical people, and (c) to function as a tool for praxis" (p. 280).[2] George Orwell offered four reasons for why he writes that may often apply appropriately to the motivations of social scientists as well:

(a) Sheer egoism. Desire to seem clever, to be talked about, to be remembered after death . . . , (b) Esthetic enthusiasm. Perception of beauty in the external world, . . . (c) Historical impulse. Desire to see things as they are, to find out true facts and store them up for the use of posterity, . . . and (d) Political purpose – using the word "political" in the widest possible sense. Desire to push the world in a certain direction, to alter other people's idea of the kind of society that they strive after. (Orwell, 1954, pp. 315–316)

Orwell's reasons for writing cover the kinds of reasons that are offered for engaging in scientific activity: self-promotion, beauty, truth, and societal improvement.

The preceding structural sketch – rough and incomplete – can be used to draw several useful implications. An important common thread that runs through all three levels of analysis is the expectation that social scientific research will contribute to the improvement of practice. The image of how that contribution will be realized may be different for each level, but each includes a motivation to improvement as part of its intent.

The structural separation of the interests of the researcher and the research tradition from the societal expectations provides some important insights into their interactions. Narr and Orwell's descriptions make it clear that individual interests for doing research cannot be reduced to the interests of the research tradition or a society – even if these interests overlap on some points. Conversely, societal interests cannot be reduced to individual interests. Even if (some) individual researchers are not particularly interested in the societal significance of their work, this does not mitigate the societal interest and expectation that social scientific research be worthwhile for the public good, nor the reasons why societal institutions (e.g., research foundations, governments, universities) are supporting these research activities. Universities in general or social science in particular are not supported primarily for aesthetic reasons (e.g., because something beautiful might be created) or intellectual reasons (e.g., because the store of human knowledge is increased), even if this is a primary or sole motivation for (some) individuals who work within scientific traditions.

A focus on the research tradition provides a useful intermediate level for thinking about how social scientific practice mediates between individual and societal interests. We do not need to consider the personal motives and interests of specific researchers in analyzing the motivations of research efforts. A societally useful social science is understood to be a collective responsibility of a research tradition and not the specific responsibility of any individual researcher who works within that tradition. This is an interesting situation. Individual researchers can personally absolve themselves from not satisfying the societal expectation of contributing to the public good because we (and "they") believe that something will emerge from the collective activity. Thus, no single scientist has the responsibility to realize the responsibility of the tradition to address the societal goals that support the research tradition, and in practice individual researchers usually do not directly try to address these goals. At the same time, the collective development of the tradition responds to the societal interest.

Similarly, no single study within a research tradition can be expected to bear responsibility for the whole tradition. Some research studies in a theoretical tradition may have clear objectives to intervene directly into a particular practice, but it is not common. It is not necessary, or even that useful sometimes, to evaluate whether the results of a particular study will contribute to the improvement of the human condition. A particular study focuses on a question that is relevant to the problem at hand. For example, in this volume, we have studies of a blacksmith at work, two artificial intelligence researchers working together, mothers doing a task with their children. It is not particularly useful to interrogate these specific studies (or other chapters in this volume) to see how their specific results alone are going to be a basis for significant modification or improvement of the practices they studied.

In short, it does not seem informative or useful to enter into debates about whether a single individual is trying to improve human practices, or whether a particular study has done so. More useful is to consider the theoretical objective of a research tradition, rather than individuals or particular studies.

The structural analysis illustrates a general principle that reflects a spirit found in this volume's chapters. There is a dialectic between the actions of individuals and the more collective units of analysis, such as members of a research tradition or a society. We cannot reduce individuals to mechanical actors of societal demands, but at the same time we cannot understand individuals completely independent of them either. An important problem for future development is to develop our theoretical and practical understanding of how to work with these relationships in the context of analyzing particular practices.

If social improvement through social scientific research is recognized as an essential part of our interests, and not just a random, fortunate consequence of this work, then it would be worthwhile to reflect about how the knowledge produced by our research traditions can accomplish this goal. Some of the authors were quite explicit that they wanted their work to contribute to the improvement of

societal practices (Dreier; Engeström; McDermott) or to the design
of environments for human use (Fuhrer). However, it is worth noting
that in the context of this volume, no one wrote so as to intervene
directly in particular practices. Of course this reflects, in part, the
manner in which these chapters were prepared, but it also emphasizes that one can work with questions of practice in a theoretical way
to develop theoretical concepts, empirical, or analytic methods that
help to understand a practice. The general question here is what is
the logic by which research traditions expect to satisfy societal expectations.

One way to approach this question is to consider a general historical development in the views about the relation between knowledge
and practice. This approach can help to set a general frame for
understanding social science practice, although in the long run it will
be better to work out these historical analyses within the logic and
history of specific research traditions and the practices they have
investigated.

Historical views of scientific knowledge and practice

The idea is to consider briefly the historical development of
Western views about the relation between scientific knowledge and
improving human practices. The first problem one encounters is to
decide where and when to begin the analysis. One possibility is to
start at the beginning of the 17th century, which marked the first
appearance of arguments that scientific efforts have some claim to
the possibility of transforming human life (Zilsel, 1945). Francis
Bacon was particularly noteworthy for articulating and developing
this argument. However, Bacon's attention was directed to the natural sciences with the idea that by understanding basic physical and
chemical principles, one could develop the "mechanical arts" in
agriculture, shipbuilding, and other economically valuable areas. The
same can be said about the mid-18th-century views, as expressed in
the *Encyclopédie* of Diederot and d'Alembert, which was partially and
directly inspired by Bacon's philosophy. During this period, there
was an emphasis on the use of reason as being adequate to address
human problems, and that unhampered accumulation of knowledge
and general education would contribute to the general improvement

of the human condition (Goldmann, 1973). Bacon and the *philosophes* recognized that knowledge could be used for bad purposes, and that human action is needed to apply this knowledge to good ends, but in general this relation was not problematized. This problematic arose more clearly in the late 18th century with the work of Immanuel Kant. He was disturbed by philosophical developments that viewed knowledge as having no moral responsibility in it. His solution was to separate a sphere of moral thinking that cannot be addressed by scientific knowledge (as Kant conceived of it). In other words, Kant's analysis tends to separate how we can know things from the decisions about how to act in practical situations.

Perhaps it is not relevant to consider these thoughts from the 17th and 18th centuries because the development of intellectual activities that could (broadly) be called "empirical social sciences" did not occur until the end of the 18th century. In the beginning of the 19th century, Auguste Comte, inspired by Bacon, developed philosophical arguments that tried to apply Bacon's principles to the social sciences. But even here Comte, who was trained as a mathematician, did not make any significant empirical work to speak of. His programmatic views, and those of immediate predecessors (e.g., Destutt de Tracy, Condorcet) still expressed a Baconian view that if we can find ideas that are validated by experience, then we would be able to act better.

In the middle and later 19th century three philosophical traditions appeared – Nietzschean, dialectical, and pragmatic[3] – that reproblematized the relation between knowledge and practice. For example, Nietzsche, using historical analyses, tried to show how the development of knowledge can be used for repressive ends as much as for improvement. Marx, also using historical methods, tried to understand the processes by which social and political conditions come into being. Peirce and Dewey in the pragmatic tradition were directly responding to the split between scientific and ethical knowledge developed by Kant (as I will describe). Also present in the thinking of these three traditions is an "activist" element: Nietzsche's creator of values, Marx's eleventh thesis on Feuerbach,[4] the epistemology of Peirce and James that emphasized the consequences of beliefs for future action as the sole criterion. Finally, there is an important shift in relation to the 17th- and 18th-century thought where knowledge and reason become conceptualized as developing within life, rather than something first developed and applied.

This brief mention of some historical developments can be used to make the following points. First, we can see that in trying to use a historical analysis, it is not always apparent where one should start, and what elements to include in that analysis. Second, one can see that the history is not always a smooth, continuous development in which present practices can be directly traced to preceding ideas. Third, even though the interest in this chapter is the practice of social sciences, it was still useful to consider periods that preceded the practice of social sciences in order to understand better the philosophical views that appeared around the start of social sciences. And finally, this historical review helps to illuminate some problems that need further development. In particular, the philosophical analysis of the role of knowledge has not been specifically developed in relation to the application of social sciences, and the relation between social scientific knowledge and ethical or moral questions has not been developed considerably either, especially at the level of detail found in the chapters in this volume. This state of affairs continues into the present (cf. Haan, Bellah, Rabinow, & Sullivan, 1983).

Theory/practice as a research strategy

The structural analysis about the societal and individual expectations from social science research and the historical review of some 17th-, 18th-, and 19th-century thought about the relation of knowledge to practice yield the following image: There has been a long-standing expectation that scientific research and the knowledge it develops will be useful for addressing and improving our living conditions, but over the centuries our views of *how* this knowledge will help has become more complicated and problematic, although without a corresponding reduction in our desires, as societies, research traditions, or individuals, to improve human practices.

The historical review points to a development in the 19th century where rational or theoretical knowledge becomes embedded as part of practices, rather than preceding it. Continuing in that vein, instead of seeing our research as aiming at a comprehensive description of the practice we study, we take a more modest (and historically accurate) view that social science research has the potential to illuminate and clarify the practices we are studying as well as the possibility to be incorporated into the very practices being investigated.[5]

I will use the term *theory/practice* to denote this idea of a social science that aims to develop a theoretical account of societally significant practices. Theory and practice (sometimes called basic and applied science) are often opposed to each other in the history of philosophic and scientific thought. It is important to note that the value of theoretical knowledge is expressed clearly and consistently in the philosophical thinking discussed previously. However, the goal is usually to understand principles that go beyond or underlie the particular practices that are being studied.

There is no reason why both aspects cannot be developed in the context of the same research program, but this has not usually been expressed. The potential value of this view can be explained analogically from Säljö and Wyndhamn's study in this volume. Their study illustrates the difference between applying knowledge in a theoretical way in the course of a school exercise that posed no problem beyond itself versus solving the exact same task but now construed in relation to a meaningful societal context. They found, as have others, that the knowledge used to solve a task is used more effectively and sensibly when it is approached in relation to a meaningful problem. By analogy, research that attempts to understand human practices with attention to the societal context in which this practice is carried out is likely to develop descriptions that could be directly useful in that practice.[6]

In addition to their reflections about the relation between knowledge and practice, the 19th-century philosophical traditions also provide some conceptual resources for analyzing human practices in a theoretical way. For now I only illustrate what should be more fully developed. Here are two basic strategies, corresponding to the Nietzschean and dialectical traditions.

An important feature of the Nietzschean tradition is the focus on the historical analysis of concepts, searching for their origins in the codification of social practices. Nietzsche's genealogy of morals (1887/1956) and Foucault's archaeology of mental illness (1961/1965) and genealogy of criminal punishment (1975/1977) are examples of historical analyses of the formulation and change in the meaning of societally important concepts. These analyses show that we are no longer able to find external criteria to justify some practical relations as fundamental and others as not.

In a Nietzschean tradition, analytical descriptions are a means of identifying the problems from and processes by which societal formations and practices are constructed. Foucault, for example, was concerned with identifying and characterizing societal problems as opposed to prescribing solutions (Gandal, 1986; Rabinow, 1984). The studies in this volume inspired by an ethnomethodological tradition fit this characterization very well. McDermott describes the daily moments of interaction that help to constitute the "fact" of learning disability. Similarly, Mehan analyzes the influence of social structures on the social interactions of persons who are deciding the future handling of a school child; Suchman and Trigg characterize the social interactions that yield the representations of two artificial intelligence researchers.

The dialectical tradition also works with a historical focus on the development and change of concepts and practices, as well as the contribution of societal and social aspects as important sources for understanding the organization and change of practices. This perspective describes a second basic strategy for investigating persons engaged in societally significant practices. An important concept in the dialectical tradition is the idea that development occurs through the resolution of contradictions and conflicts in a situation. This principle orients researchers to search for such contradictions. Moreover, it may inspire researchers to intervene into a practice as a means of illuminating these processes. Engeström describes a plan of research for actively changing the practices of a medical clinic, based on the analysis of contradictions in the working situation. Dreier describes how therapists can work to develop an understanding of individual problems in their societal relations as part of developing new comprehensive forms of action. In these two projects, the theoretical developments are intended to be used by the very practitioners that are being theorized about. Using dialectical concepts alone does not necessarily mean research follows this second strategy. The chapters by Keller and Keller, Levine, and Minick each use dialectical concepts, but have taken a more descriptive approach in the spirit of the first strategy.[7]

An issue that must be addressed with both strategies is the relation between scientific knowledge and ethical values. This issue was particularly important in the pragmatic tradition. A main point that was developed, partly in response to Kant's split of scientific thinking and moral conduct, was that scientific thinking was an example of moral conduct, and that the meaning of scientific statements had to be understood in relation to future action. From this point of view, Peirce (1905/1989) wrote of the "inseparable connection between rational cognition and rational purpose" (p. 103). Similarly, Dewey (1929/1989) wrote that for philosophy the "central problem is the relation that exists between beliefs about the nature of things due to natural science to beliefs about values – using that word to designate whatever is taken to have rightful authority in the direction of conduct" (p. 291). These quotations only indicate what one can see from further study of their writings, that their primary concern was to find a way to integrate scientific knowledge and moral conduct, but their solutions still have a quality of trying to integrate two separate spheres of knowledge (rational and moral).

If one accepts the idea that structural and historical aspects of practices must be understood as part of understanding individual practices, then one must acknowledge that moral and political[8] aspects are part of this context, and may contribute in significant ways to the organization and structure of the practice under investigation. In other words, the moral and political content has to be a part of the scientific investigation – not just a problem of trying to relate this investigation to moral conduct. This conclusion comes from the demands of the theoretical perspective – independent of the personal political or moral interests of the researchers.

Traditionally moral and political aspects have been seen as distorting the validity of scientific analysis. It may be alright to conduct a study that is motivated by a moral or political question, or to reflect about a moral or political question using the results of social scientific research, but the conduct of the investigation itself should not be "biased" by these considerations. This is sensible methodological advice. Processes of observation and data collection should be motivated by the content of the general questions under investigation and not the personal interests and desires of the researcher. However, this reluctance to admit political or moral aspects is usually extended to exclude the *content* of political or moral interests as well.[9] Perhaps this exclusion reflects the fact that theoretical traditions, especially in psychology, that have traditionally focused on individual practices have not typically had theoretical concepts for conceptualizing the relation or role of moral or political interests in the conduct of practices.

The relevance of political aspects in the study of societally significant practices can be seen in the chapters in this volume. For example, Minick's chapter addresses a question of what is valuable to be taught in school. Without such a political analysis in relation to societal goals, we cannot formulate a research program to evaluate how to achieve this goal. Second, when one ignores possible political origins of problems, then one tends to resort to "natural" reasons that locate the source of problems in the individuals themselves. For example, both Mehan and McDermott discuss the labeling of a child as learning or educationally disabled. Although Mehan did not discuss this in his chapter, it turns out that the school district gets financial support for a certain number of "educationally disabled" children. This has a potential motivation for discovering the right number of "educationally handicapped" children. Similarly, McDermott tries to locate the "learning" failure of (some) individuals in societal institutions, as embodied by the expectations of participants in these institutions, rather than primarily in the individuals themselves. The questions raised by these studies highlight the importance of considering the political interests of participants and institution as critical for understanding individual practice.

If our research has the potential to be incorporated as part of the practice under study, then it should try to address moral and political aspects present in the practice. This does not mean that a researcher must always assert a political position. These aspects might be incorporated in the design and conduct of the research, where different points of view are actively solicited and possibly even confronted with each other. The kinds of analyses described in Engeström's chapter were subsequently used as a basis of discussion with the physicians in the health clinic. Keller and Keller did not discuss the consequences of their study on Keller's subsequent smithing work, but one could imagine that it could open new dimensions for formulating craft training. By focusing on practices as the unit of study, it becomes possible to produce results that can be directly meaningful to the people engaged in those practices. At the same time, the political aspects are often the most important in significant practices, and the knowledge produced from the research should ideally be in a form that can be understood in relation to those issues. The inclusion of historical and structural aspects in the analyses of practices provides a way for integrating moral and political aspects as an explicit part of the scientific analysis.

What was sought?

This chapter applied structural and historical methods to analyze the chapters in this volume as examples of social scientific practice. The idea was to use the same kinds of methods to investigate these examples of individual research practices as would be used to investigate and understand other societally significant human practices. I have tried to understand what we are seeking, in general, as a community of scholars concerned with understanding individual human practices. I have argued that we participate in a long-standing Western tradition of systematically investigating and analyzing our societal and individual conditions and characteristics, even if we are using theoretical perspectives that have not been common. The reflections presented here outline the idea of a science of societally significant practices, discuss its historical significance, illustrate some strategies and philosophical traditions that could be used, and note some problems for further investigation. Put in summary form, the goal of a science of societally significant practices can be expressed in my thesis on Marx's eleventh thesis on Feuerbach: "The point is not to interpret nor change the world, but to live in it." The goal is to continue building our tools for understanding individuals engaged in meaningful practices in a way that acknowledges and builds the human values contained in those practices, and with a view for these ideas to be potentially incorporated as a part of the practice.

If taken seriously, it calls for a different relationship between the social scientific researcher and the object of research. An important tenet of the pragmatic (e.g., G. H. Mead) and dialectical traditions (e.g., Marx & Engels, 1970; Holzkamp, 1983; El'konin & Davydov,

1966/1975) is that forms of thought are determined by forms of practice. For new forms of thought to develop, changes in practice are sometimes required. In addition to financial resources, researchers work in relation to societal expectations and demands. To develop new ideas, one must have possibilities to test these ideas and to interact directly with those engaged in the practices under study. The organization of the possibilities for research and the relation of these institutions to other societal institutions may have a greater importance for supporting or hindering those possibilities than is commonly noted.

Notes

1. *Social* refers to direct interactions between individuals, whereas the concept of *societal* refers to actions in response or relation to institutions and traditions. The term *structural* will refer to descriptions that potentially encompass both social and societal elements.
2. Narr's analysis does not clearly separate between the individual scientist, a research tradition, and social science in general; therefore, it is unclear whether to read this list as referring to an individual or collective. I include it under an individual perspective because one does not usually talk about a social science trying to gain a reputation. The structural analysis in the present chapter may provide a way to express Narr's intentions more clearly.
3. Each of these philosophical traditions is better understood as a movement of thought that has formulated particular kinds of problems and methods for addressing them and not as a specific doctrine.
4. "The philosophers have only *interpreted* the world in various ways; the point is to change it" (Marx & Engels, 1970, p. 123).
5. It is interesting to note that this modest view of rational knowledge was prevalent in the 16th century (Toulmin, 1990).
6. This does not mean that other approaches cannot yield useful knowledge. As discussed earlier, the issue is more usefully approached in terms of what methods are appropriate for addressing what problems.
7. Given my earlier remarks about the value of focusing on a tradition, I do not mean to put too much responsibility on these single studies for representing an entire research strategy. One can easily imagine these studies as a part of a larger research program designed for intervention. The main point is that these strategies are not equivalent to the use of particular theoretical concepts or research traditions.
8. Where *political* is broadly understood to include not only the actions and interests of elected and appointed public officials, but also the policies reflected in the actions of institutional representatives. See also Orwell's definition given earlier.

9. Except, of course, when political views or moral thinking is the direct object of study.

References

Barker, R. G. (1968). *Ecological psychology: Concepts and methods for studying the environment of human behavior.* Stanford, CA: Stanford University Press.

Dewey, J. (1989). The construction of good. In H. S. Thayer (Ed.), *Pragmatism: The classic writings* (pp. 290–315). Indianapolis: Hackett. (Original work published 1929)

El'konin, D. B., & Davydov, V. V. (1975). Learning capacity and age level: Introduction. In L. Steffe (Ed.), *Soviet studies in the psychology of learning and teaching mathematics* (pp. 1–11) (A. Bigelow, Trans.). Stanford, CA: School Mathematics Study Group. (Original work published 1966)

Foucault, M. (1965). *Madness and civilization: A history of insanity in the age of reason* (R. Howard, Trans.). New York: Vintage. (Original work published 1961)

Foucault, M. (1977). *Discipline and punish: The birth of the prison* (A. Sheridan, Trans.). New York: Pantheon. (Original work published 1975)

Gandal, K. (1986). Michel Foucault: Intellectual work and politics. *Telos, 67,* 121–134.

Garfinkel, H. (1967). *Studies in ethnomethodology.* Englewood Cliffs, NJ: Prentice-Hall.

Goldmann, L. (1973). *The philosophy of the Enlightenment: The Christian burgess and the Enlightenment* (H. Maas, Trans.). Cambridge, MA: MIT Press. (Original work published 1968)

Haan, N., Bellah, R. N., Rabinow, P., & Sullivan, W. M. (Eds.). (1983). *Social science as moral inquiry.* New York: Columbia University Press.

Holzkamp, K. (1983). *Grundlegung der Psychologie.* Frankfurt: Campus.

Ilyenkov, E. V. (1977). *Dialectical logic* (H. C. Creighton, Trans.). Moscow: Progress. (Original work published 1974)

Levitin, K. (1982). *One is not born a personality: Profiles of Soviet education psychologists* (Y. Filippov, Trans.). Moscow: Progress. (Original work published 1982)

Marx, K., & Engels, F. (1970). *The German ideology* (C. J. Arthur, Ed.; W. Lough, C. Dutt, & C. P. Magill, Trans.). New York: International.

Narr, W.-D. (1983). Reflections on the form and content of social science: Toward a consciously political and moral social science. In N. Haan, R. N. Bellah, P. Rabinow, & W. M. Sullivan (Eds.), *Social science as moral inquiry* (pp. 273–296). New York: Columbia University Press.

Nietzsche, F. (1956). *The genealogy of morals* (F. Golffing, Trans.). Garden City, NY: Doubleday. (Original work published 1887)

Orwell, G. (1954). *A collection of essays.* Garden City, NY: Doubleday Anchor.

Peirce, C. (1989). What pragmatism is? In H. S. Thayer (Ed.), *Pragmatism: The classic writings* (pp. 101–120). Indianapolis: Hackett. (Original work published 1905)

Rabinow, P. (1984). Polemics, politics, and problematizations: An interview with Michel Foucault. In P. Rabinow (Ed.), *The Foucault reader* (pp. 381–390). New York: Pantheon.

Rossi, P. (1968). Baconianism. In P. P. Weiner (Ed.), *Dictionary of the history of ideas* (Vol. 1, pp. 172–179). New York: Scribner.

Spiegelberg, H. (1978). *The phenomenological movement: A historical introduction* (Vol. 2, 2nd ed.). The Hague: Martinus Nijhoff.

Toulmin, S. (1990). *Cosmopolis: The hidden agenda of modernity.* New York: Free Press.

Zilsel, E. (1945). The genesis of the concept of scientific progress. *Journal of the History of Ideas, 6,* 325–349.

Author index

403

Subject index

408

Continued from the front of the book

Situated Cognition: On Human Knowledge and Computer Representation
WILLIAM J. CLANCEY
Communities of Practice: Learning, Meaning, and Identity
ETIENNE WENGER
Learning in Likely Places: Varieties of Apprenticeship in Japan
JOHN SINGLETON
Talking Mathematics in School: Studies of Teaching and Learning
MAGDALENE LAMPERT and MERRIE L. BLUNK
Perspectives on Activity Theory
YRJÖ ENGESTRÖM, REIJO MIETTINEN, and RAIJA-LEENA PUNAMÄKI
Dialogic Inquiry: Towards a Sociocultural Practice and Theory of Education
GORDON WELLS
Vygotskian Perspectives on Literacy Research: Constructing Meaning Through Collaborative Inquiry
CAROL D. LEE and PETER SMAGORINSKY
Technology in Action
CHRISTIAN HEATH and PAUL LUFF
Changing Classes: School Reform and the New Economy
MARTIN PACKER

Printed in the United States
68052LVS00001B/61-78